COUNTERFACTUAL THOUGHT EXPERIMENTS
IN WORLD POLITICS

Sponsored by the Committee on International Peace and Security
of the Social Science Research Council

COUNTERFACTUAL THOUGHT EXPERIMENTS IN WORLD POLITICS

LOGICAL, METHODOLOGICAL, AND PSYCHOLOGICAL PERSPECTIVES

Edited by Philip E. Tetlock and Aaron Belkin

PRINCETON UNIVERSITY PRESS   PRINCETON, NEW JERSEY

Published by Princeton University Press, 41 William Street,
Princeton, New Jersey 08540
In the United Kingdom: Princeton University Press, Chichester,
West Sussex

Library of Congress Cataloging-in-Publication Data

Counterfactual thought experiments in world politics : logical,
methodological, and psychological perspectives / edited by Philip E.
Tetlock and Aaron Belkin.

    p.   cm.

  Includes bibliographical references and index.

  ISBN 0-691-02792-7 (cl : alk. paper). — ISBN 0-691-02791-9 (pb :
alk. paper)

  1. World politics. 2. History—Philosophy. 3. Counterfactuals
(Logic). I. Tetlock, Philip. II. Belkin, Aaron, 1966–
D16.9.C645   1996
901—dc20   96-6396
                                          CIP

This book has been composed in Times Roman

Princeton University Press books are printed on acid-free paper and
meet the guidelines for permanence and durability of the Committee
on Production Guidelines for Book Longevity of the Council
on Library Resources

Printed in the United States of America by Princeton Academic Press

10 9 8 7 6 5 4 3 2 1

10 9 8 7 6 5 4 3 2 1
(Pbk.)

Contents

Contributors

AARON BELKIN
Doctoral candidate, Department of Political Science
University of California, Berkeley

GEORGE W. BRESLAUER
Professor, Department of Political Science
University of California, Berkeley

BRUCE BUENO DE MESQUITA
Senior Fellow, Hoover Institution
Stanford University

LARS-ERIK CEDERMAN
University Lecturer in International Relations, Somerville College
Oxford University

ROBYN M. DAWES
University Professor
Carnegie Mellon University

RONALD J. DEIBERT
Assistant Professor, Department of Political Science
University of Toronto

JAMES D. FEARON
Assistant Professor, Department of Political Science
University of Chicago

MICHAEL P. FISCHERKELLER
Doctoral candidate, Department of Political Science
The Ohio State University

RICHARD K. HERRMANN
Associate Professor, Department of Political Science
Director, Program in Foreign Policy Analysis, Mershon Center
The Ohio State University

ROBERT JERVIS
Adlai E. Stevenson Professor of International Relations,
   Department of Political Science
Columbia University

YUEN FOONG KHONG
Fellow, Nuffield College
John G. Winant University Lecturer in American Foreign Policy
Oxford University

EDGAR KISER
Associate Professor, Department of Sociology
University of Washington

RICHARD NED LEBOW
Director, Mershon Center
Professor, Department of Political Science
The Ohio State University

MARGARET LEVI
Professor, Department of Political Science
University of Washington

JAMES M. OLSON
Professor, Department of Psychology
University of Western Ontario

NEAL J. ROESE
Assistant Professor, Department of Psychology
Northwestern University

BRUCE RUSSETT
Dean Acheson Professor of International Relations and Political Science
Yale University

JANICE GROSS STEIN
Harrowston Professor of Conflict Management, Department of
    Political Science
University of Toronto

PHILIP E. TETLOCK
Harold E. Burtt Professor of Psychology and Political Science
The Ohio State University

MARK TURNER
Professor, Department of English
Member, Center for Neural and Cognitive Sciences
University of Maryland

STEVEN WEBER
Associate Professor, Department of Political Science
University of California, Berkeley

BARRY R. WEINGAST
Senior Fellow, Hoover Institution
Professor, Department of Political Science
Stanford University

Acknowledgments

As THIS VOLUME ATTESTS, judging the plausibility of counterfactual arguments is a tricky business. Nonetheless, we place great confidence in the following counterfactual: if we had not received generous intellectual and financial support from a variety of colleagues and institutions, this volume would not exist.

On the financial front, we owe a special debt of gratitude to the Committee on International Peace and Security of the Social Science Research Council, the John D. and Catherine T. MacArthur Foundation, the Center for Advanced Study in the Behavioral Sciences, the Institute of Personality and Social Research, the Institute of International Studies at the University of California, Berkeley, the Institute on Global Conflict and Cooperation, and the National Science Foundation Training Grant to the Mershon Center at the Ohio State University.

On the collegial front, our debts are even more numerous. Most important, we want to acknowledge the help given by contributors to this volume as well as the other participants in the conference on counterfactual thought experiments held at Berkeley in January 1995. Although many participants at that conference do not appear in this book, their ideas do at various junctures. We appreciate the intellectual guidance of Henry Brady, David Collier, Barry Eichengreen, Fred Greenstein, Robert Keohane, Nelson Polsby, Robert Powell, Eleanor Rosch, Brian Skyrms, and Peter Woodruff. We single out Daniel Kahneman for thanks. Although he does not appear in this volume, he had a major impact on how we now think about thought experiments.

We also want to acknowledge the constructive comments that we have received on various aspects of this project (including our introductory chapter) from Christopher Achen, Robert Bates, Alexander George, Albert Fishlow, John Gaddis, Ernst Haas, Peter Katzenstein, Deborah Larson, Elisabeth Lloyd, Scott Sagan, Paul Sniderman, and Peter Suedfeld. And we owe a debt of considerable gratitude to the numerous anonymous reviewers who examined our manuscript for both Cambridge University Press and Princeton University Press.

Shifting to the administrative dimensions of the project, we would like to acknowledge the support of the Social Science Research Council and the assistance of Steve Heydemann, Robert Latham, and the editorial staff of Princeton University Press, including Malcolm DeBevoise, Malcolm Litchfield, and Heidi Sheehan, and Cambridge University Press, in particular John Haslam. We would be terribly remiss if we did not remember the highly professional copyediting of Madeleine B. Adams and the enormous logistical, word processing, and editorial assistance that we have received on this project from Helen Ettlinger, Leslie Lindzey, and Ann Parker. Without their patience, it would have been much more difficult to orchestrate this project.

Finally, the first editor would like to acknowledge the love of his wife, Barbara Mellers, and of his son, Paul, and his daughter, Jennifer, without whom his life would be much less fun (a sound counterfactual). The second editor is grateful for the love and support of his parents, Jeff and Jane Belkin, sister, Joanna Belkin, and grandparents, Roen and Sid Phillips and Ann Simon, and the guidance and opportunities provided by James G. Blight, Mark Garrison, Jan Kalicki, Martha Weinberg, the late Richard Smoke, and my family at the Center for International Security and Arms Control at Stanford.

Part One ————————————————————

COUNTERFACTUAL INFERENCE:

FORM AND FUNCTION

1

Counterfactual Thought Experiments in World Politics

LOGICAL, METHODOLOGICAL, AND PSYCHOLOGICAL

PERSPECTIVES

PHILIP E. TETLOCK AND AARON BELKIN

THERE IS nothing new about counterfactual inference. Historians have been doing it for at least two thousand years. Counterfactuals fueled the grief of Tacitus when he pondered what would have happened if Germanicus had lived to become Emperor: "Had he been the sole arbiter of events, had he held the powers and title of King, he would have outstripped Alexander in military fame as far as he surpassed him in gentleness, in self-command and in other noble qualities" (quoted in Gould 1969). Social scientists—from Max Weber (1949) to Robert Fogel (1964)—have also long been aware of the pivotal role that counterfactuals play in scholarship on such diverse topics as the causes of economic growth and the diffusion of religious and philosophical ideas. Nevertheless, some contemporary historians still sternly warn us to avoid "what-might-have-been" questions. They tell us that history is tough enough as it is—as it *actually* is—without worrying about how things might have worked out differently in this or that scenario. Why make a difficult problem impossible? In this view (Fisher 1970; A. J. P. Taylor 1954), we do scholarship a grave disservice by publishing a volume on counterfactual reasoning. We are luring our colleagues "down the methodological rathole" in pursuit of unanswerable metaphysical questions that revolve around the age-old riddles of determinism, fate, and free will (Fisher 1970, 18).

The ferocity of the skeptics is a bit unnerving. Moreover, they are right that counterfactual inference is dauntingly difficult. But they are wrong that we can avoid counterfactual reasoning at acceptable cost. And they are wrong that all counterfactuals are equally "absurd" because they are equally hypothetical (Fisher 1970, 19). We can avoid counterfactuals only if we eschew all causal inference and limit ourselves to strictly noncausal narratives of what actually happened (no smuggling in causal claims under the guise of verbs such as "influenced," "responded," "triggered," "precipitated," and the like). Putting to the side whether any coherent and compelling narrative can be "noncausal," this prohibition would prevent us from drawing the sorts of "lessons from history" that scholars and policy makers regularly draw on such topical topics as the best ways to encourage economic growth, to preserve peace, and to cultivate democracy. Without counterfactual reasoning, how could we know whether state intervention accelerated growth in country x, whether deterrence prevented an attack on country y, or whether the courage of a young king saved country z from sliding back into dictatorship? Counterfactual reasoning is a prerequisite for any form of learning from history (cf. Tetlock 1991). To paraphrase Robert Fogel's (1964) reply to the critics of "counterfactualizing" in the 1960s, everyone does it and the alternative to an open counterfactual model is a concealed one.

This volume surveys the many roles that counterfactual arguments play in the study of world politics. A useful place to begin is by clarifying what we mean by counterfactual reasoning. A reasonably precise philosophical definition is that counterfactuals are subjunctive conditionals in which the antecedent is known or supposed for purposes of argument to be false (Skyrms 1991). As such, an enormous array of politically consequential arguments qualify as counterfactual. Consider the following rather representative sample of counterfactuals that have loomed large in recent scholarly and policy debates:

> If Stalin had been ousted as general party secretary of the communist party of the Soviet Union, the Soviet Union would have moved toward a kinder, gentler form of communism fifty-five years before it actually did;

> If Yeltsin had followed Sachsian fiscal and monetary advice in early 1992, Russian inflation in 1993 would have been a small fraction of what it was;

> If the United States had not dropped atomic bombs on two Japanese cities in August 1945, the Japanese would still have surrendered roughly when they did;

> If all states in the twentieth century had been democracies, there would have been fewer wars;

> If Bosnians had been bottlenosed dolphins, the West never would have allowed the slaughter of innocents in the Yugoslav civil war to have gone on so long.

The contributors to this volume approach counterfactual inference from both normative/epistemological and descriptive/cognitive science perspectives. The normative issues—which we explore in the next two sections of this chapter—focus on how students of world politics *should* use and judge counterfactual arguments. We break these issues into two categories:

(1) In what ways do counterfactual arguments advance our causal understanding of political events? Are such arguments—as the skeptics insist—

merely forms of rhetorical posturing? Or can such arguments sensitize us to historical and theoretical possibilities that we might otherwise have ignored? Although we do not doubt that true believers often use counterfactuals to justify predetermined conclusions, it is a mistake to dismiss all such arguments as thinly veiled tautologies. We advance a provisional taxonomy of five constructive functions of counterfactual arguments in world politics, illustrating each with examples drawn from chapters in this volume.

(2) Once we settle on the appropriate purposes of counterfactual inference, what criteria should we use to distinguish plausible from implausible, insightful from vacuous arguments? Although we recognize the need for somewhat different criteria for distinctive "ideal-type" functions of counterfactuals, we see an even more pressing need to be explicit about the standards that scholars use in evaluating competing claims. There is an unfortunate tendency in the scholarly literature to oscillate between the extremes of dismissing dissonant counterfactuals as hopelessly speculative and of proclaiming favorite counterfactuals as self-evidently true, indeed as factual. This reaction is understandable, but unhelpful. The choice is typically not dichotomous; as we shall see, counterfactuals vary along a plausibility (or, if you are a Bayesian, subjective probability) continuum. If debates over competing counterfactuals are not to reduce to expressions of theoretical or ideological taste, we need to articulate standards of evidence and proof that transcend rival schools of thought. In this spirit, we advance a provisional list of six standards for judging counterfactual claims, illustrating each standard with examples drawn from later chapters.

The final section of this chapter shifts the focus from "how *should* we generate, use, and judge counterfactual arguments?" to "how *do* we generate, use, and judge counterfactual arguments?" One key cognitive-science question concerns when people are prone to think about possible worlds. Of the infinity of past events that people could "mentally undo" and insert as antecedents into counterfactual arguments, why do they devote so much attention to certain causal candidates and so little to others (Kahneman and Miller 1986; Commentary 2, Olson, Roese, and Deibert)? A natural next question concerns when people are likely to be persuaded by counterfactual claims concerning the consequences of altering particular antecedents. Given that people have no way of directly determining what would have happened in these hypothetical worlds, why do they defer to some counterfactual arguments but disdain others (Commentary 1, Turner)? Finally, we explore the potential for double standards in so subjective a domain as thought experiments. Is there evidence of cognitive and motivational biases in how people judge claims about possible worlds, tendencies to raise standards of evidence and proof for dissonant counterfactuals but to lower standards for claims consonant with one's beliefs and goals?

Normative Issues in Evaluating Counterfactual Claims

Our contributors generally agree that counterfactual reasoning is unavoidable
in any field in which researchers want to draw cause-effect conclusions but
cannot perform controlled experiments in which they randomly assign "subjects" to treatment conditions that differ only in the presence or absence of
the hypothesized cause. Try though we do to control statistically for confounding variables in large-N multivariate studies or to find matching cases
in comparative designs or to search for the signature of hypothesized causes
in process-tracing studies, the potential causes are simply too numerous and
too interrelated in world politics to permit complete escape from counterfactual inference. Researchers must ultimately justify claims that a given cause
produced a given effect by invoking counterfactual arguments about what
would have happened in some hypothetical world in which the postulated
cause took on some value different from the one it assumed in the actual
world (Fogel 1964; Fearon 1991).

The consensus among our contributors, however, begins to unravel beyond this point. They emphasize distinctive, albeit largely complementary,
functions of counterfactual reasoning. The arguments they present have persuaded us to adopt a stance of epistemic pluralism that acknowledges the
variety of ways in which counterfactual arguments can prove enlightening
and the need for different standards in judging counterfactuals that serve
different scholarly goals. We organize these distinct styles of counterfactual
argumentation into five ideal types:

1. *Idiographic case-study counterfactuals* that highlight points of indeterminacy
at particular junctures in history (reminding us of how things could easily have
worked out differently and of how difficult it is to apply abstract hypothetico-
deductive laws to concrete cases);

2. *Nomothetic counterfactuals* that apply well-defined theoretical or empirical
generalizations to well-defined antecedent conditions (reminding us that deterministic laws may have been at work that were invisible to the original historical
actors as well as to contemporary scholars who insist on a radically idiographic
focus on the particular);

3. *Joint idiographic-nomothetic counterfactuals* that combine the historian's interest in what was possible in particular cases with the theorist's interest in identifying lawful regularities across cases, thereby producing theory-informed history;

4. *Computer-simulation counterfactuals* that reveal hitherto latent logical contradictions and gaps in formal theoretical arguments by rerunning "history" in
artificial worlds that "capture" key functional properties of the actual world;

5. *Mental-simulation counterfactuals* that reveal hitherto latent psychological
contradictions and gaps in belief systems by encouraging people to imagine possi-

ble worlds in which causes they supposed irrelevant seem to make a difference, or possible worlds in which causes they supposed consequential seem to be irrelevant.

Five Styles of Counterfactual Argumentation

1. Idiographic

Several authors use counterfactuals to explore "possibility-hood"—whether history had to unfold as it did. For instance, Breslauer (Chapter 3) explores the several junctures in the history of the Soviet Union that have sparked the most intense counterfactual debate within the expert community: Was the Bolshevik revolution inevitable given the Russian defeat in World War I? Was Stalinism inevitable given the vanguard-party legacy of Leninism? Was Gorbachevism inevitable given the repressive stagnation of Brezhnevism? And was the disintegration of the Soviet Union inevitable given the liberal reforms of Gorbachevism? Khong (Chapter 4) attempts to assess whether any conceivable British prime minister would have adopted a policy of appeasement toward Nazi Germany, at least up to March 1939. Herrmann and Fischerkeller (Chapter 6) examine several counterfactual controversies in which the positions taken by policy makers on "what would have happened?" shaped American policy toward Iran during the Cold War. Lebow and Stein (Chapter 5) construct an exhaustive inventory of the counterfactual beliefs that apparently guided American and Soviet policy during the Cuban missile crisis—the crisis during which, it is often asserted, the world "came closer" than ever before or since to nuclear war.

These diverse applications all use counterfactuals to focus on "conceivable" causes that could have easily redirected the path-dependent logic of events (cf. Hawthorn 1991; Chapter 2, Fearon). In each case, the investigators want to know what was historically possible or impossible within a circumscribed period of time and set of relations among political entities. To make this determination, they draw upon combinations of: (a) in-depth case-specific knowledge of the key players, their beliefs and motives, and the political-economic constraints under which they worked; and (b) general knowledge (nomothetic propositions) concerning cause-effect relations in human behavior and political-economic systems. Moreover, our case-study authors seem to agree that counterfactual speculation should be constrained by some form of "minimal-rewrite-of-history" rule that instructs us to avoid counterfactuals that require "undoing" many events—counterfactuals that, for instance, ask us to imagine a democratic Soviet Union at the end of World War II or Soviet possession of strategic nuclear superiority at the time of the Cuban missile crisis. A more fruitful way to proceed is to ask what could have worked out differently if we introduce *easily imagined* variations into the causal matrix of history. Might the murderous tyranny of Stalin have been averted if Trotsky had not gone duck hunting, caught a cold, and missed a key politburo meeting or if Bukharin had been a savvier politician? Might World War II have been nipped in the bud if British opponents of appeasement had had one or two additional cabinet seats during the Munich crisis? And might World War III have been triggered in October 1962 if Kennedy had followed the advice of his more hawkish advisors and immediately ordered air strikes against Soviet missile sites in Cuba?

These idiographic counterfactuals are not idle exercises in social-science fiction; they are a useful corrective to simple deterministic forms of theory. They compel us either to abandon determinism by acknowledging the role of chance or to abandon simplicity by acknowledging that factors outside the purview of our deterministic models—viruses, skillful or inept leadership, group dynamics, a well-timed or ill-timed persuasive argument—can decisively alter the course of events.

Beyond their heuristic contribution to social science theory, idiographic counterfactuals are an integral part of the process of passing moral judgment on individual leaders and even entire political systems such as Marxism-Leninism. We rely on them in attributing responsibility (Hart 1961). Would a reasonable person, confronted by these circumstances, have acted differently? Should a particular leader be praised for performance above the norm (spectacular prescience or courage) or condemned for performance below the norm (stubborn refusal to recognize trends apparent to others or cowardly failure to protest immoral conduct)? Neville Chamberlain, John Kennedy, Nikita Khrushchev, and Lyndon Johnson are all, in a sense, in the docket with their reputations as wise leaders hanging in the balance on counterfactual judgments of what they could or should have done at certain junctures in history.

2. Nomothetic Theory-Testing

Whereas idiographic investigators are interested in conceivable causes that they can readily imagine taking on different values within a specific historical context, nomothetic investigators usually show little or no concern for the plausibility of switching the hypothesized counterfactual antecedent on or off in any given context. From this perspective, counterfactuals are the inevitable logical by-products of applying the hypothetico-deductive method to an historical (nonexperimental) discipline such as world politics. Whenever we combine a well-defined Hempelian covering law (say, relating money supply to inflation) with well-defined antecedent conditions (the Russian economy in January 1992), we can deduce specific counterfactual conclusions (e.g., if the Russian central bank had adopted this or that monetary policy, then, *ceteris paribus*, inflation would have taken on this or that value). Note that these counterfactuals are in no way constrained by the historical plausibility of the Russian central bank adopting one or another policy. The counterfactual "predictions" follow from the context-free logic of macroeconomic theory, not from the context-bounded logic of what was psychologically or politically possible at that juncture in Russian history. Adopting Fearon's (Chapter 2) terminology, these nomothetic counterfactuals invoke miracle causes. Even if our theory requires us to posit an extremely implausible hypothetical world, we do what our theory tells us to do. The goal is not historical understanding; rather, it is to pursue the logical implications of a theoretical framework. For instance, Kiser and Levi (Chapter 8) note that influential sociological theories of revolution imply that if there had been a large, educated middle class in the France of 1789 or in the Russia of 1917, revolution would not have occurred. Russett's (Chapter 7) democratic-peace hypothesis implies that if all states in the twentieth century had been democracies, war would have been less frequent. Keohane's (1984) theoretical work on regimes claims that if international regimes did not exist, there would be markedly less international cooperation. Waltz's (1979) structural neorealism implies that if we transformed a multipolar state system (e.g., pre–World War I Europe) into a bipolar one, the stability of the system would have increased.

What makes these counterfactuals anything more than dogmatic reassertions of faith in a theory that stipulates "cause x facilitates outcome y and, in the absence of cause x and all other things being equal, the likelihood of y diminishes by some amount"? A fuller answer to this question emerges in our later discussion of the statistical and projectability tests of counterfactuals. For now, it must suffice to note the root difficulty: namely, history is a terrible teacher. Key events occur only once, whereas for purposes of valid causal inference we would like to rerun history many times and to examine the resulting distribution of outcomes in contingency tables that reveal how strongly causes and effects covary. But time-machine experimentation of this sort is impossible, so we are stuck with the covariation data available in the real world (a world in which the numbers of democratic states and wars are both constants). We then have to rely on the imperfect statistical means at our disposal to estimate the degree to which democracy inhibits war, controlling as best we can for confounding variables. From the Dawesian perspective (Commentary 3), the democratic-peace counterfactual can be only as true as the covariation data in the real-world contingency tables permit. In King, Keohane, and Verba's (1994) framework, there is additional latitude for learning about the truth-status of counterfactuals (see also Chapter 7, Russett). As good theorists, it is incumbent upon us to go beyond mere observations of covariation and to stipulate the causal mechanisms underlying the democratic peace and to derive a host of testable predictions from these hypothesized mechanisms. For instance, if heightened accountability constraints on leaders are responsible for the democratic peace, what independent evidence do we have of the workings of this hypothesized cause? Are democratic leaders who advocate war against fellow democracies more likely to fail than their less bellicose colleagues? Do we see more references to accountability constraints in the private deliberations of democratic than nondemocratic leaders? The more elaborate the network of corroborative correlational evidence, including time-lagged and partial correlations, the greater our justifiable confidence in the nomothetic counterfactual.

3. Idiographic-Nomothetic Synthesis

The tension between idiographic disciplines (history and area studies) and nomothetic disciplines (general social science) is well known and need not be belabored. A not uncommon way of proceeding is to acknowledge that the idiographic and nomothetic represent complementary "ways of knowing" that may in the fullness of time be conceptually integrated, but do not hold your breath. It is worth noting, however, that such conceptual integration is the norm in natural history, where there is much less controversy than in the social sciences over what counts as a well-established statistical or theoretical generalization.

Our favorite example of idiographic-nomothetic symbiosis is the manner in which biological and physical scientists have gone about deriving and testing rival hypotheses concerning the extinction of dinosaurs. Perhaps the most influential hypothesis is the doomsday-asteroid conjecture which, in counterfactual form, runs as follows: "If a six- to twelve-mile-wide asteroid had struck the Earth at a velocity of approximately 44,000 miles per hour sixty-five million years ago, then a host of predictions would follow (including the size of the crater, the effects on the atmosphere and climate, the distribution of various trace elements in particular geological strata, antipodal volcanism, . . .)." This line of work captures the best in both the idiographic and nomothetic traditions. Investigators focus on a well-defined "conceivable" cause (meteors and asteroids hit our planet frequently over long stretches of time) but rely heavily upon deductive theory, empirical observations, and computer simulations to assess the soundness of the connecting principles that permit us to deduce empirical consequences such as climate change of sufficient magnitude to wipe out the dinosaurs. Investigators also try to tease apart testable predictions from rival hypotheses such as "endogenous volcanism alone is sufficient to account not only for this specific mass extinction but for nine of the ten other mass extinctions in the fossil record over two billion years." As a result of this vigorous research program, many scientists argue that a once highly speculative counterfactual conjecture is now better viewed as a quite-probable fact of natural history—yet another illustration of how blurry the boundary between factual and counterfactual can be (Chapter 6, Herrmann and Fisherkeller).

There are no idiographic-nomothetic syntheses of comparable scope and sweep in world politics. But there are some elegant demonstrations of how one can weave together idiographic and nomothetic objectives—in particular, by the game theorists in this volume. Bueno de Mesquita and Weingast both use game-theoretic models to enhance our understanding of particular historical episodes (Philip Augustus versus the Pope; medieval merchants versus towns; federal bureaucrats versus Congress), to identify intriguing cross-case regularities, and to make predictions about how behavior will change as a lawful function of alterations in the probabilities or payoffs attached to courses of action. In so doing, the game theorists remind us that social scientists are not the only creatures roaming this planet capable of thinking counterfactually. Policy makers do it all the time, constructing mental representations of how others would respond to one or another move and making decisions on the basis of those mental models. Policy makers can identify equilibrium solutions (solutions in which no one stands to gain from unilateral defection) only by computing off-the-path behavioral (OTPB) expectations concerning what would happen if they or the other side acted differently in response to a given move. Assuming both sides act rationally and stay on the equilibrium path, these OTPB expectations eventually become counterfactual assertions about what would have happened under this or that contingency (Chapter 9, Bueno de Mesquita; Chapter 10, Weingast). The mental representations of these now-counterfactual worlds were once, however, causally consequential; they constrained rational decision makers to go down particular branches of the game-tree.

Game theorists integrate the idiographic and nomothetic by applying "strong theory"—expected utility maximization and criteria for identifying equilibrium strategies—to complex historical situations that can then be understood by modeling the options available to each side and the expected payoffs associated with all logically possible combinations of moves. In judging what else could plausibly have happened, game theorists use nomothetic laws to answer the idiographic question: How much history do I have to rewrite to "undo" a particular policy? If the counterfactual simply shifts us from one equilibrium path to another (as is possible in games with multiple equilibria), the counterfactual does no violence to the rational-actor axioms of the underlying theory and may be quite acceptable. But if the counterfactual requires us to imagine a world in which, for stochastic reasons ("trembling hand") or psychological reasons ("bounded rationality," motivational perversity), players stray from an equilibrium to a non-equilibrium path so that one or both are worse off than they otherwise could be, the counterfactual is suspect. These ground rules for judging the permissibility of possible worlds are commendably precise, albeit rather procrustean. There is no guarantee that history is efficient in the sense of quickly identifying equilibrium solutions; history may be better viewed as a "path-dependent meander" (March and Olson 1995) in which accidents, fortuitous opportunities, and miscalculations often lead us into culs-de-sac from which it is difficult, even impossible, to extricate ourselves.

4. Pure Thought Experiments: Logical Proofs and Computer Simulations

Our contributors often use counterfactuals to reinforce a causal argument (be it an idiographic one concerning the impact of a particular belief, person, or policy, or a nomothetic one concerning causal processes that theoretically transcend context). But they also sometimes use counterfactuals to reveal previously hidden contradictions or ambiguities in the logical structure of the causal arguments that others have advanced.

Using counterfactuals to probe the logical completeness and internal coherence of claims is commonplace in mathematics, the physical sciences, and economics. A prototype is Euclid's elegant proof that the number of prime numbers must be infinite because if we take the counterproposal seriously, we are compelled to make contradictory claims. For example, if and only if the number of prime numbers were finite, then there would exist a nonprime number x such that x equals the product of all primes plus 1 ($x = (p_1 p_2 \ldots p_n) + 1$). But if this were true, x as a nonprime number must by definition be directly factorable into either nonprimes or primes and, if factorable into nonprimes, those nonprimes must eventually be factorable into primes. But this is impossible given the method of constructing x, so the number of primes must be infinite and the antecedent must be false.

We know of no comparable *reductio ad absurdum* in world politics or indeed of thought experiments that are as decisive in shaking theoretical convictions as those of Galileo and Einstein in physical science or of Ricardo, Coase, and Arrow in economic theory. But we do see some interesting parallels with the computer simulations of complex adaptive systems that Cederman and Fearon discuss in their respective chapters. One interpretation of these simulations is that they highlight logical lacunae in currently influential approaches to world politics. The qualification "one interpretation" is critical; one is not obliged to accept this interpretation for the simple reason that the simulation-based counterfactuals lack the "if and only if" delivering power of rigorous mathematical proofs in well-defined axiomatic systems. For example, one could argue that if balancing were inevitable in anarchic international systems, then global hegemons would not emerge in simulated worlds which, according to Cederman (Chapter 11), capture the key functional attributes of anarchy within a neorealist framework. But because hegemons do emerge, and emerge especially frequently when defense-dominance prevails (an additional unwelcome surprise for some theorists), this neorealist prediction may (not must) be wrong. Cederman's simulations of artificial histories suggest that we may have just been lucky that an Alexander or Hitler or Napoleon has not yet conquered the world! Or, shifting to Fearon's chapter, one could argue that if long-term forecasting were possible in complex interdependent systems, then we could predict the long-term consequences of minor variations in initial settings for cellular automata. But because we cannot make accurate long-term predictions even in these simple, well-understood systems, perhaps long-term predictability also breaks down in the much more complex and poorly understood domain of world politics. These simulation-driven counterfactuals are not deductively decisive but they are intellectually seductive. They nudge us gently toward the conclusion that something is awry with key assumptions that serve as starting points for influential analyses of security issues.

5. Mental Simulations of Counterfactual Worlds

Not all counterfactual simulations of possible worlds need run through the logical structures of computer programs; some run through the psychological structures of the human mind. The classic thought experiments of physicists and economists illustrate the point in the abstract, but it is possible to make the same point with examples more directly relevant to world politics. Asking people to imagine and work through the detailed implications of hypothetical worlds is a powerful educational and rhetorical tool. Like their formal epistemological kin (logical proofs and computer simulations), mental simulations can highlight critical contradictions and ambiguities in one's own and others intellectual positions (see also Turner's notion of spotlight counterfactuals in Commentary 1). As Kahneman (1995) points out, mental simulations derive their persuasive force and power to surprise by revealing previously unnoticed tensions between explicit, conscious beliefs and implicit, unconscious ones. In this sense, people discover aspects of themselves in mental simulations that would otherwise have gone undiscovered. We find it useful to distinguish three specific ways in which mental simulations can yield insights into our own thought processes: by revealing double standards in moral judgment, contradictory causal beliefs, and the influence of unwanted biases such as certainty of hindsight.

COUNTERFACTUAL MORALITY TALES

Mental simulations can compel people to acknowledge embarrassing or even shameful inconsistencies in their application of moral rules. The paradigmatic example is the identity-substitution thought experiment that manipulates either the perpetrator or victim of a deed and asks the audience to contemplate whether they had the same emotional reaction to what actually happened as they would have had to various hypothetical events. For instance: "If Bosnians were bottlenosed dolphins [Rwandans white, Chechnyans Lithuanians . . .], we never would have tolerated the slaughter of innocents so long." Insofar as the audience detects a discrepancy in their reactions to the two scenarios, and insofar as the audience firmly believes that the mentally manipulated cause should be irrelevant, the audience will deem the discovery of a differential emotional reaction to be a disturbing *fact* about themselves. Moreover, the thought experiment is easily translated into an actual experiment. For example, survey researchers often perform actual identity-substitution experiments to gauge the influence of "socially undesirable" causes of policy preferences that, it is assumed, people would not be willing to acknowledge if they were asked directly (Sniderman, Brody, and Tetlock 1991).

COUNTERFACTUAL CONSISTENCY PROBES

Here the mental simulation reveals contradictions between causal beliefs that may have previously coexisted peacefully within a belief system. The paradigmatic example is the syllogism that traces through the logical implications of one set of beliefs to the point where the contradiction becomes undeniable. For example:

> If you really believe that there is so much indeterminacy at the micro level (battles, firms, bureaucratic subunits of government), you cannot plausibly argue for so strongly deterministic a position at the aggregate or macro level (wars, economies, government decisions);

> If you commit yourself to an extreme structural-realist position that denies any significant causal role to domestic politics in shaping properties of the international system, then you would have to believe that even if the Soviet Union had been a democracy in 1945, the Cold War would still have occurred.

The thinker then has the dissonance-reduction options of changing one or both sets of beliefs, introducing new cognitions that neutralize the contradiction, or disengaging from the simulation exercise by simply ignoring the contradiction (cf. Abelson 1959; Festinger 1957).

It is important to be explicit about the likely long-term impact of repeated counterfactual-consistency probing of expert belief systems. Certain belief systems are much more vulnerable to this type of conceptual challenge: specifically, belief systems organized around strongly deterministic claims (if x, then y must occur) and strongly exclusionary claims (x and only x influences y). The greater vulnerability can be traced to the greater ease of generating and justifying "could" versus "would" counterfactuals. A "could" counterfactual merely requires showing that there is at least one plausible story about a possible world in which x did not automatically lead to y or in which some other cause, z, also influenced y. By contrast, an unqualified "would" counterfactual requires showing that an outcome would have occurred in all possible worlds that pass some threshold of plausibility. The burden of proof is obviously much higher in the latter case.

COUNTERFACTUAL EXERCISES AS DEBIASING TOOLS AND MEANS OF STIMULATING THE IMAGINATION

Retrospective scenario generation is mental simulation in which the goal is to prevent premature cognitive closure induced by certainty of hindsight. Some scholars (e.g., Weber 1949) have long suspected, and cognitive psychologists have recently demonstrated (e.g., Fischhoff 1975; Hawkins and Hastie 1990), that "outcome knowledge" contaminates our understanding of the past. Once people learn the outcome of an event, they not only perceive that outcome as more likely ex post than they did ex ante (which might be defended as a rational Bayesian updating of subjective probabilities), they often fail to remember their ex ante assessment of what was and was not likely to happen. Backward and forward reasoning in time are, in this cognitive sense, deeply asymmetrical.

Counterfactual thought exercises can check the "creeping determinism" of certainty of hindsight. Asking people to think of how things could have worked out differently becomes a means of preventing the world that did occur from blocking our views of the worlds that might well have occurred if some antecedent condition had taken on a different value. Indeed, there is a small "debiasing" literature in experimental psychology that assesses the usefulness of encouraging people to imagine that the opposite outcome occurred (Fiske and Taylor 1991). There is also a small literature in literary studies on the concepts of sideshadowing, foreshadowing, and backshadowing in narratives that makes a strikingly similar normative point (M. A. Bernstein 1994; Morson 1994). Sideshadowing calls attention to what could have happened, thereby locating what did happen in the context of a range of possibilities that might, with equal or even greater likelihood, have taken place instead. Sideshadowing serves as a valuable check on foreshadowing (the tendency, in extreme form, to reduce all past events to harbingers of the future) and backshadowing (the even more insidious tendency to judge historical actors as though they too should have known what was to come).

Bernstein cautions us about the dangers of adopting a condescending "back-shadowing" attitude toward participants in past events—such as the victims of the Holocaust—that were neither inevitable nor perhaps even predictable.

Of our contributors, Weber (Chapter 12) is most concerned with the potentially liberating effects of allowing our counterfactual imaginations freer rein than they are usually given. He suggests that a partial explanation of why international relations theorists are so often surprised by events is a failure of divergent thinking—a failure to give due weight to the variety of possible pasts that could have occurred as well as to the variety of possible futures that might yet occur. Confronted by a complex probabilistic world in which the tape of history only runs once, prudent decision makers should entertain multiple plausible scenarios of how events might have unfolded and might yet unfold, hedging their policy bets accordingly (Schoemaker 1991). Weber also criticizes methodologists and epistemologists, including us, who try to constrain our counterfactual imaginations by invoking the sorts of plausibility tests advanced in the next section. We agree with Weber that deterministic tunnel vision is a serious problem but worry about the viability of the proposed solution. Weber may be right that lack of creative divergent thinking is a more serious deficiency in world politics than proliferation of false hypotheses, but if the field took Weber's advice to heart, the opposite might well soon be the case. Any self-respecting academic community must offer the attentive public criteria for distinguishing scenario snake oil from serious scholarship.

Six Criteria for Judging Counterfactual Arguments

There should now be no doubt that scholars use counterfactual arguments for a variety of distinct, albeit interrelated, purposes. It should also come as no surprise that there is no single answer to the question of what counts as a good counterfactual argument. The obvious rejoinder is, "Good for what?" A counterfactual that is idiographically incisive (advances our understanding of a particular case) might be nomothetically banal (devoid of interesting theoretical implications) and vice versa. A counterfactual grounded in an elegant computer simulation might blow a gaping logical hole in an influential theoretical argument but tell us precious little about the actual world it supposedly simulates. A counterfactual that stimulates us to think of new hypotheses might run afoul of the received wisdom on what counts as a trivial or influential cause.

Given the diverse goals that people have in mind when they advance counterfactual arguments—from hypothesis generation to hypothesis testing, from historical understanding to theory extension—our contributors convinced us that the quest for a one-size-fits-all epistemology is quixotic. Different investigators will inevitably emphasize somewhat different criteria in judging the legitimacy, plausibility, and insightfulness of specific counter-factuals. It would be a big mistake, however, to confuse epistemic pluralism (which we accept up to a point) with an anything-goes subjectivism (which we reject and which would treat all counterfactual claims as equally valid in their own way). The study of world politics has suffered from a lack of self-consciousness about the counterfactual underpinnings of causal claims (Fearon 1991). Indeed, different schools of thought sometimes seem precariously close to establishing their own implicit norms for deciding what is and is not a "trivial" argument (Chapter 12, Weber)—an outcome that would be disastrous because it would permit rival schools to disengage altogether from constructive arguments with each other. A science or, more modestly, quasi science of world politics is possible if and only if advocates of conflicting hypotheses embrace at least some common standards for judging the plausibility of each other's counterfactual claims. Otherwise, we are fated to talk past each other.

To avoid this fate, we advance six normative criteria for judging counter-factual arguments that appear to command substantial cross-disciplinary support. To be sure, we do not expect universal consent; we do seek, however, to initiate a sustained conversation within the research community on what should count as a compelling counterfactual argument—a conversation that will allow us to explore the strengths and weaknesses of specific standards in the abstract, in isolation from the dominant debates of the moment (when the temptation to play favorites is often irresistible). There should, more-over, be plenty to talk about. Each standard we propose is open to some interpretation. Certain standards will provoke resistance from those who de-nounce it as impossible (Chapter 3, Breslauer) or undesirable (Chapter 12, Weber) or irrelevant (Chapter 5, Lebow and Stein). And some standards will clash with each other. For example, consistency with well-established historical fact sometimes conflicts with consistency with well-established statistical or theoretical generalizations. There are at present no generally accepted principles for adjudicating such disputes and we do not claim to offer a well-defined "method of counterfactual argument" that researchers can deploy in an off-the-shelf fashion to solve any and all problems.

With these disclaimers, we list six attributes of the ideal counterfactual thought exercise (where "ideal" means most likely to contribute to the ultimate social-science goals of logically consistent, reasonably comprehensive and parsimonious, and rigorously testable explanations that integrate the idiographic and the nomothetic):[1]

---

[1] Readers may wonder how these six criteria for good counterfactual reasoning map onto the five ideal-type patterns of counterfactual reasoning sketched earlier. Although the answer is complex and the subject of some disagreement among contributors, we can offer the following observations:

(1) The first two criteria—logical clarity and cotenability—have widespread acceptance

   1. *Clarity:* Specify and circumscribe the independent and dependent variables (the hypothesized antecedent and consequent);

   2. *Logical consistency or cotenability:* Specify connecting principles that link the antecedent with the consequent and that are cotenable with each other and with the antecedent;

   3. *Historical consistency (minimal-rewrite rule):* Specify antecedents that require altering as few "well-established" historical facts as possible;

   4. *Theoretical consistency:* Articulate connecting principles that are consistent with "well-established" theoretical generalizations relevant to the hypothesized antecedent-consequent link;

   5. *Statistical consistency:* Articulate connecting principles that are consistent with "well-established" statistical generalizations relevant to the antecedent-consequent link;

   6. *Projectability:* Tease out testable implications of the connecting principles and determine whether those hypotheses are consistent with additional real-world observations.[2]

---

across ideal types and are perhaps the best candidates for the status of universal minimum standards;

(2) The third criterion—consistency with well-established historical fact (also known as the minimal-rewrite rule)—is carefully observed by most idiographic researchers (ideal type 1) but frequently ignored by many nomothetic researchers (ideal type 2);

(3) The fourth, fifth, and sixth criteria—consistency with well-established theoretical and statistical generalizations and projectability—are more widely acknowledged among nomothetic than among idiographic researchers (although a significant contingent of idiographic researchers do apply these standards in their own work).

[2] Some logicians (Stalnaker 1984; Lewis 1973) have proposed a seventh test—the semantics of possible worlds—for judging the truth or falsehood of counterfactual claims. To test a proposition of the form "if p, then q," possible-worlds semantics directs us to do three things: (1) identify the set of possible worlds $\{p\}$ in which the counterfactual antecedent, p, is true; (2) identify that possible world $\{p^1\}$ that is "closest" to the actual world; (3) determine whether that possible world $\{p^1\}$ falls in the intersection of the set of possible worlds in which p is true, $\{p\}$, and the set of possible worlds in with q is true, $\{q\}$. We should judge "if p, then q" to be true if and only if the "closest" p falls in the intersection of $\{p\}$ and $\{q\}$. In other words, we should judge "if p, then q" to be true if and only if the closest world in which p is true is also a world in which q is true.

This logical calculus provides an elegant framework for evaluating counterfactual claims. It assumes, however, a vastly more sophisticated knowledge of the causal workings of the world than social scientists currently possess (or are likely to possess anytime in the next century). We need to partition the universe of possible worlds into overlapping sets, to locate the actual world in the universe of possible worlds, and to quantify the "distance" between the actual world and each possible world. Not surprisingly, none of our contributors could implement this test. We differ from Lebow and Stein (Chapter 5) in that we distinguish the Lewis-Stalnaker approach from the minimal-rewrite rule. Even if the antecedent p is an historically implausible miracle cause (Chapter 2, Fearon), the closest world in which p is true could still be a world in which q is true, in which case the counterfactual violates the minimal-rewrite rule but passes the Lewis-Stalnaker test.

1. Well-Specified Antecedents and Consequents

Our first recommendation might strike readers as a tad obvious. Like actual experiments, thought experiments should manipulate one cause at a time, thereby isolating pathways of influence. Although excellent advice in principle, implementing it is often deeply problematic. There is no way to hold "all other things equal" when we perform thought experiments on social systems that are densely interconnected (cf. Jervis 1993; Commentary 4, Jervis). To invoke the terminology of experimental design, we cannot manipulate the "independent" variable in interconnected systems without creating ripple effects that alter the values taken on by other potential causes in the historical matrix, thereby creating "confounding" variables that render interpretation of the original thought experiment problematic.

At this juncture, radical wholists take the systems-theory argument even further and insist that if we want to advance coherent and defensible counterfactuals, we will have to reconstruct an entirely new hypothetical world for each new counterfactual proposition—a new world that specifies all other things that would also have to change in order to accommodate the hypothesized antecedent (otherwise the counterfactual is underspecified). This position strikes us as too extreme. Causal interconnectedness is a matter of degree. In the words of one systems theorist: "Everything is connected but some things are more connected than others. The world is a large matrix of interactions in which most of the entries are very close to zero" (Pattee 1973, 23). The analytical challenge then becomes estimating interconnectedness and designing our counterfactual thought experiments with due consideration for the complexities created by interconnectedness. Sometimes we will discover that the wholists are right: the causal antecedent that we mentally manipulated is so deeply embedded in a recursive network of causation that simply positing that "if cause x took on a different value, then y" is deeply uninformative. Consider two examples:

(1) Cederman (Chapter 11) criticizes the structural-realist claim advanced by Mearsheimer (1990, 14) that "*ceteris paribus*, war is more likely in a multipolar system than a bipolar one." In Cederman's view, other things probably cannot be held equal in the post–World War II case, and Mearsheimer glosses over the problem by failing to articulate what else would have had to be different in counterfactual post–World War II systems in which multipolarity prevailed. As soon as we try to specify the alternatives to a bipolar world more precisely, we begin to appreciate the need for domestic-political boundary conditions on the polarity counterfactual. For instance, the identity of the third power—be it Great Britain, France, or China—might matter. Given the special historical relationship between Lon-

don and Washington, it is not intuitively obvious that a tripolar world composed of the Soviet Union, the United States, and Britain would have been less stable than the actual bipolar world.

(2) Shifting to economic history, Gould (1969) complains about the counterfactual, "If the Industrial Revolution had not occurred, the British standard of living would have been lower than it was." He observes:

> We cannot decide what we must subtract from the real past along with the Industrial Revolution. . . . In order to know what would have happened to income per head had the Industrial Revolution not occurred we need to know, amongst other things, what in such circumstances, would have happened to population. But to know what, in those same circumstances, would have happened to population we need to know, amongst other things, what would have happened to income per head.

It is not clear that we can escape this "vicious circle." At a minimum, we need to clarify the counterfactual antecedent by creating a "compound" (e.g., if the Industrial Revolution had not occurred *and* if British population grew at the same rate between 1750 and 1850, then . . .) and by specifying what else would have to be different about this hypothetical Britain from which we have now "subtracted" two fundamental causal processes: industrial growth and rising population.

These arguments are grist for the wholists mill. But in other cases, causal interconnectedness seems much thinner. Perhaps one reason why assassinations attract so much counterfactual attention is that it is so easy to imagine "getting away with" changing only a few causal antecedents and producing a consequential result. It requires little rewriting of history to posit hypothetical worlds in which Oswald missed his target or in which Kennedy chose to ride through Dallas in a car with a bulletproof roof. These possible worlds are only a muscle twitch or nightmare removed from the actual world.

We run into similar conceptual problems on the consequent side of counterfactuals. Consider a variation of Pascal's conjecture on the causal impact of Cleopatra's nose on the course of Western history. Fearon (Chapter 2) concedes that "if Cleopatra had an unattractively large nose, World War I might not have occurred" but argues that the counterfactual hardly belongs in any reasonable explanatory account of World War I. If Cleopatra's nose were that consequential, the hypothetical world of 1914 is almost certainly not just a minor variant of the actual world of 1914, but rather a radically different world in which the nonoccurrence of World War I is but one of countless points of difference that go back 2,000 years. There might also be no Germany or Great Britain. Fearon proposes, as a pragmatic rule of evidence, that we seriously consider only those counterfactuals in which the antecedent seems likely to affect the specified consequent *and* very little else. This argument invokes a surgical-strike model of counterfactual infer-

ence in which we not only manipulate one thing at a time, we give priority
attention only to those causes specifically relevant to the consequent of interest (if and only if the hypothesized causal variable takes on the value x',
then the effect occurs *and* everything else in the hypothesized world is pretty
much identical to the actual world).

Fearon's proposal is open to challenge on the ground that it arbitrarily
rules out causes that, because of their location in complex systemic networks
of causation, do not have effects that can be conceptually isolated. For our
part, we see no easy resolution of the tension between the desire of methodologists to "hold other things equal" and the insistence of latter-day Leibnizians that once we tamper with one element from the past, we have to
trace through the causal implications for all other elements, in effect creating
a full-fledged alternative world for each counterfactual. The argument is best
engaged on a case-by-case basis, with a minimum of metaphysical posturing. Investigators should obviously be sensitive to systemic effects and be
precise about the implications of implementing their hypothesized causes in
hypothetical worlds. In some cases, the grounds for suspecting systemic
effects will be weak and the counterfactual exercise can approximate the
austere parsimony of the thought experiment; in other cases, the grounds for
suspecting systemic effects will be powerful and counterfactual exercises
will acquire the rich narrative trappings of scenario generation, with detailed
stories and subplots elaborated around why certain historical paths were not
taken and what would have had to be different to activate them (Chapter 12,
Weber).

2. Cotenability: Logical Consistency of Connecting Principles

Every counterfactual is a condensed or incomplete argument that requires
connecting principles that can sustain, but not imply, the conditional claim
(Goodman 1983). When explicitly articulated, these connecting principles
are often complex, even in the case of such seemingly simple counterfactuals as "If the match had been scratched, it would have lighted." The connecting principles specify, within reasonable limits, everything else that
would have to be true to sustain the counterfactual, including the necessary
amount of friction generated by the scratch, the chemical composition of the
match, the absence of water, the presence of oxygen, and so forth.

In our view, connecting principles should satisfy three minimal criteria.
They should be specified reasonably precisely, be consistent with each
other, and be consistent with both the antecedent and consequent. Unfortunately, as several contributors point out, counterfactual arguments in
world politics often fail the first test so badly that it is impossible to tell how
well they might have fared against the second and third tests. Focusing on

the Cuban missile crisis, Lebow and Stein (Chapter 5) note that liberal "revisionists . . . provide no compelling justification for their expectation that had Kennedy made a secret overture to Khrushchev before choosing the blockade, Khrushchev would have responded positively." It is just as plausible that he would have stood firm and accelerated the construction of the missile sites—as the Soviet military in Cuba did initially in response to the blockade. Although some liberal revisionists do advance the connecting-principle rationale that it would have been easier for Khrushchev to back down in the absence of a public confrontation, they cannot rebut the counterargument that Khrushchev needed a serious confrontation to justify a withdrawal to hard-liners in the politburo. They cannot do so because they lack a sound basis for specifying when the Soviet political leadership would have responded in an accommodative or confrontational fashion.

Conservative revisionists have similar problems. They are fond of counterfactuals in which a president who displayed greater resolve prevented the missile crisis of 1962. In this view, Khrushchev doubted Kennedy's resolve for two reasons: the president's poor performance, and Khrushchev's view of Americans as "too soft, too liberal, and too rich to fight." The counterfactual hypothesizes that Khrushchev would not have sent missiles to Cuba if Kennedy had displayed greater resolve at the Bay of Pigs, at the Vienna summit, and in Berlin. It does not specify, however, how presidential displays of resolve would have altered Khrushchev's view of the American people. Although Khrushchev might have revised his alleged estimate of the American public had it enthusiastically supported a hard-line strategy, it is also plausible that had Kennedy committed American forces to the Bay of Pigs, he might have embroiled his administration in a politically divisive and militarily costly quagmire that only reinforced Khruschchev's view of Americans. Here again, no compelling political logic connects antecedent to consequent.

The complexity of the connecting principles underlying counterfactual arguments creates plenty of opportunities for running afoul of the cotenability standard (Goodman 1983; Elster 1978). Consider, for example, one part of Jon Elster's (1978) critique of Robert Fogel's (1964) classic counterfactual that "if the railroads had not existed, the American economy in the nineteenth century would have grown only slightly more slowly than it actually did." Elster argues that it is nonsensical to postulate as a supportive connecting principle that the internal combustion engine would have been invented earlier in the America without railroads because the postulate presupposes a theory of technical innovation that undercuts the original antecedent. If we have a theory of innovation that requires the invention of cars fifty years earlier, why does it not also require the invention of railroads? (Of course, Fogel's core counterfactual claim concerning the limited economic impact of railroads may still be correct even without speeding up the invention of automobiles. It rests on complex comparisons of the actual world with an elaborate counterfactual model of a nineteenth-century American economy that relied on waterways instead of railroads.)

In a similar spirit, Lars-Erik Cederman (Chapter 11) criticizes John Mueller's (1989) claim concerning the "irrelevance" of nuclear weapons. Mueller constructs a counterfactual non-nuclear scenario to demonstrate that nuclear weapons did not contribute to the postwar peace. Cederman notes that "the problem with Mueller's account is that he explicitly traces postwar history as it actually happened, including the Cuban missile crisis, while merely subtracting nuclear technology." This procedure illustrates the perils of superficially rewriting history. It is not at all clear that cotenability obtains between the counterfactual antecedent of a non-nuclear world and any connecting principle that posits the occurrence of the Cuban missile crisis in 1962. Why would the Soviets go to all the trouble of placing conventionally armed intermediate-range missiles in Cuba? Why take so large a risk for so small an advantage? There is something odd about the hypothetical world that Mueller created.

The two standards considered so far—logical clarity and cotenability—are helpful for screening out ambiguous and oxymoronic counterfactuals; purely formal (content-free) standards are not helpful, however, for screening out counterfactuals that invoke bizarre antecedents or connecting principles. What, for example, should we make of the suggestion that "if Napoleon had possessed a Stealth bomber, he would have won the Battle of Waterloo," or that "if Oswald did not shoot Kennedy, then someone else would have done so, because Kennedy was astrologically fated to die by assassination"? An adequate normative theory of counterfactual inference should give us principled grounds for rejecting conjectures of this sort. We see four ways of preempting such nonsense and we take up each in turn.

3. Consistency with Well-Established Historical Facts

Several scholars have proposed a "minimal-rewrite-of-history" rule designed to eliminate far-fetched counterfactuals that radically transform the temporal landscape (cf. Hawthorn 1991, 158; Weber 1949). They propose that, in principle, possible worlds should: (a) start with the real world as it was otherwise known before asserting the counterfactual; (b) not require us to unwind the past and rewrite long stretches of history; (c) not unduly disturb what we otherwise know about the original actors and their beliefs and goals. As noted earlier, these guidelines represent ground rules for assessing historical "possibility-hood." Operationally, investigators might agree to constrain counterfactual speculation in a host of more specific ways: by considering as antecedents only those policy options that participants themselves considered and (ideally) almost accepted, by giving extra weight to counterfactual antecedents that "undo" unusual events that appear to have made the decisive difference between the occurrence and nonoccurrence of the target event (and perhaps only the target event), by ruling out counterfactuals in which the antecedent and consequent are separated by such wide gaps of time that it is silly to suppose that all other things can be held equal, and by linking antecedent and consequent with connecting principles that are faithful to what we know about how people at the time thought and about the constraints within which people at the time had to work. This complex set of rules contains potential contradictions, but it does capture the flavor of most idiographic forms of counterfactual analysis (Chapter 3, Breslauer; Hart and Honoré 1959; Nash 1991).

Variants of the minimal-rewrite rule appear at several points in this volume. Scholars often invoke the rule to challenge or defend the legitimacy of considering certain counterfactual antecedents. For example, Lebow and Stein (Chapter 5) use this criterion to eliminate the "early warning" counterfactual that "had President Kennedy issued a timely warning in the spring of 1962, Khrushchev might not have sent missiles to Cuba." According to Lebow and Stein, the antecedent is implausible because it requires rewriting too much history. They note that "in April, before the conventional buildup began, Kennedy had no reason to suspect a missile deployment, and months away from an election campaign, had no strong political incentive to issue a warning." To sustain the antecedent, then, we have to rewrite history to alter both the political incentives and the evidence confronting the U.S. government. Using a similar standard, Khong (Chapter 4) argues for the plausibility of the antecedent in the counterfactual that "if Britain had confronted Hitler over Czechoslovakia, he would have backed down and World War II might have been avoided." According to Khong, the decisive factor in Britain's unwillingness to risk war at the time of Munich was neither the memory of World War I nor the unfavorable military balance, but Chamberlain's personal conviction that he could negotiate a diplomatic solution with Hitler. Khong finds historical evidence that influential politicians, including Eden, Cooper, and, of course, Churchill, favored a strong stance against Hitler as early as 1937. Hence, to the extent that any of these men could have been prime minister at the time of Munich, the antecedent becomes plausible.

Scholars also use the minimal-rewrite rule to assess the plausibility of connecting principles. For instance, Lebow and Stein (Chapter 5) assess Khrushchev's counterfactual claim that had the Soviet Union not deployed missiles in Cuba, the United States would have invaded the island. Lebow and Stein point to recently uncovered evidence that even before the missile deployment, no influential members of the Kennedy administration wanted to attack Cuba. The option had been considered but decisively rejected. Kennedy and Secretary of Defense McNamara had been impressed by Cuban popular support for Fidel Castro and the ability of the Cuban militia to overwhelm the invasion force at the Bay of Pigs. Revised intelligence estimates indicated that a successful invasion would require massive U.S.

forces, which would have to remain in an occupational role for an indefinite period. Kennedy and McNamara were deterred by these costs and resolved not to attack unless there were dramatic political changes inside Cuba.

It is worth emphasizing that consistency with well-established historical facts may often be a necessary but is rarely a sufficient condition for establishing the plausibility of counterfactuals. As Breslauer (Chapter 3) notes, most counterfactual claims advanced in the Sovietological literature were consistent with historical evidence. He observes that "the problem was not invention of facts, but gaps in established bodies of facts, which allowed for multiple interpretation of the meanings of those pools of evidence."

4. Consistency with Well-Established Theoretical Laws

Just as we need historical and logical constraints on counterfactual reasoning, we also need theoretical constraints on the connecting principles we use to link antecedents and consequents. Otherwise, we cannot rule out counterfactuals that start from reasonable antecedents but end in far-fetched consequences by invoking preposterous principles of causality such as: "If Oswald had not shot Kennedy, then someone else would have done so, because Kennedy was astrologically fated to die by assassination," or "If North Korea had conquered South Korea in 1950, the economy of the South would have grown even more rapidly than it actually did because of the wisdom of the policy of self-sufficiency of the Great Leader Kim Il Sung."

Ideally, we could ground all counterfactual inferences in extensively validated scientific laws of the sort we drew upon in the match-lighting conditional. But do we have theoretical laws of comparable scope and power in the behavioral and social sciences? Some contributors, such as Lebow and Stein (Chapter 5), reject the notion that there are *any* well-established theories of international politics. They evaluate counterfactuals concerning the Cuban missile crisis by relying largely on case-specific political and historical standards. Other contributors, such as Kiser and Levi (Chapter 8), enthusiastically embrace deductive theory as a means of disciplining otherwise unruly "what-might-have-been" speculation.

The economic historian Robert Fogel is perhaps the preeminent advocate of the view that it is reasonable to rely on strong theory to fill in the missing counterfactual data points. Theory-guided counterfactuals are absolutely essential for assessing the economic impact of policies and technologies:

> The net effect of such things on development involves a comparison between what actually happened and what would have happened in the absence of the specified circumstance. However, since the counterfactual never occurred, it could not have been observed and hence is not recorded in historical documents. In order to determine what would have happened in the absence of a given circumstance, the economic historian needs a set of general statements (that is, a set of theories or

model) that will enable him to deduce a counterfactual situation from institutions and relationships that actually existed. (Fogel 1964, 224)

In this view, counterfactual reasoning is a straightforward application of Hempel's (1965) covering law of historical explanation: "Counterfactual propositions [in quantitative economic history] are merely inferences from hypothetico-deductive models" (Fogel 1964).

Following the Hempel-Fogel neopositivist tradition, many game theorists, neoclassical economists, and structural realists display impressive confidence in their counterfactual claims. They know that if one changes the incentives confronting rational actors, those actors will quickly identify the new utility-maximizing course of action. If a currency is under- or overvalued, arbitrageurs will seize upon profit-making opportunities. If state regulations reward inefficiency and punish efficiency, aggregate economic output will fall. If a status quo power offers weak or incredible promises of extended deterrence to its allies, aggressors with much to gain and little to lose will strike. The calculus of rational action is not, however, the only theoretical logic that we can use to infer what would have happened in this or that counterfactual scenario. We can draw upon sociological theories that stress normative and institutional rules of fairness, cultural theories that stress group values and identifications, political theories of bureaucratic and interest-group competition, and cognitive theories of belief systems and bounded rationality.

Consider this sampling of the range of theories that political observers draw upon to "fill in" missing counterfactual data points:

(1) Keohane (1984) supports his claim that "if there were no international regimes, there would be less cooperation" by appealing to the Coase-Williamson tradition of institutional economics that stresses the role that institutions play in reducing the transaction costs of cooperation and in increasing the reputation costs of defection.

(2) Breslauer (Chapter 3) reviews the work of comparativists and area specialists who bolstered counterfactual claims about the causes of the Russian Revolution and the impact of Stalin's modernization policies by invoking theories of economic development.

(3) In their recent book, Lebow and Stein (1994) use Janis and Mann's (1977) psychological theory of decision making under stress to defend their claim that even if Kennedy had displayed more resolve at the Vienna summit, Khrushchev still would have deployed missiles in Cuba. Lebow and Stein argue that Khrushchev confronted a strategic dilemma that may well have induced a psychological state of defensive avoidance that, in turn, would have rendered Khrushchev insensitive to any plausible American signal of resolve.

(4) Kiser and Levi (Chapter 8) note how large classes of "agency" coun-

terfactuals are ruled out by structural theories of revolution. If we view revolution as inevitable when certain structural preconditions are satisfied— intense international and demographic pressures on the state, fiscal crisis, deep divisions within the dominant class, and mass mobilization of discontented groups—then there is little point in contemplating counterfactuals that assign decisive roles to the actions of individuals. Within structuralist frameworks, it is impossible to undo the English, French, or Russian revolutions by simply positing wiser kings.

(5) Cederman (Chapter 11) draws on cartel theory to support his critique of neorealism and his claim that if defense-dominance had prevailed throughout history, there would have been less stability.

(6) Herrmann and Fischerkeller (Chapter 6) invoke Huth and Russett's theory of extended deterrence (a theory indigenous to political science, not an import) to argue that even if Truman had not threatened Stalin, the Soviets still would have withdrawn from Iran.

(7) Perhaps the most systematic use of theory to assess counterfactuals occurs in the chapters by Bueno de Mesquita and Weingast. These authors argue (among other things) that possible worlds become plausible only insofar as they are logically consistent with the equilibrium conditions of the game that captures the strategic interdependence obtaining between actual historical actors. For example, it does not make much sense to posit a hypothetical world in which both players cooperated in a single-round game if one or both of the players could have been much better off by defecting whenever the other player cooperated. Using this game-theoretic screening rule, it is possible to eliminate vast numbers of counterfactuals.

This overview is, however, disturbing. It suggests that each school of thought can foster its own favorite set of supporting counterfactuals (Chapter 12, Weber). Moreover, these schools of thought will sometimes prescribe contradictory rules for assessing counterfactuals. Where does this leave us? Consistency with *well-established* theory is a reasonable standard for gauging the plausibility of counterfactuals but we should expect disagreement about what counts as well-established theory in world politics. To prevent competing schools of thought from simply inventing counterfactuals of convenience, we need reality constraints. Counterfactuals must not only fit existing historical and statistical data (the emphasis in our third and fifth standards), they must stimulate testable predictions that hold up reasonably well against new data (the emphasis in our sixth standard, projectability).

5. Consistency with Well-Established Statistical Generalizations

In many contexts, we rely not on theoretical laws but on statistical generalizations to fill in "what would have happened if this rather than that event had occurred." One obvious form such reasoning takes is reliance on base rates and patterns of covariation. For instance, we might justify the counterfactual, "If Bill Clinton had lost the presidential election of 1992, he would have been disappointed," by observing in a two-by-two contingency table that when people fail to achieve a goal for which they have worked long and hard, the overwhelming majority experience disappointment, but when people do achieve their goals, there is markedly less disappointment.

The "discovery" is hardly startling; more startling, however, is the strong stand that some scholars take on both the *necessity* and *sufficiency* of statistical justification for assessing counterfactual claims. In his commentary, Dawes, for instance, treats statistical evidence as trump when he declares that counterfactual inferences are justified *if and only if* they are embedded in a system of statistical contingency for which we have reasonable evidence. He offers an intriguing example:

> Suppose that someone is required to wager her entire wealth on a single roll of a pair of fair dice. Her wealth will be doubled if she wins the bet; if she loses, she will be bankrupt. Her choice is to bet either for or against a roll of snake eyes. Being wise, she bets against snake eyes. The dice are rolled and they come up snake eyes. She loses. She is bankrupt. Is it normatively valid to state that "if only" she had bet on snake eyes, she would have won? Well, it is true that she bet against snake eyes and that she lost. But does the "if only" add anything to the analysis? I suggest the answer is no. But suppose she had bet on snake eyes and lost. Here, I suggest that the regretful counterfactual inference that "if only" she had bet against snake eyes she would have won is normatively justified. Why? Because the odds are thirty-five to one against snake eyes, and those odds justify the expectation that she would have won had she bet against snake eyes. It's an expectation; one can insert "probably won" if one wishes.

The plausibility of the snake-eyes counterfactual hinges on the aim of inquiry. From an historical point of view, the counterfactual is plausible. We do not have to rewrite much history to reach a hypothetical world in which the woman threw the dice slightly differently and won her bet. The bet against snake eyes is an easily imagined and easily reversed cause of bankruptcy. To statisticians of both the Bayesian and frequentist schools, however, the counterfactual is implausible because it posits so unlikely an outcome. We certainly do not want people drawing the lesson from history that it is a good idea to risk their fortunes on long-shot wagers.[3]

---

[3] Dawes's snake-eyes problem bears a deep resemblance to Newcomb's paradox, which pits statistical intuition against causal intuition through an ingenious thought experiment that calls upon us to imagine a being who has demonstrated a phenomenal capacity to make accurate predictions ($R^2 = 1.0$) and who has asked us to make a choice involving two boxes, $B1$ and $B2$. $B1$ contains $1,000; $B2$ contains either $1,000,000 or nothing. Our choice is between two actions: (1) taking what is in both boxes; (2) taking only what is in the second box. Furthermore, we know, and the being knows we know, and so on, that if the being predicts that we

One need not, of course, accept the radical epistemological argument of Dawes to agree with the more moderate mainstream view that canons of sound statistical reasoning should constrain our judgments of counterfactuals (King, Keohane, and Verba 1994) and, indeed, that we should be alert to the psychological fact that people are flawed intuitive statisticians who fall prey to various biases in detecting and using covariation data. The experimental literature warns us that people often draw inappropriately strong conclusions from observing only the cause-present/effect-present cell of contingency tables and see strong relationships between variables that they expect to be correlated but are in reality only weakly correlated (Nisbett and Ross 1980). A good start in implementing our fifth criterion would be simply to improve the accuracy of intuitive estimates of covariation, with special attention to sensitizing people to the problem of missing counterfactual data. Accurate covariation estimates would, however, be just the beginning and would not protect us from accepting many false counterfactual claims (Type I errors) and rejecting many true ones (Type II errors). We also need to beware of biases produced by nonrandom selection, confounding variables, and omitted variables, as well as a host of other familiar obstacles to meaningful statistical inference (King, Keohane, and Verba 1994). These statistical issues play an especially prominent role in Russett's chapter, which grapples with the controversial counterfactual that if all states in the twentieth century had been democratic, there would have been markedly fewer wars. Skeptics of the democratic-peace hypothesis challenge this counterfactual on various grounds, including the inadequacy of the available statistical samples (too few democracies, too few wars, and too truncated a range of time), the inadequacy of the operational definitions of democracy and war (the self-serving suppleness of certain judgment calls), and—perhaps most important—the collinearity problems created by confounding variables that, once controlled for in regressions, may "explain away" the democracy effect. Russett responds by rebutting these objections, in the process illustrating the enormous overlap between traditional procedures for hypothesis testing and

---

will take what is in both boxes, he will not put the $1 million in the second box; if the being predicts we will take only what is in the second box, he will put the $1 million in the second box. The rules are straightforward. First the being makes his prediction; then he puts the $1 million in the second box or not, according to his prediction; then we make our choice.

The problem is paradoxical because powerful epistemic intuitions push us in opposite directions (Nozick 1993). Statistical intuition tells us that if we take what is in both boxes, the being almost certainly will have predicted this choice and will not have put the $1 million in the second box, whereas if we take only what is in the second box we will almost certainly get $1 million. Therefore, we should take only what is in the second box. Causal intuition tells us, however, that the being has made his prediction and has already either put the $1 million into the second box or has not. That fact cannot be undone. Therefore, we will receive more money, $1,000 more, by taking what is in both boxes.

Thought experiments of this form provide a useful means of clarifying our intuitions about how to resolve clashes between epistemic standards.

those for evaluating an important category of counterfactual (our ideal type 2, the nomothetic).

Statistical tests of counterfactual plausibility also play a pivotal role in the chapters by game theorists. Weingast's notion of comparative statistics reminds us of the need to build appropriate time lags into our assessments of covariation. And Bueno de Mesquita's work on medieval church-state relations reminds us of the need for probabilistic tests of hypotheses concerning mixed-strategy equilibria.

6. Projectability

Theory evaluation and counterfactual evaluation are inextricably entangled. Sound counterfactuals require sound theories that provide the lawlike generalizations that fill in the missing data points in our thought experiments. How can we judge, however, whether these lawlike generalizations are robust enough to support counterfactual inferences? Here Nelson Goodman's (1983) concept of projectability is helpful. Goodman draws a sharp distinction between coincidental generalizations that just happen to be true at a particular time and place (and are therefore unprojectable) and robustly lawlike generalizations that hold up over a range of circumstances and permit projection into the past and future. An example of a merely coincidental generalization is "All the coins in my pocket yesterday were silver." Nothing follows from this observation—certainly not "If this penny were in my pocket yesterday, it would be silver." The counterfactual fails because "if this penny were in my pocket yesterday," we would simply assume that the original generalization—"all the coins in my pocket yesterday were silver"—was false. By contrast, a robustly lawlike generalization—such as that oxygen is a necessary but not sufficient condition for fire—inspires confidence when we move either backward in time (if there had been no oxygen, the Great Fire of London would not have occurred) or forward in time (if we cut off any future fire's source of oxygen, the fire will expire).

Most social-science generalizations, of course, qualify as neither merely coincidental nor robustly lawlike; they take the form of either contingent generalizations (under this set of boundary conditions, x causes y; under that set, x causes z) or statistical generalizations (x increases or decreases the likelihood of y) or contingent statistical generalizations (cf. George and Smoke 1974; George 1993). From Goodman's perspective, however, whether the generalization is bounded or unbounded by moderator variables and whether the generalization is deterministic or probabilistic, it is subject to the same acid test of scientific legitimacy: namely, its projectability or its ability to predict what will happen in new, hitherto unobserved cases. The same causal principles that allow us to retrodict the past should allow us to

predict the future. Indeed, the strong Popperian form of this argument asserts that we should take counterfactual claims seriously if and only if the
lawlike generalizations supporting the claims yield falsifiable forecasts. We
see this classic philosophical argument resurfacing in the recent methodological advice of King, Keohane, and Verba (1994), who urge scholars
to search aggressively for the observable implications of their causal constructs by regularly asking themselves, "If my argument is correct, what else
should be true?" Counterfactuals that are devoid of testable implications in
the actual world leave us marooned in hypothetical worlds of our own subjective making. Projectability, from this vantage point, stands as the preeminent criterion for judging the value of counterfactual speculation.

Perhaps not coincidentally, the most outspoken advocates of the projectability standard in this volume tend to be the most nomothetic in their
overall approach to social science. Bueno de Mesquita and Weingast are not
content with post-hoc exercises in which they fit game-theoretic models to
data; they derive testable implications from their models and show how
those predictions can be statistically or historically disconfirmed. In a similar
vein, Russett is not satisfied with showing that the democratic-peace hypothesis captures an intriguing regularity in the brief slice of history that we call
modern; he seeks out alternative data sources—Greek city-states and tribal
societies—into which we can project the hypothesis. In his computer simulations, Cederman explores the replicability and robustness of his counterintuitive result that defense-dominance increases rather than decreases the
likelihood of the emergence of hegemons. And in their critique of structuralist theories of revolution, Kiser and Levi raise the suspicion that structuralist
theories—with their emphasis on complex conjunctions of preconditions—
are ultimately exercises in post-hoc data-fitting that will never pass the projectability test.[4]

---

[4] The strong version of the "projectability" argument treats backward and forward reasoning
in time as symmetrical. There are good reasons, however, for suspecting that even when we can
construct compelling explanations of the past, we will often do a terrible job of explaining the
future (Dawes 1993; Chapter 2, Fearon). When we look back into the past from the present, we
occupy a privileged but also easily abused position. We know which one of the many futures
that were once possible has actually occurred. With the benefit of this retrospective knowledge,
it becomes relatively easy to find antecedents that depict the consequence as the inevitable result
of some "inexorable" causal process. Yet we risk capitalizing, indeed massively capitalizing, on
chance. By contrast, when we look forward into the future, we cannot avoid the complexity and
indeterminacy of possible relationships among antecedents and consequences. We can draw
upon our knowledge of past causal relationships to anticipate the future, but are often disappointed by the results. The causes we identified retrospectively for a class of consequences
prove to be anemic predictors of the same class in the future. Dawes (1993) illustrates this
argument with the crash of a passenger airplane into a parked truck on a runway under repair at
Mexico City airport on October 31, 1979. The FAA flight investigators easily constructed a
causal story for the outcome that invoked such plausible antecedents as poor weather, smog,
pilot fatigue, radio malfunction, cryptic communication by traffic controllers, and stress. But

Psychological Perspectives on Counterfactual Reasoning

Up to this juncture, we have focused on normative perspectives on counter-factual reasoning—on the criteria that people should use to generate and judge counterfactual arguments. We now turn to psychological perspectives. There is a thriving research literature in both cognitive psychology (Commentary 2, Olson, Roese, and Deibert) and linguistics (Commentary 1, Turner) on how people actually generate and judge counterfactual claims. These normative and psychological arguments should not, of course, be viewed as two self-contained, hermetically sealed domains of discourse. The psychological literature highlights a host of determinants of spontaneous counterfactual reasoning that raise serious questions about the reliability and validity of counterfactual thought experiments in world politics. Indeed, when the topic is thought experiments, it is hard to say at what point epistemology and methodology end and psychology begins.

From a broadly psychological perspective, it is difficult to imagine avoiding serious bias in thought experiments. Bias can creep into every stage of this inherently subjective process, from the initial selection of antecedents (for "mental manipulation") to the evaluation of connecting principles to the willingness to entertain counterarguments and alternative scenarios. Bias appears inevitable, in part because of the cognitive limitations and motivational inclinations of the thinker in whose mind the thought experiment "runs," and in part because of the extraordinary complexity and ambiguity of the task. The population of past events from which one can draw counterfactual antecedents is effectively infinite, from the flapping of butterfly wings to the "structural polarity" of the international system. And the task of assessing what would have happened in these hypothetical worlds (to which no one has access) is obviously highly subjective. Consider the potential for epistemic mischief.

Cognitive Biases

A useful starting point is the principle of bounded rationality (Simon 1957). People, it is now widely conceded, are limited-capacity information pro-

---

the causal variables identified in that story will probably not help FAA investigators to predict future crashes. For example, pilots are often tired, but rarely crash, and many crashes occur when pilots are well rested. This argument suggests that counterfactuals in world politics often fail the projectability test not because the underlying claims are false, but rather because there are such complex interactions among causal variables and so much potential for randomly distributed small causes to be amplified into large effects (a point reminiscent of chaos theory). In this view, projectability is most likely to break down for explanations of low-likelihood and low-frequency events (exactly the sorts of surprising events that, psychologists argue, are most likely to attract counterfactual speculation).

cessors who rely on low-effort strategies to simplify an otherwise intolerably complex world (Kahneman, Slovic, and Tversky 1982). The price of cognitive economy is, however, steep: increased susceptibility to systematic biases and errors. We itemize several ways in which reliance on simplifying strategies might distort the conclusions we draw from counterfactual thought experiments.

(1) *What gets mutated?* This is the ground floor for the entry of psychological bias into thought experiments. As Kahneman and Miller (1986) argue in their influential norm theory, the human perceptual apparatus is attuned to notice change. The more abrupt or discontinuous the change, the more likely people are to notice it, to try to explain it, and to generate counterfactual scenarios in which they "mutate" the departure from normality to the more customary and expected default value (Commentary 2, Olson, Roese, and Deibert). For example, experimental subjects generate more "if only" thoughts and experience more regret upon learning that the victim of a traffic accident had departed from her regular route to the office than they do upon learning that the accident victim had adhered to her regular route. It is easier to "mentally undo" accidents or indeed other events that constitute deviations from the routine.

Translating this well-replicated finding from the experimental literature into the realm of world politics is no simple exercise. This volume, however, contains much evidence that departures from normality or the status quo do indeed attract especially vigorous counterfactual speculation. These departures can take diverse forms, including leadership transitions (Chapter 3, Breslauer; Chapter 6, Herrmann and Fischerkeller), revolutions (Chapter 8, Kiser and Levi), assassinations (Chapter 3, Breslauer), and unusually intense policy debates in which the argument might easily have gone either way (Chapter 4, Khong; Chapter 5, Lebow and Stein). Routine events fade into the perceptual background and are rarely selected for mental manipulation in thought experiments. Of course, not all social scientists conform to the predictions of norm theory. Nomothetic investigators often invoke background conditions that change almost imperceptibly slowly (such as the size of the middle class in early twentieth-century Russia or the "polarity" of the pre–World War I balance of power). And chaos and complexity theorists specialize in demonstrating the sensitive dependence of major outcomes on minor background conditions, such as the flapping of butterfly wings. Norm theory fits idiographic better than nomothetic "counterfactualizing."

(2) *Once constructed, which counterfactual scenarios are judged plausible?* The simplifying strategies that people use to impose cognitive order carry a price tag. These strategies can tilt the playing field (arguably unfairly) in favor of certain counterfactuals over others. Consider the much discussed trilogy of judgmental heuristics: anchoring, availability, and representativeness (Tversky and Kahneman 1974). The anchoring heuristic could lead people to be too quick to dismiss scenarios about hypothetical worlds

that deviate dramatically from the perceptual anchor of the actual world with which they are already so familiar (making it difficult to appreciate the arbitrariness of the status quo); the availability heuristic could lead people to be too quick to embrace vivid, easily imaginable scenarios that link all the component events into a compelling story (even though the compound probability of all the narrative's components taken together is vanishingly small); the representativeness heuristic could lead people to be too slow to concede plausibility to counterfactuals that posit dramatic nonlinearities in cause-effect relations (making it difficult to appreciate that small causes can sometimes produce big effects and vice versa).

Perhaps the most lethal threat to the validity of counterfactual thought experiments comes, however, from theory-driven thinking. We have already noted that counterfactual reasoning will inevitably be theory-driven to some degree. Indeed, we treated "consistency with well-established theory" as a defining feature of sound counterfactual reasoning. But the cognitive perspective leads us to be suspicious of people's capacity to apply standards of evidence and proof in an evenhanded fashion (Nisbett and Ross 1980; Fiske and Taylor 1991). People often succumb to the temptation of applying strong tests to dissonant arguments and weak tests to consonant ones—a temptation that may be especially pronounced when the arguments invoke possible worlds that no one can ever enter and that can never be decisively disconfirmed. The perceived plausibility of a counterfactual hinges on how hard one looks for shortcomings. Few counterfactual arguments will not have points of vulnerability when we subject their antecedents and connecting principles to close scrutiny. As a result, we are much more likely to recognize the collapse of cotenability in our opponents arguments than in our own—a recurring theme in several chapters.

The cognitive perspective also leads us to be suspicious of people's capacity to transcend (avoid contamination by) outcome knowledge. As theory-driven thinkers, people automatically try to assimilate "what happened" to some prior knowledge structure or schema that specifies cause-effect relationships for events of that type (Fischhoff 1975; Hawkins and Hastie 1990). The result is a deep, and arguably unjustifiable, asymmetry between backward and forward reasoning in time. On average, political experts see fewer possible pasts than they do possible futures (Tetlock 1994). When they look backward in time, they mobilize their finite mental resources to explain the one outcome of the many possible outcomes that actually occurred, selectively recruiting the most plausible (theory-consistent) antecedents that will allow them to tell a good causal story for that outcome (Commentary 3, Dawes; Chapter 12, Weber). By contrast, when experts look forward into the future, they are typically unsure of what will happen. In part for contingency planning and in part to avoid the embarrassment of making blatantly wrong forecasts, experts often survey in a reasonably open-minded way the panoply of possibilities and conditions for their occurrence. This cognitive analysis helps us to explain an otherwise paradoxical pattern in expert judgment: bold counterfactuals and timid forecasts. Experts often assert that they know what would have happened in the past but modestly demur on what will happen in the future.

Motivational Biases

Thus far, we have focused on only cognitive sources of bias. People are not, of course, just information-processing devices; they are animated by wishes, hopes, and fears that shape their perceptions of what might or could or should have been (Commentary 2, Olson, Roese, and Deibert). These emotional needs can take many, sometimes conflicting forms (Tetlock and Levi 1982). Consider the following possibilities suggested by the psychological literature:

(1) *Needs for predictability and controllability*: On the one hand, people might allow their desire to believe that the world is fundamentally predictable to rule out butterfly-effect counterfactuals, which imply that, no matter how hard we try, it is in principle impossible to anticipate the future because so much hinges on small causes that are beyond our measurement grasp. On the other hand, people might allow their desire to believe that the world is controllable to rule out "inevitability" counterfactuals, which imply that, no matter what people do, our fates are ultimately under the sway of powerful geopolitical, macroeconomic, and technological forces beyond individual mastery. Indeed, this psychological need to believe in a "controllable world" may lie at the heart of Kissinger's conversion from his belief as an academic observer in deterministic arguments that minimized policy makers' latitude to influence events, to his world view as a policy maker which assigned a much more prominent role to individual human beings who could be persuaded—through the right combination of arguments and inducements—to change their minds (Chapter 3, Breslauer; Kissinger 1993).

(2) *Needs to avoid blame and to claim credit*: On the one hand, people might allow their desire to avoid blame for bad outcomes to override their desires for predictability and control. In such cases, people will argue that they should not be blamed for having failed to foresee the unforeseeable or having failed to control the uncontrollable. On the other hand, people might allow the desire to claim credit for good outcomes to enhance the plausibility of counterfactuals that take the form "had it not been for my superior predictive ability and courageous willingness to act on the basis of that insight, this good outcome would never have occurred."

(3) *Needs for consolation and inspiration*: People might use "downward" counterfactuals to comfort and console themselves ("Things may not be

great, but think how bad things could have been if x or y had occurred") or "upward" counterfactuals to inspire greater effort ("Do not be complacent about the present, think how good things could have been and, by implication, could yet become").

(4) *Need for cognitive consistency*: The well-documented aversion to imbalanced or dissonant couplings of events should motivate people to rule out counterfactuals that link bad causes (like Stalin) to good outcomes (like accelerated economic growth) or that link good causes (like foreign aid) to bad outcomes (like increased dependency and corruption of recipient regimes). Pressures for cognitive consistency should also motivate people to defend "core beliefs." For example, people who believe that "evil is avoidable" should be strongly motivated to generate counterfactuals that undo moral catastrophes. But people of different political persuasions may define moral catastrophe differently. For many conservatives, the root of evil in Soviet history goes straight back to the Bolshevik revolution of 1917 (which should be a focal point of "if only" speculation); for many social democrats, a noble socialist experiment was corrupted by Stalinist tyranny (which should be a focal point of "if only" speculation). These predictions fare reasonably well against the evidence (Chaper 3, Breslauer).

The list is a lengthy and unparsimonious one. Here we simply want to add that there are always two levels at which motives may influence counterfactual reasoning: private thought (affecting what we truly believe) and public posturing (affecting what we say we believe and want to induce others to believe). Most psychologists think that the motives listed here do indeed shape privately held plausibility judgments of counterfactuals, but few would deny that public impression management is also at work (Tetlock and Manstead 1985)—a judgment with which most of our contributors seem to concur. This volume contains suggestive evidence that the closer we get to prescriptive policy debates, the greater the temptation to use counterfactual arguments as rhetorical tools to justify either what one plans to do or has already done (Chapter 3, Breslauer; Chapter 5, Lebow and Stein; Chapter 6, Herrmann and Fischerkeller).

How should we respond to this extended list of cognitive and motivational threats to the validity of thought experiments? We urge a middle-ground response between arrogance and despair. The arrogant response is, of course, to argue that although mere mortals may fall prey to these biases, serious professionals are surely immune. We judge this response arrogant because there is already abundant evidence that a wide range of professionals working on important tasks are susceptible to many of the effects discussed here (Dawes 1991). Moreover, some of our contributors report evidence of certain hypothesized biases in the scholarly literature (Chapter 3, Breslauer; Chapter 8, Kiser and Levi). The despairing response is, of course, to argue that the biases identified by psychologists are inevitable—

COUNTERFACTUAL THOUGHT EXPERIMENTS

that they have hopelessly contaminated all counterfactual arguments advanced thus far and will contaminate all counterfactuals advanced into the foreseeable future. The former response is too dismissive of the psychological literature; the latter takes it too literally. The appropriate response in our view is to acknowledge cognitive biases and to make good-faith efforts to hold each other accountable to standards of evidence (such as those sketched in this chapter) that check the most serious and pervasive of these biases (Tetlock 1992b). All research methods are subject to contamination and misinterpretation; it is only prudent to beware of potential biases in the most subjective of all methods of inquiry, the counterfactual thought experiment.

Conclusion

There is something about the topic of counterfactual thought experiments in world politics that makes people feel a bit uneasy, even defensive. To be blunt, it feels like epistemological slumming. As social scientists, we are all too familiar with the prestige hierarchy for methods of drawing causal inference. At the top of the scientific pecking order is experimentation in which we can manipulate hypothesized causes and then either hold everything else constant or randomize extraneous influences across treatment conditions. Experimental control of this sort is obviously out of the question for most questions in world politics. We cannot rerun the tape of history: splicing a Gorbachev in or out, delaying or accelerating key technological development, or tinkering with this or that aspect of macroeconomic policy.

Social scientists often resort to statistical control when experimentation is ethically or practically problematic. But statistical arguments themselves often rest on counterfactual assumptions (Fearon 1991) and are, in any case, extraordinarily difficult to make for many issues that loom large in security debates. For example, what kind of regression or time series analyses will allow us to estimate the causal contribution of nuclear weapons to the "long peace" between the United States and Soviet Union between 1945 and 1991? There are simply too many confounding variables—a problem we can alleviate but not eliminate through judicious selection of comparison cases and meticulous process-tracing of decision-making protocols.

So where does that leave us? Probably still feeling uneasy: we seem to be stuck with quite literally a third-rate method, counterfactual thought experimentation. The control groups exist—if indeed "exist" is the right word—in the imaginations of political analysts who are left with the daunting task of reconstructing how history would have unfolded if causal variables of the past had taken on different values from the ones they actually did. The whole exercise starts to look hopelessly subjective, circular, and nonfalsifiable. What is to stop us from simply inventing counterfactual outcomes that justify our political biases and predilections? There appear to be large classes of questions in the study of global conflict and cooperation for which experimental control is out of the question and statistical control is of limited usefulness (assuming we can find a reasonable set of comparison cases and can reliably operationalize the theoretical constructs). These questions are too important to ignore, but apparently too difficult to answer in a fashion that commands transideological consensus.

Too often, the response to the dilemma is to embrace extreme solutions (Strassfeld 1992): either to reject categorically all counterfactual arguments as fanciful suppositions, mere conjecture, and frivolous figments (counterfactual dread) or to assume confidently that we know exactly what would have happened if we had gone down another path, sometimes going so far as to project several steps deep into hypothetical causal sequences (counterfactual bravado). The former response leads to futile efforts to exorcize counterfactuals from historical inquiry (Fisher 1970); the latter response leads at best to error (we ignore the compounding of probabilities at our peril) and at worst to the full-scale politicization of counterfactual argument (as advocates claim carte blanche to write hypothetical histories that advance their favorite causes). This book tries to articulate a principled compromise between these extremes. On the one hand, we acknowledge that thought experiments inevitably play key roles in the causal arguments of any historical discipline. On the other hand, we acknowledge that thought experiments are often suffused with error and bias. But, that said, we do not conclude that things are hopeless—that it is impossible to draw causal lessons from history. Rather, we conclude that disciplined use of counterfactuals—grounded in explicit standards of evidence and proof—can be enlightening in specific historical, theoretical, and policy settings. And that, we suspect, is the most important lesson of this book.

2

Causes and Counterfactuals in Social Science

EXPLORING AN ANALOGY BETWEEN CELLULAR AUTOMATA AND HISTORICAL PROCESSES

JAMES D. FEARON

FOR A VARIETY of purposes, social scientists and historians take the discovery of causes of events in the human world as a goal—perhaps the principal goal—of their work.[1] Some research communities are shy of the word "causes," preferring words like "influences," "determinants," "sources," "origins," "roots," "correlates," "factors that shape or give rise to," and so on. But these are all forms of language that is basically causal.[2]

When trying to argue or assess whether some factor A caused event B, social scientists frequently use counterfactuals.[3] That is, they either ask whether or claim that "if A had not occurred, B would not have occurred." Most often, such claims are little more than unelaborated rhetorical devices—throwaway lines—deployed as part of a larger rhetorical strategy to convince the reader that A caused B. Less frequently, researchers actually develop and explore the counterfactual scenario as a means of testing the causal hypothesis.

Whether counterfactual argument should be considered a valid method of testing causal hypotheses is not clear. Considerable skepticism has been expressed over the years, focusing on the objection that it is difficult or impossible to know with any certainty what would have happened if some proposed cause had been absent in a particular historical case. This is a strong objection. Who can say with any assurance what would have happened if

---

[1] I wish to thank Mark Hansen, David Laitin, participants of the conference "Counterfactual Thought Experiments in World Politics," and especially Aaron Belkin, David Collier, Philip Tetlock, Mark Turner, and Peter Woodruff for valuable comments.

[2] I am aware that there is significant debate among philosophers about whether valid explanations are all "causal" and have the same basic form, or fundamentally differ, for example, from causal explanations of physical events to intentional explanations of actions. When I say that all social scientists seek to discover causes, I do not mean that they all think about causes the same way; I would like to include intentionalist explanations, however they are precisely characterized. On the debate see Wright (1971) and Davidson (1980).

[3] See Tetlock and Belkin (Chapter 1) and Fearon (1991).

Neville Chamberlain had not pursued a policy of appeasement, or if nuclear weapons had not been invented, or if the Reagan administration had not engaged in such a large defense buildup?

Nonetheless, there are also reasons to believe that social scientists, who generally cannot conduct true experiments, may have no choice but to rely on counterfactual assertions in one way or another. If some event A is argued to have been the cause of a particular historical event B, there seems to be no alternative but to imply that a counterfactual claim is true—if A had not occurred, the event B would not have occurred. And it can be shown that causal claims evaluated with regression and related methods applied to nonexperimental data must assume the truth of a counterfactual proposition concerning other causes of the phenomenon in question (Fearon 1991, 174–75).[4]

In this chapter I focus on two problems that bear on the questions of whether and how counterfactuals should be used by social scientists. The first is the objection noted above: How can we know with any confidence what would have happened if the hypothesized causal factor had been absent? I argue that for most social science problems we simply cannot know and, moreover, we cannot know in principle. Further, the difficulties involved in peering into possible worlds put fairly strong constraints on how much solid empirical confirmation we can get from any conceivable method of counterfactual argument.

Nonetheless, although it is frequently impossible to say with much precision what would have happened if A had been different, it is often easy and plausible to argue the negative case that whatever would have happened, it would *not* have been *B*, and therefore that *A* was a "cause" of *B*. This raises the second problem. For *too many* factors *A* it can be plausibly argued that but for *A*, *B* would not have occurred. How do we select among all the possibilities? Why is it not totally arbitrary to select one factor and argue for its causal status on counterfactual grounds if similar arguments can be advanced for myriad other factors and events? Are there criteria by which some counterfactual antecedents should be judged legitimate while others should not be considered because they are illegitimate to vary counterfactually as potential causes? For example, should we say that the length of Cleopatra's nose was a cause of World War I, and Napoleon's lack of a Stealth bomber a cause of his defeat at Waterloo? Or that it is illegitimate to consider the 1930s without a British policy of appeasement because Chamberlain could not have pursued any other policy given the constraints he faced?

This second problem, I will suggest, turns on ambiguity or confusion

---

[4] For arguments that social scientists and historians cannot avoid relying on counterfactuals see Fogel (1964), Fearon (1991), and Tetlock and Belkin (Chapter 1).

about the meaning of the word "cause" as we understand it when discussing historical phenomena. I offer two arguments. First, when we say that "*A* caused *B*" we seem to mean not just that if *A* had not occurred, *B* would not have occurred. Rather, we mean that if *A* had not occurred, *B* would not have occurred and the world would otherwise be similar to the world that did occur. This takes care of the Cleopatra's nose example and other factors that might be argued to be causes on "butterfly effect" grounds.

My second argument is that what we understand by "cause" differs in different explanatory environments and problems.[5] In particular, I argue that what we accept as a cause differs according to whether we are trying to give causes of a particular historical event, such as World War I, or of a class of events, such as wars in general. In the case of particular events, we often seek what I will call *conceivable causes*, factors that could actually have been different, according to the best of our knowledge about how the social and physical worlds work. On the other hand, when we argue that some factor causes some event (such as war) across cases, we do not typically require that in each case it be actually or "objectively possible" that the factor not occur. I call such factors *miracle causes*.[6] For example, one might maintain that imbalances of power cause war across cases and use the late 1930s in Europe as a supporting case, even if historians claim that the British and French could not conceivably have rearmed faster than they did. Thus, giving the causes of a singular event and of a class of events may be different sorts of explanatory exercises, and what can be "legitimately" accepted as a counterfactual antecedent may differ according to the exercise. One implication is that a researcher's purpose of inquiry may reasonably determine what factors should or should not be varied counterfactually, and thus what the causes of the phenomenon are!

In developing these arguments, I have found it helpful to use a model known as a cellular automaton as an analogy for the sort of historical phenomena about which social scientists make causal arguments. Independent of the arguments sketched above, this analogy is valuable for thinking about counterfactuals and historical processes.

Cellular Automata

The following is an example of a two-dimensional cellular automaton: Imagine a computer screen divided by a grid into a large number of cells, for example, one hundred cells on each side. In each of a successive number of

---

[5] This general observation is made by Hart and Honoré (1959, 17), who find the first treatment of it in Mill (1900).

[6] The idea of a "miracle" explaining how things could have been different comes from Lewis (1973, 76).

periods $t = 0, 1, 2, 3, \ldots$, every cell on the screen will take on one color from a set of colors—in our simple version, there are two possible colors, green or yellow. Next, there is a rule that determines what color a cell will be in period t as a function of its own color and the colors of its immediate neighbors in period t-1. For instance, a rule might say "green if two or three neighbors were yellow, yellow otherwise."

If the rule is deterministic—that is, the rule determines cell colors with certainty rather than with some probability—then given any initial ($t = 0$) distribution of cell colors the system will evolve along a deterministic path. Even for very simple rules, however, it may be impossible to write down an equation that will give the color of a given cell in a given period t as a function of the initial pattern of colors. It should be stressed that this is not due to any random element in the automaton. Rather, there simply does not exist a formula or any other simplified model of the system that can project the system's behavior. As Stephen Wolfram (1984, 32) puts it, for some transition rules the behavior of a cellular automaton is "essentially unpredictable, even given complete information about the initial state: the behaviour of the system may essentially be found only by explicitly running it."

Early computer experiments with cellular automata showed that even quite simple deterministic rules could generate highly elaborate images that appear over time to move, grow, shrink, envelop, explode, spiral, "eat," and contort all over the screen. Tiny differences in the initial pattern might have enormous implications later on. For example, for many rules, changing a single cell from yellow to green in period $t = 0$ would mean that one hundred generations later the pattern would be unrecognizably different. For many rules there is no long-run equilibrium pattern that the system gradually evolves to regardless of the initial state. Systems may constantly change and evolve, like a pattern of sunlight through the leaves of a tree on a windy day.[7]

We owe the idea of a cellular automaton to the mathematicians John Von Neumann and Stanislaw Ulam.[8] While thinking about computers, Von Neumann apparently had some ideas about self-reproduction in biological systems, which he tried to express via cellular automata. The best-known example of an interesting rule for a two-dimensional cellular automaton is

---

[7] Of course, in a finite cellular automaton there is only a finite number of possible patterns for the screen, so all initial patterns either converge to some equilibrium or end up cycling through a finite set of patterns. For a large automaton, however, the number of possible patterns is enormous, so a "cycle" can easily take longer to complete than anyone would have time to observe.

[8] For Von Neumann's essays, see Von Neumann (1966). For a more recent overview see Wolfram (1983). This paper, along with other technical works on cellular automata, are collected in Wolfram (1986). Thus far I have only been able to find a technical literature on automata and a small, computer-hobbyist, mathematical-games literature. For the latter see Gardner (1970) and, more recently, Sigmund (1993). In both literatures authors almost invariably note that the behavior of automata seems to mimic natural, historical processes, but I have yet to see this analogy developed in more than a passing comment.

"The Game of Life," created by John Conway. Using the above example, the transition rule for the Game of Life is: (1) a cell is yellow in period t if less than two or more than three of its neighbors were green in the last period; (2) if exactly two neighbors were green in the last period, the cell stays the same color it was; and (3) if exactly three neighbors were green, a cell turns green or stays green. The interpretation Conway suggests is that green represents a living organism, while yellow represents a dead one or an empty space. The logic behind the rule is that an organism needs a certain number of living neighbors to survive or be born, but too many yields overcrowding, resource depletion, and death. The Game of Life can then be thought of as a model of the evolution of a bacteria population in a petri dish, for instance.

The Game of Life yields dynamic behavior like that described above. There may be no long-run equilibrium state and the patterns that evolve are very sensitive to initial conditions. Self-reproducing "structures" (i.e., patterns within the whole pattern) are typically generated and may endure for many periods, until they encounter other structures that may absorb or disintegrate them. Note that all this variety, complexity, and chaos can follow from a very simple, deterministic transition rule.

Cellular automata of this sort provide an appealing and fruitful analogy to the historical processes studied by historians and social scientists.

The Analogy

Imagine a large and fairly complex cellular automaton, in which the cells can assume many different colors and for which the transition rules are stochastic rather than deterministic. That is, part of a rule might specify something like the following: if exactly two neighbors were green in the last period, then the cell will be green with probability .3 and yellow with probability .7 in the current period. With a stochastic rule, the path of the patterns that evolve from an initial state will obviously no longer be deterministic. Instead, there will be a hopelessly complex implied probability distribution on possible patterns (which number $2^{10,000}$ in the two-color, 100-by-100 example used above). Now it is not even clear how much one learns from observing a single simulation. At each period t, there will be a range of actually possible successor patterns in period $t+1$, with chance deciding which occurs. And as in the deterministic example, if a single cell just happens to flip green rather than yellow in one period, this can have enormous consequences one hundred or even ten periods later.[9]

[9] Why should an automaton that is analogous to the human world be pictured as stochastic rather than deterministic? We might think that (1) the world is "truly stochastic" at some micro, atomic level; (2) mechanisms of human choice sometimes involve randomization, or "random-

An event in the social world is analogous to the appearance, disappearance, or change of some pattern within this automaton. For example, a war might be analogous to the appearance of a ring of red cells against a blue background, while the disintegration of a government might be analogous to the disappearance or fragmentation of a cluster of black cells. Each "event" might have its own historically unique aspects. The colors of nearby cells might be novel, or the ring might be shaped, shaded, and growing in ways that were slightly different from any previous ring that had been observed. But nonetheless it might still be sensible to speak of recurrent patterns that are identifiable as such (e.g., red rings). In other words, because every "case" might look different in particular respects, it might be difficult to code some of them, but nonetheless we could recognize categories.

A transition rule is analogous to a set of causal mechanisms that explain social, political, or economic interactions. For example, perhaps the most commonly employed mechanism in historical explanation is: People choose actions that make sense ("are optimal") in light of their beliefs and objectives. The various psychological biases in decision making discovered by cognitive psychologists provide another class of examples. A causal mechanism might also be less microlevel—it could be constructed or based on such microlevel components. For instance, the proposition that states will fight wars when both sides are overly optimistic about their chances of winning might be seen as a transition rule that is built up from more primitive rationality or psychological-bias mechanisms.

What follows if historical processes are "like" a stochastic cellular automaton of this sort? What I find most attractive about the analogy is that it pictures historical and social processes as simultaneously characterized by (1) local predictability and regularity, given information about some local domain, and (2) global unpredictability, chaos, and history dependence.[10]

The global unpredictability part is easy to see based on the discussion above. Even if one could know the whole pattern at time t and if one knew the full set of transition rules—by analogy, more than any social scientist could possibly aspire to—it would be impossible to predict whether a war (a red ring) would appear in a particular place at time $t + 50$. Will there be a

---

ization for all we can possibly know about what happens in an individual's head"; or (3) the stochastic element reflects the social scientist observer's lack of information about facts or causal mechanisms at some more micro level.

[10] I stress that I do not think the comparison of historical processes to cellular automata is anything more than an analogy. I can think of virtually no real social process that could be naturally or constructively modeled in this way, with the possible exception of housing and segregation patterns. And I certainly do not mean to say that all of history could be constructively modeled by an automaton. This is just an analogy. Further, it is meant as a loose analogy, in that I do not want to commit to saying that a "cell" is analogous to a state, a group, a person, a neuron, or a particular location in space. The level of application of the analogy is left open.

war in Europe in the year 2053? What will the U.S. economic growth rate be next year, or two months from now? The inflation rate, the Dow Jones, the murder rate, the level of "consumer confidence" or societal alienation? Insofar as all such variables are determined by the actions of myriad agents making myriad choices in response to "local" conditions, and whose choices feed back to each other in highly complex ways over time, these variables are determined by cellular-automatonlike processes. So if the analogy holds, we can forget the goal of making highly accurate point predictions about such things.

According to the analogy, however, this unpredictability and hopelessness of point predictions follow from local-level rules and mechanisms that may be highly regular and predictable. Take, for example, a human life.[11] Locally, my life is highly predictable and so are those around me. I can predict with a high degree of confidence who will come to work at the department tomorrow, for instance. Every day, I and everyone else make thousands of extremely accurate predictions about other peoples' choices and behavior. When we drive, we regularly stake our lives on the accuracy of these predictions. Beyond our immediate environs, we can often make quite sharp predictions about international political events. In late August and early September 1994, many were able to predict with a high degree of confidence that the Clinton administration would not completely "back down" in its confrontation with the Haitian military leadership—Clinton could not have done so after having created all the audience costs he would have suffered for not following through in some way on his massive display of force.

At a longer range, however, lives are highly unpredictable and subject to enormous variation due to very small and often random factors. Children, whose production involves a natural lottery, are a prime example. So are the often accidental circumstances that tip a person towards one career or another. I can predict a few things about what my life will look like in thirty years (if I last that long), but many others are globally unpredictable in the sense discussed above. At a "local" level one can give coherent and convincing causal explanations for life patterns and choices, but for a whole life from start to finish the best we can do is often narrative ("this happened, then this happened, . . .").

The analogy suggests a program for social scientists: Discover and explain the mechanisms, or local transition rules, that make things somewhat predictable at "local" levels.[12] For more global or "macro" levels, the analogy would suggest that all we can do is describe or narrate how various essen-

---

[11] Reisch (1991) uses the same example, although he draws out quite different implications.

[12] I view game-theoretic models as tools for discovering, exploring, and clarifying arguments about local (versus global) mechanisms of this sort. The idea of social science as seeking to discover and understand local mechanisms and how they work has been consistently developed by Elster (1989; 1993).

tially accidental conjunctions of mechanisms selected one historical trajectory from many other possible ones, which may not even be imaginable in any useful detail.[13] Thus there may be grounds for both the social scientist's view that one can discover meaningful causal patterns and relations in the social world and for a view typically held by historians, that the empirical evidence of history reveals tremendous contingency and essentially unique sequences of events.[14]

Before developing this analogy in regard to counterfactuals and causal arguments about social events, I wish to note two other general aspects that I find appealing and that speak to some issues that often arise in discussing counterfactuals.

First, while the evolution of the patterns on the screen might be highly sensitive to some small events—for example, whether a particular cell happens to flip yellow or green in a given period—this would not necessarily be true of all small events. It could be that in a given period, some cells are positioned in the whole pattern in such a way that their color is highly influential for future states, while others are positioned so that it does not matter at all whether yellow or green occurs. In a deterministic automaton, for instance, two distinct patterns can have the same successor pattern, so that either one yields the same future sequence.

My intuition is that this is also true of historical processes. Whether Khrushchev wore a blue shirt rather than a white shirt on October 25, 1962, probably made no difference whatsoever to the resolution of the Cuban missile crisis. But I can imagine that whether the day was sunny or cloudy, or incidental things that relatives or other politicians said to him, might conceivably have mattered.[15] Assassinations seem to provide the best class of examples here. For these one can often construct plausible arguments about the world-shaping importance of very "small" events, such as whether Lee Harvey Oswald had his morning coffee or not. The analogy suggests that one might simultaneously agree with the historian who asked rhetorically "Can one seriously believe that if my dog whose name is 'Trailer' had been called 'Tiger' everything else would have been affected?" and with the view that some "small" events have enormous consequences (Hook 1943, 121). Everything need not be connected to everything else, especially in the short term. What some Malaysian farmers were doing in 1960 need have had no

---

[13] Almond and Genco (1977) criticize "behavioralist" political scientists for treating politics as analogous to clocks rather than clouds; they say the latter is more often a better analogy. In Almond and Genco's language, the point of this paragraph can be expressed as follows: Many little clocks can produce big clouds. Discover and study the clocks, describe the clouds and how they were produced from clocks.

[14] For a fairly typical recent statement of this view see Gaddis (1992).

[15] On the influence of the weather: Saunders (1993) shows that New York Stock Exchange prices are systematically lower on cloudy days in Manhattan.

effect on the occurrence or resolution of the Cuban missile crisis, even if in 300 years the world historical consequences of some very small choices by these farmers will be enormous (for example, by influencing who their myriad descendants are and what they will do).

Second, the automaton analogy admits the possibility of statistical regularities, and thus statistical predictability, at the global level. It could be, for instance, that on average ten red rings appear every hundred periods and that this is quite regular. Thus it is not the case that all sorts of events in a cellular automaton need be locally predictable but globally unpredictable—some phenomena may be globally predictable in the statistical sense but locally unpredictable for an observer lacking factual information or the relevant transition rules. Analogously, the suicide rate for a country may be quite predictable year to year even though it would be impossible for an observer with no information about individuals to predict precisely which ones would commit suicide. Nonetheless, few would call a statistical regularity at a global or macro level an "explanation" by itself. Rather, we usually want some reference to transition rules or mechanisms that give rise to the regularity (for example, Catholics have lower suicide rates than Protestants because they are bound more tightly within an integrated religious community) (Durkheim 1951).[16]

Applying the Analogy

In this section I use the analogy of historical processes to cellular automata to consider the two questions identified in the introduction. First, how can we know with any confidence what would have happened if some factor had not been present? And second, are some factors "illegitimate" as counterfactual antecedents, and under what circumstances?

We can distinguish two types of explanatory tasks. First, a researcher may be interested in discovering or testing a factor that is proposed as a cause of some class of events, such as wars, revolutions, national income across countries, protectionist trade policies, and so on. Second, a researcher might be interested in discovering or testing a factor that is proposed as a cause of a single, particular event. By analogy, these tasks correspond to asking

---

[16] Peter Woodruff (personal communication) has pointed out another sense in which a deterministic automaton may be considered globally predictable but locally unpredictable: In the deterministic case, one can predict the full (global) pattern in period $t+1$ given knowledge of the global pattern in period t, but one cannot predict the $t+1$ pattern for any ("local") contiguous subset of cells without knowledge of the neighboring cells' colors in the period t. I mean "locally predictable" in the sense that to predict the color of a cell in period $t+1$ one needs to know only the colors of the eight immediate neighbors, while to predict the same cell's color in $t+i$, for example, one needs to know the colors of $(2i + 1)^2 - 1$ neighboring cells in period t (if this does not already encompass the whole automaton).

about either the causes of the appearance of red rings in general or about the appearance of a particular red ring.

There are essentially two approaches one can take. First, one might try to evaluate whether the proposed causal factor is regularly associated with the event to be explained across cases. That is, one tries to learn whether the event always or usually occurs when the causal factor is present, but rarely or never occurs when the factor is not present. This is the essence of Mill's method of difference, the approach at the base of all statistical methods for causal inference. Second, one might try counterfactual argument. Here one begins by taking a single, particular event, and then asks whether the event would not have occurred if the proposed causal factor had been absent but all else had been the same.[17]

It is worth noting that either approach can be used for either explanatory task. One might try to explain a particular event by looking for causal factors that were present in this particular case and which are known (or found) to be causal factors by an examination of frequencies of association across cases. Or one might try to show that, for example, imbalances of power cause war in general, across cases, by arguing counterfactually case by case for a sample of wars. It should also be stressed, however, that even when the counterfactual approach is employed in the hope of testing or making a general argument about cause and effect, it does so by focusing on single, particular cases. In the counterfactual approach, evidence always comes from consideration of particular cases, rather than from blunt regularities of association across multiple cases (Fearon 1991, 175–76).

Using the analogy to cellular automata, exactly how does the counterfactual approach work? Suppose we are trying to explain the appearance of a particular red ring pattern in a particular period t. The counterfactual approach proceeds by arguing that the colors of some set of cells $w, x, y, \ldots$ in previous periods "caused" the red ring, on the grounds that if these cells had assumed different colors (perhaps specified), the red ring would not have appeared. This claim is then evaluated or rendered plausible by refer-

---

[17] The underlying logic is the same in either case (Fearon 1991). The question is whether comparison cases are found in actual or possible worlds.

Political scientists who rely on case studies frequently take Mill's method of agreement as another valid approach, and use it to justify research designs where all cases had the same outcome on the dependent variable. As Mill (1900, 286ff) noted, however, the so-called method of agreement *does not work* when there is more than one cause of the phenomenon in question. Because there is no a priori way of knowing how many causes a phenomenon has, and because in political science problems we invariably think there are multiple causes, the method of agreement becomes in effect a rhetorical device that rationalizes bad research designs. Consider the following example. Suppose we want to learn the causes of fatal car accidents, and we observe two cases in which drivers went off the road and into a tree late at night. In one of the two cases the driver was drunk. Using the method of agreement, we conclude that alcohol cannot be a cause of fatal car accidents. This is obviously nonsense.

ring to our knowledge of, or beliefs about, the relevant transition rules (the "local" mechanisms), which may take the form of theories or statistical generalizations from observation of past occurrences of red rings. If we know or have some confidence in the relevant transition rules, we may then be able to deduce that given different "initial" colors for cells $w, x, y, \ldots$, the red ring would not have appeared. The rules plus initial conditions imply that something else would have appeared, or that the status quo would have continued.

So, as many have argued, in the counterfactual approach the test of an empirical claim (A caused B) makes crucial and deductive use of some set of theories or statistical generalizations about how the world works. Our grounds for considering these empirically valid must derive either from deductive counterfactual analysis of other particular cases or from the inductive method of comparing across sets of cases. Presumably, at some point the theories or generalizations must be based on the method of induction. For example, if we observed the operation of a cellular automaton and initially had no idea what any of the transition rules were, we could not begin to figure them out by using the counterfactual approach. Instead, we would have to draw inferences by looking for regularities across cases.

How Can We Know What Would Have Happened If . . .

So it appears that the only possible answer to the question "How can we know with any confidence what would have happened if the proposed causal factor had been absent?" is: By deduction using transition rules (local mechanisms or theories sometimes understood only as statistical generalizations) in which we already have some confidence.[18]

If the analogy of historical processes to cellular automata is reasonable, however, then this answer implies a bleak assessment of the prospects for knowing "what would have happened" in many counterfactual analyses. It is in the nature of automatonlike processes that one may not be able to predict what will happen several steps ahead without explicitly "running" the system. Attempting to proceed by deduction from rules plus initial conditions will take one only a very short distance forward before complexity overwhelms the effort. Moreover, this can be true *no matter how good our knowledge of the transition rules or theories used to draw out the consequences of a particular counterfactual antecedent.* Indeed, even in the impossible case of perfect knowledge of all "social science transition rules," we would not be able to say what would have happened without access to a

---

[18] The Stalnaker-Lewis "possible worlds" approach may represent another feasible answer, or may simply restate this argument in different language; I am not qualified to judge. See Stalnaker (1968) and Lewis (1973, 57, 65–72).

model that was just as complex as the social world itself. In other words, we would need a map just as large as the terrain it described.

From this perspective, the problem of determining "what would have happened if . . ." is fundamentally similar to the problem of forecasting specific political and economic events. If we had the ability to forecast with a high degree of confidence whether and where, for example, the United States will be at war in two years' time, or what GNP growth will be, then we would also have the ability to delineate counterfactual scenarios on such matters with a high degree of confidence. And wherever we are unable to forecast political and social events with confidence, there we will also be unable to develop counterfactuals with much plausibility. The ability to forecast—that is, to make point predictions—entails an ability to use causal theories plus knowledge of initial conditions to spell out a narrative, a chain or succession of events. Often this is precisely what is needed to render a counterfactual claim plausible. But if the automaton analogy holds, then the only successful point predictions social scientists will be making will be quite local or short-range. One might successfully use theories about decision making and strategy to predict the Gulf War in September 1990, but no theories could reliably predict in 1989 the war that occurred in 1991 (let alone predict it in 1945). If this line of argument is correct, then detailed counterfactual scenarios will have a chance at being rendered plausible only if the proposed causes are temporally and, in some sense, spatially quite close to the consequents.[19]

If we think specifically about the analogy of historical processes to *stochastic* cellular automata, a new issue arises that yields new problems. In the paradigm of the perfect thought experiment, we try to imagine the world without the proposed causal factor *A* but with all else the same as in the world that actually occurred.[20] But if we think that historical processes have random components, then the meaning of "all else the same" is not clear. Do we try to sketch the counterfactual scenario so as to be as close as possible to what actually did happen, or do we presume that what did happen was just one of many possible paths, and not necessarily the most likely one? For instance, consider the claim that "if I had not gotten stuck in a

---

[19] For arguments on the difficulty of forecasting in international politics see Jervis (1991). I should note that making point predictions is not the be-all and end-all of social science. Social scientists seem to do better at making comparative statics analyses of ongoing regularities of behavior or institutions—for example, at explaining why intra-alliance politics takes one form under bipolarity and another under multipolarity.

[20] Mill's (1900, 256) definition of the method of difference suggests just such a perfect experiment: "If an instance in which the phenomenon under investigation occurs, and an instance in which it does not occur, have every circumstance in common save one, that one occurring only in the former; the circumstance in which alone the two instances differ is the effect, or the cause, or an indispensable part of the cause, of the phenomenon."

traffic jam, I would have arrived on time." Should we evaluate this claim by using information about how other drivers actually did behave, for example, on the way to the freeway where the jam was, or should we imagine all counterfactual worlds where they might have acted differently due to random variation? I do not see any obviously correct answer here.[21]

As a more applied example, consider the counterfactual claim that if Khrushchev had "stood firm" in the Cuban missile crisis for two more days, Kennedy would have offered a more attractive compromise that Khrushchev would have accepted; thus the risk of nuclear war was really not very great in the crisis. One might support this claim by citing evidence that Kennedy was indeed secretly planning to make a more generous and public compromise offer, and evidence that he was not at all sanguine about the prospects for a disarming attack on Cuba (Blight and Welch 1989, 83–84, 173–74). But in offering this scenario we assume that (1) in the two-day interval that did not actually occur, other events would not have happened that might have influenced Kennedy's or Khrushchev's decision calculus; and (2) events that did occur in the actual world would also have occurred in the counterfactual world. We implicitly extend the pattern of the previous actual days forward into the counterfactual two days, and we also presume that events that occurred in the actual two days would have occurred in the counterfactual two days. How warranted is this? Perhaps if Khrushchev had not offered to settle when he did, there might have been a dispute between Cuban and Russian officers in Cuba that U.S. leaders would have interpreted as seriously threatening and calling for a preemptive strike. And suppose that in the actual world a Cuban and Russian officer happened to have a sharp personal conflict the day after Khrushchev signaled his willingness to withdraw the missiles; does this conflict also occur in the counterfactual world where Khrushchev "stands firm"?

The point is that if we think historical processes evolve stochastically—or stochastically for all we can possibly know—then counterfactual antecedents do not imply determinate paths for counterfactual scenarios, as we often assume in sketching them. Rather, changing a factor counterfactually implies a probability distribution over many counterfactual paths, in which the evidence provided by the actual world that did occur may not be relevant for saying what would have occurred in unprecedented counterfactual situations.

---

[21] Using the analogy, the problem may be expressed as follows. We ask what would have happened in period t if cell x had been a different color in time t-3 (for instance). Suppose we know that in the actual unfolding that occurred, in time t-2 a nearby cell z happened to flip green instead of yellow, and that this bore on the outcome in question. Does "all else the same" mean that our counterfactual scenario should leave z green (assuming that the counterfactual change of cell x does not affect z one way or the other), or should we allow for the possibility that yellow might have occurred?

This raises a difficult question about the meaning of "all else equal" in a counterfactual scenario, and adds to the difficulties involved in knowing how plausible our counterfactual assertions are.[22]

To summarize, we will be able to judge the plausibility of and have confidence in counterfactual arguments in precisely those domains where we are confident about making forecasts and predictions. Thus, I may have considerable confidence in the claim that "if I had not gotten stuck in the traffic jam, I would very probably have arrived at class on time." This is plausible because it is asserted in a highly predictable, "local" domain where the causal mechanisms are well-understood and relevant intervening factors are few. Accidents may happen, but I know them to be rare from past experience.[23] By contrast, the claim that "if Gorbachev had lost the succession struggle in 1985 the Soviet Union would not have disintegrated before 1992" is asserted in a domain where causal mechanisms are less well understood and, moreover, *even if they were well-understood* a forecast such as this one might be impossible because it is too "long range."[24] The greater the number of steps and the more time passes, the more automatonlike chaos will intervene.

So what do we do with counterfactuals like this one about Gorbachev? These are often precisely the counterfactuals in which we have the most interest. If there is no way even in principle that one could say precisely what would have happened in 1992 if Gorbachev had lost the succession struggle in 1985, then what is the value of making such claims? Or consider the claim that if nuclear weapons had not been invented, the post-War world would still have seen major-power peace. There is absolutely no way of anticipating a forty-five-year path of counterfactual events with any confidence, so what empirical evidence relevant to assessing whether nuclear weapons caused the "long peace" can be gathered by exploring such a scenario?

---

[22] This is exactly the problem posed by Robyn Dawes in his "betting on snake eyes" example (Commentary 3), where he insists that "all else equal" should allow for stochastic variation. Likewise, King, Keohane, and Verba (1994, 76–85) give a definition of causality that comes down on the side of always allowing for counterfactual stochastic variation. It seems to me that this may make sense if, in thinking counterfactually about one particular case, one is trying to extract a generalizable "causal effect." But if one is asking "what would have happened *in this particular case* if such-and-such had been different?" then our intuition demands that we try to hold all other things equal as we knew they actually happened.

[23] Alternatively, one might say that we can assess counterfactual claims in precisely those areas where we can also use the method of difference on multiple actual cases. "I would have arrived on time" may be plausible in light of the comparison to many other typical driving days I have experienced.

[24] Arguably the relevant "local-level" mechanisms *are* well understood—we rarely have much difficulty explaining why any particular politician made a particular choice at a particular time, given enough information. It is in aggregating all the various decisions and situations that complexity overwhelms.

My sense is that counterfactual claims such as these two rarely or never act as independent empirical tests or sources of empirical evidence. Rather, they are typically rhetorical devices—"spotlights" in Mark Turner's (Commentary 1) terms—that at best point the reader towards bits of evidence relevant to assessing causal claims that may be somewhat different from the one suggested by the counterfactual. We cannot say with any confidence what would have happened in 1992 if Gorbachev had lost out in 1985, but the counterfactual claim may serve to direct our attention to the political programs being offered by Gorbachev's rivals, to the sources of their support, and to a comparison of their strength to the strength of Gorbachev and his camp. The counterfactual claim is thus a rhetorical flourish directing attention to another, more "local" and empirically assessable claim: that the political program of Gorbachev's closest rival was quite different, and he would have had a good chance of implementing it, at least in the short run. Thus, had Gorbachev lost the succession struggle, the Soviet Union would not have started down the specific path that we saw lead to disintegration. Where it would have led by 1992 will always be difficult or impossible to say.

Similarly, while we cannot hope to describe a post-War world without nuclear weapons in any convincing detail, making the rhetorical claim directs our attention to the somewhat more assessable question of what factors prevented war between the United States and the Soviet Union in the actual world that did occur. One can ask, for example, how large a role nuclear weapons played in actual superpower crises.[25] If one answers "very little"— most or all crises would have worked out the same way even without nuclear weapons—then this would count somewhat against the view that nuclear weapons caused the long peace. It could hardly be decisive, of course, because nuclear weapons might still have been responsible for moderating superpower behavior so that the crises that did occur were fewer and less serious than would otherwise have been the case. On the other hand, if one finds evidence that concerns about nuclear war were a significant factor moderating U.S. and/or Soviet behavior in the actual crises, then this would count in favor of the claim. Again, the evidence would not be decisive, because it could be that nuclear weapons were themselves a principal source of war-threatening friction, and so gave rise to dangerous crises that would not have otherwise occurred. To some extent this possibility might be assessed by asking about the principle interests in dispute in the several major crises that occurred, which would lead in turn to counterfactual speculation at a more "local" level. For example, would a crisis over Cuba have occurred at all but for nuclear weapons? The immediate cause of the missile crisis was, of course, the introduction of nuclear missiles, but absent these a

---

[25] Some relevant evidence is presented in Betts (1987).

war-threatening crisis might have arisen if the United States in a non-nuclear world had tried harder to overthrow Castro. Perhaps in this world the Soviets would have viewed the option to take Berlin more favorably.

My general point is that the value of counterfactual claims often does not lie in the possibility that empirical evidence can be adduced by explicitly exploring the counterfactual scenario. Complexity means that for all but the most local-level claims, we simply cannot say with any confidence what would have happened. Instead, unassessable counterfactuals typically act as rhetorical devices or "spotlights" that direct us to look at other, more local sorts of evidence relevant to assessing related causal claims.

Are Some Counterfactual Antecedents More Legitimate Than Others?

Although it may be difficult or impossible to describe in any detail the world that would have followed if causal factor A had not occurred, it is frequently easy to support a weaker claim that whatever would have happened, it would not have been effect B. For example, in an article attempting to explain the failure of the August 1991 coup against Gorbachev, Stephen Meyer (1991, 5) writes that "there can be little doubt that had the military establishment actively supported the putsch the outcome would have been far different." He makes no effort to say exactly what would have happened—presumably it would be difficult to predict much beyond the immediate success of the plotters and the crushing of demonstrations. But he asserts with justifiable confidence that the coup would not have collapsed as it did.[26]

The automaton analogy suggests why this is the case. Consider the problem of explaining the appearance of a red ring in period t. The number of cells in prior periods that, had they been different, would have caused B not to occur may be tremendously large, and we may be able to assert this with confidence even if we cannot say exactly what would have occurred. Indeed, the farther back we go the more cells will matter "causally" in this sense. Pascal's example concerning Cleopatra is of this type: We cannot know exactly what would have followed if Anthony had not fought a war on her behalf, but we can be reasonably confident that history would have taken a very different course. Thus we face the prospect of finding the claim "if Cleopatra's nose had been a different length, World War I would not have occurred" more plausible and defensible than "if Lord Grey had sent a stronger signal of Britain's willingness to fight, World War I would not have

[26] Max Weber's (1949, 164–88) example of an important counterfactual argument in history also takes this form: Eduard Meyer claimed that if the Athenians had lost at Marathon to Persia, the West would not have developed with many of the features that seem to distinguish it from the East. Meyer does not attempt to fantasize about the specific course that would have been followed if the Persians had won, only to show that evidence suggests that from this starting point the trajectory would have been very different.

occurred."[27] Ironically, "butterfly effect" counterfactuals of the Cleopatra's-nose type may be among the most defensible and plausible even as they seem intuitively wrong, or not what we are after in seeking causes.

There are other cases of counterfactual claims that seem highly plausible but whose antecedents strike us as wrong or "illegitimate." The claim that "if Napoleon had had Stealth bombers at Waterloo, he would not have been defeated" may be plausible in that if we grant the antecedent, the consequent might very well follow (that is, we could make a strong argument for it). But we are very reluctant to grant the antecedent, which seems illegitimate because we think that Napoleon "could not possibly have had" Stealth bombers.

Ruling out antecedents of this sort puts us on a slippery slope, however. To do so consistently we need criteria for distinguishing between legitimate and illegitimate antecedents. In effect, we need criteria for deciding what factors or events should be considered as possible causes of a phenomenon, and what factors should not be considered as causes. Such criteria are not easy to produce.

The standard suggestion is that the counterfactual antecedent must have been "actually" or "objectively" possible.[28] Even assuming that we can say what it means for something to be "actually possible" at a given time, this criterion leads to substantial difficulties. Most importantly, in both ordinary language and in social science research we often call factors "causes" that do not meet this criterion. We may say that a person's death was caused by old age even if it was not actually possible that the person had been younger. Or consider a study of voting behavior that uses regression analysis to assess the causal impact of factors such as race, religion, party identification, and income on vote choice. The study may conclude from the data that race has a significant causal impact on individual voting behavior, even though it is not actually possible that any individual survey respondent could have been a different race. The same applies for large-N studies of deterrence, which may find that a balance of forces causes deterrence even if it was not "objectively possible" that the balance could have been much different than it was for particular cases in the sample.[29]

[27] If the reader has doubts about Pascal's specific example, then substitute any event in ancient times that can be plausibly argued to have had a major impact on the course of all subsequent history (e.g., the Battle of Marathon).

[28] The argument is most powerfully and emphatically expressed by Elster (1978, 185). Barry (1980) argued against this view in his review of Elster's book. For other authors taking the "counterfactuals must have been actually possible" position see Hawthorn (1991, 158–59) and Tetlock and Belkin on "minimal-rewrite rules" (Chapter 1). It is worth noting that this criterion does not help for examples of the Cleopatra's nose sort—butterfly-effect causes may be "actually possible" and so legitimate in this sense.

[29] In their discussion of causality, King, Keohane, and Verba (1994, 78) endorse the view that the counterfactuals employed in either large- or small-N research should be "reasonable and it should be possible for the counterfactual event to have occurred under precisely stated cir-

There are two problems of "legitimacy" here. First, are butterfly-effect causes—which include more than fanciful examples like that given by Pascal—legitimate as counterfactual antecedents? Second, in using counterfactuals to assess proposed causes, can we vary factors that either "had to be as they were" or "could not possibly have been"? I will suggest that there are no hard and fast, "scientific" answers to these questions because they are really questions about what our intuition will accept as a cause, and to answer them we have to ask about what we mean by the word in different contexts. I will consider each problem in turn.

BUTTERFLY-EFFECT CAUSES

When we explain why an event B occurred, we explain why B occurred *rather than* some other alternative or set of alternatives. As Alan Garfinkel (1981, chapter 1) has argued, explanation always takes place relative to a "contrast space" of alternatives, and how this space is implicitly imagined strongly influences what a satisfactory explanation will be. For example, consider the question "Why did the Soviet Union disintegrate?" A political scientist might reject the explanation that "a modern economy simply cannot work with central planning rather than markets" on the grounds that this does not explain why the Soviet Union fell apart when it did. But the central planning explanation might be perfectly acceptable if the question is asking why the Soviet Union disintegrated at all rather than surviving indefinitely. We imagine a different contrast space when we ask "Why did the Soviet Union disintegrate in 1991 rather than at some other time?" and this affects what is acceptable as an answer.[30] Similarly, the claim that "ancient hatreds are a cause of the war in Bosnia" may be a respectable part of an answer to the question "Why is there an ethnic war in Bosnia *rather than* in France, Britain, the United States, etc.?", but it would not answer the question "Why is there a war in Bosnia now rather than at other times?" Particularly when asking about the causes of a specific event, social scientists frequently fail to specify the contrast space, and this often leaves crucial ambiguity about what question is being asked.[31]

Invariably, however, when we try to explain why some event B occurred,

---

cumstances." But this would rule out much of what the authors take to be paradigmatically good social science! Authors estimating causal effects using regression analysis on nonexperimental data *never* ask whether it would have been actually possible for each case in the sample to have assumed different values on the independent variables.

[30] In the first case, the contrast space is {Soviet Union exists indefinitely, Soviet Union collapses at some time}. In the second, the space is {Soviet Union collapses in 1991, Soviet Union collapses at some other time}.

[31] Indeed, the principle benefit of explicitly specifying the counterfactual implicit in a causal claim may be that doing so forces the researcher to articulate the contrast space and thus exactly what he or she is trying to explain (cf. Fearon 1991, 194).

we implicitly imagine a contrast space in which B is absent *and the rest of the world is similar to the world in which B* is present. To show that A caused B, the relevant counterfactual to make plausible is not "if A had not occurred, B would not have occurred," because this admits a contrast space that includes worlds where B did not occur and the rest of the world was entirely dissimilar to the world that did occur. Instead, the relevant counterfactual should be, "if A had not occurred, B would not have occurred and the world would be otherwise similar." The goal is to explain the presence or absence of B against a fixed, actual "background," rather than B in the context of all conceivable backgrounds.

Butterfly-effect "causes" seem intuitively peculiar for precisely this reason: They admit a bizarre contrast space, one different from what is implicitly assumed in our idea of explanation. World War I may not have occurred if Cleopatra's nose had been different, but the butterfly-logic behind this claim also implies that all aspects of the world in 1914 would have looked tremendously different. Because the implicit assumption was that we were looking for causes of the occurrence of World War I in a world that otherwise looked as it did in 1914, Cleopatra's nose does not work as a "cause" in our standard (intuitive) sense.[32]

Thinking in terms of the automaton analogy, we can acknowledge that an enormous number of prior events (cell colors in previous periods) may have been necessary to determine the appearance of a particular red ring at a particular time, while at the same time denying that the vast majority of these were "causes" of the red ring in the normal sense of the word. For thousands and thousands of prior events it may be true that if the color of the cell had been different, the red ring would not have appeared when and

[32] In my earlier paper, I proposed a somewhat different resolution for the butterfly-effect problem: Cleopatra's nose length was not a "cause" of World War I because the probability of the war occurring conditional on a different nose length was no different from the probability of the war occurring conditional on the nose being as it was (i.e., almost zero in both cases) (Fearon 1991, 191). King, Keohane, and Verba's (1994, 82) definition of causality works the same way: "The causal effect is the difference between the systematic component of observations made when the explanatory variable takes one value and the systematic component of [here, counterfactual] comparable observations made when the explanatory variable takes another [counterfactual] value." Thus, if the independent variable is nose length, there is almost no covariation with a dummy variable for the occurrence of World War I. In the thought experiment of many hypothetical "runs" of the world with different nose lengths, the war virtually never occurs, so its "causal effect" is judged to be almost zero.

Although they work for this example, conditional probability definitions seem to have problems with others. For example, consider the proposition that the presence of oxygen in the atmosphere was a cause of World War I. It might be true that over many hypothetical "runs" beginning in July 1914 the war never occurs when there is no oxygen and that war almost always occurs when there is. So by a conditional probability definition, oxygen counts as having a large causal effect on the war. More in accord with intuition, it does not in the definition suggested above, because the world is not "otherwise similar" if oxygen is subtracted.

where it did. But for a much smaller number would this proposition be true and it would also be true that the rest of the pattern on the screen would be similar to what did occur with the red ring. I would argue that only events of the latter type meet our intuitive notion of cause.[33]

This suggestion is problematic in that it relies on an unelaborated metric for judging similarity across worlds, and also assumes that we can assess moderately well whether the rest of the world would be sufficiently "similar" following a change of the proposed causal factor. At a certain temporal or spatial range, these distinctions and forecasts are hard to make. Consider the claim that social Darwinism was a cause of World War I. Suppose Darwin had died young, and that a theory like Darwin's did not develop until some-time in the mid-twentieth century. Without Darwin and Darwinism in the 1860s, it is entirely plausible that what we call World War I would not have occurred, although perhaps some other big war might have. The "rest of the world" would look in many respects like the Europe that did exist in 1914, but it might be very different in other respects (for example, more uniformly liberal or socialist, and less imperialist). By my criteria, it is hard to say whether social Darwinism ought to count as even a possible cause of the war.

How one judges whether the world would have been "otherwise similar" depends in large part on how narrowly one defines the event being ex-plained. Using the example above, does "World War I" mean (1) a war between the five European great powers that begins in 1914; (2) a war be-tween at least four great powers beginning in the period 1890–1920; or something in between? If Darwin had not occurred, it seems entirely likely that (1) would not have occurred, for butterfly-effect reasons. But (2) might or might not have occurred. So if "otherwise similar" means a world as narrowly defined as that described in (1), then the criterion given above rules out Darwin as a cause. By contrast, if we take a broader class of "World War I's" and late-nineteenth century Europes, then Darwinism might or might not be judged a cause, depending on how much one thinks social Darwinist thought contributed to the practical views of European leaders on war.

This discussion raises a more general and very important point: What we will accept as possible causes of an event (or class of events) depends cru-cially on the level of detail with which we specify the event. As Alan Gar-finkel (1981, 28–32) has argued, when we try to explain some particular

---

[33] When historians and social scientists argue that each event is historically unique and pro-duced by an infinite stream of particular prior "causes" as far back as one wishes to go, they are employing a "butterfly-effect" notion of cause rather than our ordinary language one. See, for an example, Weber's (1949) discussion, which makes several references to particular events being caused by an "infinite succession" of prior events and circumstances.

occurrence we always implicitly imagine a class of events that would qualify. For example, it would not disqualify an explanation of the occurrence of the French Revolution if the explanation did not account for Robespierre's choice of clothes on a particular day, even if this does make up part of the specific occurrence that was the French Revolution. Rather, by "French Revolution" we implicitly have in mind a large class of occurrences, all of which we would accept as "essentially equivalent" to the revolution that did occur, for the purposes of the explanation. Depending on the explanatory focus, an explanation of World War I might have in mind an equivalence class that included only wars begun in the fall of 1914 over a dispute between Austria and Russia in the Balkans, or it might be broader, accepting any great power war in a twenty-year interval. What one will accept, or even imagine, as causes will of course depend on how broadly the "equivalence class" is defined.[34]

Thus the assassination of Archduke Ferdinand might be reasonably judged a cause of World War I, if the event "World War I" means "a general war among the European great powers beginning in the fall of 1914 over a dispute in the Balkans." But it might not be a cause of a World War I if the event to be explained is less narrowly drawn, meaning, for example, "a general war between the Triple Alliance and Triple Entente beginning sometime between 1910 and 1920." In addition to often failing to specify the relevant counterfactual claims, scholars making causal claims about international politics often fail to specify what would qualify as the event they are trying to explain. Because this obviously affects the truth or falsity of counterfactual arguments used to support or disconfirm possible causes, it is critically important to be careful about it.[35]

CAUSES THAT "HAD TO BE AS THEY WERE" OR "COULD NOT POSSIBLY HAVE BEEN"

As noted above, many writers on the use of counterfactuals in social science have argued that some counterfactual antecedents are more "legitimate" than others, and thus that some counterfactual propositions should not be entertained in seeking to learn or assess the causes of an event. Examples range from the relatively fanciful (but still problematic) Stealth bomber sort to

---

[34] See A. Garfinkel (1981, chapter 1) for the term "equivalence class" and a discussion. Another implication of Garfinkel's insight is that historians and social scientists who claim to be explaining "particular" or "unique" events are never really doing this, in a literal sense. Instead, they must have in mind a class of hypothetical events that are all essentially equivalent as far as their explanatory purpose is concerned.

[35] Thus, a principal reason for the methodological rule that the antecedent and consequent in a counterfactual need to be clearly specified is that the precise definition of the consequent crucially determines what may have caused it (Chapter 1, Tetlock and Belkin; Fearon 1991).

more difficult questions concerning whether certain decisions by state leaders were "actually possible" or not at a given time.[36]

Criteria for deciding the legitimacy of counterfactual antecedents are really criteria for saying what should or should not be considered as a cause of the consequent in question. As I suggested above, the standard suggestion that counterfactual antecedents are "illegitimate" if we have theories and arguments implying that they were objectively impossible cannot make sense of our usage of "cause" either in ordinary language or in typical social science practice. The automaton analogy suggests a distinction that, I believe, is less problematic and generates more insight.

For a stochastic cellular automaton, we explain the appearance of a particular red ring by arguing that if some set of cells x, y, z, . . . in previous periods had taken different colors, the ring would not have appeared and the overall pattern would have been otherwise similar. Beyond this, I put no constraints on how we propose to vary counterfactually the colors of cells x, y, z, and so on. There are two possibilities here. We can either restrict ourselves to color changes that actually could have occurred given the stochastic transition rules, or we can imagine ourselves intervening and changing colors of cells as we please, paying no special attention to the transition rules. In the first approach, we say that if cell x had flipped black rather than yellow, which it actually might have done under the rules, the red ring would not have appeared. In the second approach, we say that if cell x had flipped blue rather than yellow—which was impossible under the rules—the red ring would not have occurred.

I will call causes in the first approach *conceivable causes*, because they could conceivably have happened according to the "rules of the game" as we understand them. By contrast, I will call causes in the second approach *miracle causes*, because we imagine their counterfactual occurrence as resulting from an intervention from outside the system (the hand of God, as it were).

In ordinary language and in social science practice we rely on both types of cause in different contexts. I doubt that either one can be justified as a uniformly correct notion of cause, considering that explanatory purpose and context seem to determine which one we adopt. Conceivable and miracle causes are supplied in response to different sorts of questions.

More specifically, when we try to give or assess the causes of a particular event, such as Napoleon's defeat at Waterloo, the end of the Cold War, or the collapse of the Soviet Union, we are sometimes asking for conceivable causes and sometimes for miracle causes. In some contexts and for some authors, the question "Why did the Soviet Union collapse?" may be asking "What about the world could actually have been different and led to continuance of the Soviet Union?" Or the intention of the question may be less

[36] See, for example, Hawthorn (1991, chapter 3); Breslauer (Chapter 3).

restrictive. The author may intend to answer "What changes in the world, whether actually possible or not, would have prevented the Soviet Union from disintegration?" Just as there are two different ways to imagine cell colors in a cellular automaton being different, there are two different ways of imagining making counterfactual changes in the thought experiments we use to argue causality.[37]

In what contexts do we expect one type of cause rather than the other? I do not think there are any very sharp rules here, but at least two rough generalizations can be offered. First, when we are treating the specific event to be explained as an instance of a class of events, we are generally quite ready to accept miracle causes. For example, in regression analysis and other statistical means of testing causal hypotheses, one assumes that if any particular case in the sample had taken a different value on one of the independent variables, the dependent variable would have differed by a systematic component that is the same across cases plus a random component. One never even contemplates whether it would have been actually, historically possible for any particular case to have assumed different values on the independent variables. Thus, in research of this sort that seeks causes of recurrent events rather than particular events, there is nothing peculiar about statements such as "if John Smith had been black, he would have been 30 percent more likely to have voted for Clinton than he actually was." By contrast, if we were asking the question "What could conceivably have been different and would have led John Smith to vote for Clinton?" it would seem absurd to use Smith's race as a cause, or to vary Smith's race counterfactually.[38]

Some recent work on deterrence provides a more dramatic example, one fundamentally similar to the supposedly ridiculous Stealth bomber case. In order to assess the causes of successful deterrence in a certain class of international disputes, Paul Huth and Bruce Russett collected data on fifty-eight interstate crises in the period 1885–1983. One of the possible causes they wished to evaluate was nuclear weapons—does the possession of these weapons make it more likely that efforts by a defending state to deter an attack on a smaller protégé by a challenging state will succeed? For each case in the sample, the independent variable was coded "1" if the defender had nuclear weapons, and "0" otherwise. Using a probit model, they then

---

[37] When we use miracle causes in an explanation, we seem implicitly to have in mind the idea of an experiment. In true experiments, the experimenter acts literally as the "hand of God" that intervenes from outside, assigning causes to cases.

[38] In this example, race "explains" a person's vote in very much the sense of Hempel's covering-law model: John Smith's vote is explained by subsuming this case under the "lawlike" principle that whites are more likely than blacks to vote Republican. The covering-law model may be particularly friendly to miracle causes, while narrative or genealogical models of explanation are more friendly to conceivable causes.

estimated an average effect of nuclear weapons on the probability of successful deterrence (along with the effects of other independent variables).[39]

The model thus produces estimates of what would have (probably) happened if, for example, Britain had had nuclear weapons during the July crisis of 1914! But Britain "could not conceivably have had" nuclear weapons in 1914, just as Napoleon could not conceivably have had a Stealth bomber. Does this make inclusion of nuclear weapons in the model "illegitimate"? I think the answer should be no, because what Huth and Russett are doing is only an extreme instance of a sort of inductive reasoning we practice all the time. In this form of empirical assessment, evidence comes from regularities of association across cases, and "cases" are understood not as historical particulars, but rather as ahistorical configurations on independent variables. In the regression analysis, the case of "Britain-Belgium-Germany 1914" is just a list of values of the independent variables being assessed, and is implicitly assumed to be the same (absent the random "other causes") as any case that has these values, regardless of when or where it occurred. It is important to realize that this procedure is not bizarre and unusual—we use it all the time in a less formal way when we give explanations. Particularly when we seek to assess causes of a class of events by looking for regularities across cases, we do not worry about whether in each case it was "actually possible" for the proposed cause to have been present or not. For example, when we say that a particular person's death by lung cancer was caused by smoking, we do not worry about whether the person may have had an "addictive personality" or constitution such that he could not actually have quit (or that he smoked in a social environment that supported smoking and was not aware of the link to lung cancer).

So we may be more likely to expect and use miracle causes when trying to explain classes of events than when explaining singular events. This does not mean, however, that miracle causes are never invoked in efforts to give causes of particular events.[40] In fact, this is a common strategy, especially when a researcher is arguing that the particular event in question was "inevitable" and had such-and-such causes. For example, if I argue that World War I was caused by inevitable shifts in the distribution of military and economic power in Europe in the preceding twenty years, then I am invoking a miracle cause, and nothing seems peculiar about this claim. Similarly, the "ultimate" or "underlying" cause of Soviet collapse is often given as a factor that, it is assumed, could not have been different—the supposedly inherent, inescapable inefficiency of Soviet-style economic planning.[41]

[39] See Huth and Russett (1984) and Huth (1988). For a reanalysis of the data from a different theoretical perspective see Fearon (1994c).

[40] Or that conceivable causes never appear in studies of recurrent phenomena.

[41] The automaton analogy suggests a plausible interpretation of the idea of historical inevitability, which is sometimes viewed as problematic or incoherent. In a stochastic automaton,

Nonetheless, the more fine-grained a researcher's effort to give causes of a particular event, the more likely that he or she will tend to look for conceivable causes. Typically historians focusing on particular sequences of events and political scientists contemplating counterfactual scenarios are asking about conceivable causes. They want to know what about the world could actually have been different and could have led to a different outcome. Part of what is funny about the Stealth bomber example is that it provides an outlandish miracle cause in a context in which intuition wants a conceivable cause—what we really want to know is whether and what could actually have led to a Napoleonic victory. Stronger evidence for this proposition is that virtually every analyst who has written on counterfactual thought experiments in history or social science has argued or accepted without question that it is "illegitimate" to counterfactually change things that "had to be" as they were—this despite the fact that we do it all the time in framing explanations that we take to be valid.

If this generalization holds, then researchers who seek to evaluate their theories using case studies and counterfactual arguments, or who develop their theories by trying to generalize from particular cases, may tend to be biased towards conceivable causes. Further, because conceivable causes are more likely to be specific to each case, these researchers will be biased against finding causes that generalize across cases, which are by and large what social scientists are most interested in. Historians, who frequently dismiss the whole enterprise of finding causes that generalize across cases, may provide the best example of this bias in action. Historians tend to look for conceivable causes and these rarely generalize much.

From a methodological standpoint, then, it may be valuable to keep the distinction between miracle and conceivable causes in mind when one is trying to use counterfactual argument to assess the causes of some particular event or general phenomenon. Counterfactual analysis may bias one towards conceivable causes by implicitly defining the explanatory problem in a certain way (that is, by making the question "How could things actually have been different?"). But since we are often interested in learning what are the factors that regularly produce some outcome, such as war, democracy, or economic growth, then we probably should not rule out miracle causes by methodological fiat.

Simply saying that in making counterfactual arguments scholars should not restrict themselves to conceivable causes (unless, of course, conceivable causes are what they want to learn) is not enough, however. Because for any particular case there may be a huge number of "miracles" that might have

---

almost no event is "inevitable" in the sense that, for butterfly-effect reasons, if something had happened differently many periods earlier, the event would not have occurred. However, it may still make sense to say that if the event occurred in period t, it was "inevitable" (or very probable) in period $t-i$ given the nature of the transition rules and conditions in period $t-i$.

precluded the consequent while leaving the rest of the world otherwise similar, I may have worsened one of the problems noted at the outset of the paper: When one takes a counterfactual approach to hypothesis testing, far too many valid "causes" may appear. There is also the problem of exactly how one imagines the miracle occurring. Exactly how do we picture the British with nuclear weapons, or the British and French with larger militaries in 1935, or nineteenth-century America without railroads? The specific way we imagine the counterfactual antecedent may strongly condition the conclusions we draw from the counterfactual exercise. At least when we restrict ourselves to conceivable causes there are implicit guidelines about how the counterfactual antecedent is to be introduced—as suggested by Tetlock and Belkin, Hawthorn, and others, conceivable causes should be rendered consistently with historical facts, well-established theories and statistical generalizations, and so on. For miracle causes it is not clear what the guidelines, if any, should be.

I see no easy resolution to these problems, and can offer only some incomplete suggestions. First, because miracle causes seem relatively unproblematic in large-N research designs, we might try to follow this example when employing miracle causes in counterfactual arguments about particular cases. In the large-N, regularity of association approach, the range of what might be called "permissible miracles" is given by the range of outcomes on the dependent variable for all cases in the sample. Thus, we might make it illegitimate to introduce miracle counterfactual antecedents that have not been realized for any other actual case.

Second, some miracles are easier to contemplate than others due to the fact that there are sufficiently many "like" cases that both we and the decision makers involved would have a sense of the meaning and implications of the counterfactual change. For example, it is less problematic to imagine Britain and France with counterfactually strong militaries in 1938 than to try to imagine Britain with nuclear weapons in 1914, even if we are committed to the view that only by a miracle could Britain and France have been stronger than they were. For the case of nuclear weapons, it is almost impossible to imagine how European leaders in 1914 would think about these devices, or how Continental leaders would react to a British announcement and test, and so on. We have only one instance of the invention of nuclear weapons to go by. By contrast, if Neville Chamberlain awoke one morning in 1938 and was told that, due to an extraordinary failure of military accounting, the reserves and air force were in considerably better shape than had formerly been believed, we can imagine how Chamberlain and others might have responded to this knowledge. It was certainly within their comprehension, considering that people at the time explained events in foreign policy by referring to relative military strengths.

Regarding the second problem of how we should imagine the miracle cause being inserted or subtracted in the counterfactual scenario, I can only suggest a Lewislike closeness criterion: introduce the miracle by making as few changes as one can in the actual world. For instance, suppose one thinks that railroad technology had to have been invented around the time it actually was, so that Fogel's counterfactual exercise in *Railroads and American economic growth* considers what I have called a miracle cause. How best to envision the nineteenth-century United States without railroads? One might imagine counterfactually that for some obscure and purely technical reason, railroads were not feasible; perhaps in a "close" counterfactual world there is no way to lay tracks that can endure more than a few trips by heavy locomotives. Or perhaps for obscure reasons Americans are systematically deluded and believe that canals are much more efficient than railroads, so they never really try railroads. With miracle causes the problem is not to suggest a counterfactual that "actually could have happened" but rather to introduce the counterfactual antecedent so as best to capture the sense and intent of the question "What would have happened if . . . ?"

Conclusion

For diverse reasons, many political scientists who study international relations consider small-N sets of case studies the best or only feasible way to test causal hypotheses. Moreover, they frequently choose cases that all have the same outcome on the dependent variable or try to explain the occurrence of more or less "one-time," "unique" events. This approach is maintained despite standard and largely uncontested statistical arguments that say such research designs cannot actually test hypotheses. For example, in the conventional, regularity of association approach, selecting on the dependent variable will produce biased estimates of the impact of the independent variables in question, and considering only one case (i.e., one "data point") makes it impossible to draw causal inferences at all.[42]

As I have argued elsewhere (Fearon 1991), reliance on counterfactuals may be a way that users of case studies seek (mainly unconsciously) to increase their N. Counterfactual scenarios may provide the controlled comparisons necessary to support causal inferences when researchers restrict themselves to a small number of actual-world cases. If this is so, and considering that scholars employing case studies for the most part are not very explicit about their use of counterfactuals, we should ask if there are meth-

[42] On the problems created by selecting on the dependent variable see Geddes (1990). Doug Dion (1995) has argued that selecting on the dependent variable is a perfectly appropriate research design if the goal is to test for necessary conditions. See also Collier (1995), who suggests several reasons why research designs that select on the dependent variable may be worthwhile and justifiable.

odological guidelines or even a method of counterfactual argument that would help in this kind of work.

The arguments developed in this chapter lead me to be somewhat pessimistic about the possibility and usefulness of any method of counterfactual argument. The chief problem is that its domain would necessarily be very narrow. As the analogy to the cellular automaton suggests, for typical social science problems we will only be able to judge the plausibility of counterfactual arguments for highly "local" situations. That is, we will be able to assess plausibility only where the counterfactuals invoke causal mechanisms and regularities that are well understood and that are considered at a spatial and temporal range small enough that multiple mechanisms do not interact, yielding chaos. As Sidney Hook (1943, 134) put it years ago, "When we draw the line of possible eventuality too far out of the immediate period, the mind staggers under the cumulative weight of the unforeseen." Better theory may push back the limits of what is "too far" a bit. But if the automaton analogy holds, then even a perfect understanding of the local mechanisms would not allow us reasonably to assess the plausibility of important counterfactuals such as "if Gorbachev had lost the succession struggle, the Soviet Union would not have disintegrated by 1992" or "even without nuclear weapons, the post-War world would have been peaceful."

I would thus suggest adding a *proximity criterion* to the list of guidelines proposed by Tetlock and Belkin for assessing the plausibility of counterfactual thought experiments. The criterion may be stated as follows: Consider only thought experiments in which the hypothetical antecedent and consequent are close together in time and are separated by a small number of causal steps. A great many counterfactuals that are, unfortunately, of great interest will be deemed unassessable by this criterion. This does not mean that they should never be posed—such counterfactuals may serve as valuable "spotlights" directing our attention to more local and assessable counterfactuals. Rather, exploring counterfactual claims that fail the proximity criterion is unlikely to yield any very defensible judgment on the causes of the event in question.

The real payoff for carefully specifying social science counterfactuals will probably not be found in some generalizable method of empirical evaluation. There may be occasions when exploring a counterfactual scenario will allow a highly plausible test of a hypothesis, but I doubt the circumstances are very general or that there exists a method of general application.

Rather, the main benefit of being careful about counterfactuals is that doing so forces one to be clearer about, or to "unpack," the nature of the explanatory exercise one is engaged in. Specifying and exploring the counterfactuals implied by a causal claim forces one to be clear about (1) the precise delimitation of the event being explained; (2) the "contrast space" or set of alternative outcomes from which the event that occurred is explained;

and (3) the type of causes one is looking for. Regarding (3), I have proposed distinguishing between conceivable and miracle causes, and have suggested that we should only consider counterfactual antecedents that might affect the consequent while leaving the rest of the world otherwise similar.

Exploring counterfactuals opens up a range of difficult and often philosophical questions concerning what we are doing when we try to explain particular or recurrent international political outcomes. A final benefit of thinking about counterfactuals is that doing so brings some of these foundational issues out into the open. Failing to carefully specify the requisite counterfactuals is a way of sweeping such questions and problems under the rug. The more we keep these problems hidden from view, the more our "explanations" will have the character of persuasive rhetoric rather than empirical discovery.

Part Two

COUNTERFACTUAL ANALYSIS OF PARTICULAR
EVENTS

3

Counterfactual Reasoning in Western Studies of Soviet Politics and Foreign Relations

GEORGE W. BRESLAUER

WESTERN DEBATES about Soviet politics and foreign relations have been vocal and visible since the Bolshevik revolution of 1917.[1] They have been
conducted by journalists, political activists, and academic scholars alike,
with some participants combining these roles. Many debates have been of
the kind that are not typically cast in counterfactual terms: descriptive re-
portage of what "actually" happened and conceptual debates about the "nature" of the Soviet system. But many other debates or disagreements have
focused on the *causes* of events, making them prime candidates for recasting
as counterfactual questions or claims. Thus, inquiries into the decisive
causes of the collapse of czarism and the Russian Revolutions of 1917 can
be rephrased as "What if there had been no World War I? or no Lenin? or no
Rasputin?"

Causal debates among specialists on Russian and Soviet history have typically revolved around the explanation of dramatic turning points in the history of that country. Yet, in practice, although rich and intelligent discussion
has informed many of these debates, the field has paid little attention to the
methodology of causal reasoning, and even less to the methodology of counterfactual thought experiments. We have seen little in the way of sustained
thought experiments that would force one to rank the relative importance of
several contributory causes of the turning points in question.

Causal claims are the stuff of historical analysis, and counterfactual
claims are implicit in all causal assertions. Yet historians as a collectivity
tend not to treat counterfactual thought experiments as particularly worthwhile exercises. To be sure, the historical profession is not monolithic on
this score. Some treat counterfactual reasoning as a "parlor game" or "idle
speculation," while others treat it as a logical and worthwhile step in knowl-

[1] I am very grateful to David Engerman, Department of History, University of California,
Berkeley, for valuable research assistance and stimulating discussions of materials. For com-
ments on an earlier version of this chapter, I would also like to thank Aaron Belkin, David
Collier, Alexander Dallin, Robert Jervis, Nicholas Riasanovsky, Yuri Slezkine, Philip Tetlock,
Robert C. Tucker, Mark Turner, and Steven Weber.

edge accumulation.[2] But the latter tend to be those who are more theory oriented, or nomothetic, in their approach to knowledge building, while most historians show greater appreciation for idiographic contributions.

Social scientists tend to be more nomothetic in orientation. And yet the political scientists, economists, and sociologists working on the USSR, with a few exceptions, showed scarcely more interest than the historians in the methodology of causal and counterfactual reasoning. This may have been a product of distinctive features of Soviet studies as a field: its single-country focus, its (relative) data poverty, and the field's collective uncertainty as to the comparative referents or theoretical analogues most appropriate to understanding the nature of the system. These are features that Soviet studies shares with certain other area studies (China studies, in particular) and with many fields of single-country historical analysis. But the failure to resolve disputes by subjecting them to "hard" counterfactual thought experiments has also been a product of the unusually demanding—often perhaps unrealistic—nature of that exercise.

This chapter is divided into four sections. Section 1 is normative in thrust: What standards for judging the plausibility of counterfactual claims are reasonable to apply in the social sciences in general and in Soviet studies in particular? Section 2 is descriptive: When have specialists on the USSR in fact engaged in counterfactual thought experiments under the conditions that mark their field of study? Section 3 is evaluative: How does the nature of counterfactual discussion in the Sovietological field square with the standards invoked in Section 1 and with human tendencies reported in the cognitive-psychological literature? And Section 4 discusses opportunities that have become available since the collapse of communism for raising the quality of counterfactual reasoning to heights of which we previously could only dream.

1. What Are Reasonable Standards for Counterfactual Reasoning?

The defense of strong counterfactual claims probably requires some minimal combination of: (1) a data-rich evidentiary base sufficient for tracing causal connections within and among social, economic, and political processes; and (2) a theoretical apparatus based on assumptions or analogies that are sufficiently relevant to the empirical context under discussion to permit one plausibly to bridge the inevitable gaps in the evidence. This apparatus may be based upon deductive models or statistical generalizations, but the critical issue will be its contextual relevance: Are the assumptions built into the

---

[2] For disparagement of counterfactualism see Carr (1961, 127). For championing of counterfactualism and employment of it in systematic fashion see Nash (1991) and Fogel (1964).

models relevant to the context at hand (e.g., revolutionary Russia or the Soviet Union in the 1920s or 1980s)? Are the statistical generalizations based on contexts sufficiently analogous to the Russian/Soviet context in question? In short, is the theoretical apparatus based on a tight analogical fit, a loose fit, or a nonfit? There are no obvious standards for determining the optimal tightness of fit of *real-world* comparative referents.

Optimally, one would wish to advance causal and counterfactual propositions when in possession of "all the facts" and a perfect fit between theories and context. But this is a practical impossibility. The minimal requisite proportions between evidence and theory required for "fruitful" counterfactual thought experiments may be an arbitrary stipulation—or at least a purely abstract one. In the real world of the social sciences, disciplines and subfields will surely vary in the extent to which they can realistically achieve whatever minimal requisite proportions are stipulated. The strongest counterfactual claims can be made in the most data-rich and reductionist social sciences, such as experimental cognitive psychology, and in realms of the natural sciences that are richest in "established" theoretical laws. Good examples of such claims may be found in Tetlock and Belkin (Chapter 1). These may provide standards to which we all should aspire, if only as thought experiments to keep us methodologically self-conscious. But they can hardly provide realistic standards for judging the quality—or social utility—of scholarship in most realms of the social sciences.[3] Thus, a third requirement for fruitful counterfactual thought experiments in the social sciences should be the construction of standards that are commensurate with the availability of data and grounded theory in the given realm of study.

Western studies of the Soviet Union have been handicapped on each of these scores. Most of the issues have been marked by an extreme scarcity of data about the critical causal relationships under investigation. And the novelty of the Soviet Union as a political order forced scholars to live with immense uncertainty as to the analogues and theories applicable to the context.[4] More specifically, this combination of data scarcity and theoretical-

---

[3] Stephen Jay Gould (1981, 262) refers to "physics envy" among certain types of social and natural scientists. (My thanks to Marc Garcelon for drawing my attention to this passage.) On the limitations of social science inquiry see Lindblom (1990). Many counterfactual claims about historical turning points hinge on theoretical preferences, explicit or implicit, regarding the role of leadership versus the role of impersonal forces in history. This is one of the oldest, and still unresolved, issues in the social sciences. My favorite quotation, a *non sequitur* that teaches us more about the sociology than the philosophy of knowledge, is from Henry Kissinger, who stated in January 1974, five years after entering government: "As a professor, I tended to think of history as run by impersonal forces. But when you see it in practice, you see the difference personalities make" (quoted in Isaacson 1992, 13).

[4] This was further exacerbated by the fact that for almost thirty years the Soviet Union was essentially the only Leninist state in the world, and when communism came to Eastern Europe and Asia after World War II, many of the regimes were controlled by Moscow. It took decades

analogical uncertainty made it hard to define the character and political dynamics of the system and to distinguish the genetic from the developmental features of the system as it evolved over time.[5]

Which methodological standards are reasonable to invoke under these conditions? Many of the standards listed by Tetlock and Belkin are quite reasonable: clear specification of independent and dependent variables; cotenability of antecedents and connecting principles; consistency with well-established historical facts; and invocation of theories or statistical generalizations that are in principle falsifiable. These standards strike me as logical requirements for any sustained discussion of counterfactual claims by informed and methodologically self-conscious participants.

Others who have written about the methodology of counterfactual reasoning provide us with additional useful standards to apply, even in the face of data scarcity and theoretical uncertainty. I borrow them from Nash's (1991) review of the literature on counterfactual reasoning: The counterfactual antecedent must have been an available option, considered but rejected; the consequent must stand in relatively close temporal proximity to the antecedent; and the focus should be on identification of the *decisive* factor in a historical sequence, by considering which factor, if removed, would have made the sequence inconceivable.[6] Note that these standards attempt to restrict counterfactual analysis to the explanation of fairly time-bound, discrete historical sequences.

Concerning theoretical requirements, the emphasis should be on explicit theory, carefully specified to conform to actual initial conditions. But how much conformity is needed to constitute a sufficiently tight fit? Here Elster's (1978, 184–85) stipulation about the optimal "strength" of theory is useful: "For a successful counterfactual analysis a delicate balance must be struck: the theory must be weak enough to admit the counterfactual assumption, and also strong enough to permit a clear-cut conclusion."[7]

These logical, empirical, and theoretical stipulations are somewhat weaker than several of those suggested by Tetlock and Belkin, but still sufficiently strong to constitute very "hard tests" of counterfactual or causal claims in any nonreductionist social science. And if any *single-country* field of historical study can come close to meeting the conditions I have conceded

---

of observation before we could clarify the features that *independent* Leninist regimes held in common and that were not likely to change short of a revolution from below.

[5] On genetic versus developmental attributes of Leninist regimes see Jowitt (1992, 162–73).

[6] The criteria I borrow are cited by Nash from the works of Jon Elster, H. Stuart Hughes, and Lance Davis.

[7] As we shall see, the dominant forms of debate in Soviet studies have been between antagonists who embraced extremely strong theories and those who embraced extremely weak theories.

to be "reasonable," it will have met a very high methodological standard indeed!

2. When Have Specialists on the USSR Employed Counterfactual Reasoning?

Specific counterfactual claims dot the pages of almost any historical work on the USSR. What if Rasputin had been killed earlier? What if Lenin had been successfully assassinated in 1918—or had not been shot at all? What if Stalin had lived five years longer than he did? What if Khrushchev had not denounced Stalin? What if Khrushchev had not been overthrown? What if Brezhnev had died earlier? Although these and many others gain mention, they tend not to be the objects of lengthy discussions or debates among scholars.

In some cases the lack of debate is a product of consensus about the likely consequences; for example, if Stalin had lived longer, few observers deny that there likely would have been another terroristic purge of the leadership, for all the signs of such an impending purge were accumulating in the months before his death, and there was no obvious reason to believe Stalin could not have implemented his will. In other cases, lack of debate reflects the fact that the specific issue is subsumed in discussions of broader counterfactuals: Rasputin's role in the czarist court is a contributory consideration in debates about the survivability of czarism, especially among those who treat the low quality of leadership choices as determinant of the fate of that system. Similarly, the hypothetical disappearance of Lenin in 1918, three or four years short of his initial incapacitation from stroke in December 1921, is subsumed within the debate about the causes of Stalinism.

In Soviet studies, isolated counterfactual claims turn into sustained counterfactual debates, supported by a growing empirical literature, when specialists address the causes and consequences of major discontinuities in Soviet history. In the realm of internal affairs, such debates have included:

1. The causes of the revolutions of 1917: the collapse of czarism; the collapse of liberalism during February–October 1917, the ascendancy of Bolshevism and its ability to retain power through the Civil War of 1918–21
2. The causes of Stalinism and its causal relationship to Leninism and Marxism
3. The consequences of Stalinism as a strategy of "modernization"
4. The causes of the "Gorbachev revolution"
5. The causes of the collapse of the USSR.

In the literature on Soviet foreign policy, these include:

1. The causes of the Cold War

2. The causes of the alternating warming and chilling of US-Soviet relations throughout the 1950s–1980s

3. The causes of the Sino-Soviet split

4. The sources of Gorbachev's "new political thinking" about international affairs.

I will evaluate most of these debates in this chapter.

Debates about the Trajectory of Internal Development

Why have these substantive issues led scholars to adopt a counterfactual approach? Let us deal first with the internal issues. The causes of the revolutions of 1917 and of the Bolshevik consolidation of power thereafter have been the object of sustained debate in the field for many decades; that debate continues to this day. Archival access, even before *glasnost*, was sufficient to allow for a substantial empirical base on the period 1914–17 (though this remained thin compared, say, to the empirical base for studies of Nazism or Italian fascism). Counterfactual claims have been framed in several ways: (1) *Absent* World War I, would czarism have survived? Alternatively, would it have evolved into a liberal-democratic regime? (2) *Given* World War I, and its continuation after the collapse of czarism, could liberalism have consolidated itself (in today's parlance, could the "democratic breakthrough" have been "consolidated")? (3) *Given* the collapse of liberalism, could Bolshevism have been avoided as the alternative to liberalism?

The second issue—the relationship between Leninism and Stalinism—also has distinct features, though of a different kind. Among historians of the era, the question is typically posed in causal-probabilistic terms: Given Leninism, what was the likelihood of Stalinism? Or, in the awkward phraseology in which the debate was framed: "Was Stalinism a logical continuation of Leninism?"[8] But portions of the debate were cast in counterfactual terms: Would Lenin, had he lived another ten years, have acted as Stalin did? Given Lenin's early death, could Bukharin have defeated Stalin? Regardless of who sponsored it, could an evolutionary strategy of "building socialism" have emerged victorious in Soviet policy making? What would have happened had Stalin, say, suddenly passed away in the mid-1920s or, as Tucker (1977a, 78) framed it, died in the flu epidemic of 1918–19?

The third issue treats early Stalinism (1928–35) as cause, rather than effect, and seeks to evaluate the consequences of those policies. Specifically, the issue is posed: "Was Stalinism a 'rational' strategy of 'modernization'"? This question raises issues of effectiveness and efficiency that are expressed

---

[8] As one skeptical participant quipped, "It didn't develop out of Buddhism" (in Tucker 1977b, 321).

in a combination of causal and normative terms: Did Stalin's policies achieve modernizing goals at a reasonable cost? But the issue could only be extensively *argued* or rebutted in counterfactual terms: Would a different strategy of modernization have achieved more in the way of modernizing goals at the same or lower cost?

The fourth and fifth issues—the sources and effects of the Gorbachev phenomenon, including its relationship to the collapse of the USSR—often invokes the counterfactual: Would the radicalism embraced by Gorbachev have emerged victorious even in his absence? If, for example, Gorbachev had not won the power struggle in 1985, would policy have continued for long to reflect the conservatism of other politburo members? Or would it have become radicalized anyway, under the pressure of social forces and reform communists within the upper reaches of the political establishment? Next, the counterfactual posed by those writing after 1991 has often been: Given Gorbachev's ascension to power and the radicalization of his program, did the collapse of the USSR have to ensue? Was a semidemocratized and semimarketized USSR a possibility? Might things have turned out differently had Gorbachev pursued a somewhat different, but still radical, reform strategy?

There is one grand counterfactual that, remarkably, has not generated a debate within the field: What if there had been no World War II? This omission is intriguing in part because there has been such immense debate about what would have transpired had there been no World War I. One would think the field primed to replicate the other debate, albeit with somewhat different substantive concerns. The omission is also intriguing because of the immense impact the Second World War had on the USSR in terms of lives lost, nonlethal casualties, material damages, demographic shifts, changes in social stratification, the role of the Communist Party during the war, changes in industrial location, and changes in the USSR's relative position in the international order.

Perhaps a glance again at the four explanatory counterfactuals that *were* debated at length will yield insight into the reasons for this. These share a parallelism in the outcomes to be explained. In all four cases, the outcome is an *extreme change of long duration*: the collapse of czarism, and then of liberalism, issuing in a Bolshevik revolution; the victory of Stalinism over less extreme alternatives; and the emergence after Brezhnevism of a radical reformism that would lead to the collapse of the USSR. Indeed, the counterfactual that was not discussed—what if there had been no World War II?—provides a confirmatory negative case: That war was followed by fundamental continuity, by a quick reconsolidation, not collapse, of the Soviet system.[9]

---

[9] Presumably, had Gorbachev's radical reformism been short-lived and resulted in a conservative reaction or restoration in the late 1980s, rather than in the collapse of the USSR, it too

But why was the collective mind of Sovietologists focused on sharp discontinuities of long duration? Perhaps the choice of issues for debate and discussion was a product of the intense political emotions generated by the Soviet experience. Counterfactuals entertain the possibility that something that happened might not have happened. Psychologically, therefore, we could imagine a tendency to be attracted to discussions of how "bad" outcomes might have been avoided.

This hypothesis fits much of the pattern noted thus far. That is, heated discussions of counterfactuals about a Russia without World War I were largely driven, on one side at least, by a normative commitment to discern how either liberalism or Menshevism might have averted the victory of Bolshevism.[10] Not the collapse of czarism but rather the victory of Bolshevism were the outcomes to be avoided (put differently, monarchists were not prominent figures in these debates!). Similarly, discussions of Stalinism in counterfactual terms were largely driven by the concern of many scholars to determine whether a more moderate regime could have won out in the 1920s.[11] And discussions of the collapse of the USSR in counterfactual terms may have been driven by a desire to show that the system could have survived or reformed itself, or that Gorbachev could have "succeeded."[12]

I hesitate to attribute hidden motives to scholars, and therefore resist arguing the stronger ("the more . . . the more . . . ") form of this case. It may or may not be true that the more an observer detested Bolshevism or Stalinism, the more likely he or she was to entertain scenarios that averted the victory of these forces. And it may or may not be true that the greater the sympathy for Bolshevism or Stalinism, the more likely the observer was to view these outcomes as overdetermined. The most heated and polarized debates in the field did indeed display these characteristics, but the evidence is too thin to document degrees of sympathy or aversion.

The focus on grand discontinuities may also have been a matter of con-

---

would not have been the object of lengthy counterfactual discussion. Continuity would have been confirmed and the causes of that continuity assumed to lie in the power of entrenched interests within the system.

[10] Thus, Alexander Gerschenkron argued that economic westernization that was proceeding until World War I put Russia on a different trajectory; absent World War I, he foresaw "Germanization" of Russia's developmental state (see, for example, Gerschenkron 1960). Arthur Mendel (1965) makes an analogous claim in the political realm. He sees much progress toward liberal constitutionalism, which was aborted by World War I. Leopold Haimson (1964; 1965) rejected these perspectives, arguing that, absent World War I, a revolutionary overthrow of czarism would still have taken place, but of a Menshevik, not a Bolshevik, variety. Debates surrounding these issues were numerous and rich; I will not attempt to cite them exhaustively.

[11] The milestones of this concern were S. F. Cohen (1985b) and Lewin (1968; 1974).

[12] See, for example, Dallin (1992). Conversely, those who refuse to entertain the counterfactual consideration patently reject the proposition that the system could have survived or reformed itself, i.e., that Gorbachev could have "succeeded" on his own terms. See, for example, Malia (1994).

venience. On certain specific counterfactuals (e.g., "What if Sergei Kirov had not been assassinated in 1934?"), the data about the policy-making process are so scarce that observers recognize the need for archival openings to further advance our thinking. But on matters of grand discontinuity in regime type or policy, we may look at both longer-term and immediate causes and explore these in social, cultural, economic, international, and domestic-political realms; hence, many discrete pools of evidence become relevant, and can be found, that at least bear upon the larger debate, even if insufficient data exist to trace the interaction of social, economic, international, and political processes.[13]

Thus, the three factors that seem to have determined whether an issue elicited a grand debate *cast in counterfactual terms* were: (1) the amount of historical evidence available to be mined that bore on the question; (2) the magnitude and staying power of the change in trajectory to be explained; and (3) the level of political partisanship elicited by the question. When rich data became available, counterfactual claims could be addressed, whether or not widespread personal motivation existed to undertake them.[14] When reasonably useful data were joined to far-reaching changes that excited political passions, a grand debate was likely to be sustained for decades. When such data were not available but the question concerned far-reaching changes and/ or excited political passions, sustained debates about counterfactuals were conducted by means other than historical research; that is, by theoretical deduction, sophisticated or not, or by polemics. When data were poor and the issue was not of high political stakes, scholars might make casual counterfactual claims, about which they might disagree with each other, but a sustained debate did not ensue.

A constant in all of this was theoretical dissensus. Theories that would be relevant to the above-mentioned debates are theories about the driving forces of history: revolutions, their origins and evolution; regime change and collapse; strategies of modernization. Explicitly or implicitly, participants in these impassioned debates embraced theoretical perspectives that informed or buttressed the conclusions they reached. In the case of the causes of the revolutions of 1917, comparativists entered the debate and discussion among the area specialists became more theoretically explicit and somewhat richer.[15] In the case of evaluations of Stalinism as a strategy of modernization, com-

[13] The tendency for scholars to mine discrete veins of evidence on one or two aspects of the larger interaction is a characteristic of all the debates about grand discontinuities, and may be a powerful argument for well-conceived team research when counterfactual discussion of these turning points is at issue. For the classic article introducing the theory and method of "process-tracing," see George (1979).

[14] Presumably, however, the incentive structure within Western academia, and the sheer number of scholars competing for research topics within the academy, would lead us to expect that rich new sources of data will be mined by somebody.

[15] See, for examples, Hagopian (1974), Skocpol (1979), and McDaniel (1988).

parative perspectives and theoretical (economic-developmental) models were brought to bear, enriching—but not deciding—the debate.[16] But in debates about the causes of Stalinism, the causes of the Gorbachev phenomenon, and the causes of the collapse of the USSR, the analogical referents have been less clear, and theoretical disputes have been less explicit components of the debates, a point to which I will return in Section 3.

Debates about Foreign Policy

Debates about Soviet foreign policy have entailed a number of highly charged and sustained disagreements cast in counterfactual terms. The grand debate about the origins of the Cold War, of course, hinged on a counterfactual: Had the United States followed a different course of policy toward the USSR, could the Cold War have been averted? Similarly, all debate about "missed opportunities" to end the Cold War in the 1950s, 1960s, or 1970s were intrinsically counterfactual, for the very concept of "missed opportunity" is a counterfactual claim. Thus, had the United States followed a more conciliatory foreign policy in 1953–54, would Malenkov's more conciliatory orientation have won out in the leadership, whether under Malenkov or under some other leader? Analogous debates or disagreements can be found in the literature concerning alleged missed opportunities in 1957, 1959, 1961, and 1965.[17]

This concern with missed opportunities, of course, extends throughout the twentieth-century history of U.S.-Soviet or East-West relations. From the Stalin period we wonder whether Western acceptance of Litvinov's proposals for collective security in 1938 might have avoided the Molotov-Ribbentrop Pact of 1939. From the more recent years, we wonder whether different negotiating terms during the Nixon-Brezhnev detente—such as U.S. willingness to negotiate away its lead in MIRV technologies—might have averted the Soviet military buildup of the mid-1970s and the collapse of detente later in the decade. As in domestic affairs, so in foreign affairs, some of these specific debates are subsumed within grand debates about major historical turning points. Both the specific and the grand debates continue to spark interest in new sources of evidence that might help us to fill in empirical gaps and thereby reduce uncertainty about whether there were actually "opportunities" that were "missed." The uncertainties also continue to nourish interest in the development of a theory of Soviet politics, or of

[16] See, for examples, Erlich (1960), Hunter and Szyrmer (1992), Gerschenkron (1960; 1966), Jowitt (1971; 1978; 1992), Wilber (1969), and Nove and Newth (1967).

[17] See, for examples, Dinerstein (1959), Schurmann (1974), Deutscher (1970), Richter (1994), and Lebow and Stein (1994).

Soviet-American relations, that would allow us to build still more plausible counterfactual arguments.[18]

Another grand debate in the Soviet foreign relations literature concerned the causes of the Sino-Soviet split. Some scholars emphasized personality differences between Soviet and Chinese leaders. Others pointed to ideological disputes arising from differences in the stages of development of their respective revolutions (Chinese communism having come to power thirty-two years after Soviet communism). Still others emphasized Chinese and Soviet nationalism, while some emphasized national security differences. Occasional scholars would revert to the overdetermined listing of all these allegedly mutually reinforcing factors. As in many other issue areas in which evidence about political processes was scarce, the choice was typically between single-factor explanations and the overdetermined listing of all possible, allegedly reinforcing, reasons, with no empirically rich database available for weighting the causes, and little in the way of a theoretical-deductive framework to guide us.[19]

For these reasons, chroniclers of the Sino-Soviet split typically avoided reformulating their causal claims in strong counterfactual terms. Each mono-causal claim could logically have been rephrased as a counterfactual (absent x, there would not have been a Sino-Soviet schism); and each might have been investigated accordingly, were the data available. But the data were not available. So most scholarly energies were devoted to proving descriptive claims: whether a split in fact existed and how it manifested itself in published polemics.

Returning to East-West relations, the grand debate surrounding the origins of the Cold War has been going on for almost fifty years.[20] And although the debate has hinged on contrasting counterfactual claims, there have been few empirical studies of Soviet behavior that allowed for strong counterfactual conclusions. The data about Stalin's intentions and perceptions have always been exceedingly thin, even more so than on Soviet domestic issues, and most claims that "the United States was to blame" are based on little evidence about the Soviet policy-making process. Instead, the empirical tests have delved principally into U.S. foreign policy decision making, in order to

---

[18] Richter (1994) combines new evidence with a theory of Soviet leadership and policy making that makes for an especially powerful combination. For analogous combinations of new evidence and new theory, again with a focus on leadership, see Anderson (1993) and Goldgeier (1994).

[19] A suggestive theoretical framework was proposed in Deutsch (1954). More recently, see Dittmer (1992). For literature that displays diverse perspectives on the decisive causes of the split see Zagoria (1962), Schurmann (1974), Griffith (1964), Floyd (1963), and Hudson, Lowenthal, and MacFarquhar (1961).

[20] The literature is vast. For a useful early review see Graebner (1969); for a more controversial, recent review see Gaddis (1992).

demonstrate U.S. aggressive or benign intent, U.S. perceptions of Soviet behavior, and the specific timing of U.S. actions; and most of these claims about U.S. responsibility have been advanced by specialists on U.S., not Soviet, foreign policy. To the extent that Sovietologists have sought to characterize Stalin's reactions to these acts, they have relied on arcane, ambiguous clues from the Soviet press. Those clues, although intriguing and suggestive, were insufficiently "hard" to provide the basis for a counterfactual claim that had the United States behaved differently the Soviet Union would have been willing to reach an accommodation based on superpower collaboration.

Because of Soviet censorship, we have had less data about Soviet foreign policy-making processes than about almost any other issue. But if the data have been thin all along, why have foreign policy issues been so frequently marked by counterfactual arguments? The answer, I think, may lie in one feature that foreign policy issues share equally with domestic issues (a high level of passion and partisanship about the grand turning points in relations) and one factor that is more explicitly prevalent among foreign policy issues (the felt need to engage in policy prescription).

The foreign policy literature, more so than the domestic, is suffused by an apparent sense of obligation or desire to be policy prescriptive.[21] Such prescription forces the analyst to engage in both backward thinking (counterfactual-historical) to specify the appropriate lessons of U.S.-Soviet interaction to apply to current circumstances, and forward thinking (counterfactual-predictive) to justify the need for a particular U.S. policy ("if you discontinue your current policy toward them, they will react differently from the way they have"). When explicit policy prescription is required, some form of counterfactual justification will also be required.[22]

Interestingly, this hypothesis is reinforced by the negative example of the Sino-Soviet split. I have noted that little or no counterfactual debate took place over that issue, due to lack of data. But lack of data, though perhaps necessary, is not a sufficient condition for the gap, considering that crucial data were lacking on almost all other foreign policy issues. During the 1950s and 1960s, at least, this literature *did not have to be policy prescriptive* because of the assumption that, if there was a schism between the two communist giants, there was little or nothing the United States could do about it. Only in the 1970s, when the "China card" became an instrument of U.S. policy, did counterfactual-predictive and counterfactual-prescriptive claims

[21] Consider how many articles, even in scholarly journals, end with a section called "Implications for U.S. policy."

[22] My claim about the difference between domestic and foreign policy issues is relative. Many debates about domestic policy may have been driven by policy-prescriptive motives or borne policy-prescriptive implications. But foreign policy debates were explicitly suffused with policy prescription per se.

enter the literature with regularity (Garrett 1979; Lieberthal 1978). But this was no longer a debate about the origins of the Sino-Soviet dispute; rather, it was a debate about the current character of the dispute and the ways in which its manipulation by Washington could affect the terms of U.S.-Soviet competition and collaboration. Thus, the issue of the Sino-Soviet dispute had evolved from a descriptive and explanatory challenge to a partisan-prescriptive challenge, ripe for speculation cast in counterfactual terms.

Predictably, high levels of partisanship induced passionate disagreements about almost all East-West issues noted above. Yet the passions seemed to be in inverse proportion to the quantities of data available to resolve the disputes. This suggests still another factor driving the *content* of counterfactual claims (as opposed to the *fact* of debates cast in counterfactual terms). The greater the paucity of reliable data, the greater the dependence of counterfactual claims on the analyst's theoretical apparatus, cognitive imagery, or philosophy of history. That is, bridging the huge gaps in the data about Soviet foreign policy making required primary reliance on deduction from, say, one's theory of international politics (idealist versus realist versus liberal-institutionalist; bandwagoning versus balancing), or one's image of the nature of the Soviet system (totalitarian/expansionist versus authoritarian/competitive versus authoritarian/status quo-oriented), or one's assumptions about the relationship between personal and impersonal forces in history ("voluntarist" versus "determinist"; cybernetic versus mechanistic).[23]

For these reasons, we find in the foreign policy debates a tendency analogous to what we often find in the great debates about the causes of the Russian revolution and of Stalinism: a split between "determinists" and "possibilists," with the data insufficient for probability testing. Those who argued that the Cold War could have been avoided did what they could to demonstrate that Stalin was not necessarily irreconcilably antagonistic, and that he could have misunderstood or misperceived U.S. actions. Thus, as with the wistful Bukharinite alternative, the limit of the claim typically stopped with the assertion that it did not necessarily have to turn out that way.[24]

---

[23] Indeed, if there is a human need for cognitive structure and closure, this would reflect a broader psychological tendency to compensate for shortages of data with heavier reliance on theory.

[24] David Engerman, of UC Berkeley's Department of History, has suggested the evocative term "wistful counterfactuals" to characterize conclusions advanced by those possibilists who go no farther than demonstrating the existence and availability of a preferred alternative that was at least "in contention" at the time (e.g., Bukharinism or Trotskyism in the 1920s as an alternative to Stalinism), without exploring in much depth the probability of that alternative emerging ascendant. The same term might be applied to Alexander Kerensky's (1934, 208) claim that liberalism could have survived in Russia in mid-1917 ("indubitable truth: without Rasputin, there could be no Lenin"), or to the claim that the Soviet Union could have avoided collapse after August 1991 (Dallin 1992). But caveat emptor: Depending upon one's theoretical

3. On the Quality of Counterfactual Reasoning

The quality of counterfactual reasoning in the field of Soviet studies has surely been affected by the nature of the issues and the purposes of the participants. The foci of disputes have been some of the most momentous turning points of the twentieth century. And the participants have ranged from journalists to partisan-political activists to academic entrepreneurs to ivory-tower scholars. Hence, the passions and stakes in the debates have been high and the purposes diverse. Under these circumstances, it was likely that violations would abound of the high methodological standards for counterfactual testing listed in Section 1 of this paper.

The Impact of Partisanship on Methodological Standards

The very terms of debate were often a product of the search for partisan advantage, which often, willy-nilly, sacrificed clarity in the specification of independent and dependent variables. For example, Soviet ideology constantly trumpeted the notion that its triumphs had been historically "inevitable" and had conformed to "historical necessity." These concepts entailed both a nonprobabilistic causal claim and a conflation of the normative and the analytic, trumpeting the long-term inevitability of the desirable. Unfortunately, Western participants in Sovietological debates at times imported these methodologically suspect concepts into their scholarship. This tended to create confusion, as when Alec Nove entitled his discussion of the *likelihood* of Stalinism emerging ascendant in Bolshevik Russia, "Was Stalin really necessary?," which elicited misplaced rebuttals about the *utility* of Stalinism as a strategy of modernization (Nove 1964 and 1976; rebuttal in Millar 1976).

To take another example, each of the counterfactuals comprised several subsidiary counterfactuals, some purely causal and analytic, others normative in their implications. Thus, in the Lenin-Stalin debate, the issue was often framed according to partisan purposes. The question "Would Lenin have acted as Stalin did?" became a matter of partisan importance among those concerned to absolve Lenin personally of Stalin's "betrayal" of the revolution. By contrast, "Did Lenin's organizational and ideological legacy greatly facilitate Stalin's victory?" was quite a different question.

Perhaps the most egregious violations of methodological standards, not to

---

apparatus and the weight one accords to personal versus impersonal forces in history, one could apply the term "wistful" to any number of counterfactuals that might in fact be less tenuous than those noted here. Malia (1994), for example, considers the Soviet Union to have been doomed to collapse once Gorbachev began his radical reforms in 1987, and argues that those who disagree are ideologically motivated dreamers ("wistful"?).

mention academic collegiality, have surrounded the framing of the causal claim being rebutted and the tendency to caricature the positions of one's opponents. Thus, a recent thrust in the intellectual wars over the Russian Revolution is entitled "Did the Russian Revolution have to happen?" (Pipes 1994). Participants in these debates have at times polarized into camps based on these framings, with each camp trying to pin the extremist label on the other, or to attribute motives for the adoption of scholarly positions ("Cold Warrior," "apologist for Sovietism").[25] Those who assigned a high probability to the Bolshevik victory in 1917, or to the victory of Stalinism in 1928, or to the collapse of the USSR in 1991 are dubbed "determinists" wedded to a perspective of inevitability, while those who ask how the revolutions or Stalinism or Soviet collapse might have been avoided are dubbed "wishful thinkers" engaged in "idle speculation" in order to justify their preconceived ideological or theoretical preferences.

Whatever the motives of individual participants, and however subtle their statements, the grand debates about 1917–29 were not notable for a predominance of probabilistic thought. In part this was due to data poverty and theoretical uncertainty, in part to the search for partisan advantage. Thus, debates often pitted "determinists" of many stripes (political-organizational, social-structural, cultural, economic, international) who generally disagreed among themselves—usually vehemently—about the decisive causal factor but who were united in their opposition to "voluntarists" who stipulated ways in which better or different leadership initiatives might have averted the given outcome.[26] The voluntarists insisted upon the need to think in counterfactual terms, but did not have much in the way of a methodology for testing the counterfactual claim. As a result, their position might be described as "possibilist": insisting that "it didn't have to come out that way" by pointing to the existence of an alternative that was considered but rejected,[27] but without a means of conducting a probabilistic test. The so-called determinists, in turn, tended to ignore counterfactual thought experiments entirely, even to sort out differences among themselves as to which causal factor was decisive in determining the outcome. Determinists tended to embrace available theoretical perspectives that buttressed their claims, while voluntarists tended to be largely atheoretical.

[25] For diverse perspectives on this tendency see Carr (1961, 126–27), S. F. Cohen (1985b, chapter 1), Malia (1994), and Laqueur (1994, chapters 5–6). I have tried to sort out some of this, and have discovered that polemical titles and accusations often coexist in the same piece of scholarship with much more subtle, probabilistic claims (Breslauer 1992).

[26] For example, within the Leninism-Stalinism debate, those who emphasize impersonal (social, cultural, economic, or international) forces in history have been in mortal combat with those who emphasize the causal decisiveness, not of individual leaders (in which case they would not be "determinists"), but of Bolshevik political organization and ideology.

[27] This was one of the criteria proposed by Elster (1978) and included in our list of "reasonable" criteria in Section 1 of this chapter.

Polarization between determinists and possibilists/voluntarists, in both the domestic and foreign policy literature, is indicative of a persistent violation of Elster's rule concerning the optimal strength of theories invoked in counterfactual reasoning. As noted earlier, theories must be "weak enough to admit the counterfactual assumption, and also strong enough to permit a clearcut conclusion" (Elster 1978, 184–85). Determinists propose theories that are so muscle-bound as to rule out the counterfactual assumption, while possibilists and voluntarists offer at best a philosophy of history that implicitly treats turning points as almost totally open-ended and contingent as to outcome. Moreover, in both cases, the approach largely rules out the relative weighting of diverse causal influences, and the construction thereby of a probabilistic series of claims.

To be sure, probability analysis is more easily advocated than executed, all the more so when the object of study is a single turning point in a single country's evolution. Probabilistic causal analyses typically require time-series data and/or interspatial comparative analysis, neither of which has played a dominant role in Sovietological discussions.[28] Hence, the failure to meet Elster's rule and the division between determinists and possibilists may be characteristic of disputes over counterfactual claims in many areas of study that focus on the historical evolution of individual countries.

It does appear to be the case that those who insisted on counterfactual "possibilism" (the voluntarists) tended to be those who insisted that "bad outcomes" were avoidable. Carr (1961, 126–27) asserted that precisely such a tendency existed in early literature on the causes of the Russian Revolution (through the 1950s), and his defensive assertion was subsequently supported by a review of that literature published by Billington (1966).[29] Similarly, in the literature on the causes of Stalinism, possibilists tended to be hostile to Stalinism (a trait they shared with political-organizational-ideological determinists), but to define Stalinism as a betrayal of Leninism.[30]

Thus, partisanship has had the most damaging impact on clarity of specification of causal, counterfactual, normative, and theoretical claims, and on

---

[28] For a complex methodological discussion of the demands of probabilistic analyses see Skyrms (1988).

[29] Billington (1966, 457) writes that until the mid-1960s, those who treated the Revolutions as a pathetic accident included "most Anglo-American scholars and commentators, whose skeptical empiricism inclines them to reject deeper patterns . . . and whose native political traditions subtly incline them to regard sudden and convulsive change as a distasteful aberration," making them particularly susceptible to "dwelling on turning points that might have gone the other way." Notwithstanding this sober reflection and his expressed admiration for the scholarship of E. H. Carr, which shared a Marxist emphasis on impersonal forces, Billington (p. 463) could not resist characterizing Carr's methodology and tone as analogous to that of an apologist for the Bolshevik Central Committee.

[30] Note that the very concept of betrayal reveals both the partisan and the volitional content of their perspective. The classic recent statement is S. F. Cohen (1985a).

the maintenance of a fruitful dialogue in which participants do not talk past each other and do not bastardize the intellectual history of the field.[31]

On other scores, however, the record has been better. Thus, lack of consistency with well-established historical facts was not generally a problem in these debates. Except for partisan politicians and irresponsible journalists, most of the participants cited in this article were accomplished historians of politics, economics, and/or society. The problem was not invention of facts but gaps in "established" bodies of facts, which allowed for multiple interpretations of the meanings of those pools of evidence. The meanings could not be clarified by process-tracing that would reveal more about the causal connections among social, economic, political, and international action. Conclusions, therefore, typically hinged on the authors' theoretical assumptions.

For example, the social history of Russia from 1917 through 1929 became the object of study for large numbers of young scholars during the 1960s, continuing to the present. Their data attempted to show that a social base for Bolshevik rule (1917) or a Stalinist turn (in the late 1920s) existed. Most of them did not explicitly advance claims about the relative weights of different causes of the Bolshevik revolution or of Stalinism. But *some* of them did use their data to argue that Bolshevik party organization, or Stalinist usurpation of power, were insufficient conditions for those victories, social factors were also necessary conditions, and perhaps themselves even sufficient ones. The boldest disputants (minority viewpoints among social historians, to be sure) would stipulate that, even in the absence of a Bolshevik party (in 1917) or of Stalin (in the 1920s), radicalism might well have prevailed in each time period. By contrast, these viewpoints were rebutted by those scholars who treated political, not social, factors as decisive (i.e., as necessary and sufficient) in each case.[32] The debate continues to this day, but awaits new pools of evidence for purposes of tracing connections between the social and the political, and new theoretical inspirations about those connections in the given circumstances.

Partisanship notwithstanding, the debates have also been quite respectable on three other methodological scores: The counterfactual antecedents under consideration were overwhelmingly available options, considered but rejected; the consequent stood in relatively close proximity to the antecedent;

---

[31] In my opinion, two of the more unfortunate depictions of the intellectual history of Sovietology, which stand in mutual antagonism but share the propensity to homogenize the stated positions and alleged motives of those who disagree with them, are S. F. Cohen (1985b, chapter 1) and Malia (1994). For elaboration see Breslauer (1992). For a recent critique of Malia's characterization of the field see Menon (1994, 5–6). For an intellectual history that demands "confessions" and "repentance" from those who committed the "sin" of misinterpreting the nature of the Soviet system see Laqueur (1994, chapter 6).

[32] The most extensive rebuttals, with citations to the social history literature, appear in Malia (1994).

and the antecedents were generally cotenable with connecting principles. Briefly, this means that the focus was typically on discrete, relatively compact historical sequences, grounded in the disputed options of the time period under investigation, and avoiding absurdities analogous to the "Stealth bomber at Waterloo." We find no examples of czarism being only one SCUD missile away from avoiding collapse, or of Bukharin emerging victorious by demonstrating the capacity to rationally plan a mixed economy with a top-of-the-line Macintosh. More seriously, we even find little tolerance of addressing such reasonable issues as: Would the Soviet Union have been better prepared for World War II had Bukharin won the power struggle?

Social science theory and "connecting principles" have played a mixed role in these debates. Theories of the causes of the great revolutions are fairly well developed, and have been applied to the debates about Russia. But the application to that case, though useful, was not especially urgent. The greatest contention within the field was not over 1917 but over 1914. The primary scholarly debates concerned the fate of czarism had Russia or the world avoided World War I, and the fate of liberalism had the Provisional Government pulled out of the war in February 1917. Few scholars defend the proposition that either czarism or liberalism could have prevailed, given the ravages of World War I and the decision to remain in the war after the collapse of czarism.

Social science theory has played a more substantial role in the evaluations of Stalinism as a strategy of modernization, a point to which I shall return below.

The limited role of theory in the Lenin-Stalin debate, and in discussions of the rise of Gorbachev, is perhaps attributable to the lesser development of theory pertinent to those particular questions of leadership and radicalization of policy. Social science theory has more to offer in explaining the consequences of leadership than in explaining its emergence or radicalization, which obviously contain a heavy dose of contingency, especially when the standard is (see Section 1) explicit, falsifiable theories, neither too strong nor too weak, that conform to actual initial conditions. But the limited role of theory in debates about the collapse of the USSR may be a temporary phenomenon (it has only been a few years), though the peaceful nature of the collapse and the distinctive features of that political entity (unitary nation-state? multinational empire? Leninist variant of either?) have spawned a search for the most appropriate analogical fit.[33]

Then too, when one examines the entirety of debates about 1914–17 and about the causes and consequences of Stalinism, one finds a growing sophistication and self-consciousness over time, even among individual combat-

---

[33] Bruce Parrott, of the Paul Nitze School of Advanced International Studies, is conducting an ambitious comparison of the collapse of the Soviet Union with the collapse of a half-dozen empires, in search of the most pertinent empirical generalizations.

ants,[34] but certainly as new participants attempt to synthesize and test the conflicting claims in the literature they encounter when they enter the field.[35] And in debates about the relationship between Gorbachev and the collapse of the USSR, I find from personal conversations a tendency for people to change their minds about previously held positions.[36] Moreover, even in some of the impassioned historical disputes, one finds quite a few individual examples of both methodological and theoretical sophistication, especially about the causes of the Russian revolutions, about the evaluation of Stalinism as a strategy of modernization (see the next subsection) and, most recently, about the analogical referents to employ in thinking about the causes of the collapse of the USSR. Again, when one gets beyond the headlines, newspaper articles, and MacNeil/Lehrer appearances, one finds in the academic literature on all these questions a great deal of careful scholarship by very self-conscious, informed, and intelligent debaters.[37]

Cognitive-Psychological Tendencies: Congruence and Incongruence

In the *foreign policy* literature, when counterfactuals are addressed, it is fair to say that the standards have been lower than those displayed on domestic issues. Extreme data poverty, the heavy emphasis on explicit policy prescription, and the proliferation of journals in which scholars attempt to influence the policy community have led to a situation in which partisans more often embrace theoretical perspectives and invent counterfactuals to justify their preferred policies. Indeed, this probably explains a tendency first noted by Jervis (1981): extraordinary congruence between analysts' images of Soviet foreign policy motivations and those analysts' images of the nature of the international order.

This raises the larger question of the extent to which congruence of cogni-

[34] For example, the possibilist title of Pipes (1994) belies the more nuanced and probabilistic analysis within that article. Also, Malia's (1994, chapter 3) recent discussion of counterfactuals regarding the relationship among World War I, liberalism, and the Russian revolutions of 1917 is methodologically self-conscious, analytically rich, empirically sound, and theoretically innovative.

[35] See, for example, Kotkin (1991). Kotkin combines area knowledge with comparative perspectives in order to expose the limits of the explanatory power of social history and the need to complement it with cultural and political factors in order to explain outcomes in 1917.

[36] But caveat emptor: It is not clear whether minds change because of receptivity to new evidence, embrace of new theories, or the human tendency to exaggerate in retrospect the degree to which things that happened were likely to have happened (what Reinhard Bendix called "retrospective determinism").

[37] Indeed, one of the most methodologically self-conscious inquiries into the role of the individual leader in history, with application to Lenin's role in the Bolshevik victory of October 1917, was by a political philosopher and social theorist who knew and wrote a great deal about the Soviet Union (Hook 1943).

tive-psychological imagery prevails within the field, a question raised implicitly by Tetlock and Belkin's listing of experimental results in cognitive
psychology. Specifically, they ask, do scholars involved in counterfactual
debates tend toward explanations in which small causes have small effects,
big causes have big effects, good causes have good effects, and bad causes
have bad effects? To avoid confusion, let me stipulate that "small causes"
here refer either to the actions of individual leaders or to isolated events,
while "big causes" are the impersonal social, cultural, economic, and international forces of history.

Obviously, the Sovietological field was a diverse, highly disputatious
community of scholars; no theoretical line prevailed. But the greater the
polarization among disputants, the greater the prevalence of the psychology
of congruence on each side of the barricades. Even the point of dominant
consensus in the field—the ravaging effect of World War I on the prospects
for liberalism in Russia—is a case of a big, bad cause having a big, bad
effect. Only the most wistful possibilists—and they were not typically
scholars but liberal politicians trying to hold back the tide—advanced the
proposition that better leadership (a "small" cause) could have avoided the
deluge.

Consensus and congruence break down on other issues. For those who
believe that, absent Stalin the man, a moderate strategy of development
could have emerged ascendant in Soviet politics in the late 1920s, a "small"
cause is claimed to have had a very big effect. Similarly, those who view
Gorbachev's personality as having been decisive in the adoption and maintenance of policies that resulted in the collapse of the USSR postulate that a
small cause had a big effect. Is it perhaps generalizable that those who push
counterfactual thinking about the avoidance of big effects tend to run against
the grain of this allegedly human tendency to seek congruence in the size of
causes and effects? Or does this reflect an Anglo-American tendency to per-
sonalize historical evolution?[38]

But the debate about Stalinism as a strategy of modernization is a most
interesting example of incongruence about the relationship between good/
bad causes and effects. Official Soviet doctrine treated Stalinism as a glo-
rious fulfillment of historical responsibility to the toiling masses, enabling
them to combine industrialization with opportunity for upward mobility and
social justice in a new socialist order. In revulsion against this self-congrat-
ulation, many Western analysts strived to prove that alternative strategies of
modernization would have been more productive economically and more
just politically.

[38] Malia (1994, 178–81) argues that much Anglo-American scholarship tends to overper-
sonalize history; Billington (1966) makes a complementary point. But for a cogent critique of
Malia's allegedly excessive depersonalization of history see Menon (1994, 4).

The question was addressed at two levels. At one level, political economists attempted to evaluate the "rationality" of specific policies pursued by Stalin in the late 1920s and early 1930s (violent collectivization of agriculture, restratification of society, and breakneck industrialization). These studies were marked by technical analyses of resource transfers between sectors, and by inquiries into the nature of the Russian peasant mentality in the late 1920s. Some economists produced counterfactual econometric models to make the case, while others sought to demonstrate the inefficiencies within the Stalinist model and the availability of alternative strategies in the 1920s that, had they been implemented, presumably would have worked.[39]

At another level, this question has been addressed through comparative analysis, examining developmental strategies in the Third World or, historically, the First World, and thereby debating the magnitude of state power required to overcome the types of constraints on modernization found in analogous milieux.[40] Research and debate will surely continue over this issue, though revulsion against the human costs of Stalinism has made it difficult to sustain a serious discussion of whether some variant of such a modernization strategy could, in any sense, have been "necessary." And lack of consensus among comparativists as to the feasible range of effective strategies of industrialization, modernization, and nation building in the Third World has made it difficult to decide the issue by deduction.

Thus far, then, congruence reigns: Official Stalinism posited a good cause producing a good effect; anti-Stalinism posited an evil cause producing a bad effect. But there was more diversity than that in the debate, and a good deal of incongruence. Gerschenkron, for example, founded an entire school of thought to the effect that, as a late developer, Russia could only overcome its backwardness through coerced, state-directed development—not Stalinist extremism, perhaps, but not an evolutionary, organic development from below, either.[41] Other works followed in this tradition in different ways. Wilber (1969) compared the Soviet "model of development" to that in the Third World, concluding that the Soviets had much to teach the Third World about how to modernize. The same approach is central to the works of Ken Jowitt (1971; 1978) on this subject. Nove and Newth (1967) made an analogous argument with respect to Soviet Central Asia. Von Laue (1971; 1981) took the argument to a global scale, arguing that the impact of relative backwardness on Russia made imperative a Stalinist strategy of modernization to ensure Russian security in a hostile world. Thus, by "going comparative" and advancing theories based on Third World or "relatively backward"

[39] See, for example, Erlich (1960) and Hunter and Szyrmer (1992).
[40] See Jowitt (1971), Wilber (1969), and Nove and Newth (1967).
[41] The two milestones of his contribution to this debate are Gerschenkron (1960; 1966).

(rather than British, American, or French) analogical referents, a very influential school of thought evaluated Stalinism by positing a "bad" cause that had "good" effects in a cruel and imperfect world.[42]

Space limitations prevent my exploring further the cognitive-psychological tendencies displayed by disputants in Soviet studies. But one conclusion may be worth highlighting, as it recurs in the course of our discussion of domestic and foreign policy debates. The tendency for combatants to embrace, and long defend, congruent conceptions of cause and effect, whether in terms of size (big/small), valuation (good/bad), or character (e.g., images of adversary/images of international order in the foreign policy literature), may be indicative of a polarization between those who debunk and those who embrace hard counterfactual thought experiments. That polarization, in turn, may be indicative of both the politicization of an issue and the limited means available, both empirical and theoretical, for testing conflicting claims. Under those circumstances, an unobtrusive "test" of a field's commitment to counterfactual thought experiments might be the extent to which it is populated by thinkers who exhibit lack of congruence in their formulations. In the Sovietological foreign policy debates, there were relatively few of these. But in the domestic debates, although congruence was more prevalent than incongruence, substantial incongruence existed.

4. Prospects for Counterfactual Reasoning in Soviet and Post-Soviet Studies

I began this chapter with the argument that for three reasons Soviet studies have been disadvantaged in reframing debates about causation and evaluation as counterfactual thought experiments: data poverty, theoretical-analogical uncertainty, and (related to this uncertainty) the single-country focus. The collapse of the Soviet Union has now loosened all of these constraints. Archival access and, for recent issues, interviews and memoirs of participants vastly expand the empirical base available on all the issues mentioned in this article, including the most sensitive foreign policy issues as well.[43] We are now capable of engaging in forms of process-tracing, both within the

---

[42] The spirit of these schools of thought might be: "One cannot make an omelette without breaking eggs." Incidentally, I cannot readily think of *scholarly* works that evaluated Stalinist modernization strategy as a case of a "good" cause having "bad" effects. Perhaps regretful Stalinists themselves fall into this category.

[43] The recent book by Lebow and Stein (1994) is an exemplar of the diminished data scarcity on even the most sensitive of issues—foreign policy decision making—and of our new-found ability empirically to address counterfactuals that had previously been consigned to the realm of speculation. For other recent examples of how much more is now possible in tracing Soviet decision-making processes see Richter (1994) and Holloway (1994).

polity and between polity and society, or between the Soviet and non-Soviet polities, of which we could earlier only dream.

Concerning the origins of the Cold War, new Soviet archival access raises the prospect of a much more detailed assessment of Stalin's intentions, perspectives, and perceptions in the mid and late 1940s. This is certainly prerequisite to our constructing a base of evidence as rich on the Soviet side as it has been on the American. At this point, the revelations suggest greater support for the school of thought that had treated Stalin as irreconcilably antagonistic toward the West, and as too distrustful to reach a lasting accommodation.[44]

The literature on missed opportunities to end the Cold War in the 1960s or 1970s is also now beginning to acquire a richness of data, buttressed by archival revelations, that will allow us to document strong counterfactual claims. Earlier, such debates took place in policy-oriented journals (e.g., *Foreign Affairs*) as reflections on current events. They were heavily politicized because of their immediate policy-prescriptive implications. And they were suffused with conflicting claims based principally on deduction from conflicting images of the Soviet or international systems. Only recently, with the passage of time, are we starting to get data-rich studies of specific turning points that may allow us to get beyond the determinist versus possibilist divide.[45]

Similarly, we may someday be able to specify the decisive causes of the Sino-Soviet split, thus getting us beyond the monocausality versus overdetermination divide. Protocols of leadership meetings in each capital may reveal whether there were many others in each leadership who would have led their countries in different, mutually compatible directions. Or the same protocols may reveal whether each leadership was consensual, and whether the terms of the consensus were ideological or nationalistic. What Lebow and Stein have managed to do for the Cuban missile crisis we may someday be able to do for the Sino-Soviet crises of 1958–61.

Theoretical-analogical uncertainty within the field has also been reduced as a result of the collapse of communism. Both the fact of Soviet collapse and the new data sources have enriched our understanding of the nature of the Soviet system: its adaptability, internal dynamics, and "essential" features. We are now in a position to build theories and embrace analogues that more closely approximate the distinctive character of the Soviet system and context.[46]

[44] See reports of the "Cold War International History Project" (Woodrow Wilson International Center for Scholars, Washington, DC), both the *Working Papers Series* and the *Bulletin*; also Holloway (1994).

[45] Excellent examples of recent work that bears on this question include Lebow and Stein (1994), Richter (1994), and reports of the "Cold War International History Project."

[46] For major reinterpretations see Jowitt (1992), Kaminski (1992), Kornai (1992), and Malia (1994).

The more recent debates about the collapse of communism and ongoing debates about the transition from communism can benefit from elimination of the single-country constraint. This will put the field of post-Soviet studies on entirely new methodological footing with respect to counterfactual reasoning. For the grand issues of the post-Soviet era concern the relative impact in a context of collapsed Leninism of alternative strategies of transition. We can address these questions with much greater data at our disposal, including participant observation. We can do so also with a much clearer empirical and theoretical understanding of the nature of the baseline and the legacy: Leninism. And, perhaps most important, we can engage in comparative analysis using comparative referents (other post-Leninist systems in the area) that constitute "tight fits." We can ask whether the Polish version of "shock therapy" would have worked in Russia had it been applied. We can ask why Russia and Ukraine have not gone to war while Armenia and Azerbaijan or Serbia and Croatia have. We can test our path-dependent assumptions about transition strategies that work, as compared with those that led to "missed" or "lost" opportunities.[47] And so on.

The field of comparative postcommunism is much more promising than was the field of comparative communism. The latter had insufficient variation within it, and many of the units were not independent actors. The new field has much greater variation and independence among the units, while having sufficiently common features (the legacy of Leninist rule) to make comparison logical. In particular, close, empirically rich comparison of strategies of transition and their diverse results allows us to address those counterfactuals about the post-Soviet era that are sure to inform the grand debates of the future.

---

[47] For the most recent example of this tendency see Goldman (1994), who examines Russian marketization and privatization under Yeltsin and concludes that an opportunity for success was "lost." The distinction between missed and lost opportunities, I would think, is crucial in counterfactual analysis (and is fundamental to path-dependent analyses and conclusions), but is difficult to assess in a short time frame. A "missed" opportunity may not be irretrievably "lost" if a country is capable of eventually reaching a particular goal (e.g., market democracy) by a diversity of "paths."

4

Confronting Hitler and Its Consequences

YUEN FOONG KHONG

IN SEPTEMBER 1938 British prime minister Neville Chamberlain chose to appease Adolf Hitler by acceding to Germany's demands for a chunk of Czechoslovakia known as the Sudetenland.[1] The agreement was signed in Munich by Chamberlain, Hitler, French prime minister Edouard Daladier, and Italy's leader Benito Mussolini. Far from satisfying Hitler, the Munich agreement only whetted his appetite. Six months later, Germany annexed the rest of Czechoslovakia. From Czechoslovakia, Germany went on to invade Poland. Thus began World War II.

Would history have turned out differently if Britain had acted more resolutely in the face of Hitler's Sudetenland demands? Those who answer yes believe that *if Britain had confronted Hitler with the threat of war over Czechoslovakia, Hitler would have backed down. Chastised and deterred, Hitler would have exercised much more caution over Poland, and World War II might have been avoided.*

This essay examines the plausibility of the antecedent, "if Britain had confronted Hitler," and the two consequents, "Hitler would have backed down" and "World War II might have been avoided." I argue that the antecedent is reasonable and plausible. It does not take massive historical rewriting to imagine a Britain capable of adopting a confrontational strategy (see Chapter 1, Tetlock and Belkin). Even though Chamberlain was unlikely to adopt a confrontational strategy, by the time of Munich there were politicians of prime ministerial caliber such as Winston Churchill, Anthony Eden, and Duff Cooper who were willing to confront Hitler and risk war over the Sudetenland. If any one of the Churchill-Eden-Cooper trio were prime minister, or if two or more of them were in the cabinet in September 1938, Britain could conceivably have told Hitler, "Step on an inch of Czechoslovakia and it is war." The consequences of this counterfactual confrontation, however, are harder to determine. In particular, claims that Hitler would have retreated and World War II would have been avoided are not necessarily more plausible than the rival counterfactual hypotheses that

[1] The author thanks Philip Tetlock, Aaron Belkin, Steve Weber, George Breslauer, Robert Jervis, Daniel Kahneman, Barry Weingast, and James Fearon for comments on an earlier draft.

Hitler would have welcomed an early opportunity to fight and World War II would have started earlier. Paradoxically, our inability to determine which of these consequents is more probable encourages us to specify each of the possible counterfactual alternatives with greater precision. Doing so enables the analyst to arrive at an "informed" assessment of the relative merits of appeasement and confrontation.[2]

Counterfactuals and Munich: Their Policy and Scholarly Significance

A recurrent theme in post–World War II American foreign policy is the necessity of avoiding another Munich. From Harry Truman's equating inaction over North Korea's invasion of South Korea to a mistake of Munichlike proportions, to Lyndon Johnson's portraying the Vietnam War as a war to prevent future Munichs, to recent U.S. mutterings about the need to distance itself from the Munichlike policies of Britain and France towards Bosnia, the Munich analogy has served as a major script of the likely course of events if the United States failed to do X. The best documented use of the Munich script—and its implied counterfactuals—is to be found in the Johnson administration's deliberations about whether to stand firm in Vietnam, in the face of impending defeat of South Vietnam by North Vietnam and the National Liberation Front.

One of Johnson's closest advisers described the mind-set of the administration's decision makers as they contemplated going to war in Vietnam: "You will remember if we'd known then what we know now, we never would have permitted Hitler to get started when Hitler went into the Low Countries and into Czechoslovakia and Austria; if he'd been stopped then we might have prevented World War II. . . . All of this was very much in their minds" (cited in Khong 1992, 180).

Consider, for example, Dean Rusk's explanation of why the United States was tending in the direction of military intervention:

So what is our stake [in Vietnam]? . . . Can those of us in this room forget the lesson . . . in this issue of war and peace when it was only 10 years from the seizure of Manchuria to Pearl Harbor . . . 2 years from the seizure of Czechoslovakia to the outbreak of World War II in Western Europe? Don't you remember the hopes expressed those days: that perhaps the aggressor will be satisfied by the next bite. . . . But we found that ambition and appetite fed upon success and the next bite generated the appetite for the following bite. And we

---

[2] "Informed" is put in quotation marks because such an assessment is informed by, and incorporates, the actual course of events *and* an elaborate but explicit set of counterfactual assumptions.

learned that, by postponing the issue, we made the result more terrible, the holocaust more dreadful. We cannot forget that experience. (U.S. Department of State 1964, 401)

Munich also featured prominently in the development of Lyndon Johnson's thinking about Vietnam. In his 1961 vice-presidential trip to Vietnam, Johnson saw the challenge there as analogous to that faced by Britain in the 1930s. He sought to rouse South Vietnamese president Ngo Dinh Diem to take the path of Churchill instead of Chamberlain as he faced the emerging (communist) dictators of Asia. Similarly, in a critical Camp David meeting with his senior advisers just before making the decision to commit ground troops, Johnson was reported to have said, "To give in [in Vietnam] = another Munich. If not here—then Thailand" (cited in Khong 1992, 178).

As these vignettes indicate, American decision makers availed themselves of the Munich script in their deliberations and explanations about Vietnam, and arguably the script influenced their decision making. For our purposes, what is interesting about the way they used the Munich script are the counterfactuals implied. The posited counterfactuals are as follows: If Britain had taken a firmer stance against Hitler over Czechoslovakia, world history, in all likelihood, would have been different. Hitler would have backed down, Czechoslovakia would have been saved, and World War II would have been postponed or avoided. From this specific script, many U.S. policy makers also deduced a general lesson: it is important to stand firm against would-be dictators because appeasing them now would only lead to war later. This is one of several lessons that influenced Johnson's and Rusk's thinking about Vietnam.

Johnson's and Rusk's interpretations of Munich, with their focus on an irresolute and irresponsible Chamberlain and a deterrable Hitler, are consistent with early reactions to Munich. Such first-wave postmortems, beginning as early as 1940 with the polemical *Guilty Men* by "Cato," tended to portray Chamberlain and his inner circle as naive appeasers who failed to deter Hitler and who brought their country to ruin ("Cato" 1940). As Michael Foot, one of the original authors of *Guilty Men*, put it, "pride of place as Guilty Man Number One must surely always be allotted to Neville Chamberlain" (Foot 1986, 180).

With the opening of the British archives in the 1960s, a second wave of analyses rose to challenge the *Guilty Men* perspective. Access to cabinet deliberations allowed historians to paint a picture in which Britain's leaders were severely constrained by "structural factors" such as the weak military and economic position in which Britain found itself. Public opinion was on Chamberlain's side when he declared the Czechs "a far away people about whom we know nothing." Opinion in the Dominions was similar. No one was anxious to help Britain in the event of war over Czechoslovakia. In other words, the political, military, and economic context in which Britain existed precluded her exercising the deterrent option. Britain was psychologically, militarily, and economically unprepared for the consequences— war—if deterrence failed (Richardson 1988; Kennedy 1976; Kennedy 1978; Gruner 1980; Dilks 1987). Moreover, those who used German sources also found some evidence that Hitler was intent on picking a fight over the Sudetenland and may have felt "tricked" out of it by the Munich conference (Weinberg 1988).

Second-wave analyses therefore took a major portion of the blame away from individual decision makers; instead they pointed to the debilitating effects of the long-term economic and military decline of Britain. The implication was that had a different set of men been at Britain's helm, they would have felt the same constraints and acted in roughly similar ways. According to Weinberg (1988, 174), even as vocal a critic of Chamberlain as Churchill "might well have followed the same policy had he held the responsibilities of power."

The release of the Chamberlain papers at the University of Birmingham in 1975 occasioned a third wave of appeasement studies. With the help of some remarkably revealing and frequent correspondence between Chamberlain and his spinster sisters, Ida and Hilda, these studies raised questions about the second-wave structural constraints arguments. Unlike most third waves, which provide a synthesis of orthodox and revisionist accounts, the third wave in this case harked back to the *Guilty Men* hypothesis.[3] The general argument is that Chamberlain was far more credulous, naive, and ultimately mistaken than most of his colleagues. Although both his cabinet and the public were together with him on the necessity of appeasing Hitler even after Anschluss, Chamberlain became increasingly isolated by the time of Munich. More than anyone else, he continued to believe in the possibility of limiting Hitler's ambitions by satisfying his claims. More importantly, the new sources cast doubt on second-wave arguments that emphasize Chamberlain's appeasement policy as a ploy to buy time as Britain rearmed: a genuine belief in the appeasibility of Hilter, not a desire to postpone the showdown while furiously rearming, lay at the root of Chamberlain's thinking (Parker 1993; T. Taylor 1979; Aster 1989; Gibbs 1976).

In my view, the third-wave focus on choice within constraints is on the mark, although it is curiously silent on what might have ensued if a more resolute England had chosen confrontation. One supposes that one-half of one counterfactual—whether Britain had other real choices at the time—is about as far as respectable historians are willing to go.[4] The historians are on

---

[3] Post (1993) straddles and to some extent integrates the second and third waves by focusing on the machinery of British foreign policy making.

[4] T. Taylor (1979) is an exception; in chapter 33 he analyzes the possible consequences of war in 1938.

solid ground here, for the first and most critical issue that needs to be "settled" is, in Tetlock and Belkin's terminology, the plausibility of the antecedent, i.e., whether the specified (counterfactual) antecedent—"if Britain had confronted Germany"—is consistent with well-established historical facts (Chapter 1). Much of what follows deals with this issue: if our antecedent or counterfactual point of departure is not plausible, then it is neither interesting nor worthwhile to analyze its hypothesized consequents of Germany backing down and World War II being avoided.[5]

The Historical Context

In 1933 Britain began to reappraise its foreign policy. The calm associated with the "age of Locarno" was gone. Britain was increasingly concerned about the rise of National Socialism and rearmament in Germany, about Japanese threats to British interests in the Far East, and about bellicose statements emanating from Italy. In the preceding decade, Britain had been content to play the role of a mediator between France and Germany: it had been "unwilling . . . to appease the Germans to the point of ignoring French claims or to support the French at the expense of Germany" (Beattie 1977, 229).

The reappraisal led to a different strategy for the 1930s: Germany was considered to be Britain's major long-term threat and appeasement-cum-deterrence was the chosen strategy to deal with the threat. Appeasement meant a willingness to negotiate the removal of legitimate German grievances and to work toward a general European settlement; deterrence meant rearmament so that Britain could consider future German claims from a position of strength (Beattie 1977, 234). Neville Chamberlain, who was Stanley Baldwin's chancellor of the exchequer, played an important role in forging the new policy. When Chamberlain succeeded Baldwin as prime minister in May 1937, he shifted the emphasis. Even though Italy had annexed Ethiopia and Hitler's Germany had retaken the Rhineland, appeasement became Chamberlain's preferred strategy for dealing with the rising fascist powers. Deterrence fell by the wayside.

The strategy of appeasement became apparent with Anschluss, the forced union of Austria with Germany, in March 1938. From the Chamberlain cabinet's perspective, Austria was dispensable. Its chancellor, Dr. von Schusch-

---

[5] I rely on third-wave findings in this essay to reconstruct Chamberlain's reasoning and to flesh out the alternatives to appeasement. By relying on third-wave sources, I have taken a position on the scholarly debate. Obviously, my analysis should not be seen as an attempt to vindicate the third wave; it is more usefully seen as an attempt to use third-wave sources to explore the plausibility of the antecedents and consequents proposed in the second paragraph of this chapter.

nigg, was seen as unreasonably intransigent in the face of German demands; moreover, there was Austrian support for union with Germany. Germany's display of its military prowess, however, led Chamberlain to acknowledge that collective security had failed, and prompted him to consider forming alliances to counter Germany. But Chamberlain was not ready for such alliances yet:

> I don't want to get back to alliances but if Germany continues to behave as she has done lately, she may drive us to it. . . . For the moment we must abandon conversations with Germany, we must show our determination not to be bullied by announcing some increase . . . in armament, and we must quietly . . . pursue our conversations with Italy. If we can avoid another violent coup in Czechoslovakia, which ought to be feasible, it may be possible for Europe to settle down again, and some day for us to start peace talks with the Germans. (cited in Parker 1993, 134)[6]

Indeed, Czechoslovakia was next in line on Hitler's territorial aggrandizement agenda. In February, Hitler had mentioned the imperative of reintegrating Germans in Austria and Czechoslovakia. With Anschluss completed, Europe turned its attention to Czechoslovakia. Although the Czechs were ultimately dispensable as "a far away people about whom we know little," Czechoslovakia raised far more serious issues for Britain. France was bound by treaty to help Czechoslovakia if it was attacked; Russia had also agreed to join France in defending Czechoslovakia. Britain was bound by the Locarno Pact to come to France's aid if it was attacked. A German attack on Czechoslovakia was therefore likely to engulf the major states of Europe, including Britain, in a general war. Avoiding such a war was the paramount consideration guiding Britain's decision makers in 1938.

Three reasons are usually given for Chamberlain's aversion to policies that might risk war. The first is the First World War: Britain lost 750,000 men between 1914 and 1917, and the horrors of total war remained firmly etched in the minds of the decision makers as well as the British public (Kupchan 1994, 132–37). The second reason given is military strength: the government and military felt Britain was militarily ill prepared to confront Germany. The pace of rearmament, constrained by Treasury's refusal to put the economy on a war footing, was insufficient to make Britain feel invulnerable. British military planners were especially fearful of the *Luftwaffe* and its ability to rain terror from British skies should war come. Chamberlain's military advisers therefore urged him to postpone war until British defenses were considerably stronger.

The third reason given for Chamberlain's unwillingness to risk war is his

---

[6] My account of Chamberlain's policy making in 1938 is based primarily on T. Taylor (1979) and Parker (1993). Taylor's book gives the most detailed account of events leading up to Munich, including Munich itself, while Parker's book focuses exclusively on Chamberlain's diplomacy and is based entirely on primary documents.

belief in himself, diplomacy, and Hitler (in that order). Consummately certain of his abilities and of the correctness of his vision, Chamberlain believed himself the one world leader capable of taking on Hitler and restraining him.[7] In so doing, Chamberlain believed, he would bring "peace in our time." He dismissed the French as unreliable, the Americans as hopelessly isolationist, and the Russians as untrustworthy. Any movement toward formal alliances with these unreliable powers, in Chamberlain's estimation, would antagonize Germany and Italy and detract from diplomacy. Thus Chamberlain's attempt to use diplomacy to engage Hitler and to entice Germany into the world of civilized nations was very much a solo act, on behalf of himself and the country he led.

Of the three reasons why the Chamberlain government chose to appease instead of confront Hitler, the third is probably decisive. Despite the horrors of World War I, by the time of Munich close to a majority of the Chamberlain cabinet and a sizable portion of public opinion were willing to stand firm against Hitler and risk war. Perceived military weakness in 1938 definitely stayed Chamberlain's hand, but Chamberlain's handiwork—both as chancellor of the exchequer and as prime minister—was also responsible for Britain's military underpreparedness. As Telford Taylor (1979, 588) tells it, "Chamberlain's own large responsibility for that state [military weakness] dated back to the spring of 1934, when as Chancellor of the Exchequer, he had taken the lead in cutting back the arms program recommended by the Defence Requirements Committee, and making air defense the focal point of rearmament." Chamberlain was always afraid that the full armament program would disrupt "normal trade" or even bankrupt Britain (T. Taylor 1979, chapter 23).

As prime minister, Chamberlain continued to resist requests giving top priority to armaments. Although national bankruptcy remained a worry, the major reason then for not increasing apace Britain's rearmament efforts was Chamberlain's belief that it would intensify the arms race with Germany and Italy as well as derail diplomatic negotiations aimed at achieving an enduring peace. As will be apparent in the following account of the Munich negotiations, Chamberlain's overweening belief in himself and in the appeasibility of Hitler goes farthest in helping us understand the determinants of Britain's behavior.

From the perspective of Chamberlain and his "inner cabinet," which included Lord Halifax (Foreign Secretary, 1938–40), Samuel Hoare (Home Secretary, 1937–39), and John Simon (Chancellor of the Exchequer, 1937–40), Hitler's claims on the Sudetenland were not illegitimate. By allowing

---

[7] This is the dominant impression one receives from reading the Chamberlain letters and Cabinet deliberations copiously cited in Parker (1993) and T. Taylor (1979). See also Aster (1989) and Cooper (1953).

them, Britain avoided a possible military showdown which it might be ill equipped to win. Even more important, Chamberlain assumed that Hitler's ambitions were limited. Giving in on Czechoslovakia might satisfy Hitler and, if so, Britain would not only have avoided war, it would also have paved the way toward a general European settlement. In his refusal to see Hitler's power grabs for what they were, Chamberlain was not anxious to seek out allies (France, the Soviet Union, and the United States) with whom he could have forged a formidable alliance against Hitler's moves. Similarly, Chamberlain was reluctant to rearm at a pace and intensity that would have strengthened Britain's negotiating position or backed up Britain's threats.

The fate of Czechoslovakia was decided in three meetings held over two weeks, in Berchtesgaden, Godesberg, and finally Munich. At the Berchtesgaden meeting, Chamberlain agreed in principle to Hitler's demands that Czech territory with more than 50 percent Germans be ceded to Germany. In return, Chamberlain received Hitler's word that his objectives were limited. He wanted self-determination for ethnic Germans in the Sudetenland, not domination of Europe. Just as important to Chamberlain was word—planted by the führer, no doubt—that he had "favorably impressed" Hitler. As he intimated to his sister, "I had established a certain confidence [with Hitler], which was my aim. . . . I got the impression that here was a man who could be relied upon when he had given his word" (cited in Parker 1993, 162).

Before returning to Godesberg for the second Chamberlain-Hitler meeting, Chamberlain met with his cabinet and French prime minister Daladier. The brunt of these discussions was that because neither France nor Britain was prepared to go to war over Czechoslovakia, the only solution was to persuade the Czech government to cede the Sudetenland to Germany. The Czech government relented most reluctantly, especially after France and Britain threatened to leave Czechoslovakia to its own devices if it continued resisting.

What Chamberlain had extracted with such difficulty from the Czech government, he discovered upon arriving at Godesberg, was no longer enough for Hitler. Chamberlain was authorized to suggest to Hitler that the new frontiers of Czechoslovakia, based on self-determination for ethnic Germans, be worked out by an international commission. Hitler rejected that mode of transfer. Instead he demanded the immediate evacuation of Czech forces from the Sudetenland and its occupation by Germany. Otherwise Germany would occupy the Sudetenland by force on September 28.

Hitler's Godesberg demands occasioned the most impassioned debate within Chamberlain's cabinet. Back in No. 10, Chamberlain urged his colleagues to accede to Hitler's Godesberg terms. Chamberlain offered two reasons for meeting Hitler all the way. First, and by far the more important, was that giving Hitler what he wanted would lay the foundation for Anglo-German detente. As Chamberlain put it to his cabinet, "It would be a great tragedy if we lost this opportunity of reaching an understanding with Germany on all points of difference between the two countries." Chamberlain believed that "he had now established an influence over Herr Hitler, and that the latter trusted him and was willing to work with him. If this was so, it was a wonderful opportunity to put an end to the horrible nightmare of the present armament race" (cited in Parker 1993, 169).

The second reason Chamberlain offered was that it was not a good time to risk war; British defenses against German aerial bombing would be stronger in time to come. For the first time since the beginning of the Czech crisis, the cabinet demurred. Most significant was Foreign Secretary Halifax's change of mind. Halifax felt that Hilter had gone too far. Hitler was "dictating terms, just as though he had won a war." Halifax argued that it was wrong to pressure the Czechs to accept the Godesberg demands. Britain could convey Hitler's latest demands to the Czechs, but "if they rejected it he imagined France would join in, and if France went in we should join with them" (cited in Parker 1993, 171). As the historian R. A. C. Parker (1979, 171) put it, "Halifax thus found himself preferring the risk of war to acceptance of the Godesberg memorandum." Seven additional cabinet members—Walter Elliot, Duff Cooper, Edward De La Warr, Edward Winterton, Douglas Hailsham, Leslie Hore-Belisha, and Oliver Stanley—openly disagreed with Chamberlain. Public opinion was also against Chamberlain. "The great mass of public opinion," according to Halifax, "seems to be hardening in sense of feeling that we have gone to limit of concession" (cited in Parker 1993, 170).

Without strong support from his cabinet for acceding to Hitler's Godesberg demands, Chamberlain was left with two hopes. One was that the French would renege on their promise to defend Czechoslovakia and force the latter to accept the Godesberg terms. French prime minister Daladier, who had been summoned to London, informed Chamberlain of France's refusal to be party to the "strangulation of a people [the Czechs]." When pressed on what France would do in the event of a German invasion of Czechoslovakia, Daladier replied that "each of us would have to do his duty" (cited in Parker 1993, 172). The next day Daladier left no doubt what he meant by "duty": France would fight on the side of Czechoslovakia if the latter was attacked.

Chamberlain's last hope was to invite himself to Germany for a final meeting with Hitler during which he planned to beseech Hitler to modify the Godesberg demands in the name of preserving world peace. Hitler agreed to see Chamberlain; he also invited Daladier and Mussolini to Munich for final discussions on the mode of transferring the Sudetenland to Germany. After testing French and British firmness on the unacceptability of the Godesberg terms, and after discovering that France intended to fulfill its commitment to Czechoslovakia if the latter was attacked, Hitler allowed Mussolini to suggest modest modifications of his Godesberg terms.

Instead of occupying all of the Sudetenland immediately, Germany would progressively occupy it over a period of ten days, beginning October 1. An international commission composed of representatives from Germany, Britain, France, Italy, and Czechoslovakia would decide where plebiscites would be held; it would also be involved in the "final determination of the frontiers" (reproduced in T. Taylor 1979, 50–51). Of course, once German troops marched into the Sudetenland, the international commission decided little: no plebiscites were held and the frontiers were ultimately decided by Germany's annexation of all of Czechoslovakia. At the time of Munich, however, Hitler gave the impression of retreating just enough to enable Chamberlain and Daladier to return home as heroes.

If the story of appeasement ended there, with Germany pacified, the remainder of Czechoslovakia intact, and general war avoided, Chamberlain would indeed have bought peace, albeit at the price of giving up the Sudetenland. But allowing Germany to incorporate the Sudetenland did not bring peace. Like the reoccupation of the Rhineland and Anschluss, the Sudetenland was merely another move in Hitler's bid for continental hegemony. Six months after Munich, German troops took the rest of Czechoslovakia. Poland was next on Hitler's list. Chamberlain's appeasement strategy had failed utterly. Reluctantly, Chamberlain shifted back to deterrence. The line was drawn in Poland. If Germany invaded Poland, Britain and France would be at war with Germany.

On September 1, 1939, Germany attacked Poland. Five hours before the British-French ultimatum to Germany was to expire, Chamberlain was still interested in a negotiated solution. "If the German Government should agree to withdraw their forces," Chamberlain told the House of Commons the next day, "then His Majesty's Government would be willing to regard the position as being the same as it was before." A withdrawal would open the way to discussions between Germany and Poland, a discussion with which Britain was "willing to be associated" (cited in Gilbert 1976, 1109).

This narrative demonstrates the close association between Chamberlain and appeasement. More than anyone else, Chamberlain believed in the necessity and efficacy of appeasement. He also adhered to the policy longer than most. He was not against rearmament or deterrence per se, for as chancellor of the exchequer and prime minister he presided over Britain's rearmament efforts, albeit at a pace his detractors considered insufficiently fast. The problem was that whenever there was a choice between deterrence and appeasement, Chamberlain chose the latter.

As suggested earlier, that choice was partly informed by Chamberlain's pessimistic assessments of British military preparedness and the costs of war (should deterrence fail); it was mainly informed by his belief in his own diplomatic abilities and Hitler's reasonableness. As the author of the definitive study of Chamberlain's appeasement strategy put it, by March 1939 "all British policy-makers became less inclined to trust dictators; like everyone else Chamberlain became more cautious . . . but he remained the most hopeful, the most credulous of British statesmen" (Parker 1993, 205). The German ambassador in London could confidently predict for the benefit of his government: "As long as Chamberlain is at the helm, a relatively moderate course is assured" (cited in Parker 1993, 205).

As long as Chamberlain was at the helm, Britain was unlikely to chose confrontation over appeasement. To explore whether Britain could have chosen confrontation and deterrence in the 1930s, it is necessary to look beyond Chamberlain. The question "Could Britain have chosen to confront Hitler?" becomes "Were there other Englishmen who were prepared to confront Hitler in ways Chamberlain was not?"[8] In the next section, I answer the latter question with an unqualified yes. A related question follows: Under what conditions might the recommendations of these more bellicose politicians have been adopted? Or in Tetlock and Belkin's terms: How much historical rewriting need be done in order to arrive at a scenario where the confrontationists win the policy debate? Not all that much, I suggest, and in the next section I specify the conditions under which the more confrontationist policy might have been adopted. In providing these answers to the above questions, I am in effect arguing that our counterfactual point of departure or antecedent, "if Britain had confronted Hitler," is reasonable and plausible.

Who Might Have Threatened Hitler with War?

The record of the 1938 debates about British foreign policy reveals the names of three men who would have liked to pursue a more confrontational policy against Germany and Italy: Anthony Eden, Duff Cooper, and Winston Churchill. Two of these would later become prime minister, suggesting that these individuals were not outliers in the English political spectrum given to tough talk precisely because they were so distant from the helm.

When Chamberlain became prime minister, he asked Anthony Eden, Baldwin's foreign secretary, to remain in that post.[9] At the same time,

---

[8] In Tetlock and Belkin's (Chapter 1) terms, we are attempting to specify the antecedent with greater precision. Mark Turner (Commentary 1) distinguishes between counterfactuals that perform "spotlight" and "lab rat" functions. In focusing on the close relationship between Chamberlain and appeasement, and thinking about the likely consequents of replacing him with the Churchill-Eden-Cooper trio, our counterfactual analysis performs both the lab rat and spotlight functions.

[9] The following discussion of Eden, Cooper, and Churchill is taken, with adaptations, from

Chamberlain warned Eden—rather ominously in retrospect—that "I know you won't mind if I take more interest in foreign policy than S.[tanley] B.[aldwin]" (Eden 1962, 501). Before long, Chamberlain's more active role led to Eden's resignation.

Eden resigned because of fundamental disagreements with his chief about the appropriate response to Mussolini's and Hitler's policies. Two specific events were decisive. One was Chamberlain's decision to spurn President Franklin Roosevelt's offer of a joint U.S.-U.K. approach to shore up the prestige of the leading European democracies. Roosevelt was concerned about the deteriorating situation in Europe, where the smaller states seemed to be "falling away from the ideals and loyalties to which they would have preferred to adhere, in order to gravitate into the orbit of the dictators." Roosevelt saw this "bandwagoning" as a result of the "loss of influence of the democratic states" and his initiative was to be a first step in helping restore this influence (Eden 1962, 622).

Without consulting Eden, who was vacationing in France, Chamberlain immediately dismissed Roosevelt's offer. The prime minister did not want an American initiative to undercut his attempts to negotiate on a bilateral basis with Italy and Germany. Germany and Italy, Chamberlain feared, "may feel constrained to take advantage of them [Roosevelt's suggestions] . . . to delay the consideration of specific points which must be settled if appeasement is to be achieved." Eden thought differently:

> My immediate reaction was that we must accept Roosevelt's offer outright. . . . I had no doubt that the purpose . . . was to put obstacles in the way of Hitler and Mussolini by the only method open to Roosevelt. Both dictators dislike the whole exercise and want to resist being tangled in negotiations of this kind. This is no reason for deprecating them. At worst, Roosevelt's offer would gain us time and bring the United States a little nearer to a divided Europe. (Eden 1962, 626–27)

Eden was anxious to get the United States on the side of Britain for symbolic and substantive reasons. He appreciated the fact that public opinion did not allow Roosevelt to do very much in 1937, but he felt that getting the United States involved was an essential first step in confronting Hitler and Mussolini. Chamberlain, anxious to appease the dictators and convinced that they could be appeased by clever British diplomacy, felt constrained to reject the American offer.

The disagreement that precipitated Eden's resignation was over the question of whether Britain should open formal discussions with Italy. Eden was adamantly opposed. Eden felt that Italy's recent actions in Ethiopia and Spain proved that it was an aggressive power. He distrusted Mussolini and

Khong (1993). The author and editors gratefully acknowledge the permission of Linda B. Miller and Michael Joseph Smith.

argued that the latter had agreed to Hitler's moves against Austria in return for a free hand in the Mediterranean. Under such conditions, for Britain to agree to formal discussions with Italy would be both humiliating and an admission of weakness; other countries would take their cue from this action.

Chamberlain took a more benign view of Mussolini. He saw the discussions as an opportunity to be seized. He was not averse to giving implicit recognition to Italy's conquest of Ethiopia; there was not much the democracies could do anyway. In explaining to the cabinet his differences with Eden, Chamberlain stressed the need to improve relations with Germany and Italy. Rearmament was imposing too heavy a financial burden on the country; as such, arrangements conducive to a reduction of armaments were welcomed. Such arrangements were to be achieved by making concessions to Germany and Italy.

Given the threats posed by Hitler and Mussolini, the two most important individuals entrusted with Britain's fate disagreed on how best to meet them. Their differences were not over hues of the same policy. They were over fundamentals. Chamberlain had faith in the dictators; he assumed that concessions would eventually satisfy them. Eden was much more pessimistic about Hitler's and Mussolini's intentions and saw appeasement as a hopeless policy. To be sure, there are indications that Eden occasionally vacillated between confronting and appeasing the dictators. But most analysts agree that by 1938 Eden had parted ways with his prime minister. Recent work also suggests that Eden's pessimism about Hitler and his belief in the necessity of a common front to deal with Hitler can be traced back to 1935, when Eden was assistant to then Foreign Secretary John Simon. Eden noted in his diary after talks with Hitler: "Only thing Hitler wants is Air Pact without limitation. Simon much inclined to bite at this. . . . I had to protest and he gave up the idea. . . . Simon toys with idea of letting G.[ermany] expand eastwards. I am strongly against. Apart from dishonesty it would be our turn next" (cited in Dutton 1994, 50). Even Hitler's interpreter noted Eden's skepticism toward Germany (ibid., 50).

A few years later, as word of the Chamberlain-Eden disagreements over Italy slipped out, the Italians were most concerned. Mussolini began calling his informers every half-hour to find out who would prevail. The outcome, from Italy's perspective, "may mean peace or war. . . . An Eden Cabinet would have as its aim the fight against the dictatorships—Mussolini's first." (Eden 1962, 680). The Italians need not have worried. In Britain, such contests almost invariably end with the departure of the subordinate. Eden resigned. Chamberlain's assessment of Eden's departure is also revealing: "I have gradually arrived at the conclusion that at bottom Anthony did not want to talk either with Hitler or Mussolini and as I did he was right to go" (cited in Aster 1989, 245, emphasis added).

Anthony Eden was not the only cabinet minister to go because of Chamberlain's willingness to talk to Hitler and Mussolini. Duff Cooper, secretary of state for war (1935–37) under Baldwin and first lord of the admiralty (1937–38) under Chamberlain, stayed through the Munich crisis and only resigned thereafter. Cooper's participation in the cabinet's discussions about Munich makes fascinating reading for the student of international relations. Here was someone who correctly saw the issue at stake—power—and who framed his objection to appeasement in terms of the balance of power. Even before Chamberlain's three meetings with Hitler, Cooper was already counseling a firm stance against Hitler and his ambitions in Czechoslovakia. Cooper urged in a September 12 cabinet meeting that his colleagues "make plain to Germany that we would fight" (Cooper 1953, 226–27).

On September 16, Chamberlain returned from the first of his three meetings with Hitler. Briefing his cabinet the next day, Chamberlain portrayed his visit as a success even though Hitler had not yielded a single point. Chamberlain had arrived with some British proposals—such as John Simon's plan of limited autonomy for the Sudeten Germans—but none was raised because the atmosphere was "too heated" (T. Taylor 1979, 749). Hitler's army was poised to march into the Sudetenland. By giving Hitler his personal opinion, "which was that on principle" he "had nothing to say against the separation of the Sudeten Germans from the rest of Czechoslovakia," Chamberlain managed to prevent Hitler from attacking Czechoslovakia (cited in T. Taylor 1979, 742). In essence, Chamberlain had accepted Hitler's demand for the transfer of the Sudetenland to Germany; what remained to be discussed was the method of transfer, whether by outright cession or by plebiscite. As one of Chamberlain's supporters portrayed the meeting: "It was plain that H.[itler] had made all the running: he had in fact blackmailed the P.M." (T. Taylor 1979, 749).

Chamberlain sought the assent of his colleagues to the Berchtesgaden understandings; when that assent was not immediately forthcoming, Lord Maugham tried to rally support for Chamberlain by declaring that no vital British interest was at stake. To that, Duff Cooper retorted:

> the main interest of this country had always been to prevent any one Power from obtaining undue predominance in Europe. . . . We were now faced with probably the most formidable Power that had ever dominated Europe, and resistance to that Power was quite obviously a British interest. If I thought surrender would bring lasting peace I should be in favour of surrender, but I did not believe there would ever be peace in Europe so long as Nazism ruled in Germany. (Cooper 1953, 230)

The lord privy seal, Earl De La Warr, went farther by drawing out the implications of Cooper's argument. He denounced a plebiscite "forced by German threats." The plebiscite was "unfair to the Czechs and dishonourable to ourselves." Moreover, a dishonorable peace would only beget war later. De La Warr argued that Britain should make no concessions to Germany until it demobilized; otherwise, he was "prepared to face war now in order to free the world from the emotional threat of ultimata" (cited in T. Taylor 1979, 750). These objections notwithstanding, Chamberlain overcame his critics; the majority of the cabinet sided with Chamberlain.

If Cooper did not go as far as De La Warr on September 16, he went even farther after the second Chamberlain-Hitler meeting at Godesberg. Hitler's Godesberg demands included new boundaries, immediate occupation of the Sudetenland by German soldiers, with plebiscites to be held only later. In explaining to his colleagues why these demands deserved consideration, Chamberlain proffered many reasons. Among them: Hitler told him that he was "the first man in many years who has got any concessions out of . . . [Hitler]." Hitler had maintained that solving the Sudetenland crisis would be a "turning-point in Anglo-German relations." That turning point was precisely what he, Chamberlain, had sought. Finally, Chamberlain was "also satisfied that Herr Hitler would not go back on his word once he had given it" (cited in Cooper 1953, 229–40).

Duff Cooper completely rejected the prime minister's reasoning and in the next few meetings he took a consistently firm position. Cooper told his colleagues that the Germans were unconvinced that Britain would fight and the only way to persuade them otherwise was to go on full mobilization. Before Godesberg, Cooper had assumed that Britain was faced with the unpleasant alternatives of peace with dishonor or war; now, he saw a third possibility, "war with dishonour," i.e., "being kicked into the war by the boot of public opinion when those for whom we were fighting had already been defeated" (Cooper 1953, 234–35).

As in the case of Anthony Eden, when a cabinet minister held views and policy preferences so incompatible with those of his chief, the minister had to go. Cooper waited until the Munich agreement was signed—an agreement, not surprisingly, he couldn't accept—before ending his connection with the Chamberlain government. In his resignation speech before the House of Commons, Cooper came back to his theme of the balance of power:

> Had we gone to war, as we so nearly did, it would not have been for Czecho-Slovakia that we should have been fighting, any more than it was for Serbia or for Belgium that we fought in 1914. . . . We should have been fighting . . . in accordance with the sound, traditional foreign policy of England, in order to prevent one Great Power, in defiance of treaty obligations, of the laws of nations and decrees of morality, dominating by brute force the continent of Europe. (Cooper 1953, 246)

Summing up the differences between Chamberlain and himself, Cooper opined: "The Prime Minister has believed in addressing Herr Hitler through the language of sweet reasonableness. I have believed that he was more open to the language of the mailed fist" (cited in Thompson 1971, 183).

The mailed fist approach was, of course, also the approach of Winston Churchill. Churchill's speeches and writings before Munich leave little doubt that his answer to Germany's rising power resembled that of Cooper's and Eden's; his writings after the war—embellished by hindsight, no doubt—further reinforced the antiappeasement approach. So much has been written about Churchill's antiappeasement stance that it is unnecessary to dwell on the details of his position.[10]

Still, it is useful to examine some of Churchill's views and, more importantly, his actions in 1938. As the issue of Czechoslovakia emerged, he urged Foreign Secretary Halifax in late August to issue a joint British-French-Russian note to Hitler, warning the latter about the "capital issues" that would be raised for all three powers should Germany invade Czechoslovakia. The United States was also to be brought into the picture, with Roosevelt informing Hitler that he had seen the note and it was his view that "a world war would inevitably follow from an invasion of Czechoslovakia" (Gilbert 1976, 967). Churchill, in other words, was counseling the use of alliances to deter Hitler.[11]

On September 10, Churchill marched into 10 Downing Street to demand that Britain send an immediate ultimatum to Hitler; the next day, Halifax reported to the cabinet that Churchill had urged "that we should tell Germany that if she set foot in Czechoslovakia we should at once be at war with her" (Gilbert 1976, 972). All this was before Chamberlain's first meeting with Hitler; none was acted upon, of course. Churchill's confrontational style and his willingness to risk war stemmed from many sources: principle, mistrust of Hitler, balance of power calculations, personal ambition, and the belief that the mailed fist approach was likely to embolden Hitler's domestic enemies into overthrowing him.

Be that as it may, Churchill dismissed the first Chamberlain-Hitler meeting as the "stupidest thing that has ever been done" (Gilbert 1976, 974). Between this and the Munich meeting, Churchill traveled to France to encourage the French to stand firm, he hectored his government for throwing Czechoslovakia to the wolves, and he continued to urge the inclusion of Russia in British plans for confronting Germany.

Churchill's attitude toward the Munich agreement is best seen in his speech given in the House of Commons debate on the agreement. Every word in that speech painted the agreement as a political and moral defeat for Britain, and one that spelled future disaster as well. When Hitler looked

[10] For a contrary view, see Watt (1993).

[11] For a catalogue of Churchill's calls, between March and September 1938, for a Grand Alliance—Britain, France, and Russia—to deter Germany on the issue of Czechoslovakia, see Parker (1993, 323–24).

westward, Churchill maintained, and when France and Britain had to defend themselves, they would "bitterly regret" their signing away of Czechoslovakia and her formidable defenses, for her fortifications and her armies would have required no fewer "than 30 German divisions" to destroy. Churchill concluded his speech by referring to matters that the public, in their jubilation, might have forgotten:

> They should know that there has been gross neglect and deficiency in our defenses; they should know that we have sustained a defeat without a war, the consequences of which will travel far with us along our road; they should know that we have passed an awful milestone in our history, when the whole equilibrium of Europe has been deranged, and that the terrible words have for the time being been pronounced against the Western democracies: *"Thou art weighed in the balance and found wanting."* (cited Gilbert 1976, 1001; emphasis added)

In contrast to arguments focusing on how military and economic weaknesses severely limited Britain's options, thereby making the choice of any option other than appeasement "astonishing" (Schroeder 1976, 242), the above analysis of Eden, Cooper, and Churchill suggests that, structural constraints notwithstanding, there were Englishmen of prime ministerial caliber who were willing to confront Hilter—and risk war—before and during the Munich crisis of 1938.

But were the arguments of the "mailed-fist" trio taken seriously in 1938? Apparently so, and by a most important player. Slightly more than a week after the signing of the Munich agreement, Hitler opined that "it only needs that in England instead of Chamberlain, Mr. Duff Cooper or Mr. Eden or Mr. Churchill should come to power, and then we know quite well that it would be the aim of these men immediately to begin a new World War" (cited in T. Taylor 1979, 934). Hitler seemed to be saying one of two things: had Cooper, Eden, or Churchill been prime minister at the time of Munich, they would have chosen to fight; alternatively, he may have been saying that when and if any of these men should come to the helm of power, Germany would be facing a very different England, one that would not hesitate to confront Germany militarily, even if it meant a world war.[12]

Two of the trio, Churchill and Eden, did become prime ministers, Churchill in May 1940, and Eden in July 1955. And Hitler was right: Churchill

---

[12] It is, of course, possible that Hitler made the statement in the hope of influencing English elite and public opinion against allowing Churchill, Eden, or Cooper to come to power, for that would mean war. This assumes a Hitler who preferred dealing with Chamberlain and who wanted to avoid war. On the other hand, if one assumes a Hitler who felt "tricked" by Chamberlain at Munich and who was looking for a pretext for war, then Hitler's statement may be read as an attempt to encourage England to put the trio in power so that war would come sooner rather than later. Because both assumptions have support in the historical record, it is safer to take Hitler's statement at face value: as a counterfactual prediction of who he might have to deal with and the likely consequences, if it had not been Chamberlain.

led the fight against Germany and quickly brought Eden and Cooper back to the cabinet. Indeed, based on the trio's views in 1938 and their policies in 1940, it would stand to reason that had one of them been prime minister in September 1938, England would most probably have confronted Hitler with war over the Sudetenland.

But putting Churchill, Eden, or Cooper in the prime minister's seat in 1938 may be considered a sleight of hand by those who consider our (counterfactual) point of departure far-fetched. Although Churchill had held nearly all the major cabinet posts except those of prime minister and foreign secretary by 1930, and although Eden had been foreign secretary and Cooper first lord of the admiralty when they resigned, some may object that none of the trio had a chance of assuming the premiership in the late 1930s. The most powerful and well-rehearsed argument, for example, points to Churchill's reputation as a maverick and ferocious hawk (on Germany) and how that made him unsuitable for the highest office under ordinary times. Only "the rise of Hitler . . . made it possible for a leader like Churchill to become prime minister" (cited in Commentary 1, Turner). Thus to propose thinking of Churchill as prime minister in 1938 is to rewrite history massively; it is less distant from the "if Napoleon had a Stealth bomber" type of counterfactual than one realizes.

For this "only the rise of Hitler gave rise to Churchill" objection—hereafter the "Hitler hypothesis"—to be forceful, a well-specified theory about the selection of British prime ministers is needed. The theory will command belief to the extent that it succeeds in predicting who is likely to be prime minister, given its specified conditions. Otherwise the Hitler hypothesis is quite indeterminate and possesses a strong ex post facto flavor. After all, Hitler came to power in 1933 and began his aggressive policies in 1936. Why did it take until 1940 for a Churchill to assume the premiership? Why not 1937 or 1938? Without advance specification of the time lag between the rise of a Hitler and the emergence of a Churchill, and without advance elaboration of the mechanism by which such international imperatives condition the domestic political selection process, the Hitler hypothesis is not very helpful.

In its unelaborated form, the Hitler hypothesis would also lead one to expect that when Chamberlain resigned in May 1940, the King's and England's first and most obvious choice for prime minister would be Churchill. Interestingly, that was not the case. In his account of "How Churchill became prime minister," Robert Blake (1993, 264) states that "Lord Halifax, the Foreign Secretary, was in many ways a stronger runner." According to Blake, "Chamberlain [whose advice the King sought] wanted Halifax. Labour wanted Halifax. . . . The Lords wanted Halifax. The King wanted Halifax" (ibid., 270). The only problem was that Halifax did not want Halifax.

Halifax, who had sided with the antiappeasement camp after Godesberg, turned down the opportunity in part because of the constitutional complications involved in having a member of the House of Lords become prime minister. Moreover, Halifax was weary and did not feel up to the job. Thus the underlying assumption of the Hitler hypothesis, that only at the moment of gravest danger would someone like Churchill be the obvious choice, seems demonstrably false even after England had declared war on Germany: Halifax was the most obvious and popular choice, and Churchill was second. Only when Halifax took himself out of the running did the King call for Churchill.

The general point to be extracted from the above critique of the Hitler hypothesis is this: absent a good predictive theory of the conditions under which particular types of individuals will be selected as the English prime minister, it makes sense to be agnostic or open about the possibilities. This criterion of inclusiveness, necessary because of the absence of covering laws pertaining to the selection of British prime ministers, allows us to consider senior members of the cabinet and members of parliament with national stature as possible prime ministers. If this criterion is adopted, our specification of the antecedent, "if any of the Churchill-Eden-Cooper trio had been in power," will be plausible, and it is qualitatively different from the "if Napoleon had a Stealth Bomber" counterfactual.

Finally, despite the above focus on the reasonableness of the "Churchill-Eden-Cooper trio as prime minister" counterfactual, my argument does not depend on one of them being prime minister in 1938. All I need is that their recommendations fall on receptive ears and have a chance of being implemented. That chance would of course be maximized if any of them were prime minister. But it might have been enough if Churchill was taken into the cabinet by Chamberlain in 1937, as urged by War Secretary Leslie Hore-Belisha (Blake 1993, 259). As was mentioned earlier, after the Godesberg meeting, Chamberlain's cabinet began deserting him. Conceivably, Churchill, working together the other eight cabinet members who had openly disagreed with Chamberlain—Cooper, Halifax, Elliot, De La Warr, Winterton, Hailsham, Hore-Belisha, and Stanley—could have succeeded in forming a winning coalition intent on showing Hitler the "mailed fist" at Munich.

In other words, "Churchill-Eden-Cooper as prime minister in 1938" is not the only way to specify our antecedent. Our antecedent may be respecified in a less demanding but equally (and perhaps even more) plausible form:[13] Had two or more of the Churchill-Eden-Cooper trio been members of the Chamberlain cabinet in September 1938, the chances of Britain's confront-

---

[13] Less demanding in two senses: (1) It is easier to get a cabinet job than the office of the prime minister; and (2) it might be easier for proponents of the Hitler hypothesis to conceive of Churchill as a cabinet member than as prime minister in 1937–38. (1) and (2) suggest that the respecified antecedent requires less historical rewriting of British history than the original antecedent of Churchill as prime minister.

ing Hitler would have greatly increased. For those dubious about whether any one of the trio could have been prime minister in 1938, this respecification of just having two or more of them as cabinet ministers in 1938 might be closer than the original specification of one of them as prime minister to the counterfactual world in which a confrontational Britain challenges Germany.

Would Hitler Have Backed Down? Would World War II Have Been Avoided?

Suppose the Churchillian option of confronting Hitler—"Step on an inch of Czechoslovakia and we would be at war"—won the internal policy debate in 1938 and Britain threatened Germany with war during the Godesberg or Munich meeting. Would Hitler or Germany have backed down? Conventional wisdom says yes, the revisionists say no.

Conventional wisdom relies quite heavily on a theory made famous by Churchill in 1945: had Britain, together with France and perhaps Russia, confronted Hitler in 1938, the latter's enemies within Germany would have staged a coup to depose him. The anti-Hitler forces, according to the theory, were waiting for a signal of Western resolve against Hitler before acting. In this scenario, Hitler backs down by being removed from power by disgruntled military officers who felt Germany was not yet ready for war. The Chamberlain cabinet was aware of this possibility and discussed it several times. No one had sufficient confidence about the probability of the anti-Hitler coup, however, to factor it into their decision making. If Churchill had been in the cabinet, he would no doubt have propounded the theory with force; his belief in the probability of a coup was one reason why he was willing to confront Hitler. Chamberlain, on the other hand, discouraged speculation about what the anti-Hitler forces might do, largely because he saw Hitler as someone he could work with and tame (Parker 1993).

D. C. Watt, however, has argued that although there was a conspiracy in the military against Hitler in the fall of 1938, the conditions for its implementation were quite different from what Churchill anticipated. According to Watt, the coup against Hitler would only be triggered by war between Britain-France-Czechoslovakia and Germany, and only when General von Brauchitsch ordered it (Watt 1993, 210). Watt's argument raises questions about Churchill's theory that deterrence would have caused Germany to back down. War, or the beginnings of one, would not be avoided. However, Watt neglects the fact that, unlike Chamberlain, Churchill was prepared to fight in September 1938 if deterrence failed. And if there had been war in 1938, by Watt's own reasoning, a coup would have been likely. The new German leaders might have sued for peace immediately; if not, the course of the 1938 war without Hitler (and with Czechoslovakia intact) might have been quite different from the war in 1940, with Hitler in charge and Czechoslovakia absorbed.

Leaving the anti-Hitler coup aside, was Hitler himself deterrable? Critics of the deterrable Hitler thesis point to Hitler's disappointment with the outcome of Munich: it postponed a war that he would have liked to start (Weinberg 1988). In this view, if Britain had threatened Germany with war, Hitler would have rushed to war. As Gerhard Weinberg (1988, 172) put it, "In the last months of his life . . . as he reviewed what had gone wrong," Hitler felt that "his failure to begin the war in 1938 was his greatest error, contributing to the eventual collapse of all his hopes and prospects."

This view, however, is not entirely consistent with Hitler's behavior in September 1938. If Hitler had wanted a pretext for war at a time when Britain was materially and psychologically underprepared (compared to a year later), he could easily have rejected Chamberlain's request for a third meeting. Germany would then have proceeded according to Hitler's schedule and taken the Sudetenland by force; France would have gone to the aid of Czechoslovakia, and Britain would have joined France. Hitler would have had the war he wanted.

Yet Hitler chose otherwise. He invited Chamberlain, Daladier, and Mussolini to Munich to discuss the terms of the transfer. By then France and Britain (reluctantly) had conveyed to Germany that they would stand by Czechoslovakia if Hitler insisted on the Godesberg terms. At the start of the Munich meeting, Hitler apparently tried to intimidate his interlocutors into accepting the Godesberg demands by delivering an emotional diatribe against the Czechs. According to Daladier: "It was a real explosion. Spreading his arms or clenching his fists, he accused the Czechs of a frightful tyranny over the [Sudeten] Germans, with torture, and the expulsion of thousands in panic-stricken herds" (cited in T. Taylor 1979, 31).

Daladier claimed that his reaction was to ask "whether it was Hitler's intention to destroy Czechoslovakia and annex it to Germany. If so, there was nothing for him to do but return to France." That implied threat apparently calmed Hitler down, who quickly reassured Daladier that his aim was not to annex "any Czechs" but to "bring all the Germans into a common national community" (T. Taylor 1979, 31). If Daladier's reconstruction of events is correct, it seems that Hitler was responsive to tough talk. He was willing to back off from his Godesberg demands.

Backing off from the Godesberg terms, however, is different from backing down on the Sudetenland. Those who argue that Hitler would have backed down given a more confrontational Britain are not interested in the nuances between Munich and Godesberg. For them, the surrender occurred when Chamberlain agreed in principle to let Hitler have the Sudetenland. To paraphrase Churchill, the deterrent option would have been something like "step on an inch of Czechoslovakia and we would be at war." Whether Hitler would have backed down given a message like that is much more difficult to determine.

To summarize, the Churchillian option could have engendered three possible German responses. First, faced with the prospect of fighting Britain, France, and Czechoslovakia, Hitler might have backed down. If when faced with the prospect of war at Munich Hitler was prepared to retreat from his Godesberg ultimatum, it is not unreasonable to assume that he might also have backed down on the Sudetenland if he had been shown the mailed fist earlier. Second, Hitler might have started a war, but the onset of war might have triggered an anti-Hitler coup in Germany. As D. C. Watt has argued, such a coup was in the works and would be triggered by war. If the coup succeeded, the new leaders were likely to take Germany out of the war. Third, as the revisionists argue, Hitler might have jumped at the chance of war by invading Czechoslovakia. Under this scenario, a European war would have started in 1938.

It is not possible to state with confidence which of the three counterfactual scenarios would have resulted had the Churchillian option been exercised. This claim raises serious questions for those—scholars and policy makers— wont to advocate standing firm as a general rule of diplomacy because history "teaches" that a more resolute England in the 1930s would have "certainly" caused Hitler to back down. America's Vietnam policy makers, as indicated earlier, internalized the backing down scenario uncritically. Understandably, it influenced their decision to pursue a firm policy against Ho Chi Minh.

The argument that backing down, an anti-Hitler coup, and war in 1938 are three possible outcomes of the Churchillian option is also worthwhile in another sense. It permits us to carry the assessment of Chamberlain's appeasement policy one step further. We know that Chamberlain's policy did not satisfy Hitler, that Britain had to draw the line in Poland, that Hitler attacked Poland anyway, and that World War II was not avoided. While Britain was more prepared—its air defenses especially—in September 1939 than in September 1938, it was not enough to prevent Germany from conquering the rest of Western Europe and forcing a British retreat from Dunkirk in 1940. By the time the United States was poised to enter the war, Britain was not out of danger.

Comparing the actual course of events with the Churchillian counterfactual and its hypothesized consequents suggests the following question: Would any of the three conceivable consequences of confrontation have been worse than the actual result of appeasement? The first two consequents, Hitler backing down and an anti-Hitler coup, would have been enormously better. If Hitler had backed down and left the confrontation over the Sudetenland with his tail between his legs, he probably would have had to reassess his designs on Poland. In that sense, the chances of avoiding World War II might have increased. If an order for war had triggered an anti-Hitler coup, it is conceivable that the new rulers of Germany would either retract those orders or negotiate a settlement if war had begun. The reason for staging an anti-Hitler coup, after all, was to prevent Germany from going down the suicidal path of war.

It is the third consequent—war in 1938—that worried Chamberlain and that (second-wave) revisionist historians have emphasized as a major constraint. War in 1938, Chamberlain assumed and revisionist historians implicitly accept, would have been far worse for Britain (and Europe) than in 1939. Would it? Revisionist historians argue that the extra time that Munich bought was helpful in solidifying Britain's air defenses, thus making Britain less vulnerable to the *Luftwaffe* a year later. Third-wave historians like Telford Taylor (1979, 988) argue that Britain's fear of a "knockout blow" from the *Luftwaffe* was exaggerated because the planes had "neither the range nor the clout to do much" from German bases. For Taylor, it was better to fight Germany with Czechoslovakia on the side of Britain and France than to fight Germany after it had absorbed Czechoslovakia. Czechoslovakia was better armed and more defensible than Poland; moreover, prior to the conclusion of the Hitler-Stalin pact, Germany would have had to worry about Soviet intentions and its western flank (T. Taylor 1979, 984–85).

Although it is not possible to say whether Taylor or the second-wave revisionist view is correct, the question moves us closer to an informed assessment of the relative merits of appeasement and confrontation. It suggests the following probe: If confrontation led to war between Britain-France-Czechoslovakia and Germany, what must such a war (declared in 1938) obtain or avoid in order to justify the policy of confrontation? One need not go as far as Taylor in expecting a formidable and victorious resistance to Hitler's forces. One needs to assume that England would not surrender, the threat of a knockout blow from the skies notwithstanding.[14] It would be enough to assume a course roughly similar to the trajectory of the war that was actually declared in 1939. In this scenario, Norway, Belgium, Holland, and France would still be overrun, and the United States would still have to intervene, perhaps a little earlier, to defeat Germany. If this "latching on" the actual course of events in 1939 to the hypothetical 1938 war is reasonable, we arrive at an interesting conclusion: confrontation would have been preferable to appeasement because its worst outcome would have been "no worse than the course of 1939." What really tilts the balance, then, are the other two possibilities associated with confrontation: Hitler backing down without war or war triggering a successful anti-Hitler coup.

[14] For an analysis of the capabilities of the German *Luftwaffe* see T. Taylor (1979, 987–88).

Conclusion

Toward the end of Robert Zemeckis's *Back to the Future*—Hollywood counterfactual movie *par excellence*—Marty's hitherto wimpy father had to muster the courage to hit the local bully, Biff, in order to win the hand of his girlfriend (Marty's future mother). If he had not knocked Biff to the ground, Biff would have abducted his girlfriend and history would have been very different (Marty, the story's hero, would not have been born). As the story goes, he did hit Biff. And to the audience's delight, that one hit led to a "sea change" in the family's fortunes: not only was Marty born, but with a more assertive father, the family was richer, slimmer, sportier, and held more prestigious jobs. Whether Zemeckis was symbolically contrasting the price of appeasement with the rewards of confrontation, or merely lauding the payoffs of assertive individualism, we do not know.

Could England have mustered the courage to confront Hitler? The preceding analysis argues yes, but not with Chamberlain at England's helm or as the dominant decision maker; it would require the likes of Churchill, Eden, or Cooper at or close to the helm of power. If England had confronted Hitler, would he have backed down and would World War II been avoided? The answer to this question is more ambiguous. Confrontation probably would have elicited one of three reactions from Germany: Hitler backing down, an anti-Hitler coup, or war. What is interesting about these possible consequents is not so much our ability to decipher their likelihood as the suggestion that two of them are considerably better, and the third no worse, than the actual consequences of appeasing Hitler. Confronting Hitler in 1938, therefore, is a plausible counterfactual; its likely consequents, compared to the consequences of appeasement, also suggest that it would have been the superior policy.

5

Back to the Past

COUNTERFACTUALS AND THE CUBAN MISSILE CRISIS

RICHARD NED LEBOW AND JANICE GROSS STEIN

HAD THERE NOT BEEN a young student at the University of Chicago in 1960, the Cuban missile crisis might have escalated to nuclear war. Students always chuckle when they hear this counterfactual argument. Yet it is based on a long and complicated chain of causal reasoning that connects small acts to large unintended consequences.

Not yet twenty-one and too young to vote, the student worked in the Kennedy campaign. He was asked by the local Democratic organization if he would vote on behalf of a dead voter whose name was still on the rolls. He readily agreed and, refusing the small remuneration that was offered, forged the dead voter's signature and voted a straight Democratic ticket. The Illinois vote was close—Kennedy took the state by fewer than 10,000 votes—and critical. Illinois gave Kennedy the necessary electoral votes to win the presidency.

Had the student, and many other committed Democrats like him, not participated in electoral fraud in Illinois, Richard Nixon would have become the thirty-fifth president of the United States. Had Nixon been president, it is unlikely that he would have appointed many "doves" to his cabinet. His foreign policy advisors would probably have recommended and he likely would have approved air strikes against the missiles, which, the joint chiefs of staff insisted, had to be followed by an invasion. Air strikes followed by an invasion would have led to large-scale combat in Cuba between American and Soviet forces, and Soviet forces in Cuba might have used their tactical nuclear weapons against the invasion force, probably triggering American retaliation against the Soviet Union. Or, Khrushchev might have attacked the American missile bases in Turkey, provoking an American attack against the bases in the Soviet Union from which that attack had been launched. Through this chain of reasoning, it is apparent that had this one student, many of his friends, and thousands of other committed Illinois Democrats not participated in electoral fraud, the Cuban missile crisis could have escalated to nuclear war.

Why do students scoff at this argument? A counterfactual argument can be rejected because of logical flaws; yet no logical errors are immediately apparent in the chain of reasoning. Alternatively, implausible connections at any point in the rather complicated chain of causal reasoning can invalidate a counterfactual. Again, implausibility is not obvious. In all likelihood it is the long chain of causal reasoning that connects small events to large consequences that evokes skepticism. However, work in chaos and complexity has established how distant trivial events can have far-reaching consequences (Cohen and Stewart 1994; Waldrop 1992; Bak and Chen 1991; Arthur 1989). More to the point, simple, monocausal counterfactual arguments of critical events during the Cuban missile crisis have long been widely accepted. Should they have any greater claim to validity?

We begin by identifying the counterfactual arguments about the missile crisis made by policy makers in the United States and former Soviet Union. How logical, complete, and sophisticated were these arguments? Do they meet the criteria for good counterfactual argument suggested by Tetlock and Belkin? Drawing on the new evidence we have about Soviet and American decisions, we assess the validity of these counterfactuals. We then ask whether there is any relationship between the quality and the validity of counterfactuals. On the basis of this analysis, we suggest some additional criteria for evaluating the quality of counterfactuals that may be useful to policy makers and analysts who engage in forward-looking analysis as well as backward-looking explanation.

Counterfactuals: Evidence and Evaluation

Counterfactual argument is an important part of crisis decision making. As leaders consider their options, they often use counterfactual argument to structure their problem and evaluate the likely consequences of the options they are considering. In the missile crisis, American and Soviet leaders used counterfactual arguments frequently as they struggled to define and make difficult choices.

The missile crisis was also a critical moment during the Cold War and not surprisingly became the subject of extensive counterfactual argumentation after the fact by policy makers and scholars who debated the significance of the choices that were made. Their analyses frequently constructed the "plausible worlds" that might have resulted if other courses of action had been chosen by one or both parties.

The missile crisis is one of the major Cold War confrontations for which new and extensive documentation from both sides is now available. Extensive evidence does not always permit historians to discriminate among competing counterfactual arguments. In the decades following the First World

War, many of the statesmen involved in its outbreak published memoirs and the foreign ministries of the combatants or their successor states released a flood of relevant documents. This evidence fanned rather than resolved controversy and ignited new debates about what might have been if one or another of the principals had acted otherwise.

The new evidence about the missile crisis has not yet generated the same intense controversy as that surrounding the origins of the First World War. Recent scholarship on the missile crisis has provided definitive answers to some previously puzzling questions—the genesis and purpose of Khrushchev's enigmatic message on Saturday, how and why the U-2 was shot down over Cuba, and the nature of the public-private settlement worked out by Kennedy and Khrushchev. There is a near consensus about Khrushchev's foreign policy goals, Kennedy's growing unwillingness during the crisis to use force, and the gulf of misunderstanding between the leaders that helped create the crisis.

There are also disagreements among scholars. Students of the crisis have advanced different interpretations of Khrushchev's broader foreign policy objectives, the role of domestic political considerations in his decision to send missiles to Cuba, and his reasons for believing that the deployment would succeed. Some important questions remain unanswerable for lack of evidence. For purposes of validating competing counterfactual arguments, the most important gap in our knowledge is how Khrushchev would have responded had the United States attacked Soviet missile sites in Cuba. Even those former Soviet officials with strong views on the subject admit that these views are speculative. To the best of our knowledge, Khrushchev never discussed the question with any of his advisors.

New evidence makes it possible to assess the validity of some important counterfactual arguments. The counterfactual argument about the impact of the American reputation for resolve is a case in point. It contends that if Kennedy had had a firmer reputation for resolve, Khrushchev would not have sent the missiles to Cuba. Evidence that Khrushchev did not doubt Kennedy's resolve, or that his estimate of Kennedy's resolve did not influence his decision, would invalidate the counterfactual. Evidence that Khrushchev sent missiles to Cuba because he doubted Kennedy's resolve would strengthen the counterfactual's claim to validity. Of course, the possibility remains that Khrushchev would have sent the missiles for other reasons.

When we have evidence that policy makers made a choice contingent upon a hypothetical antecedent, we can also evaluate the validity of a counterfactual argument. The argument that had Khrushchev not withdrawn the missiles from Cuba within the twenty-four-hour time period, Kennedy would have invaded, is not confirmed by the evidence. The president had rejected the option of an air strike followed by an invasion and was preparing to make additional concessions if Khrushchev did not withdraw the missiles.

Even though the evidence is strong, evaluation of a counterfactual argument with this kind of evidence cannot be unequivocal. Leaders may change their mind when the situation arises and they must commit to a decision. The situation they confront can also differ in important ways from what they or their advisors had envisaged. On October 23, President Kennedy agreed to a retaliatory air strike against Soviet surface-to-air missile (SAM) sites in Cuba if any American U-2 reconnaissance aircraft were shot down. On Saturday, October 27, a Soviet SAM destroyed a U-2 and its pilot, but the president refused to retaliate, much to the surprise and dismay of the military. If the U-2 had not been shot down, historians of the crisis, aware of his standing order to retaliate, might have argued that the president would have ordered an air strike had a reconnaissance aircraft been shot down.

Lack of evidence or controversy make problematic the attempt to assess the validity of other arguments. Policy makers and scholars have debated how Khrushchev would have responded had the United States attacked Cuba. We have no evidence about how Khrushchev would have responded. Either Khrushchev did not consider his response to such a contingency, or he did not tell his associates. We have therefore tried to rely as much as possible on evidence or interpretations for which there is a consensus. Where there is controversy, we identify its nature, and provide reasons and evidence for our interpretation.

Counterfactuals also vary in their scope. Some make very specific claims about the immediate consequences of hypothetical antecedents. Many in the Soviet leadership maintained that had Khrushchev not agreed on Sunday, October 28, to remove the Soviet missiles from Cuba, the United States would have attacked Cuba within twenty-four to forty-eight hours. Other counterfactuals make broader, more diffuse claims, or posit consequences several steps removed from the antecedent. Many in the Kennedy administration maintained that had the president not forced the Soviet Union to remove the missiles, American authority would have been undermined everywhere. The weakening of American authority would in turn have placed severe strains on the NATO alliance, encouraged further Soviet challenges, and would have encouraged some allies to reach an accommodation with the Soviet Union. This kind of complex counterfactual must be evaluated at every link in the causal chain to assess the logic and the plausibility of the connections.

Where lack of direct evidence, controversy, or the nature of the counterfactual make it difficult to judge validity, indirect evidence may still permit judgments about the assumptions and political or military logic that underlie the arguments. Arguments about Khrushchev's hypothetical response to the hypothetical contingency of American military action against Cuba can be judged indirectly. The American "hawks" who insisted that had the United States attacked, the Soviet leader would have been constrained by the unfavorable military balance, greatly underestimated the size and conventional combat capabilities of Soviet forces in Cuba. Moreover, the hawks thought of Soviet military action as a consequence only of a deliberate decision made at the highest levels of government. We now know, however, that the American U-2 shot down over Cuba was fired on in violation of standing orders. We also know that Soviet forces in Cuba were equipped with tactical nuclear weapons and had the capability to use them against invading American forces without prior authorization from Moscow. This kind of indirect evidence can be very useful in evaluating the chain of causal logic that connects the counterfactual argument.

One final caveat is in order. Although the principal focus of this analysis is the counterfactual argumentation of policy makers both at the time and after the fact, we also include two arguments put forward by American scholars that have since become the object of considerable controversy (see Table 5.1: 2, 5). In the analysis of counterfactuals about the missile crisis, it is difficult to separate the arguments made by the official and analytical communities. Some of the most prominent analysts are also former officials and many analysts who were not administration officials were very much influenced by official arguments that were expressed in memoirs and conversations.

When policy makers and analysts make the same counterfactual arguments, we would expect a difference in their analytical quality. Policy makers generally advance arguments in written memoranda or orally in meetings, and are usually forward-looking. Their arguments, especially when they are verbal, are brief, usually simple if-then propositions, rarely articulate their underlying assumptions, and often fail to mention the relevant evidence. They are frequently intended to persuade, to serve rhetorical rather than analytical purposes. At times they are advanced largely to put a position on the official record.

Analysts, especially academic analysts, write for an audience that expects extensive argumentation that is logically constructed and as fully documented as possible. The professional standing of analysts depends on the quality of their arguments and the nature of the supporting evidence they present. Their arguments are past counterfactuals, with the additional advantage of knowledge of the "factual" outcome and, at times, of better evidence. We would expect, and research confirms, that the counterfactual arguments of analysts are more sophisticated and more likely to meet the criteria put forward by Tetlock and Belkin. It is fairer to make comparisons within the professions than across them.

TABLE 5.1
American Missile Crisis Counterfactuals

The Soviet Decision to Deploy the Missiles

1. Resolve:

   a. Had Kennedy displayed greater resolve prior to the crisis, Khrushchev would not have sent missiles to Cuba (Schlesinger, Sorensen).

   b. Had Khrushchev doubted U.S. resolve after the crisis, he would have challenged the Western position in Berlin and elsewhere (Kennedy).

2. Early Warning:

   a. Had President Kennedy issued a timely warning in the spring of 1962, Khrushchev might not have sent missiles to Cuba (Allison, George and Smoke).

   b. Had President Kennedy practiced deterrence more forcibly in September, Khrushchev might have aborted the missile deployment (George and Smoke).

3. Public Deployment:

   a. Had Khrushchev publicly announced his intention to send missiles to Cuba to deter an American attack before Kennedy's warnings in September, the president would have found it extremely difficult to threaten force to remove the missiles (Bundy, Sorensen).

The Soviet Decision to Remove the Missiles

4. Military Balance:

   a. Had the military balance been reversed, the United States would have been more and the Soviet Union less cautious. The United States might not have imposed the blockade and the USSR might have moved against Berlin (Bundy).

5. Private Diplomacy:

   a. Had President Kennedy made a private overture to Khrushchev and allowed him to save face, he might have agreed to withdraw the missiles and made a blockade of Cuba unnecessary (Stone, Steel).

   b. Had President Kennedy made a private overture to Khrushchev, it would have failed to persuade Khrushchev to withdraw the missiles and it would have weakened the president's hand (Sorensen, Bundy).

If the United States Had Attacked the Missile Bases

6. Escalation:

   a. Had the United States attacked the missile bases, the Soviet Union would have responded to an attack on Cuba with military action of its own against the United States, probably in Berlin or Turkey (Kennedy, McNamara, and many Soviets).

   b. Had the United States attacked, the Soviet Union would *not* have responded to an attack on Cuba with military action elsewhere (ExComm hawks, and implied by Bundy).

7. Risk of Nuclear War:

   a. Even if the Soviet Union had escalated horizontally in response to an American attack on Cuba, the risks of nuclear war were still very low (ExComm hawks, Bundy).

TABLE 5.1 *Continued*

b. Had the Soviet Union escalated horizontally in response to an American attack on Cuba, the risk of nuclear war would have been considerable (Kennedy).

If the United States Traded Missiles

8. Bandwagoning:
a. Had the United States made concessions to the Soviet Union, the alliance would have been seriously weakened (most of the ExComm and Kennedy during the first week of the crisis, Schlesinger after the crisis).
b. Had the president agreed publicly to an exchange of missiles, neither the alliance nor the president would have been weakened (Kennedy on October 27, Bundy ex post facto).

Soviet Policy after the Crisis

9. Resolve:
a. Had the United States not stood firm on Cuba, Khrushchev would have been tempted to engage in new challenges, most likely in Berlin, that would have had greater risk of nuclear war (Kennedy, Schlesinger, Sorensen, Bundy).

10. Military Balance:
a. If the United States does not maintain a strategic nuclear or local conventional advantage, Soviet leaders will act more aggressively. They are restrained by American military superiority (Schlesinger).

American and Soviet Counterfactuals

We have identified eight past and two future counterfactuals about the Cuban missile crisis generated by American officials and analysts (Table 5.1). With two exceptions, the antecedents are American policies and the consequents are Soviet policies. Six of the eight counterfactuals (resolve, early warning, military balance, and versions of escalation, risk of nuclear war, and bandwagoning) grow out of the deterrence paradigm. They are simple monocausal propositions and provide no arguments or evidence to explain why changes in American policy would have prompted different Soviet responses. Almost without exception, they are "surgical." The officials and scholars who make them change one American attribute or behavior to change one subsequent Soviet behavior, or behavioral pattern. Only after the crisis did some analysts develop more complex chains of causal reasoning.

Soviet counterfactuals are exclusively the provenance of policy makers. The Soviet Union did not have an independent scholarly community with access to information about foreign policy and the freedom to comment as they saw fit. We identified two counterfactuals from our analysis of Soviet documents, statements by former Soviet leaders at recent conferences on the missile crisis, and interviews of Soviet officials (Table 5.2).

TABLE 5.2
Soviet Missile Crisis Counterfactuals

The Impending American Invasion of Cuba

1. Deterrence:
   Had the Soviet Union not deployed missiles in Cuba, the United States would have invaded (Khrushchev and most of his advisors).

2. Compellence:
   Had the Soviet Union not agreed to withdraw the missiles in Cuba, the United States would have invaded Cuba on October 29 or 30 (Khrushchev and most of his advisors).

These counterfactuals were widely accepted by Soviet leaders and their advisors. None of the interviewees challenged their validity or knew of colleagues who had. In the late 1980s, Soviet officials who participated in one or more of the Soviet-American conferences on the missile crisis greeted with disbelief the statements of former Secretary of Defense Robert S. McNamara and National Security Advisor McGeorge Bundy that Kennedy had no intention of invading Cuba prior to the discovery of Soviet missiles on that island (*Proceedings of the Cambridge Conference on the Cuban Missile Crisis* 1988, 62–64; Allyn, Blight, and Welch 1992, 6–9; Lebow and Stein 1994, 29–32, 130–43).

Soviet officials involved in or knowledgeable about the missile crisis agree that the political assumptions that gave rise to the counterfactuals played a critical role in Soviet policy. They maintain that one of the principal reasons for the missile deployment was Khrushchev's belief that an imminent invasion of Cuba had to be deterred. Khrushchev later withdrew the missiles because he and other key officials became convinced that it was the only way to prevent such an invasion. After the crisis these beliefs were reformulated as counterfactuals. The United States, it was alleged, would have invaded Cuba if the Soviet Union had not sent missiles and then agreed to remove them in return for a noninvasion pledge (Lebow and Stein 1994, 29–32, 130–43).

How Good are the Counterfactuals?

Philip Tetlock and Aaron Belkin acknowledge that political beliefs can be an important determinant of the acceptability of a counterfactual argument. However, they suggest, there are six independent criteria that can be used to evaluate a counterfactual (Chapter 1, Tetlock and Belkin).

TABLE 5.3
American Counterfactuals

	Specify	Connect	Facts	Project
Resolve	No	No	No	No
Early Warning	No	No		No
Public Deployment				No
Balance	No			No
Private Diplomacy		No		No
Escalation		No	No	No
Risk of War		No		No
Bandwagoning		No		No
Resolve (future)	No	No	No	No
Military Balance (future)	No			No

These criteria subject counterfactual arguments to two different kinds of tests. The first two propositions—clearly specified antecedents and consequents, and cotenability of antecedents and connecting principles—treat the completeness of the argument. The next three propositions—consistency with well-established historical facts, laws, and statistical generalizations (and arguably projectability)—concern logical and substantive validity.

Of necessity, counterfactual arguments in international relations must be evaluated primarily on the basis of their logical structure. For our purposes, the fourth and fifth criteria are formally irrelevant because there are no "lawlike" and few well-established statistical generalizations in the field of international relations. As Tetlock and Belkin acknowledge, all theories are contested. Nevertheless, we can draw upon existing theories, even when they are contested, to assess the "projectability" of counterfactual arguments, recognizing that these projections are as controversial as the theories from which they are deduced. The Lewis-Stalnaker criterion (which Tetlock and Belkin discuss in Chapter 1) is also problematic because there is no precise way of measuring the proximity of hypothesized to real worlds. We use the criterion of "plausible worlds" in conjunction with the specification of the hypothetical antecedent to assess the quality of counterfactual arguments. The only external criterion that is relevant is consistency with well-established historical fact.

Accordingly, we have used only the first three tests and experimented with the criterion of projectability to evaluate American and Soviet counterfactuals (see Tables 5.3 and 5.4). In evaluating the counterfactuals against each of these criteria, we draw on some of the cases to illustrate general problems.

TABLE 5.4
Soviet Counterfactuals

	Specify	Connect	Facts	Project
Deterrence		No		No
Compellence		No		No

Clearly Specified Antecedents and Consequents and "Plausible Worlds"

As Tetlock and Belkin observe, every counterfactual is inherently ambiguous and requires compound counterfactuals. Good counterfactuals have to specify the conditions that would have to be present for the antecedent to occur. Some historians have argued, for example, that timely public health measures could have significantly reduced the mortality in Europe associated with the Black Death pandemic of the fourteenth century. For European communities to have implemented these measures, they would have had to recognize that human intervention could affect the spread of the disease, and they would have had to have the power and will to impose draconian measures on travel and trade over the objections of the wealthy and merchant classes. Both additional counterfactuals are implausible and would violate the test of a "closest possible world" (Hawthorn 1991, 31–60). In all likelihood, any good counterfactual in international relations would have to change more than one dimension of the past and these dimensions have to be specified. This specification is important because these conditions might either create an implausible world or invalidate the connecting principles of the counterfactual.

Nine of the twelve counterfactuals meet a reasonable approximation of this criterion. The American counterfactuals about the impact of early warning and the military balance clearly fail this test and it is questionable whether the counterfactual about the impact of resolve meets the criterion. Although the three conceivably approximate "miracle" causes for the purposes of theoretical experimentation, they fail the test of "conceivable" causes (see Chapter 2, Fearon).

The early-warning counterfactual hypothesizes that Khrushchev might not have sent missiles to Cuba if Kennedy had warned him about the consequences in April, before he had made his decision, instead of in September, when the missiles were already en route. Kennedy's warnings in September were a response to the mounting Soviet conventional arms buildup in Cuba, which had begun in the summer of 1962. They were also motivated by his need to appear resolute to the American public; the Republicans were attempting to make his alleged weakness on Cuba a major issue in the congressional election campaign.

In April, before the conventional buildup began, Kennedy had no reason to suspect a missile deployment, and months away from an election campaign, had no strong political incentive to issue a warning. To sustain the early-warning counterfactual, other counterfactuals would have to be introduced to provide foreign or domestic motives for warnings in April. This counterfactual fails to meet the test of careful specification of the antecedent and the criterion of a plausible world.

The counterfactual about the impact of the military balance hypothesizes that Kennedy might not have risked the blockade and that Khrushchev might not have backed down had the strategic balance been reversed. But how could the Soviet Union have achieved such a decisive strategic advantage by the early 1960s? A stunning scientific breakthrough seems extremely unlikely given what we know about arms technology and the relative technical and industrial capabilities of the two superpowers. Nor would it be realistic to expect the United States to stand idly by while the Soviet Union built up an impressive arsenal of intercontinental ballistic missiles. The American reaction to Sputnik and the fears of strategic inferiority that it triggered indicate a willingness to spend whatever it took to compete with the Soviet Union. The United States would in any case have retained the advantages conferred by its large bomber force and bases ringing the Soviet Union. Clearly this counterfactual fails to specify the antecedent and the test of plausibility.

If we grant the Soviet Union strategic superiority, we have to ask what else about the Cold War would have been different. To the extent that the strategic balance was a critical determinant of superpower foreign policy and risk taking, as the counterfactual alleges, it is possible, McGeorge Bundy speculates, that Khrushchev would have felt free to occupy Berlin, and Kennedy, in turn, would have stood even firmer on Cuba (Bundy 1988, 448–50). Strategic superiority could conceivably have emboldened Khrushchev to send Soviet missiles openly to Cuba. Alternatively, he might not have felt the need to send missiles at all, given what would have been the Soviet ability to destroy the United States with missiles launched from the Soviet Union. The prospect of Soviet strategic superiority opens a Pandora's box of possibilities, none of which are addressed by the policy makers or analysts who make this counterfactual argument.

Using these criteria, the counterfactual about the impact of American resolve is also open to serious question. Those who argue that had Kennedy displayed greater resolve prior to the crisis, Khrushchev would not have sent the missiles, generally fail to specify carefully what they conceive of as greater resolve. We have already dealt with the difficulties of early warning as a demonstration of resolve. More than one analyst suggest that Kennedy should have invaded Cuba; such an action would have created a world in which the consequent was no longer relevant. Alternatively, the president could have ordered the tearing down of the Berlin Wall. The possible consequences of this action range from a serious crisis between the two superpowers to an escalation to a nuclear confrontation. Almost anywhere along the spectrum, the world would have so changed that the subsequent deployment of missiles becomes implausible. This counterfactual fails the test of careful specification as well as the criterion of specifying the antecedents such that the "closest" possible world in which the antecedent is true is also a possible world in which the consequent is true.

Connecting Principles That Causally Link Antecedents with the Consequent and Are Logically Cotenable with the Antecedent

Some of the counterfactuals fail to specify the connecting principles between the hypothetical antecedents and consequents they hypothesize. Revisionists, for example, provide no compelling justification for their expectation that had Kennedy made a secret overture to Khrushchev before choosing the blockade, Khrushchev would have responded positively. It is as plausible that he would have stood firm and increased the pace of construction of the missile sites in Cuba—as the Soviet military in Cuba did initially in response to the blockade. Some revisionists contend that it would have been easier for Khrushchev to back down in the absence of a public confrontation, but it is also possible that he needed a serious confrontation to justify a withdrawal to Soviet militants and political adversaries (Stone 1966; Steel 1969; Nathan 1975; B. J. Bernstein 1976 and 1980; Wills 1982, 235–74). No compelling political logic or theories of Soviet political leadership are advanced to substantiate the claim that Khrushchev would have responded with concession rather than confrontation.

The counterfactual about the impact of resolve also does not establish the cotenability of the antecedent with connecting principles. Khrushchev allegedly doubted Kennedy's resolve for two reasons: the president's prior performance, and Khrushchev's view of Americans as too soft, too liberal, and too rich to fight. The counterfactual hypothesizes that Khrushchev would not have sent missiles to Cuba if Kennedy had displayed greater resolve at the Bay of Pigs, the Vienna summit, and in Berlin. It does not specify, however, how presidential displays of resolve would have altered Khrushchev's view of the American people.

It is plausible that Khrushchev might have revised his alleged estimate of the American public had it been unequivocal in its support of a strategy that risked war. It is also plausible that had Kennedy committed American forces to the Bay of Pigs to display resolve, he would have embroiled his administration in a military quagmire that could have quickly alienated much of the public and divided the country. Any attempt to interfere with the construction of the Berlin Wall could have provoked a serious crisis or even a war with the Soviet Union. A war-threatening crisis could have divided the allies and American opinion. Here too, no compelling political logic connects the antecedent to the consequent.

The counterfactual about the impact of American concessions on allied loyalty is also not connected by explicit theoretical or political logic. It assumes that an exchange of missiles, or in some versions, a public exchange, would have divided and destroyed NATO. The consequences of a missile trade for the alliance are uncertain; the reaction of NATO allies would in all likelihood have depended very much on the transparency of the arrangement and the degree of Turkish compliance. Those who made the counterfactual argument neither specified conditions nor a set of propositions drawn from theories of balancing or bandwagoning that connected concessions to the dissolution of NATO.

The counterfactual poses only two outcomes—no alliance or the status quo—yet there was a wide range of plausible consequences. Even the worst case—a public trade and public Turkish bitterness—might not necessarily have destroyed the alliance. Disappointed allies might nevertheless have chosen to remain in the alliance because they felt that Khrushchev would be emboldened by his success and, therefore, posed an even greater threat. For many European allies, NATO served another critical role: it constrained the Federal Republic of Germany. Presumably, this interest would have been unaffected by the outcome of the missile crisis.

Consistency with Well-Established Facts

Some of the counterfactuals about the missile crisis require rewriting of history to accommodate anomalies in the evidence. The counterfactual about the impact of resolve uses historical evidence selectively and ignores the anomalies. Khrushchev's alleged doubt about Kennedy's resolve because of his purportedly pusillanimous performance in Vienna is important in the chain of logic that connects the antecedent to the consequent. But all the evidence available at the time indicates that although Kennedy was troubled by the summit, he had been very firm at Vienna and Khrushchev came away impressed by his performance (Lebow and Stein 1994, 71ff).

Those who advance this counterfactual put even more emphasis on Kennedy's failure to commit American forces to the faltering Bay of Pigs invasion. Yet they ignore the president's success in standing up to Khrushchev in Berlin in 1961. Kennedy rejected Khrushchev's ultimatum outright and reinforced the American garrison in Berlin. His unyielding defense of Western access rights to Berlin compelled Khrushchev to retreat from his challenge and should have strengthened his estimate of the president's resolve.

The counterfactual about escalation also makes selective use of evidence. For ExComm militants and some analysts writing after the fact, the strategic balance was determining. They insist that American strategic superiority would have deterred the Soviet Union from responding to an American air strike or an invasion of Cuba with military action of its own elsewhere in the world where it possessed a conventional military advantage. The Central Intelligence Agency and some administration officials had made a similar argument before the missile crisis; they maintained that American strategic and local conventional superiority would deter the Soviet Union from sending missiles to Cuba. They were wrong. Yet they put forward essentially the same argument again with great confidence.

Projectability

Sound counterfactuals require sound theories that provide lawlike generalizations that fill in the missing data points in thought experiments. These theories should be able to predict what will happen in new or as yet unobserved cases. Policy makers and their advisors were uniformly confident about the projectability of their arguments to other cases. Although policy makers had high confidence in their capacity to predict to future cases, this confidence is a function of psychological dynamics rather than theoretical logic. We evaluate projectability not from the perspective of policy makers, but using the standards of normal social science.

The counterfactuals about public deployment and private diplomacy are ad hoc arguments not derived from conventional wisdom that is deduced from a set of propositions or theories. Consequently, we do not classify them as capable of generating predictions about what will happen in new or unobserved cases.

Eight of the counterfactuals—two on resolve, one on early warning, two on the military balance, and those on escalation, risk of war, and bandwagoning—drew on conventional wisdom that can be traced to a set of propositions drawn from theories of deterrence. ExComm members and analysts subsequently interpreted Soviet behavior in the missile crisis as evidence of the validity of these propositions, and made predictions about future Soviet behavior based on the logic of deterrence. Almost all of these counterfactuals, however, either fail to specify the hypothetical antecedent in ways that permit projection to new or unobserved cases or fail to make explicit the principles that connect the antecedent to the consequent (see Table 5.3). Insofar as they do not meet the criteria of adequate specification of variables and connecting principles, they cannot meet the criterion of projectability.

Soviet counterfactuals similarly drew on theoretical principles derived from Marxism-Leninism. The theory assumed that capitalist and socialist economic systems were inherently hostile and that capitalist states would use force to crush socialist revolutions. Over time, principles were reformulated to incorporate the assumption that "sober-minded realists" in the capitalist world recognized the mutually destructive nature of nuclear war. The United States could be expected to use force to overthrow the Castro regime—but not at the risk of nuclear war. Khrushchev therefore believed that a missile deployment would succeed in deterring an invasion by creating an unacceptable risk of nuclear war.

Marxism-Leninism also shaped the expectation that the United States would have invaded Cuba sometime on October 29–30 if the Soviet Union had not agreed to remove its missiles. Khrushchev and his colleagues viewed the president and other public officials as agents of capitalism, and greatly underestimated their autonomy from Wall Street (Griffiths 1984). The capitalist class was implacably hostile to Castro because of the threat he posed to American hegemony in Latin America, and their most influential organs of opinion, such as *Time* and the *Wall Street Journal*, repeatedly called for his overthrow. Khrushchev doubted that Kennedy could prevent Wall Street from exploiting the opportunity provided by the crisis to order the CIA and the military to invade Cuba and eliminate Castro.[1]

The Soviet counterfactuals derived from Marxism-Leninism, and Khrushchev and his advisors were confident in their capacity to predict to future cases even though the two counterfactuals offered opposing predictions. The precrisis counterfactual gave great weight to the deterrent capability of Soviet missile bases in Cuba. The counterfactual developed during the crisis recognized that the deployment had made an invasion more rather than less likely, and that it was necessary to withdraw the missiles to prevent the invasion. The two counterfactuals were reconciled by introducing the distinction, often made by Soviet leaders, between reckless and sober-minded realists. Khrushchev regarded Kennedy as a sober-minded realist who was committed to avoiding nuclear war. But the discovery of the missiles before they were fully operational strengthened the hands of reckless hard-liners. Marxism-Leninism was not determining, and neither counterfactual provided further logic for the differing expectations.[2] Nor, given the failure to specify conditions associated with competing predictions, could these arguments predict future American behavior.

---

[1] After the crisis, Khrushchev wrote Kennedy: "I take the liberty to think that you evidently held to a restraining position with regard to those forces which suffered from militaristic itching" (Khrushchev 1992, 62–73).

[2] On the illogical nature of Khrushchev's reasons for expecting the missile deployment to succeed see Lebow and Stein (1994, chapter 4).

Validity: Did They Get It Right?

Did American and Soviet policy makers and analysts get it right? Were their counterfactual arguments consistent with the evidence that became available after the fact? New evidence from interviews and archives now permits evaluation of the validity of some of the most important American and Soviet counterfactuals. A summary of the validity of the counterfactual arguments is presented in Table 5.5.

Resolve: The two counterfactuals about resolve (past and future) maintain that Khrushchev would not have sent missiles to Cuba if Kennedy had had a reputation for resolve, and would have been more aggressive had the missile deployment succeeded. They derive from the logic of deterrence and rest on an assumption and an inference drawn from scant and partial evidence: that Soviet aggression is (was) opportunity driven, and that Kennedy's performance as president had given Khrushchev ample reason to doubt his resolve.

New evidence from former Soviet officials suggests that this analysis of Khrushchev's motives and estimates was incorrect. Khrushchev sent the missiles to Cuba to deter an anticipated American invasion, to compensate partially for American strategic superiority, and to establish an atmosphere of "psychological equality." He may also have had strong domestic incentives that grew out of the failure of his economic and political reforms. Khrushchev's estimate of Kennedy's resolve thus appears to have had the reverse effect of that posited by the counterfactual. Khrushchev was unwavering in his belief that Kennedy was about to invade Cuba, and he worried that the president would exploit U.S. strategic superiority to try to intimidate the Soviet Union politically. Both these concerns drove him toward

TABLE 5.5
Validity of Soviet and American Counterfactuals

	Counterfactual	*Valid*
American	Resolve	No
	Early Warning	Unable to Judge
	Public Deployment	Unable to Judge
	Military Balance	No
	Private Diplomacy	No
	Escalation	Unable to Judge
	Risk of War	Unable to Judge
	Bandwagoning	Unable to Judge
	Resolve (future)	Unable to Judge
	Military Balance (future)	Unable to Judge
Soviet	Deterrence	No
	Compellence	No

the missile deployment (Garthoff 1987, 6–42; Lebow and Stein 1994, chapters 2 and 3).

Soviet and Cuban officials reveal that Khrushchev insisted on a secret deployment because he thought Kennedy resolute. Khrushchev expected Kennedy to order the American navy to stop any Soviet freighters transporting missiles to Cuba. He also worried that the announcement of a Soviet-Cuban defense pact would serve as the catalyst for an American invasion of Cuba. He intended to inform Kennedy about the missiles only after they were deployed and fully operational, and therefore too dangerous to attack (Lebow 1989; Sergei Khrushchev and Sergo Mikoyan in Blight, Lewis, and Welch 1994, 76–77, 80; With the historical truth and morale of Baraguá 1990, 2).[3] Fidel Castro and the Cuban leadership pleaded unsuccessfully with Khrushchev to deploy the missiles openly, as the Americans had their missiles in Turkey. Khrushchev was adamant that Kennedy would never accept a missile deployment (Schlesinger 1992; Jorge Risquet in Allyn, Blight, and Welch 1992, 71; Fidel Castro in Blight, Allyn, and Welch 1993, 55, 59–60, 213–15).

The new evidence casts very serious doubt on the counterfactual argument that the missile deployment could have been deterred by greater displays of American resolve. Rather, it suggests the contrary counterfactual that a more restrained American foreign policy would have been more effective; in the absence of perceived threats, it is possible that Khrushchev might not have felt the need to send missiles to Cuba.

The new evidence is not directly relevant to the second counterfactual claim about the impact of resolve on Khrushchev's foreign policy after the missile crisis. Even if Khrushchev's decision to deploy the missiles had little or nothing to do with a low assessment of Kennedy's resolve, Kennedy's failure to take a firm stand against the deployment could still have led the Soviet leader to question that resolve. In this respect, the missile crisis was very different from the Bay of Pigs or the Vienna summit. In Cuba, Kennedy had publicly drawn a line. To have accepted Soviet missiles in Cuba would have exposed his well-publicized commitment as a bluff. It could easily have raised doubts about his resolve in Khrushchev's mind, and resulted in greater domestic political pressure to pursue a more militant policy toward the Soviet Union. Alternatively, a success in Cuba could have strengthened Khrushchev's political position at home and abroad and led to a more accommodative foreign policy. In any prediction of Khrushchev's

---

[3] To this day, many Soviet officials are convinced that an open deployment, as Andrei Gromyko put it, "would just not have worked" (Allyn, Blight, and Welch 1992, 19–20). "I am absolutely convinced," former Gorbachev advisor Georgiy Shakhnazarov declared, "that the government of the United States would not have tolerated it." It would also have played into their hands by providing the administration with a propaganda tool "to win public opinion over to their side" for an invasion (Allyn, Blight, and Welch 1992, 22–23).

behavior, the number of potentially relevant variables probably was large and the interaction effects considerable.

Early Warning: Some of Khrushchev's most important foreign policy advisors thought the idea of a missile deployment ill-fated from the beginning. Deputy Prime Minister Anastas I. Mikoyan and foreign policy aide Oleg Troyanovsky warned that American aircraft would discover the missiles before they became operational. Foreign Minister Andrei Gromyko claims to have warned Khrushchev that domestic political considerations would compel Kennedy to take some kind of action against the missiles. Some members of the presidium were reluctant to approve the deployment (Lebow and Stein 1994, 86–87). Strident warnings by Kennedy in April or May might conceivably have emboldened the opposition to the deployment or led Khrushchev to reconsider his plan. But alternatively, they could have encouraged him to put more emphasis on secrecy and to decide on a smaller deployment, which would have been easier to hide. Khrushchev had initially wanted a small deployment but the military had insisted on a larger and more elaborate deployment (Lebow and Stein 1994, 76).

The difficulty with this counterfactual, as we pointed out earlier, is its failure to specify the conditions that would have led Kennedy to have issued warnings in April or May. In the spring of 1962, the Soviet Union would have had to arouse American suspicions about a missile deployment. Khrushchev, in turn, would have had to have been provoked by American actions. History has to be so extensively rewritten to create a context in which this counterfactual could be evaluated that no judgment is possible.

Public Deployment: This counterfactual asserts that Khrushchev might have succeeded in deploying missiles in Cuba if he had done so publicly and announced his intentions before Kennedy issued his warnings in September. Former National Security Advisor McGeorge Bundy and Special Counsel to the President Theodore Sorensen maintain that Kennedy would have found Soviet missiles in Cuba extraordinarily embarrassing but might have been unable to do anything other than protest verbally. They assume that Khrushchev would have justified the Soviet missiles as a response to the ongoing American missile deployment in Turkey, and that this justification would have seemed reasonable to most of the NATO allies.

We know now that Khrushchev saw the missile deployment as a direct response to the deployment of the Jupiters and almost certainly would have drawn the analogy. It seems likely that NATO members would have been less alarmed by a public deployment. The Soviet move appeared so much more ominous to them and to the president because it was carried out secretly and in violation of assurances from Khrushchev that no missiles would be sent to Cuba. Kennedy still would have been under great pressure from Republicans and some of his advisors to respond, but might have resisted these pressures because of reluctance to provoke a Soviet-American confrontation without full NATO support. It is also conceivable that the absence of NATO support and the prospect of certain domestic political loss would have prompted him to invade Cuba before any missiles reached Cuba. The evidence does not permit discrimination between these two competing predictions.

Military balance: For much of the Cold War, many Western analysts insisted that NATO's military capability restrained the Soviet Union. They attributed Khrushchev's assertiveness in the late 1950s and early 1960s to his often-proclaimed belief that the correlation of forces had begun to favor the socialist camp. Following conclusive evidence in the summer of 1961 that the Soviet Union had only a limited ICBM capability, the Kennedy administration informed Moscow about the U.S. strategic advantage. Officials reasoned counterfactually that Khrushchev might not have challenged the Western position in Berlin if he had realized the striking asymmetry in the strategic balance. Kennedy and his advisors hoped that public and private assertions of American strategic superiority would encourage Khrushchev to behave more cautiously (Lebow and Stein 1994, 32–38).

We know from Soviet sources that the Soviet military was very disturbed by administration claims of strategic superiority. Khrushchev is said to have worried that they were a precursor to a campaign of political intimidation; he had tried and failed to exploit his putative strategic advantage in the aftermath of Sputnik. Many of the Soviet officials thought that these American statements provided yet another incentive for Khrushchev to send missiles to Cuba. The Soviet first-generation ICBM had proven a failure; only a few were ever deployed. The Soviet armed forces had more reliable medium- and intermediate-range ballistic missiles. By sending them to Cuba, where they were capable of striking at targets in North America, Khrushchev and the Soviet military could partially offset American strategic superiority and more effectively resist any attempt at intimidation. If the Soviet Union had not been at such a strategic disadvantage, and if the Kennedy administration had not sought to publicize that disadvantage, Khrushchev would not have had the same incentive to send missiles to Cuba.

The hypothesized link between Soviet foreign policy and the military balance is an empirical question. To test this relationship, we examined Soviet-American relations from the beginning of the Cold War in 1947 to 1985, when Mikhail Gorbachev came to power. Drawing on formerly classified estimates of the strategic balance and public studies of the balance prepared by prominent strategic institutes, we developed a composite measure of the relative strategic potency of the two superpowers. Our analysis suggests that the nuclear balance went through three distinct phases. The first, 1948 to 1960, was a period of mounting American advantage. The second, 1961 to

1968, was characterized by a pronounced but declining American advantage. The third, 1968 to 1985, was an era of strategic parity.[4]

There is no positive correlation between shifts in Soviet assertiveness and shifts in the strategic balance. Soviet challenges are most pronounced in the late 1940s and early 1950s, in central Europe and Korea, and again in the late 1950s and early 1960s, in Berlin and Cuba. A third, lesser period of assertiveness occurred between 1979 and 1982 in Africa and Afghanistan.[5] The first and second peaks occurred at a time when the United States had unquestioned nuclear superiority. The third peak coincides with the period of strategic parity, before the years of the putative American "window of vulnerability." During the period of alleged Soviet advantage, roughly 1982 to 1985, Soviet behavior was restrained. The relationship between the military balance and Soviet assertiveness is largely the reverse of that predicted by the counterfactual argument. The United States had unquestioned supremacy between 1948 and 1952, and again between 1959 and 1962, the principal years of Soviet assertiveness. Soviet challenges were most pronounced when the Soviet Union was weak and the United States was strong.

[4] The accepted strategic wisdom, reflected in our analysis, holds that the United States had a decisive strategic advantage throughout the 1950s. It possessed an expanding capability to attack the Soviet Union with nuclear weapons without the prospect of direct retaliation. The Strategic Air Command had a large and growing fleet of strategic bombers based in the United States, Western Europe, and North Africa. This strike force was supplemented by carrier and land-based aircraft deployed along the Soviet periphery. The Soviet Union's bomber force was small, shorter range, and technologically primitive.

The relative military balance changed in the 1960s when both superpowers began to deploy ICBMs. In 1962, at the time of the Cuban missile crisis, the United States had some 3,500 warheads against approximately 300 for the Soviets. Only twenty of the Soviet warheads were on ICBMs. See *Proceedings of the Cambridge Conference on the Cuban Missile Crisis, 11–12 October 1987* (1988, 20, 40, 45–47), Allyn, Blight, and Welch (1992, 33–34), and Lebow and Stein (1994, chapter 2). By the end of the 1960s, the Soviet Strategic Rocket Forces had deployed enough ICBMs to destroy about half of the population and industry of the United States. It had achieved the capability that McNamara considered essential for MAD.

Sometime in the 1970s the Soviet Union achieved rough strategic parity. This balance prevailed until 1991, although some analysts have argued that one or the other possessed some margin of advantage. American missiles were more accurate throughout the 1970s. The United States was also the first to deploy multiple independently targeted reentry vehicles (MIRVs). It put three warheads on Minuteman missiles, and fourteen on submarine-launched ballistic missiles (SLBMs). The Soviet Union began to deploy MIRVs in the late 1970s and, in the opinion of some analysts, gained a temporary strategic advantage because of the greater throw weight of their ICBMs. The SS-18 could carry between thirty and forty MIRVs, but in practice was deployed with a maximum of ten.

[5] Soviet aggressiveness is a subjective phenomenon. To measure it, we polled a sample of international relations scholars and former government officials. They were carefully chosen to ensure representation of diverse political points of view. These experts were given a list of events that could be interpreted as Soviet challenges to the United States, its allies, or nonaligned states. They were asked to rank them in order of ascending gravity. The survey revealed a surprising concurrence among experts.

This pattern challenges the proposition that aggression is motivated primarily by adversaries who seek continuously to exploit opportunities. When Soviet leaders felt vulnerable, they behaved aggressively even though the military balance was unfavorable and they had no grounds to doubt their adversary's resolve. In the absence of compelling need, leaders often did not challenge even when opportunities for an assertive foreign policy were present (Lebow 1984).

Private Diplomacy: The new evidence offers no support for the counterfactual argument that had Kennedy made a private overture before announcing the blockade, Khrushchev would have responded positively. Khrushchev was committed to the missile deployment because it appeared to offer a solution to a series of foreign and domestic problems. He brushed aside the objections of well-informed advisors and, when the deployment was underway, chose to ignore Kennedy's warnings. Khrushchev initially regarded the blockade as a tentative response that might still allow the Soviet Union to proceed with the deployment. Only the threat of a naval clash led him to change his mind. Given Khrushchev's demonstrated propensity for self-delusion, there is little reason to suppose that private diplomacy would have persuaded him to withdraw the missiles. It seems much more likely that he would have persevered with the deployment while using private diplomacy to buy time.

More evidence for this judgment is provided by Khrushchev's policy during the crisis. He sought to exploit the risk of war to coax concessions from Kennedy. There are good reasons to believe that he considered these concessions, especially Kennedy's promise not to invade Cuba, very important to Soviet national and his own political interests. Before the crisis, Kennedy would have been in no position politically to issue a pledge not to invade Cuba. Both leaders needed the threat of war the crisis created to justify their mutual concessions.

Escalation: Officials and policy analysts disagree about whether an American attack on Cuba would have provoked Soviet military action in Berlin, Turkey, or elsewhere. The new evidence does not permit any definitive judgment. None of Khrushchev's lieutenants knew how he would have reacted to an American attack on Cuba or against the Soviet missile sites in Cuba, and Khrushchev himself may not have known how he would have responded.

Khrushchev's response would probably have been context dependent. An air strike that destroyed Soviet missile sites and killed several hundred Soviet soldiers might have provoked a different response than air attacks followed by an invasion that caused tens of thousands of Soviet casualties and toppled the Castro government. Khrushchev's response would presumably also have been influenced by the reaction of the NATO allies and the intensity of pressure within the leadership to retaliate. These factors and their interaction could not be assessed beforehand, nor can they be assessed in hindsight. Without knowledge of the context in which Khrushchev would have made a decision, it is impossible to discriminate between competing counterfactual arguments regarding escalation.

The new Soviet evidence does illuminate the political logic underlying the escalation counterfactuals. The nonescalation counterfactual asserts that Khrushchev would have been deterred from horizontal escalation by American strategic superiority. This constraint seems questionable, as Khrushchev was not deterred by American strategic and local conventional superiority from sending missiles to Cuba. Moreover, the counterfactual argument against horizontal escalation posits Soviet military action in a region where the Soviet Union had a decisive, or at least significant, military advantage. The onus of further escalation would then have been on President Kennedy, who was committed to avoiding the use of force because he feared that it would lead to a wider Soviet-American war. Soviet evidence indicates that Khrushchev had a similar horror of war and may well have eschewed escalation for the same reason. If so, it may well be that Khrushchev would not have escalated, but for very different reasons than those advanced by the counterfactual argument against escalation.

Those who predicted escalation argued that Khrushchev would be motivated by his need to uphold Soviet honor and his political position. President Kennedy took Khrushchev's need to save face very seriously. Depending on the circumstances, either motive could have been compelling and forced Khrushchev into a position where, buffeted by competing and seemingly irreconcilable demands, he would have had to make a rapid decision under conditions of great stress. It is impossible to know how he would have responded.

Risk of war: This counterfactual is linked to the escalation counterfactual. Those who posit a high risk of war assume that an American attack against Cuba would have provoked reciprocal Soviet escalation that in turn would have provoked further American military action, leading ultimately to a serious possibility of an all-out nuclear exchange. Most of those who deny the risk of nuclear war deny the likelihood of a Soviet response to an American attack on Cuba.

The positive risk of war counterfactual is several times removed from reality. It requires at least three hypothetical antecedents: an American attack against Cuba, Soviet horizontal escalation, and American counter-reprisals. As each of these steps is context dependent, and all of the contexts hypothetical, it is very difficult to evaluate. Soviet and American evidence indicates that Khrushchev and Kennedy were both committed to avoiding war and for this reason disinclined to use force. Kennedy resisted growing pressure to attack Cuba when the blockade appeared to be failing, and revoked his standing order to carry out a retaliatory air strike against a Soviet SAM site after a U-2 was shot down over Cuba. Khrushchev might similarly have resisted whatever pressures he would have faced to escalate.

Both the escalation and risk of war counterfactuals posit escalation—or its absence—as the result of conscious decisions taken at the highest levels in the White House and the Kremlin. Our evidence indicates that the most dramatic act of Soviet military escalation—the destruction of an American U-2 over Cuba on the morning of October 27—was the result of insubordination. The missile that brought the plane down was fired in violation of standing orders issued by Defense Minister Rodion Malinovsky. Other incidents that occurred that day—the overflight of the Kamchatka Peninsula by an American U-2 and the near challenge of the blockade line by the Soviet freighter *Grozny*—were the result of organizational mishaps. We also know that Soviet forces in Cuba were equipped with tactical nuclear weapons and could have used them against an American invasion force without authorization from Moscow. Both counterfactuals, as presently constructed, ignored insubordination, mishap, and loss of control as possible causes of escalation.

Bandwagoning: The counterfactual argument that had the United States made concessions to the Soviet Union, the alliance would have been seriously weakened is difficult to evaluate, in part because of the failure to specify the consequent more carefully. As we observed earlier, a wide range of possible consequents is encompassed within the term "weakened"—from the dissolution of NATO, to bandwagoning of allies with the Soviet Union, to the creation of internal strains and stresses.

The underlying political dynamics of NATO at the time were fear of the Soviet Union and a desire to constrain Germany. A public missile exchange would have had no impact on the latter and might have increased the former—had allied leaders reasoned that Khrushchev would be emboldened by the outcome of the crisis. Historians of the alliance speculate that only if no prior consultation had preceded a public exchange of missiles—an unlikely contingency—would NATO have experienced serious strain (Risse-Kappen 1995).

Deterrence and Compellence: The new evidence is of considerable value in assessing the two Soviet counterfactuals. The first counterfactual argues that the United States would have invaded Cuba had the Soviet Union not deployed the missiles. There were extensive American preparations for invasion, monitored carefully by Cuban and Soviet intelligence, but no intention by the Kennedy administration to mount an attack. President Kennedy and Secretary of Defense McNamara had been impressed by the extent of Cuban popular support for Fidel Castro and the ability of Cuban forces and militia to overwhelm the refugee invasion force at the Bay of Pigs. Revised CIA estimates indicated that a successful invasion would require several hundred thousand U.S. forces and that they would have to remain as an occupation force for an indefinite period. Kennedy and McNamara were deterred by these costs and made clear to the CIA and the Pentagon their decision not to attack Cuba unless there was a dramatic change in the political situation inside Cuba. Khrushchev and his advisors were unambiguously wrong: Soviet missiles were not necessary to prevent an American attack.

Ironically, the Soviet missile deployment made an American invasion of Cuba more likely because of the foreign policy and domestic political problems it created for President Kennedy. Kennedy resisted pressures from militants in and outside the ExComm to launch an air strike against the missiles or an invasion of Cuba. The administration nevertheless accelerated its preparations to execute an invasion as a form of pressure. Tapes of ExComm meetings indicate that as the crisis wore on, the president became increasingly disenchanted with the military option because he feared that it would set in motion a cycle of unstoppable escalation.

Kennedy became more committed to a diplomatic resolution of the crisis and searched for compromises that might be acceptable to Khrushchev and the American public. Kennedy was accordingly prepared to respond positively to Khrushchev's suggestion that the United States commit itself not to invade Cuba in return for withdrawal of the Soviet missiles. On Saturday night, October 27, the president sent his brother, Attorney General Robert Kennedy, to offer Soviet ambassador Anatoliy Dobrynin what he thought might be a concession: if the Soviet Union withdrew its missiles from Cuba, the United States would remove its missiles from Turkey within approximately six months. Robert Kennedy insisted that the arrangement would have to remain secret because of the problems it would create for the administration with American public opinion and the NATO allies. That evening, the president considered a further concession: a public missile exchange to be carried out under the auspices of the United Nations. Kennedy's most intimate advisors—Theodore Sorensen, McGeorge Bundy, and Robert McNamara—believed that Kennedy would have agreed to a public exchange rather than use force against Cuba. If so, Khrushchev and his advisors were wrong again. The president did not intend to invade Cuba in the next twenty-four to forty-eight hours. Rather than use force, it is possible that the president would have agreed to Khrushchev's demand for a public missile exchange.

Quality and Validity

The new evidence about Soviet and American policy before, during, and after the missile crisis suggests that at least five of the counterfactuals are most likely invalid. Another seven are untestable, but three of these, the counterfactuals about escalation, the risk of war, and bandwagoning, are inadequate as presently formulated. The best fit with the available evidence is the counterfactual about the public deployment, but here too, a different consequent is plausible.

It is striking that in these twelve counterfactuals, there is no relationship between the quality of a counterfactual—the specification of antecedents and consequents and the specification of connecting principles—and its validity, or fit with the evidence. If we ignore for the moment the criterion of projectability, which is extraordinarily difficult to meet, five counterfactuals meet most of the criteria, but only one of them—the counterfactual about the public deployment of Soviet missiles—has a reasonable claim to validity. The others are either unambiguously wrong (the two Soviet counterfactuals) or untestable. The evidence further indicates that the logic of at least two of the untestable counterfactuals (escalation and risk of war) is probably wrong.

One historical case comprising twelve counterfactuals cannot sustain in a convincing way the null hypothesis that there is no relationship between quality and validity. Our examination of these counterfactuals nevertheless suggests some important questions about counterfactual argument, further tests of quality, and additional use of counterfactual argument in ways that may be helpful to policy makers and analysts.

Counterfactuals and Beliefs

The American and Soviet counterfactual arguments—explanatory or predictive—were largely a function of political belief systems (Chapter 3, Breslauer). The American counterfactuals were derived from deeply-held beliefs about the nature of international politics and the Soviet Union. The Soviet counterfactuals similarly grew out of ideological beliefs about capitalism and the United States.

The American counterfactuals about resolve and military capability were expressions of widely shared political beliefs: the Soviet Union was inherently aggressive and responded to opportunity defined as a questionable commitment; commitments are a seamless web and failure to respond to a challenge will erode all other commitments regardless of the nature of the interests at stake; allies have a tendency to bandwagon and a failure to stand up to the Soviet Union would have encouraged American allies to make separate accommodations with Moscow.

Counterfactuals, like other arguments, operationalize propositions based on these beliefs. Judging from the missile crisis, beliefs shaped arguments: in the absence of compelling evidence, the beliefs of officials and scholars determined the motives they attributed to the Soviet Union for deploying missiles in Cuba; their construction of the calculations of Soviets leaders; the salient attributes of the context, which, if different, might have led to a less encouraging calculus; and what the president might have done to alter those attributes.

In the missile crisis, the belief in the efficacy of deterrence led officials and analysts to emphasize the importance of capability and resolve and to build counterfactual arguments around changes in the military balance or Soviet perceptions of American resolve. Arthur Schlesinger, Jr., a distinguished historian and important figure in the Kennedy administration, confidently and unambiguously asserted that Khrushchev's decision to deploy missiles

> obviously represented the supreme probe of American intentions. No doubt, a "total victory" faction in Moscow had long been denouncing the government's "no-win" policy and arguing that the Soviet Union could safely use the utmost nuclear pressure against the United States because the Americans were too rich or soft or liberal to fight. (Schlesinger 1965, 798)

The argument is premised on a belief in deterrence and Schlesinger offered no supporting evidence. Admittedly, no information was available at the time about Soviet decisions. The absence of good evidence should, however, have led a skilled historian to consider competing arguments and make cautious judgments.

Our broader analysis of the missile crisis indicates that there are no structural differences in the arguments made about the past, present, and future. The dominant counterfactuals about the impact of resolve and military capability are distinguished only by their timing. Before the crisis, Kennedy and many of his advisors worried that Khrushchev would challenge the United States because he underestimated the president's resolve. During the crisis, they concluded that the missiles had been deployed because of the administration's apparent lack of resolve. After the crisis, they concluded, as did many analysts, that the missile deployment could have been prevented by more timely display of American resolve and extended the argument into the future. As time passed, the argument became a past counterfactual; Khrushchev would have challenged the United States in Berlin if Kennedy had not displayed resolve in Cuba. In their assumptions and logic, counterfactuals were indistinguishable from the other arguments American leaders made during the missile crisis.

Our first and most important conclusion is that the validity of counterfactuals is more closely related to the quality of their political assumptions than to their formal logic. If counterfactuals are based on political assumptions that capture the processes responsible for specified outcomes, they are more likely to be valid. Conversely, counterfactuals that are logical and adequately specified are likely to be wrong if they are based on flawed assumptions. The two Soviet counterfactuals were at least in part theory-derived and better specified than many of their American counterparts. They were also unambiguously wrong. Before and during the crisis, Cuban and Soviet intelligence carefully monitored the American military buildup in and around the Caribbean. Those preparations could be read as convincing evidence of American intentions to attack Cuba (this was the interpretation of Cuban and Soviet intelligence and political authorities) or as a display of resolve (which is how they were intended by the Kennedy administration). "Facts" rarely speak for themselves. The American buildup was consistent with both interpretations, and Cuban and Soviet officials, guided by Marxist ideology and worst-case assumptions about their adversary, drew the wrong conclusion.

The overriding importance of political assumptions in determining the validity of counterfactual argument has serious, negative implications for theory building and policy making. To the extent that the validity of counterfactuals depends on the accuracy of organizing political assumptions as well as on their completeness and logic, counterfactuals may well be hostages to history. All theories, as Tetlock and Belkin observe, rely implicitly or explicitly on counterfactual arguments, yet their validity may not be established or challenged until decades later. Even then, many important counterfactuals are likely to remain unfalsifiable because of absent or ambiguous evidence.

Theorists are understandably unprepared to wait for history to validate the respective merits of competing counterfactuals. Policy makers can wait even less than scholars for the verdict of history. They need to address immediate problems and rely for guidance on the lessons of the past, actual and counterfactual. Their policy choices, based on counterfactual argument, can make even initially incorrect counterfactuals self-fulfilling. The far-reaching intellectual and policy consequences of counterfactual arguments make it imperative to develop timely means of assessing their validity.

It is important to recognize that the internal attributes of counterfactuals alone cannot substantiate their validity. Identifying a "good" counterfactual may be less feasible and important, however, than rejecting a poor counterfactual. The incompleteness or illogic of a counterfactual constitutes important and sufficient grounds for its rejection even if the hypothesized consequent subsequently occurs. A hypothesized consequent may occur for reasons different from those posited by the counterfactual. It is possible, for example, that Khrushchev would not have responded to an American attack on Cuba with military action elsewhere. The evidence suggests, however, that his restraint would have been dictated by his fear of war, not of American military superiority. A counterfactual that predicts the right outcome for the wrong reasons is of no use because it is the logic, not the prediction, that we export to future cases. Conversely, if the logic predicts the outcome within acceptable range, rather than with pin-point accuracy, the counterfactual is of considerable value to policy makers and in theory building.

Testing Counterfactuals

In addition to the criteria proposed by Tetlock and Belkin, we propose three further tests of counterfactual arguments. Some of these tests deal, at least indirectly, with the impact of organizing political assumptions on the structure of the counterfactual. We are tempted to argue counterfactually that had these criteria been applied at the time, they would have exposed additional logical flaws that might have led to the questioning of some of the critical arguments that drove policy during the missile crisis.

(1) *Counterfactuals must specify the political logic that connects antecedents to consequents.* All the counterfactuals about the missile crisis were based on assumptions about the motivations and calculus of Soviet or American leaders. These assumptions were rarely articulated, although they provided the political mechanisms that linked antecedents to consequents. Good counterfactuals need to explicate and justify their critical political assumptions. They should also stipulate the kind of evidence that would increase confidence in their validity or lead to their rejection.

(2) *Counterfactuals need to address the interconnectedness of events.* Counterfactual arguments routinely assume that one aspect of the past can be changed and everything else kept constant. History is not, however, made of discrete, independent actions that allow for "surgical" counterfactuals. Given the interdependence of causes and the interaction effects, when one past event or decision is changed, it is likely that other aspects of the past will change as well. History can be likened to a spring mattress. If a spring is cut, or a weight is put on one part of the mattress, all the other springs and connectors will shift their location and tension to varying degrees. Good counterfactuals need to consider and specify what else might change as a result of the changed antecedent, the interaction of these changed variables, and how those changes would affect the probability of the hypothesized consequent.

(3) *Counterfactuals must recognize the possibility of additional consequents and address their implications.* A changed antecedent may produce many consequents in addition to the one hypothesized. Some of these consequents may have a significant impact on the central consequent. After the crisis, advocates of an air strike insisted that American military action against Cuba would not have provoked horizontal escalation by the Soviet Union. Even if they are correct, their counterfactual, as presently formulated, says nothing about any of the other possible consequences of the air strike. It is possible that an air strike could have hastened Khrushchev's overthrow and replacement, not by the relatively moderate Brezhnev, but by a hard-liner committed to avenging the humiliation of the Soviet Union. An air strike might also have provoked strong anti-American sentiment in West-

ern Europe and have been more damaging to the cohesion of NATO than a public exchange of missiles. If either outcome is plausible, the air strike, even if successful and unopposed, would not have been a wise option. Good counterfactuals need to go beyond the hypothesized consequent to identify other likely consequents and their theoretical or policy implications.

The additional tests we propose, together with the tests proposed by Tetlock and Belkin, may not be sufficient to validate counterfactual arguments. They will, however, draw attention to logical flaws and incompleteness. Scholars and policy makers alike are less likely to be persuaded by counterfactuals that fail several tests. If the "goodness" of counterfactuals cannot be established, at least poor counterfactuals can be rejected.

Counterfactuals as Sensitivity Analyses: Two Gedanken Experiments

Counterfactuals are necessary to imagine alternative worlds and to construct alternative futures as well as to test explanations of the past to assess their projectability to the future. Policy makers can use counterfactuals to assess how sensitive their choices are to alternative hypothetical antecedents and social scientists can use counterfactuals to identify critical turning points in the past and assess the contingency of their explanations.[6]

Drawing on the criteria developed by Tetlock and Belkin and the three we have added, we set ourselves the task of developing a counterfactual with the consequent: ". . . , then Khrushchev would not have deployed the missiles to Cuba." A valid counterfactual should not be inherently difficult to construct. The consequent is a "local" decision, rather than a large system effect, and we searched for hypothetical antecedents that were reasonably closely connected in time to the hypothesized consequent and that are conceivable rather than miracle causes.

The counterfactual we developed argued that if Kennedy had not publicly revealed the extent of U.S. strategic superiority, if he had not invaded the

---

[6] Bundy (1988, 407ff.) uses counterfactual arguments as a self-conscious form of gedanken experiment to assess the role of nuclear weapons in the missile crisis. Scholars are divided in their judgment of the role played by American nuclear versus local conventional superiority in bringing about Khrushchev's decision to withdraw the Soviet missiles from Cuba. Their arguments are difficult to evaluate because the United States had a decided advantage at both the strategic and local, conventional levels at the time of the crisis. To deal with the problem of covariation, Bundy asks the intriguing question of how the two leaders would have behaved if the nuclear balance had been reversed. His hypothetical reconstruction of American and Soviet policy highlights the different understandings Kennedy and Khrushchev had of the political meaning of the military balance, and more interestingly, how their understanding of each other's understanding might have affected their behavior. Bundy is sensitive to the likelihood that a change in the nuclear balance would have had other far-reaching consequences.

Bay of Pigs, and if he had not proceeded with the deployment of Jupiter missiles, then Khrushchev would not have deployed the missiles to Cuba. This counterfactual specifies multiple antecedents, draws on psychological theories for connecting principles, and passes the short-term test of consistency with the best available evidence. It is also projectable onto new or as yet unobserved cases in a generic form.

It does not, however, pass the test of a plausible world and would require an extensive rewrite of history. What else would have had to happen for Kennedy not to have committed these three actions? At a minimum, Khrushchev would have had to refrain from issuing an ultimatum on Berlin. Under what conditions is it conceivable that Khrushchev would have refrained? The German Democratic Republic would have had to be a functioning economy and society. This condition would require such a massive rewriting of history that Khrushchev's decision to deploy the missiles seems insensitive to a broad range of policies other than those the Kennedy administration chose in the two years preceding the crisis.

A second gedanken experiment yields quite different results. We constructed a counterfactual with the hypothesized consequent: ". . . , then Brezhnev would not have sent the letter to Nixon in October 1973." It was this letter, with its implicit ultimatum, that provoked an American alert of its strategic forces and a major crisis between the two superpowers. Three hypothetical antecedents, very closely connected in time, and logically connected through psychological principles, were easily specified. If the Soviet leadership had had good real-time battlefield intelligence, and if Kissinger had credibly reassured Brezhnev and President Anwar el-Sadat of Egypt of his commitment to halt Israel's military advance and rescue the trapped Egyptian army, then Brezhnev would not have sent the letter to Nixon. Two of the three antecedents were in Kissinger's option set, and the third, better intelligence, can be imagined if communication between Egypt and the Soviet Union had not broken down. This counterfactual consequently requires no extensive rewriting of history, and suggests that alternative policies may well have mattered.

The comparative analysis of counterfactuals allows analysts and policy makers to perform sensitivity analysis on choices that have been or will be made. It requires careful specification, rather than unquestioning assumption, of the motives of decision makers and, consequently, explicit attention to the political logic that shapes estimates of motives and attention. More broadly, it raises important questions of volition and contingency in broad historical processes and encourages the imagination of alternative futures.

6

Counterfactual Reasoning in Motivational Analysis

U.S. POLICY TOWARD IRAN

RICHARD K. HERRMANN AND MICHAEL P. FISCHERKELLER

ON MAY 25, 1986, Robert MacFarlane and Oliver North arrived in Tehran with HAWK missiles, the intention of meeting Iranian officials, and the hope that they could open a new chapter in U.S.-Iranian relations (Tower, Muskie, and Scowcroft 1987, 19–22, 104–21). National security advisor Admiral John Poindexter, like MacFarlane and North, was convinced that in the midst of political turmoil and a post-Khomeini succession struggle, the Soviet Union would move to establish influence over the northern Gulf. Moscow had already invaded Afghanistan and the Reagan administration had committed itself to allies among Islamic mujahideen. Perhaps Iranian leaders would see the danger and "save their asses from the Soviets," as Poindexter put it (Bill 1990, 166–79). "Moderate" Iranian leaders might also compel the Lebanese Hizbollah to release American hostages held in Beirut, including CIA station chief William Buckley.

Allies of Hizbollah in Tehran opposed Iran's alliance with the secular regime in Syria. They saw the powerful Speaker of the Majles, Ali Akbar Hashemi-Rafsanjani, as ready to sacrifice the messianic mission of the revolution to geopolitical expediency (Cottam 1989; Ramazani 1989). As these rivals of Rafsanjani acted to disrupt the alliance between Tehran and Damascus, the Iranian regime accused them of treason and called for the arrest of their principle operators. When Mehdi Hashemi was arrested, he decided not to go quietly. His faction told *Al Shiraa* in Lebanon that MacFarlane had been in Tehran and that Rafsanjani was dealing with the "Great Satan" (National Security Archive 1987, 37). The revelation opened the lid on the Reagan administration's most embarrassing scandal and led to the complete undoing of the U.S. initiative toward Iran.

Policy Makers and Counterfactuals

The Tower Commission and subsequent investigations into the National Security Council (NSC) operation produced a host of counterfactual speculations that illustrate some of the ways policy makers use counterfactuals. First, there was a public relations struggle over blame for troubles and claims of success. Oliver North, for instance, argued that if the Iranian initiative had not gone forward, then Lawrence Jenco, one of the American hostages held in Lebanon, would not have been released (Tower, Muskie, and Scowcroft 1987, 46–47). Other supporters of the initiative argued that had the mission's cover not been blown, then Washington would have had more leverage inside Iran when Ayatollah Khomeini died in 1989. Both Secretary of State Shultz and Secretary of Defense Weinberger, on the other hand, opposed the mission from the outset and argued that its tactics were amateurish and the hope for moderation in Iran naive (Tower, Muskie, and Scowcroft 1987, 28; Shultz 1993, 784–85). They noted that after Jenco's release, three new Americans were seized in Lebanon—perhaps as a consequence of the perception that Washington would trade arms for hostages.

Beyond public relations, counterfactuals were used to generate alternative visions of the future.[1] The entire initiative had been partly stimulated by a special national intelligence estimate in Washington that explored the possibilities for nationalist as distinct from religious messianic leaders in Tehran. In the 1990s, Americans typically see the search for moderates in Iran as ridiculous. The "rogue state" stereotype is now firmly in place. In 1985, however, images of Iran were less rigid than perceptions of the Soviet Union. Despite Mikhail Gorbachev's "new thinking," American leaders found it easier to imagine "moderates" in Iran than nonaggressive communists in Moscow. It was partly the perceived threat from Moscow that motivated counterfactual scenarios regarding what might be possible in Tehran.

Motivational attribution is a central task in policy making. Hans Morgenthau called it "the fundamental question that confronts the public officials responsible for the conduct of foreign policy as well as citizens trying to form an intelligent opinion on international issues" (Morgenthau 1973, 64). Assumptions about motivations, defined as the compound of factors that predispose a country to move in a certain direction in foreign affairs, determine the expectations leaders have regarding the reactions of another country to their country's behavior. Morgenthau concluded that the answer to the question about another's motives "has determined the fate of nations, and the wrong answer has often meant deadly peril or actual destruction: for upon the correctness of that answer depends the success of the foreign policy derived from it" (ibid.). It is the use of counterfactuals in making these motivational inferences that we study in this chapter.

Our discussion begins in the next section by looking at the relationship between forward-looking conditional scenarios and retrospective counterfactuals. We identify two retrospective counterfactuals that played an important

---

[1] For a discussion of future counterfactuals see Weber (Chapter 12).

role in American policy formulation and remain popular, one related to Moscow's motives and the other to the predispositions of Iranian leaders. We then turn to the evaluative task and find both counterfactuals to be unpersuasive when considered in light of the Tetlock and Belkin criteria. Our final section returns to the general problem of counterfactual reasoning in motivational analysis and examines the interdependency between idiographic cases and nomothetic generalizations. We question whether an assumption about the predispositional base of another country is an idiographic claim or a nomothetic generalization, whether it is based on statistical generalizations or theory-driven schemata, and whether the construction of deductive propositional tests, as argued for by Tetlock and Belkin, will solve the dilemmas facing motivational analysis.

What If Moscow Had Been Predisposed to Expand?

Although no one in the Reagan White House questioned Moscow's desire to expand its influence into the Persian Gulf, a national consensus on Soviet motives was far from evident. Certainly, from the Vietnam era onward many Americans had begun to doubt the stereotypical picture of the Soviet Union as a totalitarian expansionist state. Some policy makers and scholars saw the Soviet Union as at worst opportunistic; others described it as defensive and even committed to the status quo (Herrmann 1985, 3–21). As George Breslauer points out, interpretations of Soviet motives had direct implications for U.S. policy (Chapter 3, Breslauer). Expansionist and opportunistic interpretations justified containment and deterrence, while defensive perspectives supported more active efforts to pursue détente and reassurance strategies.

Although policy makers may at times close the question about another state's motivation, quite often they recognize a high degree of uncertainty. When this is the case, contingency planning and scenario construction are common exercises. Forward-looking conditional reasoning becomes counterfactual reasoning as officials reflect on the paths not taken. For example, Reagan administration officials argued that if Moscow had truly been motivated by a desire for détente, then it would not have deployed new medium-range missiles in Europe and new MIRVed ICBMs, and it would not have intervened in Angola, Ethiopia, and Afghanistan. These tests of Soviet motives may have been biased and simply reinforced existing views, but they nevertheless supported arguments that many Americans thought provided insight into Soviet motives.

Policy makers, like physicians, need to engage in case-specific diagnosis (George 1993). This may include proactive tests. Vice President George Bush, for example, may have shared Shultz's and Weinberger's judgment about Iranian motives, but he held open the possibility that in the context of the war with Iraq and the struggle within Tehran, Rafsanjani in return for arms and recognition might cut a deal on Soviet policy, Afghanistan, and the hostages in Lebanon. Bush was reluctant to accept conclusions about Iran's motives as operating assumptions. Instead, policy planning involved designing incremental probes to discover the intentions and bottom-line interests in Tehran.

The case studies that follow concentrate on interpretations of both Soviet and Iranian motives. We begin in 1946 with President Truman's claim that if he had not threatened the use of force, Stalin would not have abandoned northern Iran. This counterfactual came to play a large role in American interpretations of Soviet behavior, and has often been cited as evidence that when confronted with U.S. resolve, Moscow will retreat. Our examination of the U.S. decision to support the overthrow of Mohammed Mossadegh involves assessments of Soviet motives, and we examine judgments about Iranian nationalists as well.

What If Moscow Had Wanted to Dominate Iran?

If President Truman had not threatened the Soviet Union with forceful American action in 1946, Stalin would not have retreated from northern Iran and Moscow would have kept satellite governments in Azerbaijan and Kurdistan.

Background

The crisis over Azerbaijan was one of the first Soviet-American contests in the Cold War and the argument that U.S. strength and resolve produced a Soviet retreat became a defining lesson for U.S. policy makers and American interpretations of the Cold War. Secretary of State Acheson later used the case as critical evidence of Soviet expansionist motives and the effectiveness of U.S. threats (*Foreign Relations of the United States* [FRUS] 1949, 11:519). President Truman recalled in 1952 that only his ultimatum, backed by threats of the use of force, compelled Stalin to pull back (Grosnell 1980). This counterfactual claim continues to enjoy widespread academic popularity.

The Soviet Union occupied northern Iran during the Second World War, while the British controlled the south. To keep a vital lifeline open from the allies to Moscow, the Soviet Union concentrated on protecting transportation and communication routes even when this meant suppressing ethnic groups like the Kurds. In the fall of 1945, however, Soviet policy changed. It now backed Kurdish separatism and promoted Azeri secession. When in November 1945 Mohammed Pishevari proclaimed the formation of an autonomous Democratic Republic of Azerbaijan, Soviet troops moved to prevent an Iranian military response. With U.S. encouragement, Iran made a strong case at the United Nations against Soviet interference. After several months of tense Iranian-Soviet negotiations and U.S. support for the Iranian position, Moscow agreed to withdraw its forces from Iran. In May 1946, Soviet troops left Iran as Tehran opened discussions with the Azeri and Kurd governments. Before the close of the year, Iranian prime minister Ahmad Qavam sent Iranian troops to reestablish Tehran's control in these provinces. While the Kurds resisted to no avail, the Azeri government collapsed quickly. The Soviet Union made no military move to save either.

Analysis of the Counterfactual

We examine the plausibility of the counterfactual regarding Soviet behavior using the Tetlock and Belkin criteria, dividing our analysis into three sections. First, we determine whether the specified antecedent is consistent with well-established historical facts. Second, we examine the connecting principles that sustain the link between the antecedent and the consequent. Finally, we consider whether accepted statistical generalizations enhance the plausibility of the conditional claim.

The antecedent of the conditional claim above is: *If President Truman had not threatened the Soviet Union with forceful American action in 1946.* Four key events sustain the antecedent, though not necessarily implying the consequent:

1. The United States sent two strong notes of protest to the USSR on March 5 and 8, 1946.

2. The United States strongly supported the Iranian case in the UN Security Council once it was placed on the agenda by the Iranian Ambassador to the UN on March 18, 1946.

3. The United States directed the battleship *Missouri* toward Istanbul, Turkey, on March 6, 1946. It arrived on April 6, 1946.

4. The United States supported the Iranian effort to keep the case on the UN agenda after Moscow pressed Iranian prime minister Qavam to remove it from the agenda.

None of these actions individually or in combination necessarily sustains the link between the antecedent and the consequent. That is, these four events do not constitute a threat of forceful American action that could be expected to lead to a Soviet withdrawal. Consider, for example, the content of the notes of protest. The strongest wording appears in the March 5, 1946, note in which the United States says that it "cannot remain indifferent" to the Soviet policy of nonwithdrawal (FRUS 1946, 7:340–42, 341). Furthermore, as Bruce Kuniholm points out, the battleship *Missouri* departed for Istanbul without the accompanying task force that had been proposed to signal military resolve. The *Missouri*'s mission was to return the body of the Turkish ambassador to the United States, who had died recently in Washington, and was not related directly to the crisis in Iran (Kuniholm 1980, 335–36 n. 89, 335). The conditional's antecedent, U.S. compellence, is only partly consistent with historical facts. The "forcefulness" of the U.S. threat is very much in doubt.

We are still left, however, with the puzzle of why Stalin withdrew Soviet forces from Azerbaijan and Kurdistan. If Stalin was not compelled by U.S. threats, what motivated Soviet policy? Here the relationship between motivational inference and estimates of power becomes particularly complicated. Adherents to the popular conditional could argue that the U.S. possession of nuclear weapons compelled the withdrawal, despite the absence of any explicit threat or local military options. Although there is no mention or threat to use nuclear weapons in any U.S. communication with the Soviets, nuclear relationships are sufficiently ambiguous that a threat could have been perceived. This case would then be described as one of successful extended compellence. There is not much literature on compellence per se. Nonetheless, Huth and Russett (1984) examined the deterrent aspects of this case and have concluded along with others that three factors are important for successful extended deterrence: (1) the protégé must have a share of the defender's trade; (2) an arms transfer relationship between the defender and the protégé must exist; and (3) the protégé must have significant existing local capabilities. Presumably, these would be minimally necessary conditions for successful extended compellence.

In 1946, none of the conditions prevailed. The United States did not yet have a significant trading relationship with Iran. The United States did not consider furnishing arms and ammunition to Iran until October 18, 1946, five months after the Soviet withdrawal (FRUS 1946, 7:535–36). Neither Iran nor the United States had any significant local military capability compared to Moscow's local strength. American officials at the time were well aware of their military disadvantage and unenviable options.[2] Huth and Russett (1984, 517) concluded that the role of nuclear weapons in such cases is often "marginal, not one on which to put much weight." Huth (1990) has subsequently refined this statistical generalization in circumstances in which

---

[2] A telegram from the Department of State to the embassy in Tehran, for example, reads: "Soviet troop concentrations along northern border are now, and have been for some time past, adequate to overcome speedily any resistance Iran could offer. . . . Slight possible augmentation Iranian ground defenses could not hamper Soviet airborne operations in this connection" (FRUS 1947, 5:924–27, 925–26).

mutual assured destruction does not exist. He found that in non-MAD circumstances nuclear weapons facilitate extended deterrence without local military capability and without even an explicit nuclear threat. His generalization is partly based on his reading of the 1946 case as remembered by Truman. It rests on correlation, not evidence of causation. Although it can be taken as support for the conditional, it is hardly a persuasive argument for a compellence interpretation of the Soviet withdrawal. David Holloway's study of the Soviet archives (1994, 160, 224–27) concludes, as we do, that Stalin in this case did not perceive Truman as issuing a nuclear threat over Iran and was not intimidated by the role nuclear weapons would play in war.

Overall, the conditional fails to satisfy several of the standards proposed by Tetlock and Belkin. Most important, the antecedent is not consistent with well-established historical facts, and the available statistical generalizations only weakly support the conditional. Moreover, an alternative interpretation of the Soviet withdrawal fits the historical evidence more easily and does not depend on claims about nuclear deterrence that cannot be demonstrated without better access to Soviet thinking at the time.

To resolve the puzzle of Stalin's withdrawal, we can introduce a conditional of the following form: *If the United States and the Iranian prime minister had appeased Stalin in 1946, Stalin would have retreated from northern Iran and not kept satellite governments in Azerbayan and Kurdistan.* This explanation is consistent with a number of the policies initiated by Iranian prime minister Qavam and summarized in a telegram from the U.S. Chargé in Iran to the U.S. State Department:

> He has (a) made oil deal[3] (b) offered quite liberal terms to Azerbaijan (c) vacillated in his position with reference to Security Council and ultimately yielded to Soviet pressure in asking that the case be dropped (d) Arrested Seyid Zia-ed-Din, General Arfa, and certain lesser lights hostile to Russians; suppressed most outspoken anti-Soviet newspapers and released from suspension all Left publications; transferred or dismissed many army officers and Government officials considered anti-Soviet. (e) Removed ban on Tudeh [the communist party in Iran] meetings; appointed or permitted appointment of many Tudeh members, or sympathizers to posts in Government; definitely recognized Tudeh labor organization (although labor unions have no legal status in Iran) and even appointed its leader, Rusta, as member of a new Higher Labor Council. (f) Consistently been conciliatory in his public statements regarding Azerbaijan question and issued positive orders to security forces to refrain from attacking or provoking Democrats and not to enter Azerbaijan until given specific permission by himself (FRUS 1946, 7:437–40, 439).

[3] On April 4, 1946, a Soviet-Iranian agreement promised Moscow 51 percent of a publicly owned Soviet-Iranian oil company, contingent on the approval of the Fifteenth Majles. Moscow agreed to withdraw Soviet forces by May 6, 1946.

Compiling a list of reassuring American actions toward the Soviet Union in the period is not so direct a task. Perhaps the most important characteristic of U.S. policy, as far as Stalin was concerned, was that it diverged from British policy. Washington supported neither British efforts to control all of Iran nor London's revival of the "great game" with Russia in Southwest Asia (L. C. Brown 1984). If capitalist encirclement and British competition in Iran were important concerns in Moscow (Cottam 1988, 68), then Washington's acquiescence to a Soviet-Iranian oil agreement, U.S. support for the anti-British Qavam government,[4] and the nature of U.S. representations to Qavam could have reassured Soviet leaders about benign American intentions. They would stand, therefore, as historical facts consistent with the reassurance proposition.

We have no statistical generalizations about reassurance moves, but find the appeasement argument as plausible as Truman's conditional claim. After all, important U.S. diplomats such as Loy Henderson (director of Middle East affairs at the State Department) wanted Qavam replaced with someone who would take a tough anti-Soviet line. Others, including Secretary of State Dean Acheson, saw Iranian nationalism as an important force that Washington needed to support in order to contain communism. He constrained Henderson's efforts to promote a pro-shah, pro-British strong man in Tehran.

Despite the weakness of Truman's conditional, the lessons drawn from the case by U.S. policy makers shortly afterward were: (1) U.S. force was effective in limiting Soviet action, and (2) Moscow would not risk confrontation to dominate Iran, but rather would work through subversion (FRUS 1949, 11:519).[5]

By 1953 both the Soviet and Iranian governments had changed and U.S. policy makers were faced with a new situation. Malenkov was part of a

[4] For example, as they considered removing Qavam, U.S. Ambassador Allen reported, "I have frequently cautioned him [the shah] during conversations regarding Qavam that he should consider carefully the alternative. If he should force out present Cabinet and substitute for it reactionary regime regarded by Iranians as British stooges result would be short lived" (FRUS 1946, 7:523). The U.S. Chargé in Iran wrote that the "danger is that Qavam, in pursuing his modified appeasement policy, will be forced to acquiesce in constant strengthening of Russian-backed groups to point at which he will be left only with choice of knuckling under entirely or being overthrown in favor of true puppet government" (FRUS 1946, 7:440).

[5] Dean Acheson concludes: "The evidence which we can assemble here points to the conclusion that the Soviet Union does not want to risk war in the near future and that its activities in the Near East, including Iran, will therefore not go beyond the sort of pressures and subversive attempts to which it has resorted during the past two years. The evidence also seems to lend itself to the interpretation that the Kremlin fears open aggression against Iran would involve it in grave risk of conflict in the United States. *If this were not the case, it would be difficult to explain why Soviet forces have so far refrained from entering Iran despite the obvious Russian designs on that country and the equally obvious physical weakness of Iran*" (FRUS 148, 11:519, emphasis added).

transition in Moscow and Mohammed Mossadegh was prime minister in Iran. Of course, a new government was in office in Washington, as well, and approached the scene with both new urgency and new perspectives.

If the United States had not successfully ousted Mossadegh, then Moscow would have dominated Iran.

Background

On August 20, 1953, Dr. Mohammed Mossadegh surrendered to the Iranian forces loyal to General Fazlullah Zahedi. Mossadegh's arrest signaled the conclusion of the CIA operation code-named AJAX. The planning for the overthrow had begun in February 1953, almost immediately after the Eisenhower administration took office (Cottam 1988, 103; Gasiorowski 1991, 74). The CIA and British MI-6 used propaganda, money, and other favors for nearly a year to undermine public and legislative support for Mossadegh's National Front (Roosevelt 1979). Then, on August 16, 1953, the shah issued an order, as was his monarchical privilege, replacing Prime Minister Mossadegh with General Zahedi.

Although the British had consistently opposed Iranian nationalism, the change in U.S. policy was dramatic. The most significant reason for the change was the election of Dwight Eisenhower. John Foster Dulles may have agreed with Acheson about the threat posed by the Soviet Union, but he had a radically different perspective on Iranian nationalism and Mossadegh (Roosevelt 1979, 103 n. 119). Dulles and the National Security Council compared Iran to China, saw grave risks in the nationalist government, and vowed not to lose another country to communism (Gasiorowski 1991, 82–83).[6]

Anxious to show the importance of the "New Look" in foreign policy, the Eisenhower administration decided to reverse the Truman-Acheson policy of trying to stabilize the Nationalist government in Tehran. The CIA redirected its BEDAMN operation, which had been designed to discredit the commu-

---

[6] Also see FRUS (1952–54, 10:530), where the National Security Council argues that the loss of Iran to the Soviets would

a. Be a major threat to the security of the entire Middle East, including Pakistan and India. b. Permit communist denial to the free world of access to Iranian oil and seriously threaten the loss of other Middle Eastern oil. c. Increase the Soviet Union's capability to threaten important United States–United Kingdom lines of communication. d. Damage United States prestige in nearby countries and with the exception of Turkey and possibly Pakistan, seriously weaken, if not destroy, their will to resist communist pressures. e. Set off a series of political and economic developments, the consequences of which would seriously endanger the security interests of the United States.

nist Tudeh party in Iran, toward undermining the National Front (Gasiorowski 1991, 69). Loy Henderson, now the U.S. ambassador in Tehran,
was mobilized to persuade a reluctant shah to dump Mossadegh in favor of
Zahedi (Cottam 1988, 107; Gasiorowski 1991, 76). Initially, the coup plan
Dulles put in motion failed, defeated by Mossadegh's refusal to comply.

With Zahedi protected in a CIA safe house, Ambassador Henderson, who
had arranged to be out of the country on the day the shah and Zahedi were to
make their move, quickly returned to Tehran from Switzerland (Cottam
1988, 107 n. 123). On August 17, Tudeh party supporters came into the
street to protest the American-engineered plot (ibid., 107–8). A number of
former CIA officers claim that these were actually "fake" Tudeh protestors,
part of a $50,000 plan to create a provocation that would mobilize Iranian
fear of a communist takeover (Gasiorowski 1991, 78–79). Reportedly, CIA
agents then escalated the protest by violently attacking symbols of the shah
and the clergy. As the protest escalated, Ambassador Henderson demanded
that Mossadegh stop the violence. On August 18, Mossadegh did call out
the police to restore order, but the next day, in response to the apparent
Tudeh attack on religious symbols, Ayatollah Kashani—the only figure who
might rival Mossadegh for populist support—brought his supporters into the
street (Cottam 1988, 61, 92–93, 108). Meantime, Zahedi declared martial
law and sent troops loyal to him to capture key communication and government facilities. On August 19, they attacked Mossadegh's house, forcing his
surrender the next day. A little more than a year later, the CIA leaked the
story of their "success" in Iran to the *Saturday Evening Post* (Harkness and
Harkness 1954).

Analysis of the Counterfactual

Policy makers in Washington considered several scenarios that would lead to
Soviet domination in Iran, focusing on both internal and external contingencies.[7] The National Security Council described the internal scenario as follows: "The overthrow of the present Iranian Government and the establishment of a pro-Soviet puppet government by subversive or other means not
involving the use of Soviet military force . . . the weakness of the Iranian
government and the growing activity of dissident elements, including the
Tudeh Party (despite the fact that this party is outlawed and has to function
underground) make this event a possibility" (FRUS 1952–54, 10:16).

In outlining the external scenario, the NSC focused on "an overt invasion
of Iran by the armed forces of the Soviet Union. . . . The possibility of such
an attack cannot be excluded, since the Soviet Union has the military capa-

---

[7] For a list of these scenarios see FRUS (1952–54, 10:16–19).

bility of launching an attack without warning and quickly overrunning Iran" (FRUS 1952–54, 10:18).

Although the consequent in these contingencies is Soviet domination of Iran, the counterfactual's connecting principles require scrutiny. Two key principles connect the ouster of Mossadegh to the prevention of a Soviet takeover. The first is that Zahedi's policies would provide greater socio-political stability in Iran and eliminate the otherwise likely Tudeh seizure of power. The second is that Zahedi's policies enhanced Iran's military ability to deter Soviet incursion.

Central to internal scenarios were judgments about the Tudeh Party. In November 1952, the CIA reported that "it is now estimated that communist forces will probably not gain control of the Iranian Government in 1953" (FRUS 1952–54, 10:531; Gasiorowski 1991, 80). In February 1953, Mossadegh ordered the arrest of Tudeh leaders and again in August used force against the communists (FRUS 1952–54, 10:752; Gasiorowski 1991, 74). U.S. officials concluded in early 1953 that "if he [Mossadegh] succeeds confirming the dissolution of the Majles through referendum as now seems probable . . . Prime Minister will then be in position destroy remaining opposition leaving him unchallenged and in absolute control" (FRUS 1952–54, 10:737). Reviewing the available historical material in the 1980s, Gasiorowski concluded that in early 1953 each of Mossadegh's domestic rivals were weakened or eliminated.[8] In November 1953, the CIA reached the same conclusion as it had before the ouster of Mossadegh, reporting that "Tudeh's capabilities do not constitute a serious present threat to the Iranian Government, and the Tudeh Party will probably be unable to gain control of the country during 1954, even if it combines with other extremist groups" (FRUS 1952–54, 10:837).

Certainly, after Zahedi took power he suppressed the Tudeh, closed its newspapers, and banned its demonstrations. Ambassador Henderson reported that "fears aroused that Tudeh planning to make surprise counterattack proved unfounded. If Tudeh really had such plan it foiled by police precautions which did not permit gathering large crowds" (FRUS 1952–54, 10:757). It is possible that Zahedi's martial law did prevent a Tudeh "counterattack." The critical point here, however, is that the Tudeh move at this point would have been a "counterattack," an attack that would have been made more, not less, likely by the American action against Mossadegh.

---

[8] Gasiorowski (1991, 80) supports this argument by stating that "Sayyid Zia and Qavam had disappeared from the scene; the British had been expelled; Kashani had lost much of his support in the Majles; and Zahedi had failed twice to oust Mossadegh and had gone into hiding to evade an arrest warrant." Based on these facts, he concludes: "Indeed, aside from the Tudeh party, which was still relatively weak at this time, *no* Iranian political group or figure appears to have been capable of ousting Mossadeq in the summer of 1953 without substantial foreign assistance."

Most historical evidence suggests that neither Mossadegh nor Zahedi was likely to be defeated by the Tudeh. In this regard, Mossadegh's replacement with Zahedi was *causally irrelevant* to the sociopolitical stability of Iran.[9] As an antecedent it did not make the connecting principle of a Tudeh takeover less probable. If we put heavy emphasis upon Iranian nationalist indignation over the American and British plot, we could conclude that Operation AJAX even increased the odds that Tudeh might try to seize power by force.

Dulles assumed that Iranians would accept a government led by traditional elites aligned with outside concerns as long as general economic conditions continued to improve. If Dulles's assumption was true, then Mossadegh's replacement by Zahedi could be connected to enhanced internal stability. It certainly was related to increased Iranian revenues. In the three months after Mossadegh's overthrow, the United States provided $73 million to the Zahedi regime, a figure equal to almost half of all Iranian government expenditures in 1952 (Cottam 1988, 111). Moreover, Washington transferred $45 million to Iran to alleviate the damage done by the British embargo that had followed Tehran's nationalization of the Anglo-Iranian Oil Company (AIOC). The nationalization of AIOC in April 1951 damaged British revenues and motivated London to push for Mossadegh's overthrow (Cottam 1988, 102; Gasiorowski 1991, 62).[10] The State Department concluded after the coup that it would be unwise for Zahedi to enter into negotiations with the British about the oil dispute and instead provided Iran $110 million in aid. This aid represented nearly 55 percent of Iranian government expenditures and more than three times Iran's oil revenues in 1950, the last year of full production (Cottam 1988, 112).

Although the American decision to replace Mossadegh was undoubtedly related to Washington's subsequent decision to provide aid, it is not clear that this increased revenue forestalled what otherwise would have been economic collapse and Tudeh ascendence. The historical evidence supports a connecting principle, but the relationship to the overall counterfactual is complicated. The British embargo reduced the revenues available to Mossadegh's government and in turn reduced its ability to maintain political stability. The CIA and MI-6 operations against the National Front did not help, either. But the historical record does not suggest that Iran was about to fall into economic chaos and popular revolt against Mossadegh in the midst of which the Tudeh or Moscow might move.

To the contrary, even without oil sales, which had accounted for two-thirds of Iranian foreign-exchange revenue, Mossadegh's stimulative fiscal

[9] For a discussion of causal irrelevance and purely positive causal relevance see Kvart (1986).

[10] In 1950 the AIOC earned $93 million in profit and the British government collected $142 million in tax revenues from it.

policies in 1952 reduced unemployment below 1951 levels (FRUS 1952–54, 10:878; Gasiorowski 1991, 79–80). In May 1953, the U.S. economic attaché in Tehran described business as "brisk," and just before the coup the U.S. Chargé in Iran reported: "Brightest spot in present situation is export prospects, particularly carpets, rice, and barley. Government estimates exports may be increased as much as 50 percent by volume over last year, thus providing exchange necessary for essential imports" (FRUS 1952–54, 10:743). Surely, had the U.S. government decided to shower Mossadegh with the money it provided Zahedi, the prospects for the Iranian economy under Mossadegh would have been much brighter than they were, but this does not imply that had Mossadegh stayed in power, economic collapse and internal communist takeover were inevitable or even likely. If Moscow was going to move successfully against Iran, whether Mossadegh's or Zahedi's, it would most likely need to do so from the outside with military force.

With regard to the external scenario, however, none of the factors taken as accepted generalizations regarding the effectiveness of extended deterrence were much more in evidence in 1953 than they were in 1946.[11] Moreover, Washington's monopoly on nuclear capability had been broken, thereby weakening the plausibility that implicit U.S. nuclear threats deterred Moscow. Moscow enjoyed substantial logistic and conventional military advantages in the area, whether Mossadegh or Zahedi was in power. Contrary to the counterfactual, it is possible that with Mossadegh in power the Soviets would have faced more determined nationalist resistance, but in neither case would the Soviet Union have faced comparable countervailing military power.

After developing a series of scenarios outlining how Moscow might take over Iran, American policy makers did not reflect long on why Moscow did so little to respond to the coup against Mossadegh. As in 1946, they apparently assumed that Moscow lacked the capability to respond to the coup effectively. Once again holding their estimates of Soviet motives constant, policy makers drew conclusions about Soviet power from the lack of action. The fact that these conclusions were inconsistent with their prior estimates of Moscow's internal and external options—as well as inconsistent with

---

[11] U.S.-Iranian trade was still small. There were two U.S. military advisory missions in Iran in addition to the Military Assistance Advisory Group. From its inception in 1950 to the end of 1953, U.S. military assistance to Iran had programmed $101.4 million, of which $45.9 million had been delivered. U.S. officials concluded in January 1954: "Inadequate training, maintenance, and supply capabilities, and low caliber personnel restrict Iran's capability to absorb U.S. military equipment, even at the present rate of delivery. . . . Iranian forces may be able to improve their capability for guerrilla and limited mountain operations, although it is unlikely that they could in themselves become capable within the foreseeable future of effectively delaying a strong Soviet thrust toward . . . the Persian Gulf" (FRUS 1952–54, 10:868).

empirical evidence about the military balance in the theater—did not appear to cause as much consternation in 1953 as it had in 1946. By 1953, enemy images of the Soviet Union were well developed in Washington and included the expectation that Bolsheviks would probe for opportunities and weakness but retreat in the face of American will and resolve. Although few American policy makers might have expected the United States to remain passive in the face of a Soviet-orchestrated coup in a country sharing a 1,600-mile border with the United States, there is little evidence that officials in the Eisenhower administration found Moscow's acceptance of Mossadegh's overthrow puzzling.

Moscow, of course, was not completely passive in the face of the CIA-orchestrated coup. *Pravda* and other Soviet newspapers complained bitterly that Washington, dissatisfied with a client regime in Tehran, had acted to establish a satellite government. The Eisenhower administration had sided with the British and encircled the Soviet Union precisely as Stalin had warned in 1946. Beyond the press barrage and diplomatic protests, however, Moscow did little—evidently deciding not to send troops back into Kurdistan or Azerbaijan or otherwise challenge the American move. Apparently, Iran did not command sufficient priority in Moscow to motivate committed action. Events in the periphery may have taken a back seat to central preoccupations such as the political transition following Stalin's death the previous March and the controversy surrounding the rearmament of Germany.

Iran soon came to play a role in the Baghdad Pact and American containment policy that continued throughout the 1950s and 1960s. The U.S. commitment to the shah increased over the years in nearly all dimensions, as did the Iranian public's inclination to see Washington's support as key to the survival of the shah's regime. Moreover, Mossadegh's charisma having been broken and the National Front having failed to defend the government from outside interference, conservative Islamic leaders became the main agents mobilizing opposition to the shah and Iran's "client" relationship with Washington. It is tempting to consider a counterfactual that sets as its antecedent U.S. support for Mossadegh in 1953 and as its consequent the avoidance of both an Islamic and anti-American revolution in 1978. With twenty-five years separating the cause and effect, however, the complexity of the necessary connecting principles is unmanageable and subject to countless possible intervening historical contingencies.[12] Rather than head into this tunnel, we will return to the more general problem of motivational analysis and counterfactual reasoning.

---

[12] See Fearon (Chapter 2) and Breslauer (Chapter 3) for discussions of the importance of proximity in counterfactual analysis.

What If Motivation Were an Empirical Question?

Differentiating between states with different motives remains extremely difficult. The same motives can lead to different actions and different motives can lead to the same actions. Correlational analysis will not suffice without complicated situational assessments and some way to decipher propaganda and behavioral feints. Realists simplify matters by assuming that all states define their interests in terms of power, treating means as ends. Neorealists accept a similar simplification, assuming all states seek security. These theoretical assumptions are not empirically based statistical generalizations, although they operate as nomothetic claims in international relations theory.

Actor-specific diagnostics are critical in policy-relevant theory and good science (George 1993, 125–31). The paradox is that despite the critical strategic importance of the motivational question at the idiographic level, we have no good way to answer it. In this regard, disciplined counterfactual reasoning can play a useful role for policy makers and scholars alike. In evaluating our counterfactuals, we found it difficult to rely on statistical generalizations and agreed-upon laws. There are very few laws in political science, and the 1946 case presented a problem for statistical generalizations. Interpretations of the 1946 case that accept the Truman counterfactual as true have played an important role in the data sets from which generalizations about deterrence and compellence have been drawn. We found that the archival record did not support this treatment of the 1946 case. Challenging the single case may not undermine the data sets, but it draws attention to the essential role idiographic case knowledge must play as a foundation for nomothetic generalizations.

Because motivation in world politics is difficult to determine, analysts may rely on generalizations to interpret specific cases. In 1946, for instance, a general theory of power-driven states may have led American policy makers to expect a Soviet move in Iran. By 1953 an enemy image of Moscow prevailed in Washington and provided a specific theory of Soviet behavior that resembled the stereotypical image outlined by Nathan Leites (1951) in his classic operational code of Bolsheviks. From 1953 on, this enemy image provided the interpretation of Soviet motives, often in a theory-driven way. That is, U.S. policy makers allowed the prior theory about Soviet motives to explain Moscow's action rather than looking carefully at the action to infer motivation. The generalizations that drove these interpretations might be considered nomothetic at two different levels of analysis.

At an interstate level of analysis, Moscow's motives might be compared to the motives of other states. In this regard, power determinists, who assume that all states seek maximum power, might see Moscow as expansionist and be predisposed to accept the Truman counterfactual and the 1953 counterfactual. They might also find persuasive the general counterfactual that posited, "If Moscow could have dominated Iran, then it would have." Neorealists, on the other hand, who see all states as security maximizers, might emphasize the defensive interests of Moscow and should be predisposed to see a spiral security dilemma and, in turn, entertain the reassurance interpretation we advance for 1946.[13]

Second, at a foreign policy level, we could imagine theories related only to Soviet behavior, where nomothetic refers not to all states but to the Soviet Union across multiple situations and time periods. In this way, an expansionist theory of Soviet behavior would be a generalization that supports the plausibility of Truman's and Eisenhower's counterfactual claims. The widespread appeal of such theories in the United States could explain why the counterfactuals, which are quite weak by Tetlock and Belkin's criteria, have so often been accepted as true by Americans. Generalizations about Soviet behavior that stress defensive motives would, of course, cast doubt on the counterfactuals. We could treat these competing generalizations about Soviet behavior as statistical base rates, but unfortunately, the methodologies that underpin the creation of these generalizations have not been very persuasive.

To a large degree, both expansionist and defensive theories of Soviet behavior have been formulated in ways that are not falsifiable (Herrmann 1985). Terms are not well defined and operational measures not well developed. Another part of the problem is the dilemma pointed to by King, Keohane, and Verba (1994). Rather than treating the motivational claims as competing propositions that should be connected to deduced consequences and then tested against behavioral evidence, political advocates on all sides often assert their motivational claim as if it were self-evident. Enemy stereotypes provided American policy makers with theory-driven interpretations of Soviet behavior in 1953 and 1985, and retrospectively for Soviet behavior in 1946.

Policy makers, however, are not always so certain about the adversary's motives. This was the case for the United States vis-à-vis Iran in 1985. In this circumstance, policy makers were prepared to follow King, Keohane, and Verba's advice and use diplomatic probes to test motivational propositions. When they did this, however, operationalizing competing motivational theories was not easy. The dilemma goes beyond King, Keohane, and Verba's appeal for traditional behavioralism or Tetlock and Belkin's logical criteria.

To generate a behavioral expectation it is necessary to apply a motivational theory to a complex political and regional context. It may be possible to conclude that a certain layer of mineral dust should follow from a meteorite impact, as King, Keohane, and Verba (1994) discuss, but calculating

---

[13] See, for example, Waltz (1979).

what effects should follow from an expansionist or defensive Soviet Union depends on a host of situational and regional assumptions that are just as controversial as the central motivational proposition. There is often little agreement about what the observable difference would be between an expansionist as opposed to a defensive state. This traditional problem is recognized by Barry Weingast in his discussion of how off-the-path behavior can generate an "observational equivalence" between two different worlds (Chapter 10). The problems involved in the operational specification of the expectations, especially the host of auxiliary contextual theories and assumptions necessary, are significantly more vexing than the notion of direct observation implies (Simon 1985).

Without reifying our concepts, direct observation of motivational cause is impossible. The best we can do is observe the consequences that follow from the propositional motive. In world politics, the theoretical connection between motivational causes and expected consequences is unclear and controversial. In our cases, connecting principles rested on both situational claims and complicated auxiliary propositions. Although Tetlock and Belkin had pointed in the right direction, we found it necessary to decompose the plausibility, logic, and case-specific applicability of connecting principles. A more elaborate strategy for proceeding in this direction is needed and a fully satisfactory analysis of our cases in this regard would require a book. Particularly difficult is assessing the cumulative effect of several connecting claims.

We also found that in evaluating counterfactual claims, motivational propositions were intricately connected to estimates of relative power. In constructing persuasive motivational probes, policy makers need to define the options available to the other actor. Only by doing this can they decide whether the actor's response should be attributed to dispositional motives or situational imperatives. A country's decision not to pursue a policy objective that is vastly beyond its capability carries little motivational information. Estimates of power and the options available, however, are often as controversial as motivational attributions. Consider, for instance, whether Iran in 1985 had the power to spread its messianic version of Islam beyond Iran. Could it rely on its resources and the appeal of its message to promote political change in Lebanon, Syria, and the Arab Gulf? Some secular Arab regimes, as well as conservative religious Gulf states like Saudi Arabia, feared that it did. They were ready to finance Iraq's war effort and were alarmed by the double-dealing revealed in the MacFarlane mission. The CIA, on the other hand, was convinced that the revolutionary regime could not prevail and would need outside assistance (Tower, Muskie, and Scowcroft 1987, 20–21, 112–21).

In 1946 and 1953, American policy makers' estimates of Soviet power shifted before and after the event. Beforehand, American policy makers saw

Soviet options and substantial Soviet power advantages. Afterward, they attributed the Soviet decision to withdraw or not to do more to dominate Iran to a lack of Soviet options or to some notion that the costs of domination outweighed the benefits. Of course, the costs were partly a function of the relative power relationship. Beforehand, the costs deterring or compelling Moscow were seen to be too little, touching off the general alarm and crisis in the first place. Then after the event, with no real change in the power relationship, American decision makers concluded that Moscow did not have options, learning more about Soviet power from the case than about Soviet motives. Interestingly, even though the Soviet decision not to compete aggressively in Iran, even when the costs were relatively low, could have provided information revealing that Moscow was not determined to expand there, few Americans reexamined their estimates of Soviet intentions.

Many Americans believe that U.S. nuclear threats deterred Moscow. In 1946, it appears unlikely that any nuclear threat was made, although the simple possession of nuclear capability may have conveyed the warning. In the later years, the situation was equally ambiguous. It is possible that NATO's dependence on Gulf oil was so great that this interest implied a credible nuclear threat even without explicit statements. In either case, the ambiguity and uncertainty involved in trying to determine what inaction and action can be ascribed to nuclear threats complicate the analysis of the counterfactuals and illustrate just one of the host of contextual auxiliary connecting principles that sustain the motivational and counterfactual propositions.

Finally, we found that in judging counterfactuals in world politics the prior history is not always obvious. Rather than a fixed starting point that the analyst can change to reason about alternative consequences, the original motives are often in dispute. We implied as much when we asked what Moscow would have done if it were expansionist. We are fully aware that for many readers this will not appear as a counterfactual antecedent, but as a true antecedent. After forty years of active debate, the core motivational dynamics of the Cold War are still in dispute, however. Assertions about consensus reflect political conventions more than academic agreement. This becomes immediately evident if we treat academics as a worldwide community, as physical scientists might, and not restrict the community to North Americans.

The process of examining the conditional claims that connect motivation to behavior in light of the Tetlock and Belkin criteria is useful. It can weaken the hold of prior beliefs and reopen the empirical question. We do not disagree with Robyn Dawes's preference for statistical norms and nomothetic patterns, but we are concerned that too often in world politics what is taken as a base rate or generalization about the motives of another country is too much an ideological conviction and too little a product of deductive and empirical behavioral science (Commentary 3, Dawes). Examining the conditional expectations that are said to test motives, or retrospectively looking at the counterfactual routes not taken, compels scholars and policy makers alike to reexamine the causal judgments resting at the center of their interpretations.

We doubt that the Tetlock and Belkin criteria will overcome all of the obstacles to motivational analysis recognized by foreign-policy analysts, but they provide a preliminary outline for examining causal reasoning. It is a demanding set of criteria that reminds us of the uncertainty involved in political analysis. This may frustrate those looking for deterministic parsimony and embarrass those who claim they have already found powerful and predictive theories of world politics. The criteria can help us, however, by opening questions that have been prematurely closed either by the political intrusion Breslauer describes or by self-serving and convenient psychological processes. If policy makers are encouraged to look back at the counterfactual developments they expected to occur that did not, then they might be able to improve the lessons they derive from historical experience and judge better the factors moving the adversaries with whom they must deal. The analysis of counterfactuals would not serve as evidence, but rather, play a critical role in the assessment of what the observable behavior means. If this helps policy makers avoid self-defeating strategies based on misjudgments about the motives of their adversaries, then this would be no small contribution indeed.

Part Three ⎯⎯⎯⎯⎯⎯⎯⎯⎯⎯⎯⎯⎯⎯⎯⎯⎯⎯⎯⎯

COUNTERFACTUAL ANALYSIS OF
CLASSES OF EVENTS

7

Counterfactuals about War and Its Absence

BRUCE RUSSETT

> MANY LIBERALS and socialist revisionists deny, or at least minimize, the possibility that wars would occur in a world of political or social democracies. An understanding of the third image makes it clear that the expectation would be justified only if the minimum interest of states in preserving themselves became the maximum interest of all of them—and each could rely fully upon the steadfast adherence to this definition by all of the others. Stating the condition makes apparent the utopian quality of liberal and socialist expectations. (Waltz 1959, 227)

Here is a triple counterfactual: The world was not, in 1959, composed entirely of social or political democracies.[1] It certainly was not a world without war. And that the maximum interest of all states could reside only in preserving themselves seemed an unimaginable counterfactual, a *reductio ad absurdum*. Being such a complex counterfactual, this quotation also probably represented a statement that appeared beyond any challenge through systematic empirical testing.

It is no longer so. Whereas the world is not yet—and may never be—composed entirely of political democracies, by reasonable standards approximately half the states in the international system of the 1990s are arguably democratic, if often newly and unstably democratic. War between stable democratic states is, empirically, at most a very rare phenomenon. Within that subset of the international system, therefore, the absence of war has become a fact, not a counterfactual assertion of what might in some utopia come to pass. Whether war might remain absent, or virtually so, in an international system composed entirely of democratic states is, if not known or fully knowable, at least more deserving of consideration. Could a world of sovereign democracies be a world without war? And whereas Waltz's condition about maximum interest may still seem utopian, various analysts—whether emphasizing the role of normative restraints or game theorists offering a new interpretation of rational action—have begun to specify mecha-

[1] Portions of this chapter previously appeared in: Bruce Russett. 1995. The democratic peace: "And yet it moves." *International Security* 19 (4): 164–75. ©1995 by the President and Fellows of Harvard College and the Massachusetts Institute of Technology.

nisms whereby, even in an anarchic world, democratic states might resolve their conflicts of interest by means short of war.

The empirical status of the central component of the paragraph above— that war between democracies is very rare—remains subject to challenge, however. Dissents take two forms: One holds that the number of democratic states, and the number of all wars, in the modern international system has been so small that by standard scientific criteria the absence of wars between democracies is statistically insignificant, not needing any special explanation. The other kind of challenge asserts that the absence of wars between democracies can readily be explained on other grounds. For example, there are good "realist" reasons why rich, or allied, or distant states rarely fight each other, and the attribution of the absence of wars between democracies to the sharing of democratic norms and institutions is merely an artifact of statistical collinearity. Or, many instances wherein democracies failed to go to war with each other can be attributed to other influences, primarily the absence of sufficient interest or strategic motivation. By any of these versions, the observation of few or no wars between democracies is not worthy of notice.

I contend, rather, that the assertion of few deadly conflicts existing between democracies is in reality a highly "significant" (statistically, substantively, theoretically) factual statement. I do not claim that we should jettison the insights of realism that tell us that power and strategic considerations affect states' decisions to fight each other. But neither should one deny the limitations of those insights, and their inability to explain many of the instances when liberal states have chosen not to fight or threaten one another. The danger resides in "vulgar realism's" vision of war of all against all, in which the threat that other states pose is unaffected by their internal norms and institutions. Establishing my position, however, requires addressing the set of conceptual and methodological criteria advanced in Tetlock and Belkin (Chapter 1). In doing so we would, strictly speaking, be assessing the accuracy and generality of a hypothesis about actual behavior rather than of a counterfactual per se. Whether the criteria for evaluating a counterfactual differ seriously from those for evaluating a good empirical generalization is not fully obvious to me.

Even in the process of evaluating the generalization itself, however, we will need to analyze the plausibility and relevance of particular kinds of counterfactuals about individual historical events (e.g., if states A and B had been democratic they would not have gone to war, or if X and Y had not been democratic they still would have fought). And it is a fairly short move from there to counterfactuals about classes of phenomena (e.g., if there had been more democracies in the system there would have been less war between those states). From there we can move to the more general counterfactual posed and rejected by Waltz: if the international system had been composed entirely of democracies, there would have been little war in the system.

Each of these moves nevertheless poses increasingly heavy demands on the plausibility of the counterfactuals asserted. The attempt to make the final move, from the last counterfactual to a wide-ranging conditional statement about the future (e.g., a subsequent international system composed entirely of democracies would evidence little or no war) is especially problematic but, I believe, well worthwhile.

Evaluating the Democratic Peace Proposition

A recent issue of *International Security* ran two realist counterchallenges arguing that "new conventional wisdom" of peace among democracies is, in terms of the old Scottish verdict, "not proven" (Layne 1994; Spiro 1994). But the counterchallenges are not persuasive when we apply the Tetlock and Belkin criteria to the democratic peace generalization.[2]

Well-Specified Antecedent and Consequent

The critics claim that the number of wars between democracies is somewhat higher than proponents of democratic peace admit, because they engage in "intellectual suppleness" with "continual tinkering with definitions and categories" (Layne 1994, 40), or "selectively adopt definitions of key variables so that data analysis yields the results they seek" (Spiro 1994, 55).

A defender retorts that "most democratic peace theorists are meticulous in their definitions" (Owen 1994); readers who wish to look at my criteria (Russett 1993, chapter 1) or James Lee Ray's (1993) can make up their own minds.[3] But neither critic is above suspicion. Layne avoids tinkering with a

---

[2] Because this chapter is intended to be illustrative rather than a definitive defense of the democratic peace proposition I will largely ignore some other published challenges. This is appropriate because the specific contents of most of those challenges do not differ in type—nor sometimes even in detail—from some addressed here. See, for example, R. Cohen (1994), with a reply by Russett and Ray (1995). Also, though much of the following material is drawn from my already-published reply to Layne and Spiro, I refer readers to the more extensive refutation there, in Russett (1995). In their correspondence in the same issue of *International Security*, Layne's (1995) reply consists of the novel charge that I practice postmodernism and Spiro (1995) dismisses the statistical analysis reproduced in this chapter on the grounds that citations for the data are not given (they are, in fact, noted as from the same sources used in Russett 1993) and the statistical methods are not described (they are, in fact, Spiro's methods). One smells a whiff of desperation.

[3] Spiro (1994, 56) says that various researchers have used different criteria for democracy, and implies that this weakens the case. Rather, the fact that essentially the same results hold across a range of definitions is evidence that the findings are robust.

definition by the simple expedient of never giving us an explicit definition. The closest he comes is the statement, "In the realm of foreign policy, France and Britain were no more and no less democratic than the Second Reich [imperial Germany]," with the explanation that in all three countries "crucial foreign policy decisions were taken without consulting Parliament" (Layne 1994, 43, 42). One might conclude from this that virtually no countries had democratically controlled foreign policy (would the United States pass this test in most of the twentieth century?) In that case there would not have been much opportunity for any wars between "democracies," and hence there could be no democratic peace! But he seems instead to want to include imperial Germany among the ranks of democratic powers (Layne 1994, 44)—an idiosyncratic view, rejected even by Spiro (1994, 69).

Spiro, however, wants to count Finland's role on the Axis side in World War II as war against four or five democracies in each of the years 1941–44. In doing so he seeks consistency in applying a definition—reasonable enough, but at some cost in good sense. His argument is that other democracies declared war on democratic Finland, and that those pairs of "warring" democracies should thus count. I thought it grotesque to count them. So far as I can tell there is no record of combat casualties between Finland and any democracy during World War II. The definition used by the Correlates of War Project from which we both drew our data is to count a "warring" state as part of a multilateral war only if it has at least 1,000 troops in combat or suffers at least 100 battle-related fatalities (Small and Singer 1982, 67). He seems to mean that we could properly exclude Finland only if we also looked carefully at all other multilateral wars to see if there are other instances where a particular pair of states (presumably, for his argument, not a democratic pair) were identified as participants in a multilateral war but really inflicted few if any fatalities on each other. That might be a good way to proceed—but it would be a great deal of work, so instead poor Finland is made to count seventeen times.[4]

Spiro (1994, 74) further defends this decision on grounds of consistency

---

[4] Spiro (1994, 74) decided that Finland "threw in its lot with those of fascist powers against other liberal democracies." He does not dispute my statement about no casualties, though he says (p. 61) that Manninen (1983, 166) reports that some Royal Navy planes bombed Finnish territory on July 30, 1941. Spiro does not mention Manninen's statement on the next overleaf that subsequent "declarations of war did not mean at any stage of the Second World War that Finland had become involved in real hostilities with the Western allies" (Manninen 1983, 168). This raid was four months before Britain, under great pressure from Stalin, reluctantly declared war on Finland (Churchill 1950, 526–35). The target was a German-operated nickel-mining operation in northern Finland. See Weart (1995, appendix). Finland took no hostile action against any Western ally, nor during the period of declared war did the Western allies shoot Finns. (Australia, Canada, and New Zealand joined Britain in a formal declaration of war lasting from December 1941 to 1944; the nonelected Free French government was briefly at war with Finland in 1944.)

and deference to the data's originators: "Singer and Small coded Finland as at war with the liberal alliance during World War II, and so should studies that use the data set." It is not always convenient, however, to be consistent and deferential. He chooses to drop Mecklenburg-Schwerin in 1866, and all but four states during the Korean War, because they suffered fewer than 1,000 fatalities. This allows him to cut the number of warring dyads (i.e., warring pairs of states) from twenty-nine to twenty-one in 1866, and from twenty-eight to four in each year from 1950 to 1953. Because all these dyads are nondemocratic, their deletion greatly raises the likelihood that he will fail to reject the null hypothesis. In massaging the data he tosses aside the very coding rules of Singer and Small noted above (i.e., the 1,000 troops/100 fatalities minimum for participation).

Clarity and Coherence of Connecting Principles

Consistency with Well-Established Historical Facts

Consistency with Well-Established Theoretical Laws

In application the next three Tetlock and Belkin tests overlap, and to avoid repetition are best considered together. Layne (1994, 38) argues that whereas "democratic peace theory identifies a correlation between domestic structure and the absence of war between democracies, it fails to establish a causal link." Certainly the literature on the democratic peace has gone well beyond correlation, and has postulated a variety of causal mechanisms, to postulating perceptions of shared norms, institutional constraints, and strategic behavior.[5] The theoretical arguments have been articulated to the point where variants can be tested against each other to see which is more powerful, and to seek greater parsimony.

What Layne presumably means is that until recently the democratic peace literature was light on the kind of historical case study analysis that would establish with reasonable force that the considerations identified in one variant or another of the theory actually were important motivators of individual and state behavior. To be valid, says Layne (1994, 13), democratic peace theory "must account powerfully for the fact that serious crises between democratic states ended in near misses rather than in war." He then looks, in four crises between democratic states, at a selection of statements by major figures in government or affecting governments, and finds that although the crises ended without war, the participants' calculations were exclusively

[5] Russett (1993, chapter 2) discusses two sets of causal propositions at length, and Maoz and Russett (1993) give a slightly different version; Bueno de Mesquita and Lalman (1992) develop and test an elaborate game-theoretic explanatory process; Kilgour (1991) presents another game-theory model. See also Rummel (1975–81) and Lake (1992).

concerned with matters central to realism's focus on power and strategic interest. He claims (p. 38) that "democratic peace theory indicators appear not to have played any discernible role in the outcome."

Process-tracing of decision making can be enlightening, and not enough of it has been done on this topic. But Layne's conclusions are not beyond contestation. Serious problems of interpretation are unavoidable, and difficulties regarding which statements are reported and which not, and of obtaining agreement among observers, must not be evaded. Owen, for example, interprets differently two of Layne's crises, notably the 1895–96 Anglo-American confrontation.[6] Owen finds substantial evidence that considerations consistent with the expectations of democratic peace did appear, and made a difference. Furthermore, Layne does not explain why Britain decided that its strategic interests lay in accommodation with the United States in the first instance and France in the second, rather than with Germany. Why did the British not consider America "another enemy," a threat along with other rivals like Germany, considering that they certainly thought of the United States as a latent "world power" (Layne 1994, 15)? The calculus of strategic interest is not obvious without asking why some states were regarded as intrinsically more desirable and trustworthy friends.

But suppose we were to concur entirely with Layne that democratic peace considerations really were invisible, or nearly so. From my own research, in fact, I conceded much of the case that Layne makes for realism as applied to the Venezuela and Fashoda crises.[7] In each of Layne's cases, power and strategic considerations were predominant. No vital issues were at stake over *Trent* and Venezuela, and in Fashoda and the Ruhr the weaker side had no hope of prevailing in war. Does that concession give away the game? It would if democratic peace proponents claimed that shared democracy is the only influence permitting states to avoid war—but that is nonsense. Power and strategic interest affect the calculations of all states, including democracies. States sometimes start wars they think they can profit from, and usually avoid those where a cost-benefit calculation indicates they will lose, or win but at unacceptable cost. They do not, however, always initiate a war just because they think they could win at some acceptable price.[8]

[6] For interpretations of Fashoda giving more credit to democratic peace interpretations see Ray (1995, chapter 5) and Weart (1995). An important extension of the democratic peace literature to process-tracing of Allied decisions during the Cold War is Risse-Kappen (1995).

[7] Respectively, "Although important in preventing an Anglo-American war over this bagatelle, British strategic interests do not deserve all the credit for avoiding war;" and "Considerations of any norm that these two nations should not fight each other were well in the background on both sides; war was avoided primarily for other reasons" (Russett 1993, 6, 8). I do contend, however, that the experience of near war stimulated in each case intense reconsideration of interests and the direction of foreign policy, in which the previous antagonists' views of the democratic norms and institutions they shared played a major role in changing the way they behaved toward each other.

[8] In the formal expected-utility calculation of Bueno de Mesquita and Lalman (1992), posi-

Though somewhat problematic, the language of necessary and sufficient conditions is appropriate here.[9] Neither an unfavorable strategic cost-benefit calculation nor shared democracy is a necessary condition for avoiding war. But, allowing for some possibility of irrationality or misperception, either may well constitute a virtually sufficient condition. For this reason, conceding Layne's argument does not gain him the day on the larger issue of whether democratic peace exists. Extending that argument commits the logical fallacy of inducing a principle of universal nonexistence merely by finding a few cases of nonexistence. Even if there were no evidence for democratic peace considerations in four cases, that would prove nothing about their putative absence in others.

At some point after examining very many cases my objection would become rather silly, at least for an influence (shared democracy) that I contend really is important in international affairs. But we have Owen's good case studies (twelve of them in his dissertation; cited in Owen 1994, 88–89), many of which find more evidence for democratic peace considerations. That is noteworthy because Owen's cases are all from the period 1794–1917—an era during which, I believed, such considerations were much less influential than subsequently.[10]

Moreover, any research design focusing on crises misses a kind of counterfactual: all the dogs that did not bark, the crises that never erupted or never brought the participants to the brink of war. What about the many conflicts of interest between democracies that were settled amicably, without threatening war—even though considerations of power and strategic interest might well have argued against such a settlement?[11] The Venezuelan and Fashoda crises were the last between these two pairs of states. Never since has Britain engaged in a diplomatic crisis with a democratic France or the United States that remotely approached war. Why? Might shared democratic norms and institutions possibly have something to do with it?

Problems of cotenability have not been explicitly discussed much in this literature. It is not even remotely possible, in some historical political sys-

---

tive expected utility for war is a necessary condition for a state to start a war but is far from a sufficient condition.

[9] The significance of "near misses"—wars between democracies that did not quite happen—depends on detailed evidence from case histories. Two states' status as democracies might be shown to have helped avert war between them (evidence for the democratic peace proposition), to have been irrelevant (democracy a sufficient but not necessary condition for peace), or to have contributed to the crisis and thus to have needed to be counteracted by other influences in order for war to be prevented (undermining the democratic peace proposition).

[10] One important reason may be the denial of the franchise to women in the nineteenth century. At least for the years for which we have good data, women have been much more averse than men to using military force (Brandes 1994).

[11] This last issue moves into the criterion of evaluating statistical generalizations and the need to avoid selection bias (in this instance, by ignoring the circumstances behind the crises that never erupted). See Fearon (1994c).

tems, to imagine that a state could have been democratic. In mixed systems composed of authoritarian and democratic states, the question is more meaningful. It can be asked, for example, in the form, "If state *A* had been democratic, would its territorial dispute with *B* have been more or less acute and war-promoting than it was in fact under authoritarian rule?" One needs then to invoke theoretically-based and tested propositions about how different kinds of states behave in conditions of possible crisis-initiation and escalation. This has been done, with the conclusion that democracies do not launch preventive wars, are less likely to initiate or escalate militarized disputes with other democracies, and are more likely to accept third-party mediation.[12]

Consistency with Well-Established Statistical Generalizations

Agreement with this criterion has been called problematic because wars are rare phenomena, and throughout most of modern history democracies are also rare. Thus the number of wars to be expected between democracies is so small that statistical testing may be unable to distinguish the actual number of wars between democracies from the very low number that would be predicted by chance. This argument does not claim to have disproved the hypothesis of democratic peace. It says only that the evidence is so sparse that statistical tests cannot confirm the hypothesis.

This consideration might seem less problematic but for a few democratic peace proponents who have maintained the strong proposition that democracies never fight each other. Most contributors to this literature, however, hold to a probabilistic view that avoids expectation of discovering a universal law or deterministic statement, and also avoids eternal nitpicking discussions. It is enough to say, first, that wars between democracies are at most extremely rare events and, second, that even violent conflicts, short of war, between democracies are also very rare. Application of the proposition to violent conflicts well short of war is useful in expanding the number of "events" that can be analyzed, and, more important, is integral to the theory.

Thus arguments about neither Finland nor imperial Germany would matter much save for the fact of few wars and few democracies. Even so, the notion that the data do not support the democratic peace proposition becomes possible only by procedures that make it impossible to find statis-

[12] See Schweller (1992), Leng (1993), Brecher (1993), Rousseau, Gelpi, Reiter, and Huth (1996), Dixon (1993; 1994), Bercovitch (1991), and Raymond (1994). Fearon (1994a, 585–86) offers a formal explanation for why democracies are less likely to escalate disputes with one another. Layne (1994, 14) recognizes that realism, unlike the democratic peace literature, expects a democracy to use "threats, ultimata, and big-stick diplomacy against another democracy."

tically significant results—even with zero democratic wars. My earlier full reply to Spiro shows that his alternative statistical analysis verges on the bizarre, with dubious and inconsistent assumptions. For a full consideration of all Spiro's objections see Russett (1995). Here I will merely consider briefly the statistical analyses that were already published, and some new ones stimulated by the Spiro critique. I use my own work as an example, but related work reaches nearly identical conclusions.[13]

Start with the recognition that not all dyads have an equal probability of being at war. A few states are great powers, with interests all over the globe, and the ability to land troops, naval bombardments, or nuclear weapons anywhere. For dyads including great powers, war is in principle possible. War is also possible for neighboring states or near-neighbors. As Layne (1994, 39) recognizes, but Spiro ignores, "only dyads meeting these preconditions are part of the appropriate universe of cases from which democratic peace theory can be tested." Most dyads (e.g., Ghana and Burma) are politically irrelevant, too far apart to have border conflicts or to be much involved in each other's affairs, and too weak to project power over long distances. On occasion—as in the World Wars and the Korean War—they may be drawn into conflict with distant states. But under nearly any other circumstance it is pointless to include them in an empirical test of potential war adversaries. Thus we should concentrate on the roughly 12 percent of dyads in the international system for which war is a real possibility.[14]

Furthermore, we do not begin with total ignorance about what kinds of countries go to war with each other. In addition to the effect of geographical proximity, good theory (much of it straight out of realism) suggests that rich countries are unlikely to fight each other, as are countries whose economies are growing rapidly; that states of relatively equal power are more likely to fight each other than are states of widely disparate military capabilities; and that states that share ties of military alliance do not have the same incentives to fight one another as do states not so allied. One should incorporate this knowledge into a test, controlling for the influence of these variables as well as of democracy.[15] By doing so we make it *harder* to find an independent

[13] See Russett (1993), Maoz and Russett (1993), and Bremer (1992; 1993). Bremer's work is important not only because we replicate each other's findings, but because it covers the long 150-year period. The proposition has become increasingly accepted by many scholars who initially were skeptical. See, for example, Chan (1993), Dixon (1993), Bueno de Mesquita and Lalman (1992), Rummel (1975–81), and Weede (1992).

[14] Maoz and I discussed analyzing "politically relevant dyads" at length in our publications. Whereas doing so misses some conflicts (and a few wars) between dyads not politically relevant by these criteria, it picks up a greater proportion of conflicts and wars between democratic dyads than between nondemocratic ones. Hence, it does not bias the results in favor of our hypothesis (Russett 1993, 74).

[15] Farber and Gowa (1995) argue that in the post-World War II era the relationship between joint democracy and little conflict is spurious, an artifact of alliance patterns. But they refuse to

causal relationship for democracy, because many democracies also are wealthy, allied, etc.[16] Nevertheless, we do still find it.

Equally important is the proposition cited above that not only are wars between democracies rare or nonexistent, democracies are more likely to settle mutual conflicts of interest short of the threat or use of military force. Conflicts of interest arise, but democracies rarely escalate those disputes to the point where they threaten to use military force against each other, or actually use force at all (even at a level of violence far below the threshold at which we would call it a war). Much more often than other states, they settle their disagreements by mediation, negotiation, or other forms of peaceful diplomacy. This integral element of democratic peace theory constitutes a logical extension of the research program that began nearly two decades ago with wars. A critic who restricts the discussion and evidence only to wars biases the argument in his favor, and is more than five years behind the curve.[17]

With these specifications Zeev Maoz and I analyzed the behavior of all politically relevant dyads in militarized disputes (if any) during the period 1946–86. The result was that democratic dyads were (statistically) significantly less likely to engage in conflict—whether wars or minor disputes—than were pairs of states in which one or both members were not democratic, even allowing for the effect of the control variables.

Spiro (1994, 77–79) objects to our pooled time-series analysis on the grounds that aggregating years violates the assumption of independence between observations. He does identify a well-known problem. We acknowledged that patterns of behavior in one year depend in part on behavior in the previous year, and took the standard methodological precautions to minimize the effects. There is no perfect statistical solution; the observations are neither totally independent nor so dependent that one need restrict the evidence just to what can be shown on a year-by-year basis.

Some New Analyses

Alternatively, if we concede that dependence between years raises some problems for pooled time-series—without invalidating them—different kinds of analyses are still applicable. Instead of using the dyad-year as a unit

---

run an analysis using alliance as a control—an analysis that has led others to conclude that the relationship is not spurious (Russett 1993; Bremer 1992 and 1993).

[16] Strong theory is also important because the statistical regularity appeared earlier, in bivariate form, than did a good theoretical model. See Streit (1940) and Babst (1964). Some theorists might be bothered by this sequencing, although it is very common in physical as well as social science (O'Neill 1995).

[17] For the extension to democracies' use of negotiation and third-party mediation, see Dixon (1993; 1994), Bercovitch (1991), and Raymond (1994).

TABLE 7.1
Dispute Behavior with Regime-Dyad as the Unit of Analysis, 1946–86

	War	No War	Percent with War
Democracy	0	169	0
Not Democracy	37	1045	3.4
	Use of Force	No Use of Force	Percent Using Force
Democracy	8	161	4.7
Not Democracy	229	853	21.2
	Any Dispute	No Dispute	Percent with Dispute
Democracy	12	157	7.1
Not Democracy	257	825	23.8

of analysis, take the whole regime-dyad as the unit of analysis. For example, the United States and Costa Rica constitute an always-democratic dyad. The United States and the USSR are an always-nondemocratic dyad. The United States and Argentina are a democratic dyad in the years 1966–72 and 1983–86; in all our other years they constitute a nondemocratic dyad because of the character of the Argentine regime. (For simplicity I treat all democratic dyad-years as a single unit even if the years were interrupted; ditto for nondemocratic years.) For each of these regime dyads then ask: Did they ever initiate a dispute, or escalate one? We are not counting the number of disputes or escalations within each regime-dyad, only asking if a dyad experienced at least one. The result is 1,251 units for comparison, one for each dyad over time. We then can ask, very simply, whether democratic dyads are less likely than nondemocratic dyads, over their whole "lifetimes" (up to forty-one years in these data), to begin or escalate disputes.

The answer, shown in Table 7.1, is overwhelmingly clear: yes. Comparing percentages in the last column, nondemocratic dyads were "infinitely" more likely to make war on each other. They were four-and-a-half times more likely to use force against each other than were democratic dyads. As for disputes, nondemocratic dyads were more than three times as likely as democratic dyads to engage in any sort of militarized dispute. These big differences confirm that the inhibition against violence between democracies applies at all levels, and that it is most powerful as a restraint on war. Statistical tests are fully appropriate, and these differences are highly significant—at the .004 level for wars, and the .0000001 level for use of force and for all disputes. This is powerful evidence for the relatively pacific behavior of democratic dyads.[18]

[18] Zeev Maoz has performed an analysis like this on the entire 1816–1986 period, with very similar results to be reported elsewhere. It is essential to distinguish escalated disputes from continuing ones, because if a regime changes from democratic to nondemocratic, or vice versa,

TABLE 7.2

Year-by-Year Tests of Disputes and Use of Force by Politically Relevant Dyads,
1946–86

	Democracies Significantly Lower	No Significant Difference
Use of Force	32	9
Any Dispute	34	7

Now the *coup de grace*. Take our data, but otherwise replicate Spiro's
year-by-year analysis, using the same .20 probability level and, for comparison, counting disputes that continued from the past year. We know wars are
too rare for us to expect significant results on a year to year basis, but uses
of force and all disputes are much more common. I created forty-one two-
by-two tables (one for each year), with the number of all democratic dyads
that did not use force against each other, the number of democratic dyads
that did use force, and the number of all other dyads with and without use of
force. I then did the same thing for disputes at all levels. Table 7.2 gives the
results. Using Spiro's own method of analysis, more than four-fifths of the
years showed the predicted statistically significant difference between democratic dyads and nondemocratic ones. None showed a difference—significant or not—opposite to what democratic peace theory predicts. The evidence for the democratic peace is thus stronger and more robust than ever.

Projectability

The matter of retrospective projectability can be addressed in two ways.
First, can the generalization be shown to apply to domains other than that
for which it was initially developed and tested? Here, that means in domains
other than the "modern" international system (since the end of the Napoleonic Wars). In short, one needs to find an analogously anarchic system,
composed of independent political units for which there is a substantial
range in the character of their domestic political constitution.

One such is the city-state system of ancient Greece during the Peloponnesian Wars. Another option is to look at preindustrial societies—the sort studied by ethnographers and anthropologists—within which rather small individual political units retained a substantial autonomy and capacity to wage

---

one would not want to blame the new regime simply for inheriting an old dispute from its
predecessor. Here and below I use Maoz's recently refined data set; the results would not be
substantively different using data employed for my book. Data sets for disputes and political
system type are publicly available for purposes of replication. Fischer's Exact Test gives the
probability that the difference is attributable to chance. On the concept and measurement of
enduring rivalries see Goertz and Diehl (1993).

war against other political units within the society. By analogy, these units are "states," and the society the interstate system. The question then becomes whether societies whose political units are organized predominantly on participatory or democratic principles experience less war among those units than do societies whose political units are largely hierarchical or authoritarian. Our studies found somewhat weak support for the democratic peace proposition in ancient Greece, but stronger support among the ethnographic units. In doing so, "the process of trying to falsify theories . . . is really one of searching for their bounds of applicability."[19]

A variant of retrospective projectability would seem contained in the customary requirement that a "progressive" research program be able to generate additional testable hypotheses, linked in a logical-deductive structure, beyond those initially put forward. Barry O'Neill (1995) similarly argues that a powerful theory can be identified by its capability for "unification;" that is, bringing diverse phenomena under a common systematic structure for understanding.

Here too, theories about democratic peace perform well. In addition to the aforementioned extension of the theory from war to the phenomenon of reduced escalation at lower levels of violence and threat, and the greater use by democracies of "democratic" procedures like negotiation and mediation for settling disputes among them, there are others. For example, democracies' pluralism at home leads them to favor pluralism in the international arena, and the right of small nations to self-determination. Democracies tend to ally with one another. They are more likely to win international wars in which they participate, perhaps because democratic leaders know that, if they lose a war, they are more likely than autocratic leaders to be deposed. In turn, democracies may avoid wars against each other in part because they perceive each other as particularly formidable opponents. States with competitive elections generally have lower military expenditures, which in relations with other democracies promotes cooperation; as democracies' politically relevant international environment becomes composed of more democratic and internally stable states, democracies tend to reduce their military allocations and conflict involvement (Miller 1995; Siverson and Emmons 1991; Lake 1992; Bueno de Mesquita and Siverson 1995; Brawley 1993; Schultz and Weingast 1994; M. R. Garfinkel 1994; Maoz 1996).

Yet another entry into the matter of retrospective projectability is consonant with Barry Weingast's suggestion (Chapter 10) about utilizing a com-

[19] The quotation is from King, Keohane, and Verba (1994). The analyses can be found in Russett (1993, chapter 3 [written with William Antholis] and chapter 5 [written with Carol and Melvin Ember]). Weart (1994) subsequently reviewed the Greek evidence and contends that we treated it too conservatively, i.e., that support for democratic peace is stronger than we allowed. An interesting corroboration of our work with ethnographic material is Crawford (1994).

parative statics approach. This was done in the first statistical analysis above by comparing the conflict behavior of dyads during years when both states in the dyad were democratic with their behavior when one or the other was not democratic. Here one can take advantage of the recent international relations research that focuses on enduring rivalries; that is, on pairs of states that experience, over a substantial period of time, repeated militarized disputes and violent conflicts. Some of these enduring rivalries experience enough variation in the domestic political constitution of their members to provide a valuable further test. In Russett (1993, chapter 1) I suggested that Greece/Turkey and India/Pakistan fit this criterion, and that they were most peaceful during the years when both members of the dyad were democracies. Another example is Argentina and Chile, which settled their many-decades-old boundary dispute, and dramatically reduced their military expenditures, only in recent years when both were governed democratically. A more systematic analysis of enduring rivalries along these lines offers a promising line of research.

As for prospective projectability, this difficult matter deserves discussion in a separate section below.

From Generalization and Counterfactual to Conditional

The full list of criteria, however, is not very distinctive as applied to counterfactuals rather than simply as normally applicable criteria for judging any generalization or deciding whether any theory is productive and powerful. In this I am sympathetic to the position of Fearon (1991) or of Dawes (Commentary 3). I am not sure that much value has been added by treating the democratic peace research as a counterfactual, and although the Tetlock-Belkin list usefully focuses attention on certain criteria, good researchers of democratic peace have already "been speaking prose."

If we move to the elaborate Waltzian counterfactual, however, new difficulties arise. We begin with a simple generalization, "democracies have rarely fought each other," which now seems well established. From there, we can put forth some modest counterfactual propositions, such as:

(1) If countries A and B had been democratic, they probably would not have fought each other. This seems a reasonable enough step, so long as the problems of cotenability are not too serious (as in, "if Genghis Khan's Mongols and thirteenth-century Russia had been democratic"). The statement "If the Soviet Union had been democratic there would have been no Cold War" is not outrageous, but still sufficiently suspect on cotenability grounds to generate many thoughts that challenge the imagination.

(2) If there had been more democracies in nineteenth-century Europe, there would have been less war among those states. Again this is reasonable,

probably with fewer cotenability problems than the first proposition. But some other difficulties are embedded in it, which the next proposition—a restatement of Waltz's—begins to make clear. I do want to move to more ambitious propositions such as Waltz's, but cannot avoid airing some doubts.

(3) If all states in the nineteenth-century international system had been democratic, there would have been little war in the system. Even if the generalization is judged to pass all the tests posed so far, this proposition requires stronger theory to be acceptable. It assumes, for example, that other restraints on war—in the international system as a whole, and within the individual states comprising the system—were not in general weaker than they were. It especially requires that a particular kind of restraint on democracies fighting one another be unimportant: that peaceful relations among democracies are not dependent on the existence of nondemocratic states as threats to democracies, or as "acceptable" targets of democracies' aggressive proclivities. Reservations about the importance of the Soviet threat to western democracies (and other states) during the Cold War, or about imperialism by European democracies and the United States in the late nineteenth century, are pertinent here.

These reservations cannot be completely dismissed. It is hard to find good empirical evidence that is fully applicable, but Maoz's result showing that democracies are more peaceful in general when their politically relevant environment is more democratic, and earlier work showing that democracies are peaceful toward one another even when one controls for the influence of shared alliances, certainly help (Maoz 1996; Maoz and Russett 1993; Bremer 1992). Strong and persuasive theory must also be brought to bear. In my view the theory, especially in forms that elaborate patterns of strategic interaction, is quite strong, if not yet conclusive for this purpose.

I believe Robert Powell (1995) was fundamentally correct in saying that we should care about counterfactuals only insofar as they generate interesting conditional statements about the future. The difficulties are even greater, however, when we move from counterfactuals to conditionals, and especially to a policy-relevant statement, a position of advocacy I would like to be able to stake out.

(4) If all states should in the future become democratic, there would be little war in the system. In addition to previously identified problems, this proposition assumes that various other restraints and preventive measures that limit the resort to war in the present will have been adopted, or will remain securely in place, in a future world that for awhile might not experience much war. One such restraint in the contemporary system is the experience of fighting wars in the recent past, and the existential knowledge that war can be very costly and painful. Another is the knowledge of decision makers that diplomatic and military confrontations may sometimes escalate

out of control, fear of which produced the procedures of communication and crisis management that were so carefully elaborated during the Cold War. If memory fades, and the machinery of crisis management falls into disuse, would democracies remain at peace with one another? Or might an international system of democratic states start at peace, but degenerate into a more war-prone one as these historic restraints atrophied?

We simply cannot say with full confidence. My judgment is that the work on democratic peace has established a presumption against the Waltzian counterfactual proposition that a world of democracies would still be a world in which war was common. It is harder to say whether that work can soon move us to a presumption that the alternative counterfactual—a world of democracies would be a world in which war was rare or absent—is correct.

Perhaps the democratic peace proposition is in a similar situation to the claim that cigarette smoking causes lung cancer. For both propositions, some skeptics remain. For neither is the causal process yet fully specified. In any single instance, smoking (autocratic regimes) will not always lead to cancer (interstate violence). Or other influences may interact with the identified cause to make the outcome more probable (asbestos or radiation with smoking; proximity or economic stagnation with autocracy). Nevertheless, for both propositions we have a great deal of evidence that gives us a handle on a major problem, with real policy implications. The choice is between a Type I error and a Type II error, and one must decide which way to take one's chances. Realists can point to the risks that would be involved if states in a still-anarchic system lowered their vigilance against the possibility of adventurism or aggression by a democracy. Critics of traditional realist wisdom, seeing the tensions and wars arising out of the old security dilemma wherein states do not regard one another as fundamentally peaceful, may consider the democratic peace literature as not utopian, and worth the effort to pursue policies that offer a historically unique opportunity to avoid war. The choice is not inconsequential.

8

Using Counterfactuals in Historical Analysis

THEORIES OF REVOLUTION

EDGAR KISER AND MARGARET LEVI

> The judgment that, if a single historical fact is conceived of as absent from or modified in a complex of historical conditions, it would condition a course of historical events in a way which would be different in certain *historically important* respects, seems to be of considerable value for the determination of the "historical significance" of those facts. It is clear that this situation had to call forth a consideration of the logical nature of such judgments.
> *(Weber 1949, 166; emphasis in original)*

COUNTERFACTUALS PLAY a large but often unacknowledged role in social science history.[1] There has been little progress in the ninety years since Weber tried to convince his colleagues to use them more explicitly and systematically. Counterfactuals are aspects of the empirical world that are contrary to fact but not to logical or, in Weber's terms, "objective possibility."[2] They are indispensable in most historical work, because the possible causal factors are so numerous and so interrelated. It is thus difficult to eliminate confounding variables, to randomize them, or to find cases similar enough on the confounding variables to constitute a quasi-experiment. If enough cases exist or if there is another means for the analyst to vary each potential causal factor while holding all others constant, counterfactuals are unnecessary.

[1] This material was partially prepared while Levi was a Fellow at the Center for Advanced Study in the Behavioral Sciences. She is grateful for financial support provided to her through the Center by National Science Foundation grant SES-9022192. The authors appreciate the comments of Jim Caporaso, Tony Gill, and especially Ron Jepperson.
[2] We can distinguish between counterfactuals in terms of the aspect of the empirical world they alter: (1) structures, (2) events, or (3) individual attributes or actions. The first would include things like geography, class power, and rates of population growth; the second particular wars or battles; and the third things like Cleopatra's nose and particular choices made by rulers or revolutionaries. This typology may aid the analysis of counterfactuals by suggesting differences in the ways in which these different types are (or should be) used, but that is beyond the scope of this chapter.

For rare historical events, such as revolutions, counterfactuals may be an essential tool in the analytical tool bag. Not only are there relatively few revolutions, all are the product of factors that develop over a long period of time and as a result of multiple interactions. To deal with the multiplicity of factors and the unique features of each event, social science historians tend to rely on implicit counterfactuals. Because social scientists fail to recognize their reliance on counterfactuals, there is little methodological discussion of how they are (and how they should be) used in historical research (notable exceptions include Fogel 1964; Elster 1978; 1983, 34–41; Fearon 1991; Hawthorn 1991; and King, Keohane, and Verba 1994, 10–12, 76–82).

The purpose of this chapter is twofold: (1) to discuss some general theoretical and methodological issues involved in using counterfactuals in historical research; and (2) to explore the extent to which comparative historical analyses fall prey to potential methodological and cognitive biases and errors in counterfactual reasoning. We argue that counterfactuals are best seen as supplements and/or substitutes for direct empirical analysis when data availability is limited. In these cases, it is important to use counterfactuals explicitly in historical research. The lack of explicit recognition of the role of counterfactuals increases the probability that scholars will use them inappropriately or fail to use them to advantage. Used appropriately, counterfactuals can aid in the logical evaluation of theory, in part by revealing additional implications. In order to use counterfactuals to full advantage, it is necessary to begin with general deductive theory with clear microfoundations and scope conditions.

To provide a concrete empirical focus for our discussion of these general issues, we will concentrate on three of the most prominent, and in many respects exemplary, studies of revolution by comparative-historical sociologists: Barrington Moore's *Social origins of dictatorship and democracy* (1966), Theda Skocpol's *States and social revolutions* (1979), and Jack Goldstone's *Revolution and rebellion in the early modern world* (1991). These books are related not only in subject matter and historical focus (all, for example, analyze the French revolution), but they share a genealogical relationship as well: Moore was one of Skocpol's mentors, and Skocpol in turn was one of Goldstone's. By exploring their successive attempts to address the same general questions, we can assess the extent of progress in overcoming theoretical and methodological problems and cognitive biases and in improving counterfactual reasoning.

Moreover, these are fine books by first-rate scholars. Moore's *Social origins of dictatorship and democracy* is perhaps the single most important reason for the resurgence of historical sociology in the last few decades. Its combination of theoretical sophistication and broad historical knowledge demonstrated that political sociologists had something unique and important to contribute to explaining major historical transformations. Skocpol's work was seminal in transforming state theory as well as in advancing the analysis of revolution. Goldstone's reflects the most advanced current thinking in historical demography and statistical technique. All three books were awarded prestigious prizes by the American Sociological Association. Taken together, these books allow us to explore the extent to which theoretical, methodological, and cognitive dilemmas in using counterfactuals are present in even the best work in this genre. They enable us to begin to think about how to overcome the resulting biases.

Moore, Skocpol, and Goldstone do not self-consciously use counterfactual reasoning in their work on revolution, but all nonetheless implicitly rely on counterfactuals to make their claims. Our task in analyzing the arguments of comparative-historical sociologists on revolution will primarily be to identify the implicit counterfactuals in their work[3] and the costs of failing to make their counterfactuals explicit (see Fearon 1991, 170).

A necessary prelude to uncovering the implicit counterfactuals in their work is stating their most general arguments. Moore offers a version of Marxism in which he assumes the importance of class struggle. Skocpol presents an argument in which the state has autonomy as an actor and must confront pressures from both its international and domestic environment. Goldstone (1991, 175) builds on this argument but also advocates distinguishing the "seismic pressures" of population change from the "construction" of the building (in this case, the state) that is affected by these shocks. It is important to note that although they all are usually considered to be developing theories of revolution, the three arguments have three different explananda: Moore provides different causal explanations for three different types of revolutions (we concentrate on his argument for democratic revolutions), Skocpol explains "social" revolutions (political transformations coupled by large-scale economic and social change), and Goldstone addresses state breakdown (which may or may not lead to revolution). Their central arguments can be stated fairly simply:[4]

Moore: Only where there was a relatively strong bourgeoisie independent of the state and only where the aristocracy and peasantry either sided with the bourgeoisie or were negligible was there a revolution that led to democracy.

Skocpol: Only where there are pressures on states due to wars and international competition and only where these pressures result in a conjuncture of fiscal crisis, abandonment of the state by the dominant classes, and peasant revolts

---

[3] Moore (1966, 414), Skocpol (1979, 88), and Goldstone (1991, 332–34, 342, 473–75) each have at least one explicit counterfactual, but they do not discuss the nature of their counterfactual reasoning.

[4] These general implicit counterfactuals refer to the most general arguments in each book. Some of the best parts of each book are detailed historical narratives containing more specific arguments implying additional counterfactuals.

based in strong peasant communities is there the possibility of a social revolution.

Goldstone: Only where there have been large demographic shifts and increasing demographic pressures that create political stress (elite competition, fiscal crisis, and mass mobilization potential based on concentrations of youth) will there be state breakdown. When the cultural framework permits the development of an elite ideology committed to innovation there will be a revolution.

There are two types of counterfactuals implied by these arguments—counterfactuals within the theory and counterfactuals outside the theory. Counterfactuals within the theory involve counterfactually transforming one of the main causal factors posited by the theory. To take Skocpol as an example: If France had not participated in the American War of Independence, there would have been no social revolution in France in 1789. Implicit counterfactuals outside the theory refer to factors that are not part of the argument, but have been suggested by other theories or historical accounts. To stay with Skocpol: If Louis XVI had not called a national assembly (or had managed it better), there would have been no social revolution in France in 1789.

The plausibility of these scholars' arguments rests on the quality of the theory used to generate and judge implicit counterfactual claims and on consistency with methodological dicta. Moreover, it is worth exploring the extent to which the content of their implicit counterfactuals are the result of cognitive biases. The next three sections focus on theoretical, methodological, and cognitive problems associated with the implicit counterfactuals in these three arguments.

Counterfactuals in Historical Research: Theoretical Issues

Weber's (1949, 170–71) important essay on "objective possibilities" reflects on how best to offer causal explanations of historical events. He differentiates what is of interest to an historian from what may be of interest to jurists, psychologists, physiologists, or others who may analyze the same set of events. To establish the relationship between causes and effects requires, according to Weber, generalization, abstraction, and other logical tasks. Thus, "the simplest historical judgment represents not only a categorically formed intellectual construct, but it also does not acquire a valid content until we bring to the 'given' reality the whole body of our 'nomological' empirical knowledge" (Weber 1949, 175).

Despite his attempts to begin the process of formulating some general principles for evaluating the plausibility of what he labels "objective possibility," Weber flounders on the shoals of what Elster (1978, 180) labels "the problem of legitimacy." Weber has no adequate theoretical grounds for justifying and circumscribing his counterfactual assumptions. Most contemporary historical sociologists have even fewer grounds. Moore, Skocpol, and Goldstone, for example, rely on theory that is principally inductive, structuralist, and conjunctural. The next three sections explore the effects of each of these features of their theories on their implicit counterfactuals.

Induction, Deduction, and Counterfactuals

If an analyst approaches an historical problem purely inductively, or guided only by some general "orienting concepts," the number of potential counterfactuals is practically infinite.[5] In the absence of any ideas about the relative importance of different structures, events, or actions, the analyst could wonder what the consequences would have been had *any* of them been different. No one can possibly explore (or even begin to think about) all of the possible counterfactuals. In the absence of adequate theory there is no clear decision rule for choosing among them.

Weber primarily uses an inductive approach in his research, but he also clearly argues for theory in the form of logically derived principles for selecting the potentially important factors. Similarly, Moore, Skocpol, and Goldstone rely on induction while claiming allegiance to theory as a means of sorting through the myriad of factors. Moore (1966, xiv) uses the metaphor of a map of a large terrain in which some houses and pathways may not appear. Skocpol relies on what she calls comparative historical analysis that builds on Mill's methods of agreement and difference and on Moore's work. She argues forcefully "that comparative historical analysis is not a substitute for theory. Indeed, it can be applied only with the indispensable aid of theoretical concepts and hypotheses" (Skocpol 1979, 39). Goldstone's "Comparative history: A manifesto" describes a search for robust processes. What he means "is a causal statement, asserting that a particular kind of historical sequence unfolds because individuals responded to particular, specified, salient characteristics in their respective historical situations" (Goldstone 1991, 57). In all three cases, however, it is less the logic that preceded research than the generalizations that emerge from the historical comparisons that ultimately produce theory. Moore most clearly admits the finding of generalizations to be his aim. Goldstone most clearly emphasizes the importance of the historical detail itself.[6]

The lack of general deductive theory in much historical work in sociology

[5] Weber (1949, 164) argues that to understand the causal importance of any particular act requires a means to evaluate its causal significance "in the context of the totality of infinitely numerous 'factors,' all of which had to be in such and such an arrangement and in no other if *this* result were to emerge."

[6] He quotes Stephen Jay Gould for justification in his claim that "good comparative history must therefore 'sink a huge anchor in details'" (Goldstone 1991, 60).

(Kiser and Hechter 1991) may be one of the main reasons for the lack of explicit counterfactuals (and may also explain why an economist, Robert Fogel, is the most prominent exemplar of the use of counterfactuals in historical work). General deductive theory focuses the analyst's attention on certain causal factors to the exclusion of others and demands a rigorous logical underpinning to the argument. The greater the clarity and precision of the theory and the more parsimonious the theoretical framework guiding historical research, the fewer the potential relevant counterfactuals.[7]

Deductive theory also facilitates meeting the criteria for the cotenability of the counterfactual with the features of the situation into which it is being inserted. Cotenability requires that the antecedent must logically imply its consequent (Elster 1978, 181–82) and that there must be compatibility between all known facts and existing theory (Fearon 1991). When cotenability is lacking, a change in one factor makes it inconsistent with many other known features of the situation—and the counterfactual fails as a device for evaluating the posited causal relationship. Deductive theory may facilitate, but it does not guarantee cotenability. By Elster's criteria, for example, Fogel's account of the role of the railroads in economic growth is less than totally successful in using counterfactuals to evaluate his central causal claims (Elster 1978, 204–8; 1983, 37–9).[8]

The relevant question is whether the counterfactual antecedent along with general propositions about such causal relations would produce the general effect. Counterfactuals are not just arguments about associations between variables but about the causes of these associations. Good counterfactuals specify not only causal relations but also the causal mechanisms responsible for the relationship (Chapter 1, Tetlock and Belkin). For example, Moore needs to specify the mechanisms by which strong states inhibit economic modernization. According to Moore (1966, 228), in Russia and China actions by a strong state produced a lack of economic modernization (and as a result the weakness of the bourgeoisie and the peasantry remaining intact). The implicit counterfactual here is that if the state had not been strong or had used its power to pursue more procapitalist policies, economic modernization may have occurred and resulted in a democratic revolution instead of a dictatorship of the left.[9] To tie the consequent to the antecedent, Moore

---

[7] Hawthorn (1991) may disagree with us on this point. He argues, "The inductively-known runnings-on of the world do set limits on what counterfactuals we can assert" (p. 77). He uses the example of variation in control of the plague in medieval Europe to make this point. Although he does find that "the limits set by these sort of runnings-on are very wide," he also claims that it is circumstance and not theory that really sets the bounds (p. 78).

[8] Elster's main criticism is that Fogel fails to meet the cotenability requirement with his counterfactuals.

[9] Of course, if progress along the road to modernization was only partial, the result would have been a dictatorship of the right instead.

needs a general theory of state policy formation. The best and easiest way to specify the mechanisms is with general deductive theory (Kiser and Hechter 1991), perhaps along the lines suggested by North (1990).

Skocpol goes a little further in offering the mechanisms that account for the choices of state leaders that bring on revolutionary reactions than Goldstone in suggesting the mechanisms by which demographic pressures translate into political stress. Although Skocpol's theoretical model does not contain explicit microfoundations, it is clear in her detailed historical narrative that her state actors are rational men acting under severe constraints that she clarifies with some precision. Her implicit counterfactuals include the absence of war, sufficient economic development to counteract the debilitating effects of war, or support of the state by the dominant class. In Goldstone's case, demographic shifts affect prices that create new fiscal problems for governments. His implicit counterfactual is either the absence of demographic shifts or the existence of a "modern" (as opposed to "traditional") state (Goldstone 1991, 287–88). The uncomfortable fit between their counterfactuals and their causal mechanisms is partially a function of failure to make the counterfactuals explicit and partially a result of being insufficiently deductive.

Structuralism, Methodological Individualism, and Counterfactuals

In the recent movie *To Live*, a Chinese couple blame themselves for the death of their daughter in childbirth. In the midst of the Cultural Revolution, in a hospital taken over by students who had sent all the experienced doctors to prison, the couple and their son-in-law decide they need one of those doctors on hand just in case something should go wrong. Cleverly, the son-in-law locates such a doctor and successfully explains his presence to the students. However, the doctor had not eaten for three days, and the couple purchase seven buns for him. He wolfs them down and is in no shape to be of help when needed, especially after he suffers debilitating bloat from water they provide him to ease his pain. When their daughter does suffer a complication and dies, the couple blame themselves for giving the doctor so many buns and then giving him water. It does not occur to them that in a normal hospital in a normal time, the issue would never have arisen.

This Chinese couple not only suffered from at least two cognitive illusions but also from bad theory. They focused on agency rather than structure and on the last effect in the causal chain. Most importantly, they had a model of the world in which one's own actions are the primary cause of one's own fate.

Moore, Skocpol, and Goldstone never make these mistakes. All three are structuralists—a theoretical framework that downplays the causal importance of agency. Structuralist theories can make one of two claims: (1) they provide a model of the macrolevel part of a multilevel causal process, without claiming to be a complete explanation of a particular outcome, or (2) they provide a complete explanation of the outcome, because the only important causal factors are at the macro level. Structuralist theories that claim to provide complete explanations of outcomes (the latter type) imply one very strong set of counterfactuals, that changes in the actions of individuals would not affect the outcomes of interest. For example, the French and English revolutions would not have been avoided by more astute choices by Louis XVI and Charles I. The classic sociological example of this type of counterfactual is Durkheim's analysis of the social determinants of deviance. Durkheim (1938) makes the counterfactual claim that even in a "society of Saints" (one in which all individuals had saintly attributes) deviance would exist, because deviance is not a product of the nature of individual action but is created by society to serve functions of defining and reinforcing value boundaries. In other words, it does not matter what individuals do. Societies will define some subset of existing behavior as deviant regardless of its content—the outcome is totally independent of the actions of individuals.

Moore, Skocpol, and Goldstone all analyze the causes of revolutions with theoretical frameworks that are both structuralist and materialist. They thus share two general sets of implicit counterfactuals: (1) if the actions of any "great person" would have changed, it would have made a difference to the outcome; and (2) a change in the ideological context prior to the revolution would have had an effect on the outbreak of the revolution. Both of these are counterfactuals outside the theory, referring to the lack of causal impact of factors not included in the argument. In each case, the relevant question is: Is the argument robust with respect to changes in these factors?

The first counterfactual denies "great person" theories of history.[10] Moore (1966, 507) stresses the fact that the "ugly side of the Stalinist era had institutional roots." Skocpol's (1979, 14–18) defense of a structuralist per-

---

[10] This form of argument also denies contingency due to the aggregated actions of multiple individuals. There are no "folk theorems" in these accounts. Kuran (1991) provides an interesting contrast, arguing that revolutions cannot be predicted because of contingency introduced in knowing and aggregating individuals' actions. In Skocpol's (1979, 96) account, it is often the case that "objective conditions allowed for no other outcome." Goldstone (1991) is alone among the three in even recognizing models of choice that help account for why individuals in similar situations might behave in similar fashion (pp. 55–56), but his conclusion is that he and Skocpol have it right in clarifying the structural conditions that produce common responses (pp. 56–57). This leaves little room for multiple equilibria or the effects of the different preferences and beliefs that he admits might exist. In Skocpol, this leads to a failure to adequately address both the fact and causes of variation in peasant response. M. Taylor's (1988) criticism and elaboration of Skocpol's argument is based on his rejection of this negative counterfactual. In Goldstone, the consequence is an attribution of all variation to the differential impact of demographic pressures and price changes.

spective against a "voluntarist" one provides another classic example; she wants to deny the importance of revolutionary leaders in "making" revolutions. Moore and Skocpol offer up names of actors, but they are simply the listing of the players who had the honor or shame of certain given roles in the revolutionary drama.

The assumption that the rulers of states or other "great people" do not shape or significantly alter the structural conditions leading to revolution is more compelling in some structural arguments than in others. For example, the long-term population dynamics that drive Goldstone's argument are not influenced much by the actions of rulers, but the wars that create fiscal crises in Skocpol's argument probably are. Although Goldstone (1991, 67) makes a point of rejecting the claims made by Russell and other "revisionists" that had Charles I altered a few critical actions, the English revolution may not have occurred, particular actors do play some role in his arguments. He actually has two different kinds of structuralist variables and, in the end, a voluntarist *deus ex machina* to explain some of the cases that do not fit. Throughout the book he insists that his theory predicts where a state breakdown is likely to occur but is not deterministic. Using his earthquake metaphor, he can tell us where there will be seismographic pressures and shaking but not if the building will fall. Thus, the second structural factor is the foundation of the building itself. Nonetheless, the wise actions of state leaders can alleviate the effects of his metaphoric earthquake. This was what William IV did in 1832 (p. 334) and what Pahlavi failed to do (pp. 473–74).

Methodologically individualist theories, such as rational choice, can produce more precise microlevel counterfactuals. We normally think of counterfactuals in terms of possible but not actual antecedents in causal propositions. In most rational-choice accounts, these propositions refer to ways in which changes in structural conditions affect individuals' actions in such a way as to produce changes in other structures or institutions, assuming the individuals act rationally and have certain goals. However, in addition to using counterfactuals to alter the structural conditions shaping action, we can also use them to alter the microlevel assumption of rationality that serves as a foundational assumption of the argument. For example, we could speculate as to how a particular outcome would have been different if actors had acted on the basis of emotion instead of rational calculation. This type of counterfactual is not relevant in structuralist theories of revolution.

The second counterfactual rejects the importance of ideas in explaining the origins of revolution. Skocpol's (1979, 32) discussion of the relationship between legitimacy and revolution is illustrative: "Even after great loss of legitimacy has occurred, a state can remain quite stable—and certainly invulnerable to internal mass-based revolts—especially if its coercive organizations remain coherent and effective." Skocpol (1979, 51) also rejects arguments that the Enlightenment was an important cause of the French revolution. Sewell's (1985) criticism of Skocpol for ignoring the role of ideology in the French revolution is an explicit attack on this implicit counterfactual in her analysis. To Goldstone (1991, 272–74), Puritanism, the Enlightenment, and other variants of an ideological clash are the results of ecological shifts; they may help explain the form of revolutionary struggles but not their outbreak. Goldstone modifies Skocpol's approach by providing ideology a role in shaping the outcome of state breakdowns, but not in causing them.

Both Elster (1978) and Fearon (1991) stress that good counterfactuals must be cotenable with known facts—the changes proposed must "fit" with everything else we know. Counterfactuals implied by arguments that explain outcomes in terms of major structural factors will often not be cotenable with existing facts. Fearon (1991, 193–94) argues that cotenability is more likely the smaller the change proposed by a counterfactual. Elster (1978, 191) requires not only that "the alternative state be capable of insertion in the real past" but also that the distance be as small as possible between the alternative and actual worlds. However, structural arguments by their nature imply very large counterfactuals and very long distances.

This is clearest in Moore, where it is long-term secular changes that lead to revolution. For example, one counterfactual implied by Moore is: if the bourgeoisie were the strongest social class in Russia in 1916, there would have been no communist revolution (and perhaps a democratic one instead). This problem is not as bad for Skocpol, because we can imagine changing one of her main causal variables without having to change many other factors. For example, an implied counterfactual in her account would be: if the French had not become involved in the American War of Independence, the French revolution would not have occurred. For Goldstone, there are also some counterfactuals that could change his central variables without cotenability problems, such as imagining a plague decreasing population pressure and thus preventing a revolution.

Conjunctural Causation and Counterfactuals

One of the main trends in recent methodological writings and substantive work in historical sociology has been toward more complicated images of causality. This leads in two quite different directions. First, many analysts have moved away from images of causality as the independent effects of single variables and toward a more holistic view of causality based on complex conjunctures of factors (Ragin 1987; Skocpol 1979). Second, many scholars have recently argued that the sequence in which events occur is causally important and that events in the distant past can initiate particular chains of causation that have effects in the present (path dependence).

Moore, Skocpol, and Goldstone are conjunctural theorists. Certain factors have to come together to produce democratization, social revolution, or state breakdown. Such an approach tends to exacerbate problems of cotenability. They have to picture numerous alternative worlds in which all the relevant factors but one come together. Conjunctural analyses, in which variables have effects only as part of large interaction terms, imply that counterfactuals should be stated in terms of hypothetical changes in combinations of variables or compound counterfactuals rather than hypothetical changes in single variables. This not only reduces parsimony but also makes it extremely difficult to apply strictures of logical and theoretical consistency.

While it is certainly the case that good theory often elaborates contingencies or points in the path where a different action or event may have changed the outcome, it is also the case that theory should delimit the possibilities. There is a tension in the work of Moore, Skocpol, and especially Goldstone. Their structuralism sometimes makes their theory extremely deterministic; on the other hand, their insistence on conjunctural analysis opens up too wide a range of possibilities. This can lead to an unmanageable number of counterfactuals.

Skocpol (1978, 298, 320) does not develop the conjunctural aspect of her argument in the text but rather in footnotes; she often uses single variable arguments in her narrative discussion. Goldstone (1991, 10–12), on the other hand, is insistent upon this complex interaction of processes as causal and explanatory. He identifies eight elements of state breakdown and then lists all their possible combinations; the result is 128 possibilities. Although he admits that many of his cells have "no attested empirical contents," his explicitness highlights the difficulties. What makes the problem worse is that he is focusing only on alternatives to the consequent, not the antecedent. If he had also considered all the possible combinations of causal elements that could produce these 128 outcomes, the number of possible worlds becomes even larger.

The Theoretical Usefulness of Explicit Counterfactuals

The result of leaving counterfactuals implicit is that the authors do not provide enough analysis to make their counterfactual claims compelling (thus the criticisms by M. Taylor 1988 and Sewell 1985). In one sense, our suggestion to explicitly examine counterfactuals is simply an elaboration of the traditional advice to pay sufficient attention to alternative explanations. Counterfactuals provide one way to help solve this old problem.

This reading of the work on revolution suggests two distinct kinds of counterfactuals that would be useful as a tool for evaluating a theory and exploring its implications:[11] (1) particular counterfactuals that have no impli-

---

[11] Our distinction seems to parallel that of the contingent versus lawlike generalizations that Goodman developed (cf. Chapter 1, Tetlock and Belkin). It even more closely parallels Fearon's (Chapter 2) distinction between conceivable and miracle causes.

cations for causal relations outside a specific setting (e.g., the famous alteration of the size of Cleopatra's nose),[12] and (2) general counterfactuals that have implications for other similar causal relations (e.g., the alteration of the size of a country to examine the effect of size on the centralization of tax administration). Particular counterfactuals are theoretically useful, but only as a "test" of the robustness of the general causal propositions: Would general cause x still have produced general effect y even if particular historical features such as z had been different? For example, would there have been a revolution in Britain in 1832 "if William IV, like Charles I, had reacted to the crisis by dissolving Parliament and failing to call for new elections" (Goldstone 1991, 332)? General counterfactuals are those that alter abstract potential causal factors; they are restatements of basic propositions of the theory that reveal additional implications. General counterfactuals yield general predictions such as: rulers who make strategic and timely concessions can head off state breakdown.

General counterfactuals offer theoretical predictions about cases and factors that are not present. They provide an additional plausibility probe of an alternative historical trajectory, one that did not and could not exist. This is the power of the Fogel (1964) argument. He has a theory about economic development in the United States that does not depend on the railroads. Thus, he uses counterfactual thought experiments to explore the empirical implications of a world without railroads.

General counterfactuals also generate expectations of what will happen if the N increases. The discovery of additional cases or information transforms the counterfactual implication into an actual empirical implication. General counterfactuals thus increase the testability of theories by revealing additional implications and decrease the likelihood of ad hoc arguments in the presence of new data or events. Kiser and Hechter (1991) criticize Skocpol (1982) for such ad hoc arguments in her analysis of the Iranian revolution, exactly such a new case for her theory of social revolutions.[13] The use of explicit counterfactuals in her initial analysis may have helped her avoid this type of ad hoc argumentation.

Goldstone (1991, 472–73) attempts to infer the causes of the Iranian revolution from his general model of state breakdown but instead comes up with

---

[12] Counterfactuals altering individual attributes or actions, such as Cleopatra's nose, are in some ways similar to the "butterfly effects" noted in chaotic systems such as meteorology. Both involve causation at a distance, with small causes producing large effects, due to tight coupling between events (path dependence).

[13] The causal factors Skocpol identifies for the revolution in Iran are significantly different from those she suggested were important for the French, Russian, and Chinese revolutions. Losses at war are absent and are replaced by a fall in oil prices; peasant insurrections are absent and are replaced by urban revolts; and subjective and ideological factors become an important part of the story.

an ad hoc list of policies that are necessary to foster state stability. These then become counterfactuals: If the shah had done x instead of not-x, then there would have been no state breakdown in Iran (Goldstone 1991, 473–74). His major causal factors, population pressures and political stress, exist in Iran, but Iran does not fit his earlier scope conditions—it is not a *traditional* state with a nonindustrial and noncapitalist economy (Goldstone 1991, 287–89). When he begins to discuss the twentieth century, however, Goldstone transforms his scope conditions into causal factors: state breakdowns are most likely where there are traditional states and economically backward economies. These factors do not exist in Iran. Iran is, by his definition, a modern state that is industrial and capitalist. These are his counterfactuals, and they are present in Iran. Moreover, whereas he earlier (pp. 148–49) made it clear that his theory could not specify when and what kinds of particular individual actions mattered, he explains the Iranian revolution by the shah's failed policies.

Counterfactuals in Comparative-Historical Analyses of Revolution: Methodological Biases

Using Belkin and Tetlock's checklist for determining the plausibility of counterfactual reasoning (Chapter 1), we find that Moore, Skocpol, and Goldstone all exhibit reasonable care in specifying the independent and dependent variables and ensuring that their antecedents are consistent with historical facts.[14] All three are weak on the tests of projectability and proximity, but the second may be an impossible or inappropriate test and the first a reflection of a more general issue for social scientists.[15]

We now turn to the question of how satisfactorily Moore, Skocpol, and Goldstone use additional cases to avoid counterfactuals, and how they deal with problems of multicollinearity.

Attempting to replace counterfactuals with additional cases: As Fearon (1991, 171–72) notes, there are only two ways to assess hypotheses when experimental control and replication are not possible; one can either imagine counterfactual cases or look for additional actual cases that are similar to the case of interest in all respects but the factor of interest. Moore and Skocpol rely on the latter strategy; they turn to facts from other cases to support their claims for the importance of the causal factors they have chosen. To take an example from Moore: it is hard to tell just by looking at Russian history whether or not the extreme poverty of the Russian peasants was a sufficient

---

[14] Although they do not always meet the criteria of cotenability, they make no outrageous or even nonplausible assertions about events and features of the historical landscape.

[15] Goldstone (1991, 58–60) goes so far as to deny the importance of prediction as a test of the validity or robustness of social science theory.

condition for the Russian revolution, because it was never otherwise and Russia in fact had a revolution. Moore does not discuss the merits of theoretical arguments that specify the causal mechanism linking the two. Rather, he supports his claim that poverty is not a main cause of peasant revolt by contrasting the peasants of Russia with those of India, where there was at least as much poverty but no revolution. In other words, this strategy does not rely primarily on theoretical argument, but only on the strength of empirical correlations (Fearon 1991, 177).

Skocpol uses Mill's methods of agreement and difference to achieve the same result, to fill in counterfactual claims concerning her main cases with facts from other cases. This strategy is an attempt to deal with situations in which counterfactuals are most prevalent and most useful, when cases are few and not manipulable. The clearest example from Skocpol's work comes when she uses cases in which a social revolution did not occur to assess the counterfactual implications of her explanations of cases that did experience social revolutions. For example, she uses evidence from Japan and Prussia (both countries that experienced political, not social, revolutions from above) to show that they lacked either nobles with "institutionalized political leverage" or strong international pressures, and thus were able to reform and avoid revolution (Skocpol 1979, 101–10). In another case, she provides a long list of differences between England and France to explain why there was no social revolution in the former (pp. 60–62).[16]

Does this comparative solution successfully resolve (or even replace) counterfactuals? To her credit, Skocpol (1979, 38–39) recognizes the main problem with this strategy:

> Often it is impossible to find exactly the historical cases that one needs for the logic of a certain comparison. And even when the cases are roughly appropriate, perfect controls for all potentially relevant variables can never be achieved. The upshot is that there always are unexamined contextual features of the historical cases that interact with the causes being explicitly examined in ways the comparative historical analysis either does not reveal, or must simply assume to be irrelevant.

The final sentence is telling. In pulling a fact out of context from a second case to deal with a counterfactual raised in analyzing the first case, she simply pushes the counterfactual back one step. The relevant counterfactual now becomes: if any of the other factors in the second case were changed, the causal relationship used to resolve the counterfactual in the first case would not change. More specifically, we must make several counterfactual

---

[16] Skocpol (1979, 60) argues that the continental geography of France was one of the main causes of its high military expenditures, which eventually created fiscal crisis. This suggests an interesting counterfactual: If England had not lost its French possessions in the Hundred Years' War, it would have experienced a social revolution.

assumptions about other factors in the Japanese and Prussian cases (all of those not mentioned by Skocpol) not affecting the outcome. The problem is especially severe when the number of differences between the positive cases and the contrast cases is large. Even in the hands of a careful and inventive scholar, this strategy can rarely be made compelling.

This comparative technique simply replaces the initial counterfactual with a "second order" counterfactual referring to the second case. Fearon (1991, 174) points out that "in statistics this is the familiar problem of whether any independent variables are correlated with the contents of the error term (which contains the effect of all unspecified, unmeasured 'other causes')." Not only does this strategy rely on counterfactuals, but on complex, compound counterfactuals (i.e., all other differences between the cases do not affect the outcome) that are much more difficult to judge than the simple counterfactuals produced by the theoretical strategy. The general point is that in most historical work it is impossible to do away with counterfactuals, and the attempt to do so by reference to other cases is usually illusory.

Multicollinearity: All three scholars turn to historically rich (for sociologists, if not historians) case studies to support their claims that the few factors they have identified as critical are, in fact, critical. Their focus on conjunctural causation raises the problem of multicollinearity. How are we to know that all factors in the complex interaction term that make up the conjunctural cause are important determinants of the outcome, and not just one of the factors?[17] Unless we have additional cases that vary in lacking each single variable in the conjunction while being similar in all other respects, this type of multicollinearity makes the use of counterfactuals necessary (Fearon 1991, 186).

Methodological Growth

All three authors are careful to ensure that their arguments are logical and that they satisfy basic methodological criteria. Moore, however, is relatively unsophisticated about what constitutes methodological rigor, Skocpol is considerably more sophisticated, and Goldstone is the most sophisticated of all. He, far more than the others, avoids some of the pitfalls of the small-N sample. Detailed examination of the histories of the revolution enables Moore, Skocpol, and Goldstone to overcome some of the methodological pitfalls of their implicit counterfactual thought experiments (Fearon 1991). These are, after all, careful and sensitive scholars, attuned to the requirements of high quality social science. Nonetheless, the failure to make their

[17] See Burawoy's (1989) criticism of Skocpol's conclusions.

counterfactuals explicit reduces the power of their argumentation and the
validity of their claims.

Counterfactuals in the Comparative-Historical Analysis of Revolutions: Cognitive Biases

In what follows, we explore the principal cognitive biases in Moore, Skocpol, and Goldstone. First, drawing on Olson, Roese, and Deibert's argument
about "naturally occurring counterfactuals" (Commentary 2), we consider
how the problem of revolution itself might trigger counterfactual thinking.
Second, we address those biases raised in Kahneman and Miller's (1986)
norm theory and in Tetlock and Belkin's more exhaustive list (Chapter 1).
Moore, Skocpol, and Goldstone suffer, as probably we all do, from theoretical commitments that make it easier to "undo" one kind of cause rather than
another. However, it is also worthwhile to explore the "extratheoretic" influences and the "psycho-logic" (Chapter 1, Tetlock and Belkin) on which they
draw. In this regard, we are struck as much by their ability to avert certain
biases as their entrapment in others.

Triggers to Counterfactual Thinking

Experimental psychologists have identified a host of factors that are likely to
trigger counterfactual thinking (Roese and Olson 1995c). Revolutions
clearly fit four of these: unexpected outcomes, negative outcomes, mutable
outcomes, and perceiver goals that are served by counterfactual reasoning.
First, revolutions are certainly exceptional events. Ex ante they are often
surprising and unexpected, even if they appear inevitable ex post. All three
theorists explicitly recognize that revolutions are extraordinary. Second,
their immediate outcomes are negative (many die, and life usually changes
for the worse, at least in the short run), and sometimes even their long-run
outcomes are negative. The debate continues over the positive effects of the
French Revolution; the debate over the Russian Revolution has reached a
clear conclusion for most; and there has been very little debate, at least in
the Western world, about how detrimental the Iranian Revolution has been.
Moore is the most explicit about defining which revolutions had negative
(those that led to dictatorships) and which had positive (those that led to
democracy) outcomes. Third, it is easy to imagine at least some of the antecedents as mutable. Although all three scholars are structuralists, they still
imagine changes in class structure or wars or state capacity that might have
forestalled revolution. Indeed, when the analysis gets detailed enough, as in
Goldstone's book, "naturally occurring counterfactuals" begin to become

more apparent, as in his comparison of Charles I and William IV. Fourth, Moore, Skocpol, and Goldstone's concern with causality is a major factor in leading them to the development of implicit counterfactuals. They mutate possible causal factors in order to highlight and evaluate their particular explanatory claims.

Two of the other potential triggers are absent. Moore, Skocpol, and Goldstone are not personally involved with the outcomes of the revolutions they study. They care intensely about the status of their arguments, and they may hope to provide guidance about future events. The revolutions themselves, however, have little, if any, personal relevance. Nor are their cases ones in which there are immediate and easy antecedents to alter. Revolutions are not basketball games whose winner was determined by two points, and they are not events like feeding buns to the Chinese doctor. Their causes are complex and often removed in time from the actual occurrence to be explained.

The last two factors, outcome involvement and antecedent mutability may affect certain kinds of scholarly questions. Scholars of the plague living at that time may have felt the force of these factors (see Hawthorn 1991), and probably students of contemporary epidemics, such as AIDS or breast cancer, do feel such force. Most of the revolutions we have been discussing are well in the past. Moreover, the structuralism of Moore, Skocpol, and Goldstone makes them unlikely to produce a sense of antecedent mutability. Nonetheless, the four factors that do apply are sufficiently motivating that it is not surprising that scholars of revolution tend to resort to counterfactual reasoning, even if implicitly.

Biases They All Avoid

Ethnocentrism: None of these authors use their own experience and cultures as the basis for evaluating those they study. All think "historically." Even so, Moore and Skocpol have certainly received their share of blasts from historians and area study specialists. There is no question that their chapters on particular countries are summaries of a vast literature and may fail to capture some of the complexity of the situation. It may also be the case, as Goldstone (1991, 23) claims, that most theorists of revolution either focus on the twentieth century or (and in this indictment he includes Skocpol) use the experiences of the twentieth century to evaluate past revolutions. Goldstone has certainly taken greater care to be conversant in the historiographical controversies. His is, in fact, a more nuanced account, but it is not necessarily a more powerful account. The issue is not who provides more detail but who provides a more plausible explanation. The overconcern with the history may be a compensatory technique for fear of ethnocentrism and it may reflect as much bias as what it is trying to correct.

Emphasis on last event: All are very self-conscious that the events most immediately preceding the actual revolutionary situation are "trigger" events rather than causes. This also follows from their structuralist perspective, which leads them to view triggering events as inevitable and replaceable (i.e., some trigger was structurally determined to occur, and many different types of triggers would be sufficient to produce revolution in those structural conditions). Goldstone does on occasion violate this condition, however, as when he introduces the importance of last-minute policies in England in 1832 (Goldstone 1991, 332).

Biases They Fail to Avoid

"Good" causes cannot yield "bad" outcomes: Moore's analysis does seem to suffer from a cognitive bias in favor of "bad" causes producing "bad" outcomes. This is clearest in his analysis of the Russian revolution. He argues that the Russian revolution "did not bring liberation," and goes on to outline the "revolting features of revolutionary dictatorships" (Moore 1966, 506, 507). This bad outcome is the result of "bad" structural conditions (the failure to modernize by commercializing agriculture) and action on the part of a "bad" group (backward peasants, who ironically become the main victims of the revolution). The situation is much different in England and France, where "good" structural conditions (modernized, commercial agriculture) and a "good" class (the rising bourgeoisie) bring about good (democratic) revolution.

Skocpol avoids the cognitive trap of assuming that "bad" effects must have been produced by "bad" causes. Like Moore, she thinks the outcome of the Russian revolution was generally "bad," as indicated by the chapter heading referring to it as a "Dictatorial Party State" (Skocpol 1979, 206). Yet its causes in her model are the same as those that produced the generally "good" French revolution.

Goldstone seeks to avoid this bias by separating out his analysis of state breakdown from his analysis of the outcome. But he succumbs to the bias nonetheless. Although the same general and extremely neutral factors produce state breakdowns in a variety of places and times, it is only certain kinds of "good" ideologies that facilitate the transition to liberal societies, clearly a "good" outcome.

Mutability and agency: In one sense all three avoid the cognitive biases of emphasizing agency rather than structure and focusing on what is mutable rather than on what is not. Indeed, we argue they suffer from exactly the opposite bias: they overemphasize structure and underemphasize mutability. The reason for their focus is not, however, atheoretical. It is precisely the kind of theory they are using that leads them to discount the role of actors and the place of contingency.

Emphasis on exceptional rather than routine events: They do, however, emphasize exceptional rather than routine events. Again, the reasons are not atheoretical but rather lie in the kind of theory they are using. The very choice of revolution as the object of study reflects a serious cognitive bias. Is it easier for these three scholars to "undo" extraordinary events than the routine outcomes that result from the ordinary and everyday behaviors of government actors, agrarian elites, financial elites, and peasants? If James Scott (1985, xvi) is correct, "everyday forms of peasant resistance" are a more important subject of analysis for understanding most agrarian societies over most of history than is the analysis of what Marc Block labeled "the flashes in the pan" represented by the great revolutions. If Levi (1988) and Kiser (1994) are correct, the more important issue for understanding the development of the state lies in investigation of changes in its fiscal and military institutions. If Geddes (1991) or Przeworksi and Limongi (1993) are correct, the key to understanding authoritarianism is not through big questions and revolutionary processes but by studying the institutions of politics.

For Moore, whose aim is to understand patterns of democratization and dictatorship, the focus on revolutions may be extremely damaging. For Goldstone and Skocpol, whose purpose is more to understand the causes of these earth-shattering events than their effects, the bias—if there is one—may be less destructive. Nonetheless, it reflects a view of history in which big events have more importance than small ones. Skocpol and Goldstone may debunk "great person" theories, but they themselves are caught in "great moment" theories.

Relationship between past and future: Is there a cognitive bias toward viewing the past as overdetermined and the future as conditional, or does this simply reflect a difference in the nature of explanation and prediction? Does the failure to predict the 1989 revolutions suggest that there is something badly wrong with our theories of revolution, or that we simply cannot predict revolutions even though we may be able to explain them after the fact? Goldstone, the only one of the three to address these issues directly, comes to two different conclusions. First he claims that it is only possible to explain but not to predict, and later he claims not only that prediction is possible but that his model has generated successful predictions (cf. Goldstone 1991, 58–60; 1994).

We argue that the difference in the way scholars view past events as determined (often overdetermined) and potential future ones as open-ended and conditional is not a cognitive bias but a reasonable way to proceed given the asymmetry between explanation and prediction. Just because it is possible to explain an event after it has occurred, it does not follow that the same theoretical model should have been able to predict it beforehand (Kuran 1991; 1994). The reason Goldstone now thinks his model can be predictive is that he essentially ignores the micro level—prediction is only possible because structural causes are viewed as determining the outcome. However, these types of pure structuralist arguments can only make loose probabilistic predictions within very broad time frames (Kiser 1995), and any attempt to make more precise predictions requires taking the micro level into account.[18] Because of the complexities of aggregation of strategic action in cases such as revolution, however, such precise predictions are unlikely (Kuran 1991). Therefore, at least given the state of our current theoretical knowledge, it is epistemologically correct (not "biased") to view the past as determined and the future as conditional.

The Role of Cognitive Biases in the Analysis of Revolution

Moore, Skocpol, and Goldstone fail to be explicit about their use of counterfactuals and are thus susceptible to certain of the cognitive illusions identified by Tetlock and Belkin (Chapter 1). Is this because the requirements of cognitive clarity are contradictory? We don't think so. Rather, we think that the reason there is so little progress in recognizing and correcting cognitive biases lies, first, in the failure to make their counterfactuals explicit and, second, in the kind of structuralist theory to which they are committed. These are criticisms to which most of us are subject—including those of us who do deductive, comparative historical work in a rational-choice framework.

There is another issue as well. When we tried to use the Tetlock and Belkin checklist, it became apparent that several of what are labeled atheoretical biases are in fact the direct consequence of the theoretical bias, that is, the commitment to a particular theory that makes it difficult for all of us who have such commitments to critique the plausibility of our own counterfactuals. For Olson, Roese, and Deibert, the "intuitive theory" of the analyst is one of the factors that affect the content of counterfactual reasoning. They argue that counterfactuals reflect perceivers' beliefs about how antecedents and outcomes are related (Olson, Roese, and Deibert, Commentary 2). This is certainly descriptive of Moore, Skocpol, Goldstone, and, we suspect, of ourselves and others as well.

[18] The problem of reflexivity may make even these structuralist predictions within broad time frames problematic. If sociological theories of revolution are correct and if rulers are aware of them (two fairly big "ifs"), these rulers may be able to take actions that would prevent the revolutions, and thus falsify the structuralist theories.

Conclusions

Abstract discussions by philosophers and very concrete analyses of particular arguments in history (especially economic history) dominate the literature on counterfactuals. In this paper we add some middle-range arguments that try to evaluate the use of implicit counterfactuals in comparative historical work and suggest ways to improve the usefulness of this tool.

In most instances additional empirical cases cannot replace counterfactuals in historical and comparative research. The failure of most people doing social science history to realize this unnecessarily weakens their work. This is demonstrated by the problems that arise when even the best scholars, such as Moore, Skocpol, and Goldstone, lack explicit counterfactuals. We argue that general deductive theory best facilitates explicitness about counterfactuals and that their inductive approach hinders both the creation and evaluation of counterfactual claims. Of course, we should note that while deductive theory is a necessary condition for using explicit counterfactuals well, it is not sufficient. Much deductive historical work, including our own, does not make adequate use of counterfactuals.

Not only is theory important for counterfactuals, but counterfactuals contribute to the development of theory, as well. The elaboration of counterfactuals increases the explicitness of a theory; it suggests additional implications. Counterfactuals can also aid in the specification of the scope of theories, by clarifying the range of "possible worlds" to which the theory applies.[19] Finally, counterfactuals can help in theory-guided case selection, because what is counterfactual in one historical period may be a factual depiction of cases that will exist in some future period. The use of counterfactuals in this way increases the likelihood of using theories in maximally diverse (within scope conditions) empirical settings.

A large part of our argument is really a plea for even more care and attention to careful logic and method in social science history. In the process of investigating examples of the best recent research on revolution, however, we identify the kinds of work in which counterfactuals are most useful as an additional theoretical and methodological tool. Relatively rare events that can be modeled as having relatively deterministic causes are particularly strong candidates for counterfactual thought experiments. Without numerous additional cases, simulation, or artificial intelligence models, the small-N problem looms large. Counterfactual reasoning offers an exploratory theoretical device to complement or help compensate for a dearth of cases and events.

---

[19] Of course, when theories are well developed enough to have clear scope conditions already, the scope conditions determine the range of relevant counterfactuals.

Part Four _____

COUNTERFACTUALS AND GAME THEORY

9

Counterfactuals and International Affairs

SOME INSIGHTS FROM GAME THEORY

BRUCE BUENO DE MESQUITA

IN 1963 I worked as a clerk in a New York City candy store, selling news-papers, school supplies, and the like.[1] One day a customer asked if I thought the Kennedys' infant son who died a few days after birth would have grown up to be president of the United States. I protested that I could not know because, after all, he had died in infancy. The customer persisted until I gave an answer. Then he insisted that I defend my answer. This was my first conscious experience in thinking about counterfactuals and their role in un-derstanding history.

The futile debate with my candy-store customer (who also introduced me to phenomenology and several other branches of philosophy) went on for some months. It was (as is evident from my writing about it now, more than thirty years later) a stimulating, exhilarating, and memorable experience. Although this customer taught me a great deal, I still insist that it was a futile discussion about a relatively uninteresting counterfactual. The counter-factual issue he raised was inadequately anchored in a clearly specified argu-ment that linked premises to conclusions. There was neither a logical nor an empirical foundation for thinking that the issue was any more plausible than that you or I would become president. Yet I also began to appreciate that not all discussions of counterfactual arguments are futile.

Counterfactual reasoning, when carefully grounded in a coherent struc-ture, can play a central role in the evaluation of international affairs. In particular, the assessment of counterfactuals provides a basis for understand-ing whether what has been (or will be) was, ex ante, the likely path of events. Here I hope to explain some natural ways in which game theory, as a coherent guide to argument, structures analytic attention to counterfactuals of particular sorts. I illustrate my main points with historical examples drawn from twentieth-century European history and from twelfth- and thir-teenth-century relations between the papacy and the king of France. In doing

[1] I am grateful to Aaron Belkin, James Morrow, Andrew Rutten, Philip Tetlock, and Barry Weingast for helpful comments on this chapter.

so I apply both nomothetic and idiographic methods, linking the application of the latter to propositions supported by the former. I also make some use of simulation techniques, though not in as great depth as can be found in Cederman (Chapter 11).

Counterfactual argument is concerned with facts that did not happen. Many historians and other scholars concerned with international (or other) relations try, therefore, to apply research methods intended to minimize their reliance on counterfactual elements. Indeed, the focus of most historical and empirical analysis is on what really did happen, not on what might have happened. Yet what really happens is often—perhaps always—the product of expectations about what would have happened had another course of action been chosen. When what really happens is influenced by judgments about the responses of others to alternative courses of action, then game theory provides a useful basis for examining the merits of rival counterfactual claims and for providing an axiomatically grounded explanation of history.

Game theory provides a useful way to structure counterfactual arguments in that the solution to extensive form games *requires* explicit attentiveness to counterfactuals in at least two central ways: the solutions or predictions from extensive form games depend on what is expected to happen "off the equilibrium path"; and games often have more than one equilibrium solution, each of which represents a plausible state of the relevant world. Equilibria not chosen in a game with multiple equilibria and off-the-equilibrium-path expectations represent two important sources of counterfactual argument that influence the chain of causality from a game-theoretic perspective. For a game theorist, therefore, counterfactuals are not to be avoided, but rather to be used as important tools in understanding reality and beliefs about it.

I begin by discussing "off the equilibrium path" counterfactuals, illustrating my central points with hypothetical and historical examples. My historical focus here is on Adolf Hitler's decision to invade Poland and that decision's relationship to expectations about how Neville Chamberlain's Britain would respond. Then I examine multiple equilibria as another source of logically rigorous and empirically testable counterfactual argument. In that discussion I turn attention to the appointment of bishops in France during the reign of Philip Augustus (1179–1223) to examine the distribution of appointments between those beholden to the pope and those with close personal ties to Philip.

"Off the Equilibrium Path" Expectations as Counterfactuals

The central means of solving noncooperative games—the Nash equilibrium—depends on each player choosing a strategy, or complete plan of action, such that no unilateral defection from that strategy can make the player expect to be better off. This means that in choosing a strategy, each player must think about the expected consequences of selecting another plan of action. What would happen under these alternative, unchosen plans of action represents counterfactual expectations "off the equilibrium path." Each such expectation involves an analysis of counterfactual realities that were rejected because some decision maker viewed the alternative state of the world as less beneficial than the *chosen* reality. Similar assessments of the dependence of causal logic on counterfactual analysis can be found in Weingast (Chapter 10) and Turner (Commentary 1).

Let me illustrate the logic of off-the-equilibrium-path reasoning with a well-known belief about international alliances. It has been widely observed (and hotly contested) that alliances are worth no more than the paper on which they are written. It has also been noted that alliances may be worse than worthless; they may be entangling, drawing nations into conflicts they might otherwise escape. The presumed limitations of alliance agreements are eloquently expressed in lines sung by King Mongkut in *The King and I*:

> Shall I join with other nations in alliance?
> If allies are weak, am I not best alone?
> If allies are strong with power to protect me,
> Might they not protect me out of all I own?
>
> (Rodgers and Hammerstein 1951, 34)

Anecdotal and systematic observations reinforce the claim that alliances are worthless or even harmful pieces of paper. Thucydides, for instance, provides a historical analysis of the problem reflected in Rodgers and Hammerstein's query, "If allies are strong with power to protect me, might they not protect me out of all I own?" Thucydides explains why allies might fight one another. His explanation depends crucially on a counterfactual supposition. Speaking through the ambassadors of the Mytilenaeans, Thucydides says:

> We held them not any longer for faithful leaders. For it was not probable when they had subdued those whom together with us they took into league but that, when they should be able, they would do the like also by the rest. . . . Now the reason why they have left us yet free is no other but that they may have a fair colour to lay upon their domination over the rest and because it hath seemed unto them more expedient to take us by policy than by force. . . . So it was more for fear than love that we remained their confederates; and whomsoever security should first embolden, he was first likely by one means or other to break the league. *Now if any man think we did unjustly to revolt upon the expectation of evil intended without staying to be certain whether they would do it or not, he weigheth not the matter aright. For if we were as able to contrive evil against them and again to defer it, as they can against us, being thus equal, what need us*

be at their discretion? But seeing it is in their hands to invade at pleasure, it ought to be in ours to anticipate. (Thucydides 1959, 3:10–12; emphasis added)

Here Thucydides makes an explicit argument based upon an off-the-equilibrium-path expectation. The alliance is broken and an apparent friend attacked based not on any action by the putative friend, but rather on the expectation of evil intended. Subsequent research provides evidence that this off-the-equilibrium-path expectation often leads to violent conflicts between allies (Bueno de Mesquita 1981; Ray 1990; for an alternative view see Bremer 1992).

Although the counterfactual argument articulated by Thucydides helps us make sense of a class of alliance entanglements—when allies fight each other—my primary concern here is with the influence of off-the-equilibrium-path expectations that deal with Rodgers and Hammerstein's earlier question, "If allies are weak, am I not best alone?"

That allies, especially weak allies, are unreliable sources of aid in wartime seems well established if we look only at what really happens in war. Sabrosky (1980), for instance, reports that about 75 percent of allies do not come to the aid of their partner in the event the partner is attacked. Bueno de Mesquita (1981) reports that there is not a significant relationship between whether war participants had allies or not and their subsequent victory or defeat. That is, alliances do not make a directly observable difference in shifting the outcomes of wars one way or the other. And yet, alliance formation is a fairly frequent foreign-policy choice of national leaders. The seeming limited utility of alliances as sources of security compels us to ask whether alliances serve some purpose other than their ostensible role in enhancing security or whether the evidence about what really happened misleads us about the reliability of alliances. Here I am not so concerned with the former possibility, although there is an excellent body of research on the multiple functions of alliances (Altfeld 1984; Berkowitz 1983; Morrow 1991; Lalman and Newman 1991). Rather, I am interested in understanding why alliances are entered into if they are unlikely to prove beneficial when the contingent event (an attack against one of the partners) takes place.

The observation that alliances apparently are worthless and unreliable ignores an important counterfactual argument about expectations off the equilibrium path. Analysis of the counterfactual reasoning highlights features of what may really happen and provides a different perspective on the seeming unreliability of allies.

Consider the simple, highly stylized game in Figure 9.1. The game depicts an international interaction involving three nations, *A*, *B*, and *C*. *B* and *C* are allies. *A* is their foe. *A* has the choice to attack *B*. If *A* chooses not to attack, the game ends and the status quo prevails. If *A* attacks, then *B* responds by giving in or by fighting. If *B* gives in, the game ends. If *B* fights

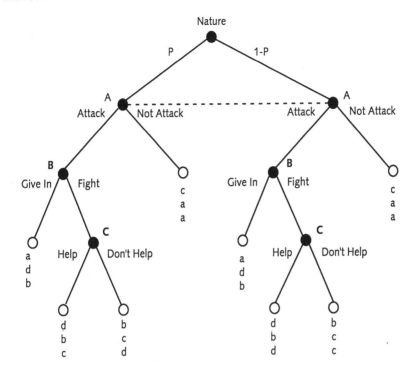

P = Probability C will help B
a>b>c>d

Figure 9.1.

back, then *C* decides whether or not to help *B*. *A* believes with probability *P* that *C* is the type who will help *B*. With probability 1-*P*, *A* believes that *C* is an unreliable ally who will not come to *B*'s defense in the event of an attack. *A*'s, *B*'s, and *C*'s payoffs (that is, their expected benefits minus the expected costs associated with each action) are listed in Figure 9.1 as values between *a* and *d*, with *a* being the largest payoff and *d* the smallest for each player. The payoffs for each complete set of actions are listed at the terminal nodes of the game, with *A*'s payoff listed first and *C*'s listed last.

Suppose *A* contemplates whether to attack nation *B*. *A* is uncertain about how *C* will respond. If *C* will help *B* (with probability *P*), then *A* prefers the status quo to an attack ($c > d$). If *C* will not help *B* (with probability 1-*P*)— that is, if *C* is an unreliable ally—then *A* prefers to attack rather than continue to live with the status quo ($b > c$). While many other sources of uncertainty are possible, I focus here only on *A*'s doubts about whether *C* will help *B* in the event *A* attacks. Assume in this hypothetical case that *A* is certain *B* prefers to fight back regardless of *C*'s type. Naturally, one can imagine extending this or related games to other levels of uncertainty and in fact this has been done (Smith 1995). What are the expected actions in this game?

To solve a game like this, assume that each player is goal-oriented and is interested in maximizing his or her payoff. Then, the players should look ahead to anticipate the responses the other players will make to the available sequence of moves and countermoves. That is, they choose from among the possible Nash equilibrium strategies only those that are subgame perfect (Selten 1975). By looking ahead and predicting what each player will do in response to each possible move by other players, each decision maker selects what he or she believes is the best reply at each juncture in the game.

In the game in Figure 9.1, for instance, A knows that B will fight back if A attacks because we have assumed that A knows B's payoffs. What A does not know is how C will react if A attacks B. A is better off attacking B only if C will not help B. So A must calculate the expected payoff associated with attacking B and compare it to the payoff associated with not attacking B. If A attacks, then with probability P, C will help B and A will end up with a payoff of d. This is the worst possible outcome for A. But, with probability $1-P$, C will not help B, so A will get a payoff of b. This is the best result A can hope for because on this occasion there is no chance that B will give in. By not attacking, A can assure itself of a payoff equal to c, the value that A attaches to the status quo. So A attacks (giving up the status quo) if: $Pd + (1-P)b > c$ or, equivalently, $(b-c)/(b-d) > P$.

All of this is rather straightforward, but notice the important counterfactual implications here. If $(b-c)/(b-d) < P$, then A does not attack. If A believes with sufficient conviction that C is a reliable ally, then C's supposed commitment to help B is not tested. A only attacks if A is sufficiently confident that C is unreliable. Naturally, when A does not attack it will have mistakenly foregone an opportunity to do better $1-P$ times. But, had it attacked when $(b-c)/(b-d) < P$, it would mistakenly have foregone a better outcome (the status quo) P times. The risk associated with attacking is just too large compared to the risk of giving up an opportunity by not attacking when $(b-c)/(b-d) < P$.

We can infer several important things about alliance reliability from this simple analysis. The observation that allies generally do prove to be unreliable when their partner is attacked tells us little about the overall reliability of alliances. What really happens may mislead us if we do not attend to what A thought would happen (the counterfactual event that does not occur) if it chose an alternative course of action. In this case, the expectation that C would retaliate is sufficient to deter A from attacking B at all. So, the prediction about A's action in this simple model cannot be made without information about A's expectations regarding the counterfactual response by C under conditions that end up being off the equilibrium path. A's actions are contingent on its beliefs about C's action if an attack takes place.

A might believe that C will not retaliate. In that instance, the action "no attack by A" is off the equilibrium path. The decision to attack B can, of course, prove to be incorrect. Again the counterfactual expectation off the equilibrium path is key to such an outcome. A attacks because it thinks that C will prove to be unreliable. Attacking in these circumstances is preferred to the off-the-equilibrium-path action of not attacking. After the fact, we might observe that A is defeated by the combined efforts of B and C. A's action was predicated on a mistaken belief. Because A's belief about C's reliability can be mistaken (and, indeed, it is expected to be mistaken P times when attacks take place), we can expect to observe some cases of fighting when the ally proves reliable and the attacker is defeated. That, of course, is consistent with the empirical regularity reported by Sabrosky that about 75 percent of the time allies prove to be unreliable when an attack takes place. That attacks against states with allies are considerably less common than attacks against nonallied states, and that attacks in general are rare, provide empirical support for the argument that off-the-equilibrium-path expectations deter attacks in cases in which allies are believed to be reliable.

The game-theoretic evaluation of actions in light of off-the-equilibrium-path, counterfactual expectations satisfies the criteria suggested by Tetlock and Belkin (Chapter 1). To solve a game, it is necessary to specify the independent variable(s) and the dependent variable. Here, for instance, the dependent variable on which I focused was whether or not A attacked B. Other dependent variables, such as whether B gave in or fought back, and whether or not C aided B after A attacked, could also have been studied. The independent variables include the payoffs at the terminal nodes of the game and the belief about C's type.

The assumptions of rationality, expected utility maximization, and the criteria for locating Nash equilibria (and its refinements) provide the basis by which the analyst connects the independent variables to the dependent variable. Game theory provides strong guidelines. It requires that the predicted actions be logically consistent with the equilibrium conditions of the game. Naturally, the logical structure of the game (or any other form of argument) does not assure that the theory is meaningfully connected to the empirical world. But, because the theory provides hypotheses that can be tested against the historical record and projected to predict future actions, the game-theoretic formulation offers a plausible foundation from which to evaluate the logic and empirical relevance of the counterfactual assessment. Indeed, the counterfactual analysis suggested above provides a way to make sense of several well-established empirical regularities that individually seem clear enough, but in combination have baffled many international relations scholars. The off-the-equilibrium-path assessment accounts for the high proportion of cases in which attacked states failed to get help from their allies, while also providing an explanation for why violent international conflicts are relatively rare between states. At the same time, the game-theoretic assessment offers an explanation of why some cases are observed in which allies do honor their commitments following an attack and provides some reassurance to those who wonder why alliances would be signed in the first place. Thus, off-the-equilibrium-path analysis not only helps us understand allied responses to attacks, but also provides propositions regarding the frequency of such attacks. In this way, the game-theoretic analysis expands the domain of dependent variables that might be explained as well as the number of cases that might be accounted for with regard to particular dependent variables. Expanding on King, Keohane, and Verba's (1994) argument, analysis of off-the-equilibrium-path expectations sheds light on the effects of causes as well as on the causes of effects.

Alliance Reliability and Germany's Invasion of Poland

A specific alliance might not prove a credible commitment for at least two reasons. An ally may lack sufficient interest to protect its putative friend, having entered into an agreement to extract benefits during peacetime believing that the contingent event of the agreement is unlikely to arise. There is always a risk that this might be the case in any formalized, explicit international alliance. Indeed, where the interest in helping an ally is unquestioned there may be no need to engage in the costly signaling associated with forming an explicit alliance (Morrow 1993). The United States and Israel, for instance, did not find it necessary before the peace agreement with Egypt to form an explicit alliance. Such formalized agreements, then, may reflect uncertainty about the credibility of the commitment of the signatories. The public aspects of making promises and then being seen to renege may, in such cases, help raise the chances that the commitment will be believed (by the other signatory as well as by rivals).

A second reason that an alliance commitment might fail under the contingent conditions is that a signatory, despite its interest in helping a friend, may lack the resources to intervene effectively (Altfeld and Bueno de Mesquita 1979). An arms buildup or mobilization, for instance, can serve as a costly signal that an ally is maintaining the capabilities necessary to punish a foe if it attacks a friend (Fearon 1994a). If the arms buildup is sufficient, then the foe may be deterred from attacking, as in Figure 9.1. If the would-be attacker believes that the arms buildup is insufficient to represent a credible threat, then that expectation leads to a failure of deterrence (Huth and Russett 1984; 1988).

In terms of the game in Figure 9.1, let us suppose that P—the probability that C is the type who will retaliate effectively—depends upon expectations that the ally is both sufficiently interested to fight and sufficiently capable that its participation would make a difference. We know that, according to the game's logic, an attack will take place only if $(b-c)/(b-d) > P$. Using this game we can explore a counterfactual analysis of the opening move by Germany in the Second World War grounded in an argument about off-the-equilibrium-path expectations.

What might we infer about Hitler's decision to attack Poland on September 1, 1939? Considerable evidence suggests that Hitler believed that Britain and France would not fight to defend Poland. He had doubts about Britain both with regard to the resolve of the Chamberlain government and with regard to the preparedness of Britain's military.

Chamberlain declared in the House of Commons on March 31, 1939, that the United Kingdom and France would aid Poland in the event that Poland resisted with force an attempt to threaten Polish independence. This declaration of resolve might have been seen in England as a vehicle to increase Hitler's conviction that Britain was serious about stopping an attack against Poland. That was its apparent intent. The declaration had several characteris tics, however, that made it an unlikely vehicle for successfully deterring Germany.

One apparent British objective behind the Polish guarantee was to encourage the Poles to negotiate with Germany over Danzig (A. J. P. Taylor 1961). In actuality, British posturing seems to have encouraged Polish intransigence instead (Newman 1976). Rather than reducing tensions with Germany, the guarantee may have exacerbated the situation. The declaration was also expected to send a strong signal that Britain was ready to guarantee Poland, but the exact wording of the declaration instead discouraged confidence in British resolve. Chamberlain specifically chose to refer to a threat to Poland's *independence* rather than to its territorial integrity. Indeed, Thorne (1967) and others argue that Chamberlain was prepared for "another Munich" (Wandycz 1986), suggesting that the guarantee was little more than a bluff. Whatever Chamberlain's intention, Hitler apparently did not believe the British would fight over Poland. For instance, Joseph Kennedy, then American ambassador to the United Kingdom, reported being informed by his colleague Anthony Drexel Biddle IV that "Ribbentrop was now pressing for immediate action against Poland, on the assumption that Britain and France would not support her" (Watt 1989, 183–84). Speer (1970, 227) maintains that even after the British declaration of war on September 3, Hitler did not believe that Britain and France would actually fight.

Hitler's doubts about Britain's type (the size of P) did not depend solely on his skepticism about Britain's interest in aiding Poland (which was clearly controversial within the United Kingdom). His doubts were also influenced by his judgment of Germany's military preparedness relative to the Allies. Speer (1970), for instance, reports that Hitler argued on the eve of the Polish invasion:

> Let us assume that because of our rapid rearmament we hold a four to one advantage in strength at the present time. Since the occupation of Czechoslovakia the other side has been rearming vigorously. They need at least one and a half to two years before their production will reach its maximum yield. Only after 1940 can they begin to catch up with our relatively large head start. If they produce only as much as we do, however, our proportional superiority will constantly diminish, for in order to maintain it we would have to go on producing four times as much. We are in no position to do so. Even if they reach only half our production, the proportion will constantly deteriorate. Right now, on the other hand, we have new weapons in all fields, the other side obsolete types. (p. 225)

Hitler concluded, against the advice of many advisors, that the time was propitious for an invasion of Poland. Apparently, Hitler's belief about the unreliability of British promises to aid Poland played an important part in his decision making. He saw concrete evidence that reinforced his belief. Not only had the English been slow to rearm, but their government had shown what Hitler interpreted as political weakness. Chamberlain's earlier performance at Munich reinforced the view that the British government's guarantee of Poland's independence was not credible.

When Churchill was brought into the war cabinet, Hitler's estimate of British credibility changed. Speer quotes Goering's remarks immediately after giving Hitler the news: "Churchill in the cabinet. That means that the war is really on. Now we shall have war with England" (p. 228). Apparently the value of P was updated; England probably was the type that would defend its Polish ally. Still, the lack of British military preparedness was thought to give Hitler a substantial advantage for the time being.

Figure 9.1 suggests that if P were large enough, Hitler would not have attacked Poland.[2] This counterfactual inference is consistent both with Goering's reaction to Churchill's entry into the war cabinet and with other aspects of Hitler's conduct of the war.[3] Chamberlain was perceived in Ger-

---

[2] Recall that I assumed that P is a function both of Britain's interest in guaranteeing Poland's security and Britain's capability to act effectively on its interests. It is possible that had Hitler anticipated Churchill's rise to the prime ministership, then Hitler would have attacked even earlier, before Churchill could have hastened Britain's military buildup.

[3] For instance, Hitler did not use noxious gases or chemicals in combat, apparently out of a concern that the Allies would retaliate in kind. He was deterred by fear of the consequences of such a retaliation. Yet he did not hesitate to use such chemicals against unarmed, innocent

many as a weak leader who preferred appeasement to war. Churchill was seen as a hawk who would fight Germany. By the time Churchill entered the war cabinet, Hitler had already invaded Poland. Before doing so, as we have seen, he took into account the credibility of Britain's guarantee from the perspectives of both resolve and preparedness. With Churchill's late entry into the cabinet, Hitler's judgment about British resolve changed (P increased), but the question of preparedness had not changed in the few days since the invasion.[4] It appears that P had not risen enough to reverse the inequality, in which case the logic suggests that Poland would not have been invaded.

Had a hawklike leader such as Churchill become prime minister years before, instead of Chamberlain, then it is plausible that Britain would have been committed to a more vigorous, early effort at rearmament. If this counterfactual is right—for which I offer no evidence here—and if it had come before Germany rearmed, then the counterfactual claim in Figure 9.1, that Hitler would have been deterred, is supported by the logic of the situation and by the empirical record we have of Hitler's deliberations. (For an alternative, more idiographic counterfactual examination of this question see Chapter 4, Khong.) What it might have meant for future world events if Hitler had been deterred is, of course, another matter entirely. To develop a well-structured counterfactual analysis of such prospects requires a much more elaborate theory than I have set down here.[5] But at least it should be clear that logic and the historical record are consistent with the counterfactual claim deduced from the game in Figure 9.1.

Multiple Equilibria as Sources of Counterfactual Arguments

The alliance game depicted in Figure 9.1 can be played under three distinct circumstances: $(b-c)/(b-d) > P$; $(b-c)/(b-d) < P$; and $(b-c)/(b-d) = P$. In the first instance, A attacks, B fights back, and the tougher type of C helps B while the weaker type of C does not. In the second instance, A does not attack while B would have fought back and the two types of C would continue to behave as in the first case. In the third circumstance, A is indifferent between attacking and not attacking. Because there is a unique equilibrium for each of these cases, the game overall has three equilibria. Despite this

---

civilians imprisoned and murdered as part of his final solution (F. Brown 1968; Bueno de Mesquita 1988).

[4] Indeed, Hitler's estimate of the time it would take the Allies to overcome German military superiority proved accurate.

[5] Such a theory would require a multiactor game in which calculations about the expected competition between communism, capitalism, and fascism would have to be taken into account in a setting in which each of the relevant regimes might have been better entrenched and more militarily capable than was true in 1939.

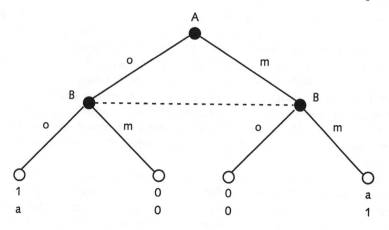

1>a>0

Figure 9.2. Multiple Equilibria

fact, we can easily separate predictions about the actions in the game if we know the value of P. Not all games, or situations in reality, have this nice property that there is a unique equilibrium for each possible configuration of expectations. Here, then, I want to consider equilibria themselves as possible sources of counterfactual reasoning.

Figure 9.2 depicts a well-known game called Battle of the Sexes. Although a rather simple game, Battle of the Sexes reflects many of the coordination problems that characterize international trade relations, alliance management, and a host of other issues common to the study of international affairs. The fundamental problem in this game is that two decision makers, A and B, each agree that they prefer to take a common action rather than go their own way, but they disagree about which action to take. A prefers an action I call o while B prefers an action I call m. A and B have an incentive to coordinate because acting independently leaves both worse off than taking joint action, but they also have a conflict of interests because each prefers a different action. The game is played under conditions that dictate that when A moves, A is uncertain about B's action and, likewise, when B moves, B is uncertain of A's choice.

Battle of the Sexes includes two pure-strategy equilibria and one mixed-strategy equilibrium.[6] The pure-strategy equilibria are for A and B each to choose o or each to choose m. It is clear that these are Nash equilibria of the

---

[6] In a pure-strategy equilibrium, players choose a given action with certainty. In a mixed-strategy equilibrium, players select actions probabilistically. In either case, the requirements of Nash equilibria must be satisfied so that a unilateral switch in strategy cannot improve a player's expected welfare.

game because a unilateral defection by either player leaves that player worse off than the strategies just identified. There is a third, mixed-strategy equilibrium. With P equal to the probability that A chooses o, and with Q equal to the probability that B selects o, the values of P and Q in the mixed strategy equilibrium are $P = 1/(1+a)$ and $Q = a/(1+a)$.

Any of the equilibria of the game are equally plausible predictions about behavior, given the axioms of game theory and the assumptions of this particular game. Naturally, in any given instance of the game, only one action can be chosen by A and by B. The actions are predicted to comply with one of the equilibria. Actions not taken that would have been consistent with another equilibrium represent perfectly plausible counterfactual claims about other likely behaviors. For instance, if we observe A playing o we can infer that we are observing a case either of the pure-strategy equilibrium o,o or a case of the mixed-strategy equilibrium, $Po,(1-P)m$; $Qo,(1-Q)m$. We cannot be observing a case of m,m, although that is an equilibrium of the game.

Mixed strategies are probably rather common forms of behavior. Most sports (golf being a possible exception), for instance, involve the frequent use of mixed-strategy equilibria. If an opponent's weakest defense in tennis, for example, is against a top-spin cross-court shot, one is still unlikely always to make that shot when it is available. To make that shot whenever it is available means that the opponent is given the chance to anticipate with certainty what the shot will be. In such a case, the opponent's defense against the shot will be improved because the opponent will not need to prepare to respond to alternative shots. Therefore, one is likely to mix shots to improve the chances of victory.

When multiple equilibria arise, an action that is a counterfactual in one observed case (that is, when the particular equilibrium's actions were not chosen) is not a counterfactual in other cases. Yet the relative distribution of equilibrium cases may be predictable across the observed behaviors. Consider an example from medieval France.

Appointment of Bishops: 1179–1223

In 1179 Philip Augustus became king of France. During his reign, he, like all kings after the resolution of the investiture struggle, was repeatedly called upon to approve or disapprove of individuals nominated by the pope to become bishops. The Concordat of Worms (1122) produced an expectation that popes would nominate and kings would approve. As part of the arrangement between king and church, it was agreed that during the interregnum after a bishop died and before a new bishop was approved, the revenues from the regalian see went to the king. As long as there was a bishop in place, the revenues from the diocese went to the church.

Naturally, the king and pope negotiated informally over the selection of a nominee every time a bishopric became vacant. The pope preferred candidates who owed allegiance to him or at least to the church, while the king preferred candidates whose allegiances were tied to the court. This question of allegiance was no small matter. The church in this period was struggling to become the dominant political unit in Europe and indeed in its broader conception of Christendom. Pope Gregory VII (1073–85) had largely staked the church's ascendancy on its ability to wrest control over the appointment of church officials, especially bishops, from secular authorities. In defense of his proposed reforms, Gregory had denounced simony and asserted the supremacy of the church over kings, including the Holy Roman Emperor. The battle over control of bishoprics may be understood as a fundamental struggle for political preeminence between the church and the nascent states of the high Middle Ages.

This is not the place to examine in depth the motivations of King Philip and the papacy. It is, however, important to recognize that both sides were cross-pressured. As noted, each preferred to see its own candidate selected as bishop. Yet at first both preferred to have a bishop in place rather than disagree over a nominee, leaving the bishopric vacant. Disagreements over candidates strained the already difficult relationship between Philip and the popes who held office during his reign.[7] Furthermore, the absence of a bishop also meant diminished opportunities for communication or bargaining between the church and the kingdom and it made it difficult to satisfy the religious wants of the people. With this in mind, I characterize the negotiations between the pope and the king as shown in Figure 9.3.

The game in Figure 9.3 implies several assumptions. The pope prefers that individual o become a bishop, while the king prefers individual m. The king is better off than the pope in the event they fail to agree on a candidate because the king derives the revenues from the bishopric during the interregnum and the pope loses those revenues. Still, in Case 1, the king prefers to agree with the church on a candidate rather than disagree. In Case 2, which is a different game, the king prefers to disagree and to keep the bishopric vacant unless the king's candidate is chosen.

Case 1 is Battle of the Sexes as in Figure 9.2. There are three equilibria: always select o, always select m, or pursue a mixed strategy between o and m. The mix, however, is different from that portrayed in Figure 9.2 because of the payoff b that the king derives and the cost $-b$ that the pope bears during the interregnum. In Case 2, the game is no longer Battle of the Sexes. Case 2 does not have a mixed-strategy equilibrium.

---

[7] It is worth noting that Philip and the pope had numerous serious conflicts. Some revolved around Philip's desire to have his first marriage annulled and his second marriage recognized by Pope Innocent III. Others revolved around Innocent III's desire to gain Philip's support in the election of the Holy Roman Emperor, around the crusade of 1190, and so on.

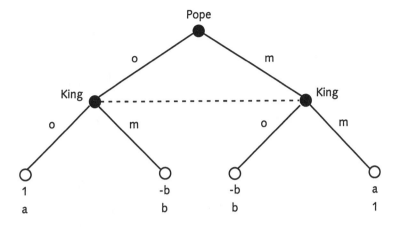

Case 1: 1>a>b>-b; Case 2: 1>b>a>-b

Figure 9.3. Selection of Bishops

In the mixed strategy for Case 1, P, the probability that the pope supports o, equals $(1-b)/(1+a-2b)$. Q, the probability that the king supports o, equals $(a+b)/(1+a+2b)$. The pope's expected utility is $(a-b^2)/(1+a+2b)$, while Philip Augustus's expected utility is $(a-b^2)/(1+a-2b)$. The probability that the pope's preferred candidate would be selected (PQ) manifests an interesting pattern. As b, the value of a vacancy during the interregnum, rises for the king, PQ increases until $b > a$. If $b > a$ (and $b < 1$), then the king has a dominant strategy: he will never support the pope's preferred candidate (o) no matter what he believes the pope will do. That is, if $b > a$, $Q = 0$, so the mixed-strategy equilibrium reverts to the pure-strategy equilibrium of m,m. In that case, the pope has no choice but to support m, because m is better for the pope than a vacant diocese. The precipitous change in the probability that o will be chosen as part of the equilibrium strategy is seen in Figure 9.4, where the value of PQ is simulated for hypothetical sets of values of b and of a. Once $b > a$, choosing o is not an equilibrium.

The reign of Philip Augustus was a period of economic expansion in France. This implies that later in Philip's reign more bishoprics would have had large enough revenues for $b > a$ than was true earlier in his reign. It is, of course, unlikely that *every* diocese would have grown sufficiently in wealth for $b > a$ to be universally true late in Philip's reign. Still, we can say that the probability that any given vacant see satisfied the condition that $b > a$ was higher later in Philip's reign than it was earlier in his tenure as king. If this conjecture is correct and if the pope and Philip played the mixed-strategy equilibrium before $b > a$, then we should see a distribution of choices for bishop that approximates Figure 9.4, although we should not

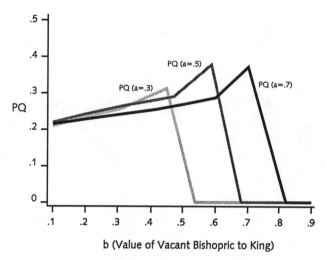

b (Value of Vacant Bishopric to King)

Figure 9.4. Probability Pope's Candidate Is Chosen

expect *PQ* actually to equal zero during the latter part of Philip's reign.[8] That is, the pope would have gotten his way with increasing frequency as time passed until the moment when the benefits for the king of the interregnum exceeded the gains from coordination with the pope. After that moment, there should be a significant decline in the pope's prospects of succeeding in having his candidates for bishop be agreeable to the king.

In fact, we can make a reasonably good estimate of the time when $b > a$ for Philip Augustus in a large number of bishoprics based on a concrete action he took that is germane to the game we are examining. In 1203, Philip renounced his regalian rights; that is, the right to the income when a bishopric was vacant. While some interpret this gesture by Philip as an act of contrition toward the church (Baldwin 1986), it might be that Philip knew that he now had a dominant strategy in most diocese that would lead to the selection of his preferred candidates for bishop. In that case, Philip could afford to appear magnanimous by renouncing his regalian rights. After all, the declaration itself was not binding and the pope should have recognized the increased need to select bishop candidates who were acceptable to the king. The game had changed from one of coordination to one of domination by Philip.

If the game structure proposed here is correct, we should on average observe a switch after 1203 from the mixed-strategy equilibrium to the pure strategy in which Philip's candidates are selected. That is, the pope is giving in to Philip, not Philip to the pope. The timing of the switch should be around 1203. If the implications of the game are correct, after 1203 Philip

---

[8] *PQ* would only equal zero according to the theory proposed here if diocesan wealth had grown to the point that $b > a$ in every diocese, a highly improbable development.

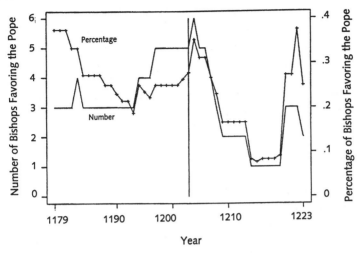

Figure 9.5. Bishops and the Mixed-Strategy Equilibrium

would no longer have cared about the income from many diocese relative to the benefits of having a supporter as bishop. Figure 9.5 displays the number and the percentage of bishops who, on ex ante grounds, were expected to support Philip over the pope.[9] As is evident, there was a dramatic shift in the likelihood that new bishops would support the pope after 1203 and the change is consistent with the switch from the mixed-strategy equilibrium to the pure strategy in many diocese, such that Philip gets his way. In fact, a statistical test for the difference in the mean value of PQ before 1203 and after 1203 yields a t-statistic of over seventeen. The probability that the post-1203 mean for PQ equals the pre-1203 mean is almost infinitesimally small.[10] Only as the period nears Philip's terminal illness and death do we see an increase in propapal bishops. The standard historical analysis of this period leads to the hypothesis that after 1203 the pope should have gotten his way more often. Had this alternate state of the world been observed, of course, that would fundamentally challenge expectations from the theory set out here.

What does this game tell us about counterfactual arguments? Given that there are multiple equilibria in Case 1, we cannot predict with certainty that any one bishop would have been more favorable to Philip or to the pope.

[9] Judgments about ex ante expectations are drawn from the appendix of regalian sees in Baldwin (1986). Newly appointed bishops are identified in terms of whether they were blood relatives of Philip, members of his court, etc., or whether they were relatives of the pope or within his circle.

[10] The test actually underestimates the consistency between the empirical results and the theory. A preliminary examination of the specific diocese where bishops favored the king or the pope suggests that those with best access to water transportation and mills were least likely to have pro-papal appointments. These are probably the diocese that experienced the most rapid economic growth.

This is true because o,o and m,m are equilibria and, of course, the mixed strategy calls for a distribution of bishops between o and m. Thus, in the selection of any single bishop we can plausibly argue for the counterfactual selection of someone who favored the pope or for someone who favored Philip, whichever was not chosen. Still, overall we expect a distribution that would favor Philip the later we get into his reign, just as we see in Figure 9.5. That Philip was conceding to the pope by renouncing his regalian rights is the disconfirming alternative hypothesis that could be supported by the pure-strategy equilibrium o,o after the regalian rights were renounced. It is, instead, apparently refuted by the evidence.

The analysis of the multiple-equilibrium game in Figure 9.3 raises several counterfactual arguments that are supported by the logic of the situation and by well-established evidence from history. In particular, because the selection of bishops was fundamental to the ascendancy of the church over secular authorities, we can ponder the likely course of church policy given greater papal success in designating bishops (choosing o) or given less success (choosing m). It is noteworthy that the church initiated policies whose likely consequence was to prolong the time when $a > b$, thereby gaining more bishops whose loyalty was to the church rather than to the king.[11] For instance, the church's antiusury laws were not generally applied to lay people prior to the twelfth century, but were vigorously pursued against the laity (and civil government) from the middle of the twelfth century on (Noonan 1957). Naturally, by retarding money lending for profit, the church helped stifle investment and entrepreneurship that could have increased regalian revenues for the king. Other policies of the church that may have retarded economic growth could also have prolonged the period when $a > b$. Had the church not enforced these policies, a plausible counterfactual implication from the game is that the church would have lost political control to the king more rapidly, possibly hastening the church's decline or leading to new policies aimed at suppressing the growth of secular authority. The Protestant reformation was the culmination of church-state competition in the Middle Ages. Had different equilibria been chosen, it is plausible that the demise of the church would have come earlier, perhaps without creating the religious schism that accompanied the decline of the church and the terms of the Treaty of Westphalia. Although I can only speculate here as to what might have happened, it is evident that other specific scenarios were plausible, at least given the logical implications of the multiple-equilibrium game that may have been played by church and state between 1075 and 1648. The

---

[11] I do not intend to suggest that there was a conscious choice by the church to retard economic growth so as to maximize its control over bishops and over kings, but I do intend to indicate that the church acted *as if* this was the objective. The chain of causality in the evolution of church-state relations and in the emergence of sovereignty as we know it today is too complex to be addressed in this chapter.

church apparently had an interest in preventing the evolution of Battle of the Sexes into the game in which the king dominates.

Conclusions

I have suggested two distinct ways in which game theory can be useful in structuring counterfactual reasoning. We have seen the counterfactual implications of off-the-equilibrium-path expectations and I have illustrated those implications with an analysis of the German invasion of Poland in 1939. These implications help account for empirical regularities that are sometimes considered surprising or even baffling to international relations specialists. We have also examined some counterfactual implications that arise in games with multiple equilibria. In these cases, several alternative states of the world are equally plausible from a logical point of view. By examining the history of the appointment of bishops during the reign of Philip Augustus in France, we have seen that behavior was generally consistent with the expectations derived from the game suggested here. Building on that empirical record, we also saw that alternative states of history were consistent with the game and that some of those counterfactual states of history carry fundamental implications about the evolution of church-state relations during a period of nearly six hundred years. The examination of church-state relations regarding the appointment of bishops also points to counterfactual implications about nondoctrinal reasons the church may have had for pursuing policies that served, whether intentionally or not, to retard economic growth in Europe. The counterfactual implications in this regard imply a number of hypotheses which, although not tested here, are broadly consistent with the logic of the game theory proposed here and the record of history. What is more, many of the hypotheses implied by the counterfactual analysis are testable, thereby supporting the requirement of a scientific theory that at least some of its particulars be predictive.

Counterfactual analysis is an inherent and explicit element in game-theoretic approaches to international relations (or any other form of relations, for that matter). Game theory is a body of thinking that encourages the systematic examination of counterfactuals. Indeed, unlike most historical analysis, game theory suggests that we cannot understand what happened in reality without understanding what did not happen but might have happened under other circumstances. "What might have happened" is a driving force behind the analysis of games in extensive form and is at the heart of the fundamental solution concept in game theory, the Nash equilibrium. Game theory is, then, one natural source for deriving theoretically meaningful and empirically relevant counterfactual claims about international affairs.

10

Off-the-Path Behavior

A GAME-THEORETIC APPROACH TO COUNTERFACTUALS AND
ITS IMPLICATIONS FOR POLITICAL AND HISTORICAL ANALYSIS

BARRY R. WEINGAST

COUNTERFACTUAL ANALYSIS has long troubled social scientists. This chapter addresses some of those concerns by focusing on a specific approach to counterfactual analysis based on game theory known as off-the-path behavior (OTPB). OTPB's importance derives from a model of how "what we don't observe" systematically influences what we do observe. Because it posits that unobserved, potential but untaken actions influence observed choices, OTPB raises several deep methodological problems. After all, how do we reliably determine which, among the thousands of possible things we do not observe, is actually of importance? One of the strengths of OTPB is that it provides a specific model for distinguishing important yet untaken, unobserved actions.

Both the importance of OTPB and its methodological difficulties are illustrated by a toy model about deterrence and the role of peacetime armies. Consider a country that is concerned about attack from a particular opponent. If it maintains an army of sufficient size and capabilities, it successfully deters all attacks. As a consequence, the army is never used.

As stated, the problem of strategic deterrence is explicitly counterfactual. From the opponent's perspective, attacking is worthwhile if and only if the home country is weak. If ever the home country appears sufficiently unprepared, the opponent will attack. Because of the opponent's expected behavior, the home country maintains its preparedness. The large army exists to repulse attacks from a potentially hostile neighbor. And yet, because the army exists, attacks never occur. Attacks by the opponents are therefore "off the path"; though attacks and retaliation are never observed in equilibrium, they are central to the analysis.

The central role of OTPB in the game-theoretic approach raises three fundamental and interconnected methodological issues. First, the causal mechanism is unobservable. For strategic deterrence, we may never observe whether the large army was sufficient to repulse an attack, let alone whether the opponent expected it to hold.

The second methodological issue concerns the problem of multiple theories about the world. In the deterrence example, because the home country is never attacked, some observers may infer that the resources going to the army are wasted. Others counter that the very presence of a large army prevents attacks. As the peacetime army illustration suggests, OTPB typically generates an "observational equivalence" between two dramatically different worlds (Weingast and Moran 1983).[1] The observational equivalence raises obvious difficulties about how to choose among the alternative views. Demonstrating that events and behavior are consistent with one is not evidence in favor of that view because the observational equivalence implies that they are also consistent with the other.

The third methodological problem is more subtle and arises in literatures that rely primarily on observations of behavior to infer underlying causal mechanisms. The observational equivalence implies that it is often easy to miss underlying causal mechanisms, as illustrated below. Yet, even in the case of deterrence where the counterfactual logic has long been understood, the complexities of the real world imply that the debate arises regularly.

For example, did the American arms buildup of the early 1980s significantly affect the downfall of the former Soviet Union? The answer is clearly not straightforward. My purpose in raising it is this: The question illustrates the interaction of counterfactual analysis and the observational equivalence. First, ascertaining the role of the United States's arms buildup explicitly requires attention to counterfactual analysis, one that is subtle and nonobvious. Second, the observational equivalence implies that, as with the peacetime army game, two polar interpretations are possible, one emphasizing the causal role of the arms buildup; the other emphasizing that the Soviet system would have failed in any case. Given that both views predict the downfall of the Soviet Union, political scientists and historians, typically working without an explicit theory of social interaction, are unlikely to take adequate steps to distinguish between these two views.

The difficulty posed by the third methodological question is not purely academic. As discussed below, debates in several literatures hinge on OTPB counterfactual analysis. Two illustrations discussed below are, first, the role of elected officials in determining bureaucratic behavior; and second, the role of political institutions in underpinning economic trade during the Middle Ages. A range of other problems also hinge on this same logic, for example, the role of political institutions in preventing the emergence of ethnic or regional conflict (Weingast 1995b).

This chapter develops the concept of OTPB and then demonstrates its central role in a variety of contexts. Section 1 provides the basic concepts.

---

[1] This does not imply that they are equivalent along all dimensions, only along some prominent ones. Moreover, the observational equivalence is often a problem for the observer, not necessarily for the participants.

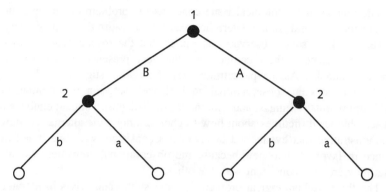

Figure 10.1. The Game-Tree

Section 2 exhibits two illustrations from particular literatures in economics and political science, the repeated prisoners' dilemma and the study of regulatory agency behavior. Section 3 provides a second extended illustration, the evolution of the merchant guild during the Middle Ages. This shows how the evolution of the ability to create the appropriate punishment helped police honorable behavior by the city. Prior to the attainment of this ability, rights of particular merchants were abused; after the ability had been demonstrated, it became OTPB, was never used again, and merchant rights were honored. Finally, Section 4 turns to the methodological difficulties raised by OTPB, including how to test models whose main causal mechanisms are unobservable. My conclusions follow.

1. Deterrence in the Peacetime Army Game

si vis pacem para bellum
(if you want peace, prepare for war)

As the opening aphorism of this section suggests, counterfactual analysis is central to the security dilemma. The simple game presented here serves to illustrate the principal concepts of the approach and is not intended as an adequate approach to international relations.[2]

Consider Figure 10.1, in which the home nation (player 1) decides whether to have a large army (A = yes, B = no), and an opponent (player 2), moving second, decides whether to attack (a = yes, b = no). Payoffs are determined as follows:[3]

---

[2] Indeed many famous works in international relations show that there are circumstances under which greater preparation increases the likelihood of war (see such diverse approaches as Jervis 1976, chapter 3; and Bueno de Mesquita and Lalman 1992).

[3] These can be adjusted if you can think of more realistic or clever combinations.

TABLE 10.1
Payoffs in the Peacetime Army Game

Outcome (H move, O move)	Payoff to H	Payoff to O
Large army, attack	10	−20
Large army, ~ attack	15	0
Small army, attack	0	10
Small army, ~ attack	25	0

For the home country:

(a) An army costs 10.
(b) Life without being conquered is worth 25.
(c) Defending an attack costs 5 *if there exists a large army*.
(d) If no large army exists, then it is overrun if attacked.

For the opponents:

(a) Successful attacks are worth 10.
(b) Attacks that fail (i.e., ones against large armies) cost 20.
(c) Zero otherwise.

This yields the payoff structure in Table 10.1. The table lists the payoffs for each of the four possible paths, that is, each combination of observed actions. Thus, in the first line, the home country chooses a large army and the opponents choose to attack. Under the assumptions above, the attack is repulsed and the payoffs to H and O are 10 and -20, respectively.

Given the payoff structure, OTPB is critical to determining the equilibrium. Because launching an attack is worthwhile for the opponents only when the home nation does not have such an army, no attacks are observed when the home nation has one. The opponents know that if they attack and the home country is prepared, they will fail; hence they do not attack. Given the home country's choice, the expected failure of an attack—never observed—determines the opponent's choice.

This conclusion is a consequence of the *perfect equilibrium* analysis, which requires that strategies specify a set of actions for the entire game, not just the equilibrium path. In the peacetime army game, the following is a subgame perfect equilibrium set of strategies (Selten 1975):

H: Choose a large army.
O: Attack if and only if the home country has a small army.

Given O's strategy, H needs an army, for only then can it repulse an attack. The paradox is that H's ability to repulse attacks implies it never needs to do so. O's strategy calls for it to attack if ever H fails to maintain its large army. The OTPB is central to this analysis of this strategic interaction.

Notice that this approach distinguishes between two types of unobserved actions, the set of all actions not taken and the set of actions that are part of the equilibrium but which are not taken. Only the latter constitute OTPB. The reason concerns the definition of a strategy, which requires the specification of an action at each information set, including ones never reached along the equilibrium path. An equilibrium strategy specifies actions for nodes that are never reached.

This provides an answer to one of the critical questions asked at the outset: If unobserved actions are an essential part of an explanation of social interaction, how are we to know which, among all possible actions not taken, are relevant? The game-theoretic approach provides an answer, for only those actions not taken that are part of an equilibrium strategy are relevant. Subgame perfection requires that these actions be in the interests of parties to take whenever they reach the relevant node in the sequential structure of interaction.

For the peacetime army game, H does not choose a small army, but this is not considered OTPB. By contrast, O never attacks H. Yet it is part of the equilibrium strategy for O when H chooses the small army (of course, H does not choose S precisely because of this expected action by O).

2. Illustrations from Modern Social Science Research

This section reveals how the logic in a number of important literatures in the social sciences relies on the concepts developed above.

The Standard Repeated Prisoners' Dilemma

Because the repeated prisoners' dilemma is commonly applied to problems of political and historical analysis, it is useful to emphasize how the approach to OTPB is central to the maintenance of long-term cooperation. In this approach, the threat of retaliation induces cooperation even though, in equilibrium, retaliation is never observed.[4]

Two central results about the prisoners' dilemma are now well known. When it is played only once, each player has an incentive to defect, so neither cooperates. When the prisoners' dilemma is repeated indefinitely, however, cooperation can be maintained. Repetition balances the short-run temptation to defect with the loss of future benefits from cooperation. When the value to each player of long-term cooperation exceeds the value of today's defection, cooperation can be maintained.

[4] Many references are relevant here. Perhaps most popular in political science are Axelrod (1984), Axelrod and Keohane (1985), and M. Taylor (1976).

Consider the standard strategies used to induce cooperation: for example, "tit-for-tat" strategy, which calls for a player to cooperate in the first period and, in all future periods, to take whatever action her opponent played in the previous period; and a "grim-trigger" strategy that requires a player to cooperate on the first play and, thereafter, to cooperate unless her opponent defects, in which case she will defect forever. Assuming some minimal conditions, these strategies induce cooperation over the long run. Although each player is tempted to defect today, the long-term consequences of today's defection check this temptation, so they continue to cooperate.

When all players adopt one these strategies, cooperation can be maintained. Somewhat paradoxically, retaliation is never observed in equilibrium; it has become OTPB. Nonetheless, this OTPB is central to the equilibrium, because it is the *expectation* of retaliation that maintains cooperation. Without that threat, the temptation to defect would be too large to avoid, and cooperation would fail.

The Role of Political Sanctions in Agency Behavior

When students of bureaucracy study particular regulatory agencies, they rarely observe sustained attention of political actors.[5] Few administrators of these agencies, for example, point to Congress as being important in their environment, and, for day-to-day decision making, Congress appears completely irrelevant (see, e.g., the detailed descriptions in Wilson 1980). Active intervention by elected officials appeared sufficiently infrequent as to be of little consequence for most agencies. This led most observers of agencies to conclude that Congress had very little influence on these agencies.

In the early 1980s, a new approach emerged, arguing that elected officials influenced agencies via an incentive system, rewarding those that served political interests and punishing those that did not (e.g., Ferejohn and Shipan 1989: Fiorina 1981; Kiewiet and McCubbins 1991; McCubbins and Schwartz 1984; Moe 1985; Weingast 1984; Weingast and Moran 1983).[6] Agencies that failed to pay attention to political officials risked various types of sanctions, such as smaller budgets and ruined careers for bureaucrats.

This interaction can be illustrated using Figure 10.1, where the agency moves first and may choose its preferred policy (A) or that desired by Con-

[5] This claim reflects students who focus on a single agency. Those studying multiple agencies or a sample of congressional committees often find different conclusions (e.g., Aberbach 1990).

[6] This literature has raised considerable controversy, for example: the role of Congress relative to other elected officials, notably the president (e.g., Moe 1987); and the precise notion of independence among bureaucrats (McCubbins, Noll, and Weingast 1989). Although there are no definitive answers to these questions, little evidence contradicts the systematic and pervasive influence of Congress and other elected officials on agency behavior.

gress (B).[7] Congress moves second and then may impose sanctions (a), altering agency policy to B (if necessary) at a cost, x. When it does so, the agency obtains the value of policy B plus some punishment costs, p.

Given this structure of interaction, Congress will intervene to punish the agency if and only if its utility difference between A and B exceeds the costs of intervention and punishment, x. Working back a node, this implies that the agency will implement the congressionally preferred policy position, B, whenever the utility difference between A and B is big enough for Congress to intervene.

As with the peacetime army illustration, the case of regulatory-agency policy making exhibits an observational equivalence. According to the first view, elected officials so rarely pay attention to regulatory agencies that these officials are irrelevant. According to the second view, elected officials do not attempt to police regulatory agencies via direct command and sustained attention. Instead, they do so via an incentive system that rewards those agencies that cooperate and punishes those which fail to cooperate.

According to the second view, in equilibrium sanctions need never be applied. Congress need not exert direct action for it to control policy making. Hence, at the very least, we have an observational equivalence between the world in which Congress plays no role and the one in which it runs the entire show.

The literature provides considerable evidence in favor of the second view, largely via comparative statics results. Although both views predict similar observations about what should be observed during normal times, they make different predictions about regulatory-agency policy change. Specifically, the second view holds that if the views of the relevant political actors change, so too should agency policy (e.g., Weingast and Moran 1983).

3. An Extended Illustration in "Real Time": The Evolution of the Merchant Guild

Greif, Milgrom, and Weingast's (1994) analysis of the evolution of the "merchant guild" presents an interesting variant on these themes. This shows how studying the evolution of the institutions underpinning cooperative behavior frequently yields interesting insights into the operation of those institutions and, in this case, OTPB.

Greif, Milgrom, and Weingast (GMW) investigate the relationship between the power of the state and the institutional foundations of markets. The standard economics view—holding that the state is an institution that should enforce contracts and property rights and provide public goods—

---

[7] For simplicity, I use "Congress" here rather than the more cumbersome term "elected officials." What follows, with some qualifications, holds for the president as well.

poses a dilemma: A state with sufficient coercive power to do these things also has the power to withhold protection or confiscate private wealth, undermining the foundations of the market economy. In the medieval world, these threats were sometimes realized, discouraging trade by foreign merchants to the mutual disadvantage of the ruler and the merchants. GMW argue that the merchant guild emerged with the encouragement of the rulers of trading centers to be a countervailing power, enhancing the ruler's ability to commit to honor contracts and property rights, thus providing an institutional foundation for the growing trade of that period.

There are two parts to the analysis. The first concerns theoretical investigation of the need and purpose of the organizational structure required to maintain efficient trade; the second concerns the details about the evolution of these institutions among German traders in Bruges, one of the major international markets during the Middle Ages.

The analysis's principal focus concerns the development of a credible punishment strategy for the merchants to use against the trading city. Once that was in place, it became OTPB and needed never to be used. As the analysis demonstrates, without this potential punishment behavior, German merchants were unable to protect themselves from the city of Bruges.

(1) *The OTPB model of the merchant guild*: To see why institutions are necessary, GMW begin by studying reputational equilibria, that is, those supported by some form of grim-trigger strategy or tit-for-tat behavior. In this context, reputation effects imply that foreign merchants trade in the city as long as the city honors its promises to provide legal protection for themselves, their goods, and their contracts. If the city defects, however, then the merchants boycott the city.

Reputational effects fail to police the city in this context because the marginal trader is worth zero to the city. The reason is that the model assumes that the city cannot costlessly expand and protect the market indefinitely. For example, after a certain level of trade, the city's costs per merchant increase with each additional merchant. This implies that, from the city's standpoint, there is some optimal level of trade in the city, x^*. The optimal trade level is defined as that level of trade where the marginal value of the last merchant exactly equals the additional costs to the city.

At the optimal level of trade, the value of the marginal trader to the city is zero: additional revenue exactly equals the additional costs. Therefore, the costs to the city of a boycott by the marginal merchant is zero. This implies that boycotts by those who experience problems are completely ineffective in policing honorable behavior by the city. Reflecting this, GMW's model shows that the efficient level of trade, x^*, cannot be supported by reputational effects whereby merchants cheated withdraw their trade.

If, instead, all merchants boycotted the city when any one merchant was cheated, merchants could police honorable behavior. In this case, the city loses not the marginal traders, but all the traders. Such a boycott is not likely to be effective, however. The reason is twofold. First, a smaller level of trade can be sustained via repeat play, even if the efficient level of trade cannot. Second, in the face of a boycott, the city has considerable incentives to encourage smugglers, in part by offering high rewards. These two points interact because the model shows that a smaller level of trade is both more valuable (per trade) to the city and, importantly, it can credibly be maintained.[8] Acting voluntarily, merchants are unlikely to react in concert to police honorable behavior by the city.

The approach also demonstrates that when the foreign merchants form a specific type of guild organization, merchants are able to police the city. The critical aspect of the stronger organization is that merchants gain the ability to punish errant members who fail to adhere to the boycott (e.g., by revoking the trading privileges of errant merchants by throwing them out of the guild). In this case, merchants are able to defeat the incentives offered by smuggling, and hence are able to sustain the type of boycott that will allow them to police the city.

OTPB is thus central to this analysis. The ability of the German merchants hinged solely on their ability credibly to threaten the city with a boycott. Until they could do so, their rights were trampled. Once they demonstrated the ability, their rights were respected and boycotts were not needed.

(2) *The evolution of the German Hansa*: We also argue that the theoretical sequence described above corresponds to the sequential stages of organization of the German Hansa in its ongoing troubles with the trading city of Bruges. In the beginning, German merchants were vulnerable because they were not organized. During this period, they were subject to ongoing abuses. Their attempts to punish the city via boycotts proved inadequate to police the city, in part because of smuggling by German merchants who defected from the boycott.

German merchants reacted by improving their organizational capabilities in two stages. In the first, they formed voluntary organizations, but still lacked the capacity to cripple the city. This failure occurred because they did not have the ability to punish one another for failure to conform to the boycott. Finally, in the mid-fourteenth century the Germans formed the mature Hansa, giving them effective power over one another. For example, any German city whose merchants were found violating guild rules or edicts could be permanently removed from the guild and potentially lose its trading privileges. This gave German merchants the effective boycott they needed,

[8] This is clear when we consider the notion that cheating a smuggler would lead to the failure of smuggling, hence to the success of a boycott. Hence the incentives for the city to honor agreements with smugglers are much larger than its incentives to honor agreements at the efficient level of trade.

put into effect only once shortly after the formation of the Hansa, and not needed again for the next two centuries.

(3) *Methodological implications*: Greif, Milgrom, and Weingast do not model the sequential development of the organizations nor the changes in equilibria over time (that is too hard!). Instead, they attempt to show, via a series of theoretical results, how the increasingly sophisticated guild organization expanded in a logical way to enable its members to boycott the city effectively.

The entire problem in protecting economic trade concerned developing a credible retaliation strategy by the German merchants. Once that was in place, it need never be used. Greif, Milgrom, and Weingast's account shows the development of a credible retaliation strategy via a series of stages and in reaction to a series of problems that emerged during unsuccessful boycotts. Once the Germans demonstrated they had overcome these problems, Bruges never again attempted to take advantage of them.

4. Methodological Issues

As a model of counterfactual analysis, OTPB raises substantial methodological problems. The very nature of the model is that the principal causal mechanisms should be unobserved. Importantly, the approach also suggests some answers. In this section, I raise two methodological problems.

The first and most important is this: Among all the possible things we do not observe, how do we decide which were really important? The game-theoretic approach to OTPB directly provides the answer. The concept of perfect equilibrium requires that each strategy specify behavior for all possible contingencies, including those never reached or observed during equilibrium play. Built into this notion of equilibrium, then, is an explicit model of the relevant counterfactuals. Further, the equilibrium nature of the model provides two internal checks on its predictions about counterfactual behavior. First, the equilibrium tells us why certain paths were chosen based on explicit expectations about what would have happened had a different path been taken. The model therefore forces the analysis to make two components of counterfactuals explicit: (a) the conjectures about the counterfactual; and (b) the hypothesized relative magnitudes between the equilibrium and the off-the-path counterfactual. Second, although the counterfactual behavior is off the path, as part of the equilibrium, it too must meet an internal check: the predicted behavior must be in the interests of actors to carry out if called on to do so. The hypothesized OTPB must be credible, that is, it must be in the interests of the relevant parties to play in the manner prescribed by the counterfactual were that path, in fact, played.

The peacetime army game illustrates the two internal checks. Recall that the home country's choice to maintain a large army rested on the expectation of its opponent's behavior: The latter would attack if and only if the home country had no army. Built into the equilibrium is the relevant counterfactual: Without a large army, the opponent will attack. The first internal check requires that the home country be better off choosing a large army than choosing no army, which results in a successful attack by the opponents. The second internal check required by the concept of perfect equilibrium is that all off-the-path behavior be credible. For the peacetime army game, this requires that the opponent's strategy be credible. In the peacetime army game, this requires that the opponent be willing to attack if (and only if) the home country fails to raise an army. The game showed this to be true.

The counterfactual analysis in the peacetime army game is particularly transparent, thus seemingly trivial. In other cases, the behavior is not so transparent and is easily missed by observers. The central importance of sectional balance during the antebellum era illustrates this point. Although historians have long known about sectional balance, its full implications were not well understood, and many historians listed it as one among many factors rather than the central factor underlying sectional peace prior to 1850.

The systematic incorporation of counterfactual analysis in the heart of game theory's equilibrium analysis thus provides an important tool for the study of behavior.

The second methodological question arises because the model predicts that central features of OTPB and its underlying causal mechanism should *not* be observed. Put another way, the model appears to predict a *zero correlation* between the independent variables and the dependent variables. The logic of the peacetime army game, for example, suggests that potential retaliation determines the opponent's behavior. And yet, the actual retaliation observed may appear perverse: to the extent that an opponent only attacks a weak country, *retaliation will be observed to fail, not to succeed* as OTPB predicts. The observation is not inconsistent with the theory. But, if so, how are we to test the model? How are we to have confidence in a mechanism that is rarely observed?

I pose four responses to this methodological difficulty. The first, and perhaps least systematically understood, is that game theory is only approximate. It is based on rational self-interest. Two implications follow if individuals pursue their self-interest most but not all of the time (for example, if they sometimes misperceive their strategic situation). First, the model should hold in most cases. Second, when this type of misperception occurs, we ought to observe behavior that is off the path. For example, if individuals sometimes fail to perceive or calculate their maximal strategies, they may veer off the path. When they do, the model predicts (assuming mistakes are not so frequent as to occur in succession) that we should observe the predicted off-the-path response. In the case of political influence over agencies, on occasion agency heads (often amateurs incompletely familiar with the ways of Washington) do not perceive the strength of the hidden congressional mechanism, and thus draw the wrath of congressional retaliation.

The second and more important response to the objection that the model predicts the importance of unobservable mechanisms concerns comparative statics results, or predictions about how observed behavior should change as underlying conditions change. Although we may not be able to observe the OTPB when conditions are stable, the model may yield additional predictions about behavior that can be tested. The case of agency behavior illustrates this point. If congressional punishment is not observed in equilibrium but is central to policy choices by bureaucrats, then, if congressional preferences change, so too should agency policy. A host of studies for regulatory agencies provides evidence for this principle in a variety of contexts.[9]

The third response to lack of ability to observe causal mechanisms concerns the study of the evolution of institutions and practices underlying the equilibrium in question. As the discussion of the evolution of the Hansa illustrates, it often takes time for the players to learn regularities in the world as well as invent appropriate responses. Systematic observation of that evolution can thus produce important insights into the implications of institutions, the structure of the game, and OTPB. In the Hansa case, for example, the initial inability of German merchants to retaliate allowed the city of Bruges to take advantage of them. Once the Germans invented the means for coordinating their retaliation—and demonstrated its usefulness—honorable behavior by Bruges became part of the equilibrium. Once the Hansa achieved its mature form, defection by Bruges and punishment by the Hansa became OTPB, and was never observed after that. But the process of evolution allowed us to see the development of this equilibrium.

Finally, to the extent that OTPB is a central causal mechanism in a particular circumstance, we should be able to find contemporary accounts that reflect this understanding. In the extended illustration of the evolution of the German Hansa, considerable evidence exists from contemporaries demonstrating that at least some understood the OTPB logic.[10] Yet accounts of this type are typically not useful for discriminating among the hypotheses. The observational equivalence noted in the context of the peacetime army game implies that we should observe contemporary accounts supporting *multiple* views, not just supporting OTPB. That certainly holds in the cases I have investigated closely (for example, agency behavior and sectional balance).

[9] For example, Moe (1985) and Snyder and Weingast (1994), using very different models and empirical approaches, demonstrate that the National Labor Relations Board is remarkably responsive to small changes in the preferences of political actors. Weingast and Moran (1983) provide similar evidence for the Federal Trade Commission.

[10] I have provided similar evidence for the influence of counterfactual logic in the case of harmony between the North and the South during antebellum America (Weingast 1995a).

The problem of the observational equivalence suggests a strength of the game-theoretic approach. The three previous answers to the second objection, especially comparative statics results, provide a potential means for going beyond the conflicting accounts of contemporaries to obtain new sources of evidence to discriminate among hypotheses. Without the theory of OTPB and the observational equivalence, empirical scholars often favor one with no theoretical or empirical reason to do so.

Conclusions

The game-theoretic concept of OTPB provides an approach to modeling counterfactual analysis. The approach addresses one of the most difficult problems with counterfactuals, namely, how do we privilege one particular event or action among many that did not happen?

OTPB does not necessarily provide political scientists and historians with the answer to questions; as the peacetime army game illustrates, the information given does not tell us whether the OTPB is really critical (the army might actually be a waste). But it does help formalize the question and suggest ways of finding whether it matters. Further, because it rests on an equilibrium analysis, OTPB requires that expectations of actions not taken satisfy a strong set of mutual consistency constraints. These mutual constraints provide a strong internal check on the use and abuse of counterfactual analysis. When counterfactual arguments are left implicit, by contrast, the occasions for such additional steps often never arise.

The analysis is especially important in the context of behavioral studies by political scientists and historians who base their causal stories, not on a general theoretical approach, but on specific observations of behavior. This often leads analysts to commit to a specific perspective without understanding or investigating another approach that yields the same observations. For the case of agency behavior, the natural inference from close observation of an agency is that political actors are relatively unimportant for agency decisions. Because errant behavior on the part of the agency is OTPB, it is rarely observed.

Illustrations of this effect could be replicated *ad nauseam*. As the discussion of the evolution of the merchant guild explicitly suggests, the problem of OTPB with respect to successful political institutions underpinning property rights makes the political component underlying economic development less visible to economists. Hence neoclassical economists, predisposed against political influence, rarely studied it. Similarly, another important phenomenon is easily brought within this type of analysis, namely the ethnification of politics as in the former Yugoslavia, Rwanda, and several of the former Soviet republics. Here too, the observational equivalence has led to strikingly divergent views and hence considerable misinterpretation of evidence (as I suggest in Weingast 1995b; see also Fearon 1994b).

OTPB also raises a series of difficult methodological problems, largely because central causal mechanisms are explicitly predicted to be unobserved. The first concerns how, among all the possible counterfactuals or actions not observed, do we privilege one (or a small number)? Game theory provides an answer to this problem, for the concept of subgame perfect equilibrium builds the counterfactual explicitly into the analysis. Further, it forces the analysis to make explicit the hypotheses underlying why the counterfactual was not taken.

A second methodological difficulty concerns testing models appealing to OTPB, given that the central causal mechanisms are unobserved. Several answers were suggested, the most important of which are twofold. First, game theory's equilibrium models often yield predictions about how particular types of behavior ought to change as some of the underlying conditions change, predictions not made by alternative approaches. Thus, for the case of the political influence over agency behavior, the OTPB model makes the following prediction not implied by the alternative, behavioral approach: If the interests of the relevant political officials change, so too should agency policy choice. Second, as the discussion of the merchant guild illustrates, an analysis of the evolution of the mechanisms underlying OTPB often provides significant clues to their operation. For the guilds, the interaction of abuses by the city of Bruges, the inability of merchants to maintain a successful boycott, and the evolution of institutions strengthening the internal organization of merchants suggest causal relationships that are not apparent from observing behavior of the mature system alone.

In sum, I believe the game-theoretic approach to OTPB is potentially one of the fundamental contributions of social science to the study of history.

Part Five ────────────────────────────

COMPUTER AND MENTAL SIMULATIONS OF
POSSIBLE WORLDS

11

Rerunning History

COUNTERFACTUAL SIMULATION IN WORLD POLITICS

LARS-ERIK CEDERMAN

WORLD EVENTS continue to influence the agenda for international relations research.[1] After several decades overshadowed by superpower strategy, the structural transformations marking the end of the Cold War have prompted a gradual shift of attention to what Charles Tilly (1984) refers to as "big structures, large processes, [and] huge comparisons." Of course, there is nothing revolutionary about the renewed interest in macroissues like regime shifts, systemic transformations, revolutions, nationalism, and integration. In the past, massive and sudden change has inspired new theoretical developments in the social sciences. It is thus inevitable that the recent transformations associated with the collapse of the Cold War order create a demand for theories covering not only comparatively stable periods but also turbulent eras.

Yet the supply of such theories does not match the demand. In recent reviews, Barbara Geddes (1991; 1994) found scholarship in historical sociology wanting. In her view, these sweeping theories all too often degenerate into an "enormous kitchen sink regression" with "variables always outnumbering observations" (Geddes 1994, 4). Because there are only relatively few great political transformations in history, the task of amassing a sufficiently large sample is hopeless. If we do not want to give up "science as a vocation," argues Geddes, we must break up these large processes into smaller and more manageable components, which can be deductively modeled and subjected to empirical tests.

Though Geddes's methodological qualms are not without justification, it is doubtful whether strict adherence to her prescriptions will promote a better understanding of Tilly's big questions. For one thing, the suggested disaggregation makes the analyst's task much easier, but at a high cost. Although concentrating on smaller problems surely yields larger samples, this redirection of analytical attention threatens to obscure important contextual

[1] I wish to thank Jennifer Milliken, Simon Hug, and David Sylvan, as well as the conveners and project participants, for their useful comments.

248   LARS-ERIK CEDERMAN

effects. Many historical processes call for an analytical focus spanning centuries as well as continents, and would thus elude the reductionist scholar.

Is there an alternative to the historical sociologist's huge but imprecise comparisons and the rational individualist's rigorous but narrow analysis? This chapter answers these questions in the affirmative by pointing to computer-supported counterfactual analysis of complex adaptive systems as a viable but often overlooked complement to the more traditional methods based on qualitative case studies and statistical inference.

How can complex counterfactual contingencies be evaluated? To answer this question, Section 1 goes through some of the criteria proposed by Tetlock and Belkin (see Chapter 1). Section 2 discusses how formal tools can be brought to bear on the methodological dilemma of complex counterfactuals. It concludes that although conventional rational-choice analysis falls short of this particular task, computer simulation offers a viable guide to counterfactual tracing of contingent, long-term macro processes. Section 3 presents a particular class of models, here called complex adaptive systems, which is particularly well suited to serve as a platform for the development and testing of counterfactuals of this type. Finally, the conclusion summarizes the implications of the present argument.

1. Simple and Complex Counterfactuals

To realize why counterfactuals pose serious methodological problems, it is necessary to distinguish between simple and complex situations. Our everyday experience of causality is based on simple settings. Everyone knows that if a ball is hit sufficiently hard and its path intersects a window pane, the latter breaks. One does not have to be a professor in solid state physics to understand this basic empirical fact. Thanks to our intuitive knowledge about balls and windows, there is no need to specify the underlying mechanisms that link the cause (the bat hitting the ball) with the effect (the broken pane). Causation is thus easily established as a straightforward link between the two events.

A simple graphical presentation may help clarify what is at stake (see Figure 11.1). Typically a counterfactual argument attempts to establish causation between an independent variable X (the antecedent) and a dependent one Y (the consequent) by showing that the actual outcome y would not have occurred in the absence of the antecedent x. This requires the analyst to construct an alternative causal path starting with $\sim x$ and leading to $\sim y$ (with "$\sim$" denoting logical negation). In the diagram, the "reality box" shows the actual course of history. The counterfactual scenario, however, lies entirely outside reality because $\sim x$ never occurred. In addition to the antecedent and

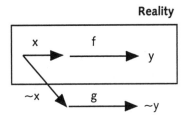

Figure 11.1. A Graphical Respresentation of a Simple Counterfactual

consequent, causal links or processes are needed, labeled f in the real case and g in the counterfactual case.

Returning to our simple baseball example, it is now possible to represent the situation graphically (see Figure 11.2a). In this case, X stands for the status of the ball, and Y for the status of the window at some later point in time. Here x can be interpreted as a ball hit by the bat, and $\sim x$ as the ball at rest. Furthermore, y symbolizes a broken window and $\sim y$ a whole one. Realizing that the window has already been broken, we look back at the chain of events from point y. The ball's trajectory f is well described by classical mechanics so there is no difficulty tracing the ball's movement back to its being hit at x. In the absence of impact $\sim x$, the ball will not move and Newtonian mechanics g (i.e., the principle of inertia) assures that the window remains intact. Under these circumstances, it seems straightforward to attribute the cause of the broken window to the bat hitting the ball.

The simple counterfactual story involving the ball and the window can be compared to a causal explanation drawn from international relations. Figure 11.2b replaces the two physical state variables by an X pertaining to the structure of an international system and a Y to collective behavior within the same system. Some theorists argue that bipolarity x promotes peace y whereas multipolarity $\sim x$ fosters instability and war $\sim y$ (e.g., Waltz 1979). Others claim the opposite (e.g., Deutsch and Singer 1964; see review in

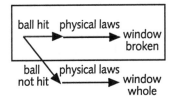

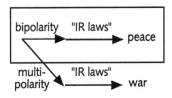

(a) Simple counterfactual   (b) Complex counterfactual

Figure 11.2. Contrasting Two Causal Scenarios

Levy 1989). Here "international relations laws," to the extent that they exist, play the role of Newtonian mechanics.

Superficially, these two situations seem to have much in common. In fact, some social scientists belonging to the positivist school downplay the difference between Newtonian physics and social interactions. For example, Milton Friedman (1953) observes that pool players behave *as if* they calculated complicated mathematical formulas in their heads. Other scholars disagree. In their view, humans and their societies are different from balls and window panes (e.g., Hayek 1967, 15–16).

In what follows, I will use this contrast to highlight the particular difficulties that must be overcome in order to answer Tilly's big questions. In particular, this requires satisfying at least three of Tetlock and Belkin's six criteria for evaluation of counterfactual arguments (see Chapter 1), namely, clarity, cotenability, and projectibility. Without clear specification of the *ceteris paribus* case, talk about big causes loses all meaning. Violations of the cotenability of thought experiments have a tendency to creep into seemingly watertight arguments, especially as the time horizon increases. Moreover, an extended historical perspective accentuates the threat that historical accidents pose to projectibility.

By contrast, Tetlock and Belkin's other three criteria are less central to our concerns. To limit the analysis to branches from actual, recorded history excludes important counterfactual inquiries into macro causes. The endemic lack of theoretically integrated and empirically confirmed generalizations in the social sciences render the evaluation of thought experiments based on these principles extremely difficult but not necessarily impossible.

Clearly Specified Antecedents and Consequents

In simple scenarios, the definition of the dependent and independent variables poses no problem. Either the window is broken (y) or it is not ($\sim y$). By the same token, the world in which the ball is hit (x) can be unambiguously contrasted to the one in which it is not hit ($\sim x$). When we say that the bat striking the ball caused the destruction of the window, we have an explicit alternative scenario in mind in which the ball would not have moved but everything else remained unchanged.

In more complicated scenarios, the distinction of independent and dependent variables becomes correspondingly more difficult. Figure 11.3 illustrates such a situation. Depending on how the independent variable X is defined, there may be more than one value that is different from x, i.e., what actually happened. If, for example, there are two alternative values (x' and x'') and the respective causal mechanisms (g' and g'') produce opposite

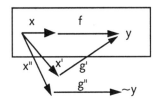

Figure 11.3. The Problem of Ambiguous Antecedents

outcomes (y and $\sim y$, respectively), everything hinges on which antecedent is chosen in the counterfactual case.

At this point, it is useful to return to the debate on polarity and stability. In a controversial contribution, Mearsheimer (1990) argues that the Cold War peace could be attributed to bipolarity and nuclear deterrence. Drawing heavily on the causal mechanisms suggested by Waltz (1979), Mearsheimer (1990, 14) claims that *"ceteris paribus*, war is more likely in a multipolar system than a bipolar one."* It is not clear, however, how "other things" could ever be held equal in the postwar case. Because Mearsheimer never attempts to sketch a counterfactual scenario, it never occurs to him that it is far from obvious what such an analysis would entail in the post–World War II world.

Leaving other possibilities aside (e.g., unipolarity), let us suppose that x stands for bipolarity and $\sim x$ for tripolarity. Complete specification of the causal argument requires us to specify a state to be added to the counterfactual story. One possibility, here labeled x', features a strong United Kingdom attaining superpower status rather than being relegated to the rank of secondary power. Another contingency x'' could feature, say, a Nazi Germany that somehow managed to strike a deal with the Allies, thus allowing it to retain most of its power in continental Europe.

Having specified the alternatives to bipolarity more clearly, we realize how hard it is to insist on other things being equal. Although some realists might claim that under x' trust would have broken down between the United States and the United Kingdom, a more likely development would feature the continuation of the "special relationship" between the two countries. This historical path would have rendered the post–World War II order even more stable than it turned out to be, thanks to the improved chances of deterring a possibly revisionist Soviet Union (cf. the link g' producing y). By contrast, in the case of x'' featuring a Nazi Germany surviving World War II, it would not be hard to envisage a postwar period sooner or later turning into a hot rather than a cold war. With two of the world's three poles being authoritarian and probably aggressively nationalistic, it is hard to imagine any room for stability (see g'' implying $\sim y$).[2]

[2] Neorealists are likely to respond that there is no need for counterfactual elaboration of this type because Waltz's (1979) "deductive" logic allegedly works irrespective of the actors' iden-

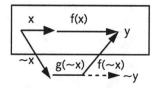

Figure 11.4. The Need to Guarantee Cotenable Counterfactuals

There can be no doubt about the importance of stating the *ceteris paribus* case clearly (Humphreys 1989). Failure to do so invites sloppy policy justifications and selective use of history. Because the need for explicit specification becomes more important with increasing complexity, this criterion is of crucial importance for our analytical purposes.

Cotenability of Antecedents and Connecting Principles

Even if the antecedent is clearly specified, the reasoning may fail. The entire counterfactual path g has to be consistent with the supposition $\sim x$. In the case of the ball and the window, this is easy to assure. There is no reason to believe that the laws of mechanics would change depending on whether the ball is hit or not. Thus we can safely conclude not only that f and g are identical but also that they do not vary with changes in X.

In complex systems, however, the assumption of the connecting principles' invariance cannot be taken for granted. As we have seen in the previous subsection, g may depend on the specific counterfactual antecedent $\sim x$. This introduces the possibility for inconsistent counterfactual scenarios in which the antecedent $\sim x$ clashes with the causal path g (see Figure 11.4).

In trying to show that $\sim x$ leads to $\sim y$, it is tempting to use the same connecting principles in the counterfactual scenario as those that obtained in the actual case. If it is the case that $\sim x$, the assumption that $g = f$ often breaks down. This is particularly serious if the correct causal mechanism $g(\sim x)$ produces y rather than $\sim y$.[3] Philosophers refer to the consistency between $\sim x$ and g as cotenability (Goodman 1983). Thus a counterfactual argument based on an inconsistent antecedent $\sim x$ that does not fit the causal link g fails the test of cotenability.

In his study of the "irrelevance of nuclear weapons," John Mueller (1988)

---

tity. Nevertheless, spelling out particular historical counterfactuals such as the possibility of Anglo-American relations turning adversarial illustrates how hard it is to sustain the argument in specific cases.

[3] I have here added an argument (e.g., the parentheses) to the functions f and g to indicate that these processes depend on the value of X.

runs into similar difficulties. To show that nuclear weapons (here x) did not contribute to the postwar peace (y), Mueller sketches a counterfactual scenario without such arms (thus assuming $\sim x$) in the hope of proving that the outcome of such a contingency would be the same as in the actual case, thus peace y. The problem with Mueller's account is that he explicitly traces postwar history as it actually happened (including the Cuban missile crisis!) while merely "subtracting" nuclear technology. This is a clear example of superficially rewritten history $f(\sim x)$ because it is unlikely that the crises that actually occurred in the nuclear postwar world would actually have taken place in the non-nuclear case, a point that becomes particularly acute with respect to the Cuban missile crisis. How could one envisage such a crisis in the absence of nuclear missiles?

It is hard to avoid the conclusion that in these cases a more holistic approach is needed. Rather than attempting to break the independent variables out of their context while holding everything else equal, it is necessary to take more than one step back and to consider entire "possible worlds."[4] In the tracing of complex counterfactuals, cotenability plays a key role in determining the consistency of the reasoning. The threats to cotenability are omnipresent, and without some type of system-oriented "accounting system," it is impossible to discover these threats.

Projectability

A counterfactual thought experiment is projectable if it is generalizable beyond the particular, single run of history. Failures to live up to projectability are common in historical accounts. In retrospect, it is tempting but fallacious to regard actual history as the inevitable causal path. This problem becomes particularly serious in complex cases that offer observers ample opportunities to select their favorite explanations.

As an illustration of the risks of such a hindsight bias in complex systems, it may be instructive to consider a somewhat more elaborate example (see Figure 11.5). Suppose that in addition to the causal paths f and g in Figure 11.1, two new alternative branches f' and g' occur with probability p and q, respectively. Under this assumption, there is always a probability p that the real case might have ended up with $\sim y$ rather than y. By the same token, the

---

[4] This point is made very effectively by Max Weber (1949, 187). For qualitative examples of this reasoning, see Glaser (1990) who compares the world of mutually assured destruction to one in which offensive strategies dominate. Stephen Walt (1987) contrasts a "world of balancing" to one of "bandwagoning." Richard Rosecrance (1986) discriminates between a "trading world" and a more traditional system marked by military competition.

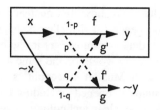

Figure 11.5. Path-Dependent Counterfactuals

counterfactual supposition produces the "real" outcome y with probability q and the opposite one with probability $1-q$.

This extension adds an element of chance to our deterministic physical scheme. For example, we could introduce the presence of strong winds f' deflecting the ball with probability p, thus saving the window ($\sim y$). Similarly, it is possible to envisage the alternative counterfactual branch g' as an earthquake, occurring with probability q, which demolishes the window (y) even if the ball was never struck.

The question is whether accidents wash out in the long run or whether their effect tends to accumulate, causing history to switch onto radically divergent paths. In linear systems, proportionality between causes and effects is preserved. In the presence of nonlinearity, however, small disturbances may spread throughout the system, rendering prediction impossible even in deterministic cases. This point has given rise to an entire literature on "chaos" (e.g., Gleick 1987; Richards 1990; Reisch 1991; Kellert 1993).

Going back to the world of international politics, it is not hard to find parallels to this windy and shaky example. Consider again the question whether nuclear weapons x explain the peaceful outcome y of the Cold War. Nuclear crises are indeed turbulent episodes, and so the probability of a fatal mistake p is certainly greater than zero. Yet John Mearsheimer (1990) implicitly discounts this probability by ruling out accidents as a matter of assumption. At the same time, he presumes that in the absence of nuclear weapon technology $\sim x$, the likelihood q of peace is vanishingly small. The latter assumption has been disputed on several grounds, because it is by no means certain that the Soviets were seriously planning to attack Western Europe (Evangelista 1982; Mueller 1988).[5]

Whatever the actual probabilities p and q were in this historical case, any empirical estimation of them would have to take into account real and potential accidental occurrences such as misunderstandings and risky decision making. To rule out these nuisance counterfactuals as a matter of assumption biases the analysis, especially if history offers only one run on which to base

[5] The actual estimates of p and q in this case depend on important theoretical assumptions. Although those adhering to the "spiral model" tend to fear a high p, to use Jervis's (1976) terminology, the proponents of deterrence fear the consequences of appeasement, i.e., a low q.

the estimation. In particular, noisy historical processes for which p and q lie close to one-half would make the task of establishing counterfactual causality difficult. Unlike large-N comparative designs, single-run thought experiments offer few possibilities to assess frequencies of association (Fearon 1991, 176).

Contemporary international relations theorizing could use a higher degree of awareness of such limitations. Not only are scholars too ready to draw sweeping conclusions about the general applicability of certain abstract principles, but they frequently transform these a priori inferences directly into policy advice. Again John Mearsheimer (1990) is a case in point. Having deductively "established" that bipolarity promotes stability, he argues that an American military withdrawal from Europe threatens to leave the continent dangerously disarmed and multipolar. To preserve stability, Mearsheimer recommends a policy of "controlled proliferation" or, more specifically, that Germany acquire nuclear weapons, advice he has recently extended to Ukraine (Mearsheimer 1993).

Here projectability of the (implicit) counterfactual depends on whether generalization is justified from the relatively stable Cold War superpower dyad to potentially fragile relations between countries that may even lack a secure second strike. Even if we believe this to be the case—by no means a self-evident assumption—the question remains whether nuclear weapons really did guarantee the "long peace" between the superpowers themselves. Mearsheimer's confidence in the stabilizing effect of nuclear arms rests crucially on the Cold War case, but it is hardly appropriate to infer anything about the causal impact of any factor based on "running the tape once." Those who argue that nuclear weapons should be relied upon in the future because everything went fine during the Cold War use the same logic as drunken drivers who refer to their clear record as a justification for refusing to give up drinking before driving.

Establishing projectability requires the analyst to sort out unimportant accidents from those that influence the course of history. This is the same as finding an answer to the tricky question posed by Carr (1961, 130): "How can one discover in history a coherent sequence of cause and effect, how can we find any meaning in history, when our sequence is liable to be broken or deflected at any moment by some other, and from our point of view irrelevant, sequence?" Henceforth, I will call causal arguments that survive this demanding test robust counterfactuals. Because historical contingency cannot be ruled out while answering "big questions" about complex systems, the criterion of projectability plays a central role in assessing the robustness of counterfactual thought experiments.

Having gone through the most important of Tetlock and Belkin's principles for assessing the validity of complex counterfactuals, we are now ready to draw several conclusions about the relevance of these criteria to the present focus on "big questions." To summarize, in order to answer "big histori-cal questions," a method is needed that *offers explicit specification of ante-cedents and consequents and guarantees cotenability and projectability in the absence of theoretical consensus or well-established empirical general-izations, while operating far from the actual historical path*. The task of finding such a method seems overwhelming indeed.

2. Simple Models and Complex Counterfactuals

Before turning to simulation as a solution to this dilemma, a few words about the strengths and weaknesses of conventional formal techniques are in order. There can be no doubt that rational-choice theory in general, and game theoretic modeling in particular, remain unsurpassed as a way to study comparatively simple behavioral systems. Though these models are usually not phrased in counterfactual terms, comparative statics analysis is nothing but counterfactual exploration (see Chapter 9, Bueno de Mesquita, and Chapter 10, Weingast). To return to the criteria highlighted by the previous section, rational-choice modeling is particularly useful in specifying ante-cedents and consequents, assuring cotenability, and checking robustness.

These points should sound familiar to nuclear deterrence theorists who, *faute de mieux*, have been forced to rely on formal and informal counterfac-tual thinking to overcome the paucity of empirical evidence in their field. Despite the abstract flavor of their models, these theorists have had a consid-erable impact on policy making (Achen and Snidal 1989). Whether one ap-plauds or deplores the particular ways in which their reasoning influenced policy, it is hard to deny the importance of model-based counterfactual ex-plorations. In fact, much of the policy debate revolved around issues of credibility of nuclear options, a theoretical problem tantamount to counter-factual cotenability. Incredible strategic plans fail this test because they rest on the assumption that if deterrence fails ($\sim x$), the defender would retaliate, thus prompting nuclear war ($\sim y$), a commitment that requires a suicidal and thus unlikely response (e.g., Schelling 1966; Powell 1990).

Rational-choice tools apply nicely to situations in which the bargaining protocol is reasonably well defined, as in voting and nuclear deterrence. Not surprisingly, these two areas are precisely the political science applications in which formal theory of this type has celebrated its greatest successes. Despite the hegemonic aspirations of many a rational-choice theorist, how-ever, game theory becomes much less useful in the realm of complexity (Binmore 1990). It may seem absurd to argue that formal voting and nuclear deterrence constitute simple research problems. Yet there is an underlying structural simplicity inherent to voting problems and nuclear exchanges.

Although many historians see nothing but single events in history, rational-choice theorists see precisely the opposite. Almost without exception, equilibrium analysis rests on the assumption that historical accidents wash out (Krasner 1988). In brief, history is assumed to be efficient. According to March and Olsen (1984, 737), "an efficient historical process . . . is one that moves rapidly to a unique solution, conditional on current environmental conditions, thus independent of the historical path." Rather than being explicitly postulated, historical efficiency usually enters the analysis indirectly as a consequence of seemingly technical assumptions. Economists almost always assume constant or decreasing returns to scale (Arthur 1990). Having precluded positive returns, the analyst need not bother about accidental factors threatening the desired unique predictions, because under this assumption, the system will rapidly return to equilibrium if ever perturbed. In international relations, neorealism, more than any other paradigm, reflects this preoccupation with stability. Neorealists assume that details on the domestic level matter little for the systemic outcomes of the system (cf. Waltz 1979).

But what if history is not efficient in this sense? As long as the analyst selects sufficiently short time slices for analysis, traditional equilibrium analysis is likely to be helpful. Yet any project whose goal is to explain long-term change must make the historical paths of the counterfactual scenarios explicit. Thus conventional formal modeling is unlikely to deliver the needed goods required to analyze large systems with large numbers of agents interacting in a complex fashion.

Although rational-choice modeling offers projectible counterfactuals in simple systems, its tendency to abstract away from "historical noise" undermines the search for robust counterfactuals in more complex situations. Moreover, cotenability problems stemming from temporal and spatial dependency may also escape the analyst unless the contextual scope is widened. Traditional formal models are often both static and nonspatial. Consequently, it seems necessary to shift the attention to a method that performs better in complex settings: simulation. By virtue of its being an experimental approach, simulation promises to produce robust counterfactuals without sacrificing the goals of precise specification and cotenability.

Simulation can be used in two ways: for predictive purposes and as a heuristic tool. In its traditional function, simulation research assists decision makers in producing forecasts in specific policy situations. This task has been largely unsuccessful in the social sciences, and I do not propose it here. By contrast, the second function is more relevant to the generation of complex counterfactuals: "Simulation is used at a prototheoretical stage, as a vehicle for thought experiments. The purpose of a model lies in the act of its construction and exploration, and in the resultant, improved intuition about the system's behavior, essential aspects and sensitivities" (Kreutzer 1986, 7; see also Sloman 1978; Hayek 1967).

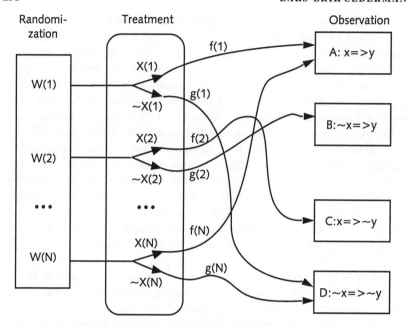

Figure 11.6. The Experimental Method of Counterfactual Simulation

The experimental method stands and falls with the ability to replay history in a structured and controlled way. Although assignment to the treatment and control groups must be random, the administration of the treatment needs to be controlled (Campbell and Stanley 1966). It is precisely this dual manipulation that allows for the deliberate introduction of historical accidents. With a sufficiently large number of replications, the accidental influences will wash out whereas the variation in the theoretically relevant variables will remain.[6]

This process requires the possibility of parameter manipulation, absent when dealing with historical macro processes. The second-best solution is to create an artificial situation in which the desired variables can be either randomized or manipulated. Such a stylized world resembles the actual social system under scrutiny without ruling out historical accidents.

A diagram helps to clarify these points (see Figure 11.6). The logic of computerized complex thought experiments follows that of traditional experiments closely. The process starts with random assignment, continues with treatment, and ends with observation. The difference is that the objects of assignment, treatment, and observation are not people, as in medical experi-

---

[6] Statistical quasi experiments rely on a similar trick. Yet, the structure of conventional regression equations impose severe, linear restrictions on the causal effects. Truly experimental studies are not limited by such structural constraints. As we will see below, the price of this flexibility, however, is paid in terms of lower external validity.

ments, but historical paths (or artificial worlds, if you wish). Randomization creates the needed variance to test the robustness of the systematically manipulated treatment variables.

Once having generated the required series of worlds, denoted $W(1)$ through $W(N)$, experimental treatment is introduced with respect to a small set of theoretically interesting parameters. This is where counterfactual logic enters the picture.[7] Each world $W(i)$ now bifurcates into two paths, one corresponding to the positive antecedent $x(i)$ and another to the negative antecedent $\sim x(i)$. If necessary, the number of treatment (or independent) variables can be increased, although one must keep in mind that each new binary variable raises the number of runs to the second power.

Now the counterfactual scenarios are unwound along the bifurcated causal paths. The positive antecedents $x(i)$ trigger trajectories denoted $f(i)$; trajectories associated with negative antecedents are denoted $g(i)$. As can be readily seen, these paths do not have to be "parallel" but may vary in a highly nonlinear and contingent fashion. Even if two paths $f(i)$ and $g(i)$ develop almost identically for some time, an accident may suddenly occur along path $f(i)$ that deflects this process from $g(i)$. In this sense, stochastic influences continue to influence the entire simulation.

The final step involves observing what difference the treatment makes with respect to the dependent variable Y. Again, this cannot be done for a single fork except by comparing the whole set of possible worlds simultaneously. For simplicity, suppose that both the independent and dependent variable are dichotomous. Then observation amounts to classifying each simulation run as belonging to one of four categories (labeled A, B, C, and D in the figure). Once the observations within each category have been added up, the causal effect can be derived by comparing two ratios. The first is the ratio between the number of outcomes belonging to groups A and C, which represent the y and $\sim y$ outcomes, respectively, generated by positive antecedents $x(i)$. The second ratio refers to groups B and D, which stand for the corresponding outcomes given negative antecedents $\sim x(i)$.[8]

As an illustration of this simulation methodology, the next section introduces a family of models called the complex adaptive system (CAS) and applies it to the problem of counterfactuals.

---

[7] Because counterfactual analysis, strictly speaking, presupposes the existence of a "factual" case, it may be stretching the term somewhat to apply it to artificial worlds. Yet if one takes some particular artificial world, e.g., $W(i)$ exposed to treatment $x(i)$, as the reference case, it becomes meaningful to talk about a counterfactual scenario, e.g., $W(i)$ exposed to $\sim x(i)$.

[8] Although Figure 11.6 describes the logic of the experimental sequence, much has been left unexplored. An important decision facing the simulation analyst is what to randomize and what to manipulate experimentally. In addition, there is also a third category: those elements of the model that will remain hardwired into the very framework and thus left unchanged throughout the tracing of the counterfactual thought experiments.

3. CAS and the Evaluation of Complex Counterfactuals

Originally a tool for the study of physical systems, the CAS concept has proved useful in exploring emergent macro phenomena in a variety of disciplines such as chemistry, biology, genetics, and economics (Holland 1992).[9] Despite the analogy between complex systems in these sciences and social systems, there have been surprisingly few attempts to employ CAS simulation in the social sciences. In a wider sense, however, the CAS approach is preceded by a long and rich tradition of modeling studies allowing for various levels of complexity. Clearly beyond the scope of this article, a full review of this literature would include references to classical work on cellular automata by Von Neumann and others (see Burks 1970), bounded rationality by Herbert Simon and James March (see March 1978 for a review), as well as Thomas Schelling's (1978) suggestive spatial models and Robert Axelrod's (1984) observations about the "structure of cooperation" and other work in the cybernetic tradition (see Alker 1981 for a review). Yet there is a growing literature focusing on "unorthodox" studies of economic systems that relies heavily on computer simulation (see Lane 1992 for a review). In political science this trend has been slower, but in recent years important work has been achieved (e.g., Axelrod 1987; 1995).

The CAS method is a particular way of studying complex systems by computer simulation. A *complex adaptive system* can be defined as *an adaptive network exhibiting aggregate properties that emerge from the local interaction among many agents mutually constituting their own environment.* Each part of this rather dense definition sets CAS modeling apart from more conventional methods (see Cederman 1996, chapter 3, for a more extensive discussion). Most important, a CAS exhibits *emergent properties*, by which we understand phenomena that "(i) can be described in terms of aggregate-level constructs, without reference to the attributes of specific [micro-level agents]; (ii) persist for time periods much greater than the time scale appropriate for describing the underlying micro-interactions; and (iii) defies explanation by reduction to the superposition of 'built in' micro-properties of the [CAS]" (Lane 1992, 3). Based on analytical nontransparency, this definition of emergence emphasizes the importance of not "hardwiring" the desired outcomes into the process (Holland, Holyoak, Nisbett, and Thagard 1986, 350).

The remainder of this section closes the circle by reconsidering Tetlock and Belkin's criteria. The aim is to find out whether CAS systems generate counterfactuals with the desired properties singled out in Section 1. Because

---

[9] Much of the research on CAS has taken place at the Santa Fe Institute. See Waldrop (1992) for a book-length, informal introduction. For a recent, fascinating example drawn from biology, see Fontana and Buss (1994).

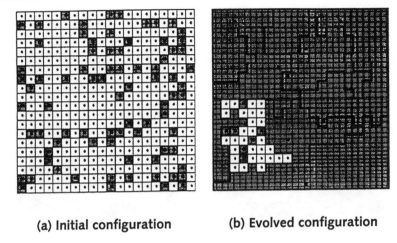

(a) Initial configuration   (b) Evolved configuration

Figure 11.7. The Evolution of a Geopolitical CAS

an extensive review of existing scholarship in the CAS tradition is beyond the scope of this chapter, I will limit myself to an unabashedly self-promotional perspective by drawing examples from my own work. For illustrative purposes, I will refer to a single example: a geopolitical model of state-formation and power politics (Cederman 1994). This CAS framework emphasizes the emergence of actors and structures in world politics. In this sense, it attempts to counter the common tendency to reify agents in international relations theory. In the conventional literature, states are usually depicted as if they were natural entities whose existence does not require any particular explanation.[10]

Figure 11.7 shows two snapshots from an artificial world consisting of many microlevel agents arranged in a square grid. The left panel shows the initial configuration featuring 400 independent states. Although the white squares represent status quo–oriented actors, the gray ones stand for aggressive powers. As the simulation progresses (see Figure 11.7b), the predators conquer their neighbors. The emerging picture is one of drastically reduced polarity. The figure also shows a state collapse; hence the patchwork of small actors in the lower left corner of the second panel.

Because a full technical description of the dynamic principles is beyond the scope of this paper (cf. Cederman 1994), the presentation has to focus on the counterfactual principle employed. As indicated in Figure 11.6, the simulation starts with the generation of parallel worlds. These initial systems

[10] Berger and Luckmann (1966) and Giddens (1984) explain what reification means in social theory. In essence, the term designates the habit of viewing social phenomena as if they were objects rather than socially constructed. See also Wendt (1987; 1992) and Cederman (1996, chapter 2) for discussions related to international relations.

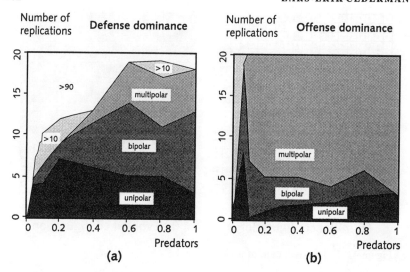

Figure 11.8. Analyzing Predation and Defense-Offense Dominance

contain 10×10 state actors and can be viewed as smaller versions of the world shown in Figure 11.7a. In this case, randomization means that the exact location of the predator states as well as the power distribution are stochastically determined.[11]

Instead of a single treatment (cf. Figure 11.6), the simulations feature variation in two parameters: (1) the frequency of predators, and (2) the offense-defense balance. Whereas the first variable governs the number of predators present in the initial configuration, the second one governs the risk-willingness of the aggressive actors. In the relatively defense-dominated system, no such state attacks unless the ratio is 3:1 in its favor. In the offense-dominated worlds, this ratio is 2:1.

For each combination of predator frequency and offense-defense ratio, the simulation model is launched twenty times, each run ending after 1,000 time periods or when one state takes over the entire system. This replication procedure produces a polarity distribution that is reported in Figure 11.8. Whereas the left panel presents the outcomes in the defense-dominated system, the right panel depicts those of the more offensive worlds. For each predator frequency the resulting polarity of the twenty replications is indi-

---

[11] Obviously, other dimensions were held fixed, such as the actors' basic strategies and the rules of combat and structural transformations following combat. As argued above, this means that simulation results should be interpreted with caution because it is impossible to predict the behavior of the model under other assumptions. Yet the claim that rational-choice modeling is superior because it produces deductive results is beside the point, because such an approach avoids complexity by "hardwiring" modeling assumptions into the game specification (e.g., the actors and their moves, preferences, and beliefs) (cf. Kreps 1990, 169).

cated. The five categories (unipolarity, bipolarity, multipolarity, more than ten, and more than ninety) are stacked on top of each other. For example, in the defense-dominated system at 60 percent predator rate, among the twenty replications five were unipolar, nine bipolar, five multipolar, and one exceeded ninety states.

To make things concrete, let us define power politics as any system that is at least bipolar but whose polarity does not exceed ten. Thus power politics obtains only in the bipolar or multipolar cases. Given this operational definition roughly corresponding to the expectations of realist scholars, the figure suggests that such outcomes seem to be rather insensitive to the actual predator frequency, at least in the offensive-dominated system. Figure 11.8b shows why this is the case, for either bipolarity or multipolarity results regardless of the actual predator density. Because this factor depends on the actual incentives of the units, this finding appears to confirm neorealist hypotheses about the structural invariance of geopolitics (Waltz 1979). Even more surprising, offense-dominated systems maintain the plurality of the geopolitical equilibrium better than defensive ones. A comparison of the two panels reveals this fact. Although power politics dominates the offense-dominated system, Figure 11.8a indicates that such outcomes are much less common when the balance tilts in favor of the defense. I will return to the reason for these effects (see also Cederman 1994 for details). For the time being, it is sufficient to note that this emergent pattern does not depend on historical contingencies in particular runs. Thus, in addition to achieving specification and cotenability, CAS methodology is helpful for testing the projectibility of complex counterfactual scenarios.

At this point, a discussion of how CAS relates to these three aspects of counterfactual analysis is in order.

Specification: Formalization automatically takes care of the specification problem because CAS methodology, like modeling in general, forces the analyst to render all categories explicit. For example, the offense-defense balance alluded to above is operationalized as the strategic factor required to launch an attack as judged by the challenging states. Instead of vague assessments of weapon systems, this precise interpretation renders the specification of the independent variable unambiguous and makes the identification of *ceteris paribus* cases straightforward.[12]

Cotenability: By virtue of its formal representation, CAS modeling also automatically generates cotenable causal paths, at least within the bounds of the artificial world. Thanks to the deductive machinery of simulation, errors

[12] See Sagan (1986) for an argument in favor of this definition and a critique of less precise measures. By the same token, Cederman (1995) uses a formal string-representation to model national identities. Under this stylized representation, the classification of identification inclusiveness becomes less problematic as a concept than if the analysis had attempted to distill an operational index of the same entity out of a wealth of empirical data.

of reasoning and other cognitive biases do not affect the result: you get whatever your microlevel mechanisms happen to produce, including counterintuitive outcomes. In view of the many obstacles that prevent manufacturing of consistent counterfactuals in complex systems, this is no small achievement.

A case in point is the counterintuitive finding about the influence of the offense-defense dominance reported above. Clearly this points to a paradox in contemporary realist scholarship (Cederman 1994). Contrary to what is usually believed, defensive mechanisms may under certain circumstances lead to hegemony and unipolarity rather than contribute to multipolar stability. The reason for this is simple: although these defensive mechanisms promote stability locally and in the short run, from a global perspective they widen the window of opportunity for potential hegemons by blocking competing great powers' attempts to catch up. Because defensive technology and alliances are likely to delay the campaigns of such competitors, the ascending power is free to absorb smaller states that would otherwise have been absorbed by its great-power enemies. If not stopped in time, the dominant power will gain control of the entire system, with unipolarity rather than balance of power as the final outcome.

Although neorealism derives much of its inspiration from economics, it has failed to carry the analogy through. Economic theory tells us that cartels and other types of collusion distort the market equilibrium, so the realists' faith in defensive technology and alliances as stabilizing factors should have become suspect. To put this argument in explicitly counterfactual terms, the contextual simulation highlights not only the immediate effects of increased defensiveness but also less obvious consequences. Such an alteration affects not only predation but also the competitive pressure of the system. Contrary to Waltz (1979), we must reject the counterfactual that if we lived in a world of defense-dominance, we would be safe from global hegemony. In other words, *to assume that defense-dominance curbs conquest and stabilizes balance-of-power equilibria is not cotenable with the indirect impact undermining competitiveness.* Apparently, modeling power politics as a complex adaptive system (CAS) alerts us to potential cotenability problems in existing qualitative theories.

Projectability: Because CAS simulation does not rule out historical accidents by assumption, it is possible to test the robustness of macrolevel relationships. Experimental replication assures that nuisance counterfactuals wash out, thus rendering visible emergent structural patterns that were previously swamped by historical details. The results reported in Figure 11.8 illustrate this point because they point to regularities that cannot be discovered in any single, path-dependent run. In this example, CAS methodology allows us to evaluate the conditions under which the neorealists' structural constancy of power politics holds in the artificial world. Unlike qualitative neorealist analysis, however, simulation also uncovers the limitations of this hypothesis.

The picture that emerges from the dynamic simulation runs, then, casts doubt on the robustness of such claims. Belief in the "invisible hand" of automatic balancing appears to rest on a number of hidden assumptions that may not be empirically valid or even logically consistent. The prevalence of power politics does not follow despite the path-dependence of power accumulation, but precisely because of this fact. More precisely, the maintenance of plurality in geopolitical systems depends on an explosive positive feedback mechanism that generates competitive conditions even in situations involving small numbers of aggressive states (cf. Wendt 1992).

Nevertheless, snowballing processes of this type may introduce either too little or too much integration for the realist predictions to hold. Because of their focus on a limited number of "great powers," realists need to explain not only how these states emerged against the backcloth of history, but also why this integrative process prevented hegemonic takeoffs. The advantage of CAS modeling is that by making the invisible hand visible, it helps identify the conditions under which structural propositions hold. This more refined research agenda highlights limitations often overlooked by structural realists who base their thinking on loose analogies and metaphors. The positivist aspirations to distill universal covering laws notwithstanding, the context-dependent approach of computational modeling offers a scientifically sounder platform for theory development and policy exploration than post hoc justifications of particular historical equilibria dressed up as "deductive" science.

Thanks to the ability to run robustness tests, CAS experiments have the advantage of being immune to retrospective bias. Here the methodology differs dramatically from a single-run thought experiment performed qualitatively in the mind of the scholar. Having defined the connecting principles, the CAS analyst relinquishes control to the computer. Because the tape is always run forward from some initial configuration there is no need to trace history backwards, thus eliminating any risk of "presentism."

So far, the presentation has concentrated on the advantages of CAS experiments. Among the drawbacks, external validity looms as the most serious threat to policy relevance. The highly abstract nature of modeling makes both CAS and mathematical approaches vulnerable to accusations of irrelevance when compared to the complexities in real social systems. These complaints usually come from empiricists and historical-minded scholars rather than from neoclassical modelers who are even less reluctant than CAS researchers to resort to drastic simplifications. The question is whether we can "infer emergence as a 'causal' mechanism in the real world, once we have identified it in the [CAS]" (Lane 1992, 9).

How, then, is it possible to find out whether the postulated processes operate in applied settings? Clearly, the solution does not lie in positivist tests of specific predictions. Such a viewpoint confuses the nature of CAS processes with simple empirical laws. Koslowski and Kratochwil (1994, 227) point out that "large-scale historical change cannot be explained in terms of one or even several causal factors but through an analysis of conjunctures." This does not mean, however, that all hope for systematic observations should be abandoned: "Although a covering law for this historical process is unlikely to be found, elements within that process do form patterns that can be perceived and analyzed, because even chaotic processes are not random." The CAS approach produces "pattern predictions" (Hayek 1967) or "robust processes" (Goldstone 1991) rather than pointlike predictions of single events.

Conclusion

By focusing on counterfactual computer simulation of complex social systems, this chapter has outlined an alternative to conventional comparative methods in international relations. Instead of engaging in large qualitative comparisons of historical cases or dividing the research question into smaller, more manageable tasks amenable to deductive analysis, the CAS approach confronts the complexity of the real world by creating an artificial world. Such an experimental solution combines the holistic focus of structural theories with rational-choice theory's emphasis on explicit and formal modeling of causal mechanisms. Thus the proposed solution opens the door for modeling of microlevel factors without committing itself to methodological individualism.

To summarize the argument, CAS modeling facilitates construction of complex counterfactuals in three respects. First, this method avoids the risk of incomplete specification by forcing the analyst to render all categories explicit. Second, computer simulations automatically generate cotenable results, at least within the boundaries of the artificial world. Third, CAS helps us determine whether or not counterfactual claims pass the projectibility test because of the possibility of modeling historical accidents explicitly. In short, viewed as conceptual sensitivity analysis, computer-assisted counterfactual thought experiments are means of highlighting hidden assumptions that may be profoundly consequential. In the process of doing so, CAS may reveal that qualitative claims framed in deterministic terms are better viewed as open-ended, probabilistic processes. Used in this way, "the computer plays a role similar to the role the microscope plays for biology" (Holland and Miller 1991, 367).

It is time to complement traditional deductive modeling approaches with methods that go beyond the prevailing orthodox parsimony. Failure to do so will continue to delay a deeper understanding of complex social systems. Although conventional equilibrium models provide useful information about stable periods, their weaknesses become obvious under turbulent conditions. Relying exclusively upon such deductive theories is like learning how to fly by using a flight-simulator that does not allow the fictitious plane to crash.

12

Counterfactuals, Past and Future

STEVEN WEBER

MANY OF THE PAPERS in this volume concern themselves with separating out
"good" from "bad," plausible from implausible, or legitimate from illegitimate counterfactual claims used in testing social science theories.[1] Together,
these papers suggest more disciplined criteria that would constrain counterfactual reasoning for the purpose of evaluating theory. But that is not the
only way we can use counterfactuals. In this chapter, I discuss a different
role for counterfactuals, which I believe in practice is at least as important.
Counterfactuals can also be used to open minds, to raise tough questions
about what we think we know, and to suggest unfamiliar or uncomfortable
arguments that we had best consider.

I am pessimistic about our chances of making counterfactuals into powerful and widely accepted tools for theory testing in social science. The implicit assumption underlying efforts to do so is that *data* are the most important scarce resource in social science. By that logic, counterfactuals are an
unfortunate necessity because we don't have enough "real" data to satisfy
reasonable epistemological criteria.[2] Of course, good data are hard to come
by, but I doubt that counterfactuals can count as good data in more than a
very few isolated cases about which we already know an enormous amount
and have a high degree of confidence. I want to emphasize a different message about counterfactuals: *theories, arguments, and ideas* are another
scarce resource, and counterfactuals can be very useful in generating them.

Playing a different game means adopting a different strategy. To use
counterfactuals as idea generators means that the "truth" of particular counterfactual statements is not at issue. What is at issue is a set of boundary
conditions for a discussion, which takes place mainly in the realm of social
psychology, about what could have been and what could be. Counterfactuals
are useful for persuasion in the midst of that strategic discussion. These

[1] For helpful discussions and feedback while writing this paper, I thank David Collier,
George Breslauer, Michael Sinatra, Deborah M. Berry, Lucy Wan, and particularly the editors,
Phil Tetlock and Aaron Belkin. Research support was provided by the Social Science Research
Council and the University of California, Berkeley, Simpson Chair in International Studies.
[2] This excludes the use of counterfactuals in causal arguments to establish the validity of
calling something a "control" case or "null hypothesis."

counterfactuals don't make causal claims; they raise questions and open up new ways of thinking when applied to the past and, perhaps even more effectively, to the future. Understanding the differences and similarities between counterfactuals in the past and in the future is an important part of justifying what we actually do with the "knowledge" gained from retrospective thought experiments as well as the "knowledge," "understanding," or "wisdom" gained from scenaric histories of the future.

Counterfactuals: For What Purpose?

Cosmologists speak of category 1 and category 2 problems. Category 1 problems can be worked on within the perimeters of current scientific frameworks. They may require new insights and new models, but they fit comfortably in Kuhnian normal science and fall under the covering laws we know and rely on. Category 2 problems sit at the outer limits or outside the boundaries and language of science as it is currently constructed: things we don't know that we don't know, or about which we don't understand what we don't understand. Counterfactuals appear in both categories, but do different things in each.

Most of this book is about counterfactuals in category 1. Tetlock and Belkin worry about people making overly facile use of counterfactuals to test arguments, and then granting themselves too much confidence in an argument that is less tested than they think. Tetlock and Belkin want to promote more careful use of counterfactuals, to increase skepticism, and to force confidence measures back down to where they belong. This is an important corrective if the social science/policy world is full of these kinds of errors. It probably is.

But what about category 2? Counterfactuals are useless for testing arguments here, because well-developed arguments (by definition) don't yet exist in this category. In world politics, category 2 may be very large and may contain many, if not most, of the questions we ask—either because the world happens to be that way, or because social science is even less well developed than we sometimes think. The constraints on counterfactuals that make good sense in category 1 are not helpful in category 2, where the ideas and arguments that precede use of data are missing.

Consider what happens when social scientists fail to foresee events of major significance that in retrospect appear to have been obvious, overdetermined, or at least highly plausible. Bayesian updating of confidence measures fails to offer much solace in this situation. The pseudoacademic and policy soul searching of 1989 centered around the question of why we failed to predict the end of the Cold War. A serious question lies behind that rhetorical one: Why didn't we consider more explicitly the possibility that the Soviet Union could disintegrate? Considering that we knew certain things about the way the Soviet system worked, and about declining productivity, birth rates, energy production, and so on, why didn't we pay more specific attention to a "counterfactual history of the future" in which the governing system of the Soviet empire ran out of steam and collapsed of its own weight? We had on hand a number of suggestive antecedents, as well as connecting principles that were consistent with well-established theory, historical facts, and statistical generalizations. Most of the Tetlock and Belkin principles were in place: apparently we had everything we needed to make a good conditional forecast. But for the most part, we did not. Some did, but they had a very hard time convincing others to pay attention.

Counterfactuals can be used to challenge mind sets, to focus attention on precisely what makes us uncomfortable, and to break apart the psychological biases that Tetlock and Belkin describe. That is a very different agenda, with a different purpose. Used in this way, counterfactuals become mind-set changers and learning devices rather than data points in explanations. The question is not which agenda is important—both are—but rather how we should divide our attention between them. The answer depends on the kinds of research problems we want to tackle and what we think the state of play is in social science as we currently know it.

A Pessimist's View on Counterfactuals

Theories about world politics rarely offer propositions that are crisply refutable by a single, a few, or sometimes even a large number of observations. Part of the problem has to do with the quality and precision of the theories we have on hand to test. Is it really possible to deduce falsifiable propositions that retrodict or predict dependent variables to a level of accuracy that falls outside the range of error of measurement or interpretation, when the independent variables in theories are concepts like power, interest, interdependence, and intentions? This is an old and familiar critique, but that does not mean that anyone has answered it adequately.

The focus on counterfactuals raises a slightly different perspective on this issue, and even more directly on the related issue of commensurability between different research programs in world politics. Debates over the legitimate use of counterfactuals could easily become a proxy for familiar theoretical cleavages between traditional schools of thought about international relations. Consider several examples of counterfactual argument offered by Tetlock and Belkin: in one case, they substitute a different individual; in another, a different strategy; in a third, a different power distribution. Are there consensual criteria for treating any or all of these counterfactuals as legitimate *subjects for discussion*, apart from and outside of the theoretical predispositions or schools of thought from which they are implicitly drawn?

Legitimacy of this kind is a prerequisite for discussion of whether the counterfactual is "good" or "bad," "valid" or "invalid." I am not sure the necessary shared legitimacy can be established. A committed neorealist would not consider counterfactuals about individuals as legitimate topics for discussion, not because such counterfactuals are invalid, but because they are trivial. The postmodernist won't debate the effects of a different distribution of power because the "same" distribution of power means nothing to her. This kind of disagreement is prior and orthogonal to any discussion aimed at increasing the validity of counterfactual reasoning. Can people who do not agree on what it means to say "cause" or even "fact" nonetheless agree on what would constitute a useful counterfactual?

The problem goes beyond the frustrations of trying to debate between paradigms. World politics is a causally complex realm with multiple conjunctural causation and (perhaps) irreducible elements of chance, possibly even randomness.[3] In addition, data in this realm are usually difficult to collect, noisy, and hard to measure. Combine these difficulties with fundamental disagreements about theory, and it becomes nearly impossible to satisfy logical criteria for the use of counterfactual arguments in all but a very few instances of interest.

The point is this: Causal complexity of the magnitude we experience in world politics butchers the minimal-rewrite principle as it applies to antecedents in counterfactual statements about history. The question becomes whether we really know what constitutes a minimal rewrite in an antecedent (see Chapter 11, Cederman, and Commentary 4, Jervis). It takes tremendous confidence in our present state of theoretical knowledge to be certain.

Consider an allegory from molecular genetics and evolutionary theory. The human genome contains billions of base pairs of DNA. Change a single base pair from adenine to thymine. Is this a minimal rewrite that would make for an acceptable antecedent in a counterfactual argument? In 1940, before we knew about the structure of DNA, the answer almost certainly would have been yes. In 1975, when we knew how genes get translated into proteins, we might have had more doubts but we still might have said yes, because changing one gene would only change one protein. Today we know about the existence of regulatory genes, single genes that control the expression of large numbers of other genes and thus can affect the production of many different proteins. Now we know that a single base pair change can easily mean the difference between a dead organism and a live one, depending on where and when the change takes place.

---

[3] On multiple conjunctural causation see Ragin (1987). On irreducible chance see Humphreys (1989).

Several implications follow from that story. If we commit the logical fallacy of saying that a minimal cause is one that produces a minimal effect, then counterfactual thought experiments become extremely conservative—dare I say boring?—and probably misleading as well. Yet to believe that we can follow a minimal-rewrite rule without that fallacy, we must also believe that we have identified the key facts and causal connections in our historical narrative. We need to know what "minimal" really means, which is a difficult problem. It might even be circular: once we knew what "minimal" meant well enough to validate counterfactuals, we would no longer need to use counterfactuals because we would already know what we want to know and understand what we want to understand.

I do not see an obvious way out of this trap, which is one of the reasons I am pessimistic about using counterfactuals in "scientific" tests of our understandings of the past. What *is* possible is to accrue evidence and arguments to convince people that some hypotheses are probably weak and others probably stronger. I doubt that we will reach agreement on many important issues by doing this, but reaching agreement may not be the only important objective, particularly with counterfactuals.

Counterfactuals and "Ideas"

What are we actually doing when we use counterfactuals? The question has intellectual, sociological, and psychological components. After all, to explain is only one goal of social science. Others are to conceptualize and to recognize. Recognition means locating unfamiliar events in stories (schemas, models) that capture more familiar patterns of temporal sequence. The social-psychological component of our use of counterfactuals points to a fourth goal of social science, to persuade.

Any debate over counterfactuals in world politics will naturally become more than just purely theoretical or scientific; it will also involve policy, political rhetoric, and public action. I take seriously and without pejorative connotation the "rhetorical" use of counterfactuals. People championing a course of action use counterfactuals to persuade; that is, to convince others that a piece of information should be conceptualized in a particular way that allows us to recognize it as part of a schema, so we can do certain things with it.[4] Confidence estimates are part of that conversation—people prefer to be more rather than less certain about what they do and do not know. But prior confidence estimates are less important than feedback and learning from action. A counterfactual can lose its luster remarkably quickly when

[4] I thank George Lakoff for showing me work in cognitive psychology and linguistics that has helped me to see this more clearly.

human action based on a sequence of reasoning from the counterfactual turns out to have unintended detrimental consequences.

Primitive evolutionary metaphors for "idea change," especially regarding counterfactuals, are troubling for precisely this reason. A "natural selection" perspective on how ideas are generated, selected, institutionalized, and overthrown is not the only useful way to think about the process. Not even the most committed defenders of Darwin still believe that natural selection is the only source of important biological change—in many (for some theorists, the most important) cases, natural selection is overshadowed by other mechanisms.[5] By analogy, I do not think that ideas in a social realm, even one as impregnated by "scientific" standards as ours is, do battle in anything like the imaginary primeval forest, nor do I see much evidence for "survival of the fittest" among ideas, either "factual" or counterfactual.

A better metaphor for what happens in the world of ideas can be constructed in the language of population ecology. Imagine populations of ideas that live together in a less draconian environment. Some populations coexist, some compete, some are synergistic, some are cooperative or symbiotic, some die of their own accord, and there is an occasional innovation. The diversity of ideas is a survival asset for a human society living in an uncertain environment with an uncertain future. Because innovation can be slow, idea diversity acts as a repository of alternative "solutions" and action plans that people can call upon if they feel they need them.[6] But this is where I think John Stuart Mill went slightly off the track.

In a population-ecology view of ideas, diversity is more than instrumental to the search for a truth, and it is more than just hedging against an uncertain future. Diversity simply is. It exists and continues to exist because there is no single truth (at least none that we can discover and agree on) either in past or future time to drive out alternative ideas. Populations of ideas wax and wane, but it is fleetingly rare for a population either to diminish to extinction or to dominate completely. Population ecology studies the dynamics of this kind of world. Beyond considering the growth or shrinkage of any single population as a function of an autonomous unit facing its exogenous environment, population ecologists think about how a population's *vital rates* (how many members are born, how many die) are affected by the presence and density of other populations.[7] Ideas, including counterfactual ideas, don't battle against a truth, or a past or future; they battle against and coexist with each other.

---

[5] For example: drift, nonrandom mating, gene flow, and mutation of regulatory genes, as well as mass extinctions that sample in a nondiscriminatory manner.

[6] The argument that diversity is a valuable hedge against uncertainty is standard in evolutionary theory, as well, but it depends on a very broad, long-term conception of natural selection.

[7] The technical terms are "founding rates" and "mortality rates." See Hannan and Freeman (1989).

This may seem an obvious point. I make it because I want to emphasize two things about that interaction. The first is that gradual change in populations of ideas is an interesting, important, and common phenomenon. Consider the recent debate over *The Bell Curve*. Think of the book's argument as less a new idea than part of a population of ideas about sociobiology that have fluctuated in popularity and social impact over nearly all of human history, a population whose ecology could be modeled over time. Population ecologists model this kind of dynamic among organizations. They study interactive effects like "liability of newness" (new organizations tend to die more rapidly than older ones), "density dependence of legitimacy" (at a certain density of an organizational form, new organizations find it easier to survive because they can draw on the legitimacy established by extant organizations), "saturation effects of carrying capacities," and so on. These concepts can be used to describe some of the ecological history of populations, be they organisms, organizations, or ideas.

But they cannot model in a useful way a more exciting phenomenon that happens in populations: the sudden, dramatic, and rapid explosion in numbers of a particular population that for a long period prior had languished in a steady state. In the world of ideas, I will call this phenomenon "idea takeoff." And it is critically important because when it happens it often heralds momentous change.

How powerful are such explosions? Most of us would agree that changing public perceptions and beliefs—a shift in ideas—can alter the course of real events in history (and the future) more quickly, dramatically, and unexpectedly than so-called structural changes, in power, military technology, etc. What of the "Washington consensus" on neoconservative economics that swept much of the developed and developing world in the middle 1980s? Or the recent interest in environmental issues and sustainability in the world political arena? Or lean production as a paradigm for organizing industrial processes? When ideas like these take hold, they change many things at once and usually in ways that catch many people by surprise. Idea takeoff brings something more like the gale of Schumpeter's creative destruction, which destroys old ways of doing things and ushers in new, than the gentle breeze of yet another discussion about race and IQ that might lead to a marginal change in public policy funding allocations.

The population ecology models that I know can generate ex post descriptions of how idea takeoff happened once the results are in, but they cannot predict timing before it happens. And most important, they cannot predict why in a world of diverse ideas one takes off and another does not. Otherwise, some sociologists would be getting extremely rich off the 1994 idea explosion surrounding the Internet. Remember that the Internet has been around for several decades, personal computers and modems for at least a decade. So what happened in 1994? The honest answer, I think, is "something we do not understand," even though we could tell an ex post story to make it look overdetermined. I am not promoting that strategy; quite the contrary. I think it is essential to develop a language to talk about this phenomenon, even if that language is not "scientific" in the traditional sense. Writing counterfactual histories of the future is one kind of language that I have found to work.

Social science fails too frequently to foresee the dynamics that can drive Schumpeterian-type change in the systems we study. This gap results in part from the fact that ideas sometimes undergo rapid expansion and grab hold of individual and collective minds. These can be world-changing processes, but we do not have "scientific models" that do more than show us, after the fact, how what came to pass was indeed possible. We may never have predictive models; we don't yet know (or agree on) whether it is possible in the abstract to create them. In the meantime, I argue that creative use of counterfactuals can help increase our understanding of these processes.

Scenarios and Counterfactuals in Future Time

It may be that the human mind cannot anticipate in a reliably predictive sense nonlinear change, but it is certainly possible to ask ourselves probing questions about the possibility.[8] Developing stories about how an idea could take off, and what the world would be like if it did, is one way to think about preparing individuals, states, or any social collectivity for futures that might happen. It is also one way to prime the pump for learning once the future becomes the past. This requires a method or procedure for seeking ideas, writing the most useful scenarios, and taking feedback away to improve the process on the next round. The method is different from what most social scientists currently do. But it is not as different in principle as some people might think.

I will point first to the notable similarities in order to ward off the objection that counterfactual histories of the future are whimsical dreams unconstrained by anything in the real world and thus useless. I argue that counterfactuals of the future are not an order of magnitude different in that respect from counterfactual histories of the past. I am not proposing that social scientists upgrade their confidence levels about future predictions to match the confidence levels they sometimes feel about their retrodictions of the past; quite the opposite. Instead, I think we can use our uncertainty about the future to remind us to be humble about what we think we know about the past. I want to establish that when we say we have "explained" an event

---

[8] Calvin (1994) makes a fascinating argument about the evolutionary neurobiology of the human mind that grounds human inability to anticipate nonlinear change in nervous-system hardwiring, not just in contemporary views of science.

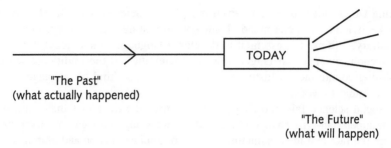

"The Past"
(what actually happened)

"The Future"
(what will happen)

Figure 12.1.

in past time, it does not necessarily mean that we have also ruled out the possibility that things could have been radically different than they were. To explain an event in a complex system like world politics is not the same as excluding alternatives.

First the premise: are there logical differences between counterfactual reasoning in the past and counterfactual reasoning in the future? Because social scientists have a vested interest in believing that there *is* a substantial difference, prudence urges caution in answering this question.[9] Unless I find a compelling reason to see a difference, I must proceed with at least some skepticism about my vested interest-backed belief. I have yet to think of or read of a reason powerful enough to overcome my skepticism. I know this will be controversial. But given the state of our theoretical understanding about how the world works and the apparent complexity of causation in that world, I believe that counterfactual reasoning in the past and in the future have to be treated as essentially identical operations in logical terms.

Consider the issue this way. Arguments about the past and the future simply fall out at different positions along a time line, with today ("the present") in the middle. The time line is single to the left of the present; to the right it has multiple branches and routes. Figure 12.1 captures the baseline assumption: although there is only a single history of the past (what actually happened) there could be more than one history of the future (because many things can happen from where we are today). So far the picture *looks* as though there is a difference between what is valid to say about events to the left and to the right of the present.

Now insert a counterfactual somewhere in the left, at time = T, as in Figure 12.2. Once you substitute a counterfactual into a historical sequence of events, you are then telling an imagined story forward from that moment, time = T. *It is not a story that actually happened.* What actually happened

---

[9] If there were no difference, how could we justify different confidence levels about prediction and retrodiction? We believe that the future is radically underdetermined, but we do not want to entertain the same conception of the past because it would make our jobs as social scientists even more difficult than they already are.

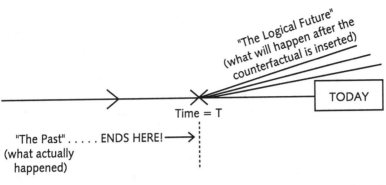

Figure 12.2.

now ends at time = T. If "what actually happened" is a working definition of "the past," *then any time to the right of T is now logically in the future.* Another way to put this point is to say that all counterfactuals are histories of the future, even when they are situated in what we normally think of as past "calendar" time. The story you tell with the counterfactual in it is about a "future" (T + 1, T + 2, T + 3) that did not really happen, even if it is situated before 1995. In other words, historical time that is ten units away from time = T is going to be T + 10, regardless of whether T + 10 falls before or after 1995.

There is an obvious objection.[10] The calendar past contains a data set that is not infinite—it is constrained by what we know about what actually happened. That is not true of the future and although the data set of the calendar future might not be infinite, it is orders of magnitude less constrained than that of the past. This should create a pragmatic asymmetry between counterfactuals that fall before the calendar present and those that fall after it.

The objection makes sense to me only if I know that the more constrained data set is not invalidated when I insert the counterfactual into its midst. Why would I think that I know that? It would have to be because I trust the validity of theories that tell me what in that data set is cotenable with what I have changed, and what is not. If I feel confident that my theories generate criteria that can do that in one data set, why not in another?[11] Why not in an imaginary data set I might create and call "the future"?

For this reason, I don't see logically why there are more or less degrees of freedom in writing counterfactual histories of the future than in writing

---

[10] As pointed out by several participants in the Berkeley conference. In particular, I thank David Collier for helpful debate on this point.

[11] This seems very close to a definition of "generalizability," which is one of the attributes that make a theory more than just a description of a single case.

counterfactual histories of the past. My objective here is to take some of the indeterminacy we feel naturally about the future and inject it into our explanations of the past—by making myself and others uncomfortable about projecting counterfactuals backward. It seems almost self-evident to say that when thinking *forward* in time in a realm as causally complex as world politics, we would be able to predict/forecast the future only when all of its major elements are predetermined. This means talking about the implications of events that have already occurred or almost certainly will occur, but whose consequences have not yet unfolded. It snowed heavily in Tahoe last winter, and I was able in February to forecast a heavy runoff in the spring because there is nowhere else for the water to go—the future consequence of an event that has already occurred. Yet when we think *backward* in time, we often seem much more comfortable retrodicting in cases where we are far less certain that we have all the major elements in hand. Why the increased confidence? Surely it is because we already know the "real" outcome, but that is hardly defensible.

In part because they recognize this hazard, Tetlock and Belkin have made a valiant effort to constrain counterfactual statements about the past. But they have made a mistake much like the attempt to predict *the* future, as if there were only one, when all the major elements of that future are *not* predetermined. It is too difficult but also too constraining to try to do this. The search for inappropriate constraints tends to drive out imagination and thoughtfulness about what could have been and (similarly) what could be. It rewards the psychologically easy and comfortable task of generating counterfactuals close to the margins of existing theories. It predisposes toward varying only the familiar variables, the ones that we think we know are tied into causal paths that we feel we know well.

This is one particular view of counterfactuals, not the only one. It may do some things well, but it predisposes to the big errors that I think we want to get better at avoiding. Arguments about technology nicely illustrate this point. It may be silly, as Tetlock and Belkin say, to imagine in isolation "what if" Napoleon had a Stealth bomber at Waterloo. But it is not so silly to imagine a different course of technological development, such that Waterloo would have been fought with different weapons. Was Elster justified in telling Fogel that a world without railroads would necessarily have also been a world without cars? Everything I know about the social history of technology suggests otherwise. What if the U.S. government had decided that building railroads would lead to a socially or ethically unacceptable concentration of population and industry in a few "hub" locations? People made the argument at the time that America was a collection of rural, local communities, and that the railroad would change that by rewarding concentration and urbanization.

This argument lost out, but not because of technological determinism (Chandler 1977, 145–87; Berk 1990; Berk 1994). If you doubt the contingency of these situations, think forward instead to the emerging architecture

of the NII.[12] Alternative futures are possible. We are on the verge of a period
in which social/political decisions get made about what kind of technology,
where, for whom, carrying what, at what price, and so on. It is precisely
because there are alternative technological trajectories, and because the
choice among them will make a big difference in what our society and lives
look like twenty years hence, that the discussion over what we want and
how to get it is first and foremost political. What a mistake it would be for a
historian in the year 2020 to look back and claim technological determinism
for what will come out of today's debates. I don't see why we need to wait
until 2020 to make constructive use of counterfactuals, however. What we
can do today with counterfactuals is to write several stories about what could
be, and use these stories to persuade people whose actions will make a
difference that they should do one thing and not another, or hedge against a
possible risk they had not foreseen, or look carefully for signs of an emerging opportunity that others will miss for lack of looking. This is what scenaric thinking tries to do.

The Scenario Process in Brief

Scenarios are not about scientific proof. The point of counterfactuals here is
to facilitate creative thinking and open minds to plausibility. The process
takes as a starting point the notion that most people (or firms, governments,
or scholars) carry around with them an "official future," a set of assumptions
about what probably will be (or what hypotheses make sense), around which
they think mostly in terms of marginal variation. Good scenarios challenge
this official future by focusing precisely on what makes people uncomfortable: discontinuities, events that don't make sense in standard theories/lan-
guage, and the like. I will briefly describe the scenario process and make
some comparisons to retrospective thought experiments aimed at yielding
"lawlike" or contingent generalizations. Then I will explore whether the Tetlock and Belkin criteria make good sense in this context. This is less a
critique of the criteria than a way to open discussion about what we might
do differently if we were to apply some of the methods of scenario planning
to thinking about the past.

Driving Forces

The first step in constructing scenarios is to identify a set of driving forces
surrounding a problem, event, or decision. Driving forces are "the elements

---

[12] NII stands for National Information Infrastructure, a less noxious phrase than "information
superhighway." The "superhighway" metaphor says much—which might turn out to be
wrong—about the infrastructure's architecture.

that move the plot . . . , that determine the story's outcome" (Schwartz 1991, 107). How this differs epistemologically or denotatively from a cause depends on what you consider a cause to be. But there are clearly connotative and practical differences. The search for driving forces is best organized as a team effort, in which one begins by putting *more* rather than *fewer* candidates on the table as being possibly important. The question then becomes: What else might matter in this decision? What else might drive this series of events? How far back toward the "causes behind the causes" can we push the discussion? If I am thinking about the future of nuclear power, for example, I would identify long-term interest rates as an important driving force, but what I really want to ask about are the driving forces behind rates.

This part of the discussion will produce a set of driving forces that includes "conventional" independent variables; indeed, I would worry if it failed to do that. But I would also worry if something new, a driving force not currently in vogue as a major independent variable in a major social science theory, were not on the list. New drivers end up on the list because people are asking themselves what else matters without yet worrying whether (and how) they could "prove" or "measure" the effects that they believe might be present. It becomes natural to search widely for driving forces that might not have received enough attention before.

Predetermined Elements

The next step is to identify predetermined elements in the story, things that are relatively certain. The driving forces suggest where to look for the relevant elements. The difficult task is to sort what is certain, or very close to it, from what people simply believe. This cognitive exercise is extremely useful in counteracting tendencies to treat routine events, "causes" of "effects," background actors, sins of omission, and "structural" (not human-agency) causes as immutable. The question of what is certain continually challenges the responder to ask herself, "Do I really know that, and how?"

People disagree, sometimes at a very basic level, about the answers to these questions. And yet the fact that there are no easy experiments and control situations in world politics does not mean that there do not exist things that are relatively certain. Peter Schwartz provides four examples of the kinds of things that can be predetermined within reasonable bounds (Schwartz 1991, 117):

Slowly changing phenomena—e.g., demographics
Constrained situations—e.g., the U.S. budget deficit
Outcomes "in the pipeline"—e.g., HIV-infected people and AIDS
Inevitable collisions—e.g., declining GNP and the Soviet "grand bargain"

In discussing the counterfactual "no-Gorbachev" case, for example, it is important to remember what we know about declining GNP and energy production in the Soviet Union. Specifying what is relatively certain in this context moves the discussion one step beyond "all other things being equal" in two ways. It makes clear that *all* other things are not on the table. And it provokes people to ask what other things might not be equal, how, and how we would know.

Critical Uncertainties

Identifying critical uncertainties means seeking out what is *most uncertain* and *most important* to making a particular decision or understanding a set of events. Critical uncertainties sometimes are closely related to predetermined elements—as in the Soviet Union story, where critical uncertainties might arise from thinking about the sources of GNP decline and what might possibly change in that equation. "Miracles" or at least what social scientists call "low probability events" happen frequently in world politics; as Tetlock once told me, what today appears impossible, tomorrow appears to have been overdetermined. That says more about the state of our understanding than about the state of the world.

At a recent conference on "Regions in International Relations," I told a story—a counterfactual history of the future—in which sophisticated telecommunications technologies reinforced peoples' ethnic/cultural identities more than their desire to engage in a "rational" economic search for efficient transactions. In this counterfactual history, current geographic borders fell victim not to trade and economic interdependence but to blood ties and culture—with a very different outcome. My story made people uncomfortable because although we are able to measure comparative advantage, productivity, transportation costs, and other factors that matter in gravity models of trade, we are uncertain how to talk about "culture and ethnicity" as a magnet for economic interaction.[13]

Telling this story is valuable because it points up a critical uncertainty about how important culture will be in a not so distant future in which human interactions are less constrained by geography than in the past. It puts the critical uncertainties out in front, ahead of the plot lines or connecting principles that I believe properly should come later. There is an important difference of emphasis here with standard social science theory "testing," in which what is mutable and uncertain is often taken to be the "independent variables" suggested by the connecting principles that we al-

---

[13] I think most political economists squirm at the idea of making culture into a mixture of transaction costs, reputational elements, and nontariff barriers—although some do try.

ready know well. In scenaric thinking, plot lines have to work with the
critical uncertainties rather than the other way around.

Plot Lines

A plot line is a story about how things happen. It describes how driving
forces might plausibly behave as they interact with predetermined elements
and different combinations of critical uncertainties. Plots have their own
logic (or sometimes more than one logic) that drive the story forward and
suggest the directions in which uncertainties resolve. The logics are sometimes quite familiar, such as a gradual response to an evolving challenge or
an entrepreneur seizing an opportunity that others were too afraid to risk.
Sometimes new logics emerge, as happens in social science theory. I think
of balance of power theory, for example, as an international-relations analogy for one such plot line. It emphasizes how a strong driving force (desire
for independence and autonomy) interacts with predetermined elements and
critical uncertainties in a social setting that could be a family, a business, a
market, or an international system. Tetlock and Belkin would call this a
connecting principle, but I see several differences of emphasis that matter
for the way in which the discussion moves forward.

The most important difference is that scenario plot lines discourage exces-
sively rigid independent-dependent variable thinking. The exemplar of a
connecting principle is one that takes an independent variable to a dependent
variable in regular fashion under specified conditions. Working in that mind
set, things like equifinality, multifinality, and complex conjunctural causation are stubborn inconveniences. They are unfortunate characteristics of the
world, which science has to try to minimize, control for, or ignore. Scenario
thinking treats these patterns differently—as natural and fundamental aspects of reality.

That ought to be as true for reasoning into the past as it seems natural for
reasoning into the future. Of course, there is always more than one scenario
of the future. And (unlike the ideal scientific notion of *an* explanation of the
past) there always should be. That is not a weakness or a liability; it is the
essence of the method. It is a way of capturing the probabilistic nature of
our arguments (counterfactual and otherwise) without necessarily having to
attach probability estimates to them (which we may not be in a position to
do). The purpose of scenario thinking, after all, is not to establish as "true"
or a "prediction" any one of these stories about the future (even after the
fact) but to persuade people of the plausibility of more than one future, to
suspend disbelief in alternatives.

The question then becomes how many alternative stories make up a good
scenaric exercise. The answer derives from the social-psychological context

in which scenario thinking is based. There is no need to lay out anything like all the possible composites, and there is no presumption that any single scenario would turn out to be "right." The idea is to identify three or four significant stories that are challenging to the official future, suggest different courses of action and consequences for the audience, and are plausible enough that audience members will carry the stories around in their minds and look for signals of the dynamics the stories contain. In a world with imperfect or noisy data that must be filtered through individual cognitive biases to small group decision-making fora and then perhaps funneled into large bureaucracies for refinement and implementation, a thousand possible futures are probably as useless as one. Computers may be able to compare the statistical validity of a thousand hypotheses against a bed of data, but most people cannot. And I have rarely been involved in a discussion in which people compare more than four ways of thinking about a problem at once. That is just as true when people discuss their understandings of the past as when they discuss their understandings of the future.

Warning Signals and Early Indicators

Counterfactual histories of the future, just like competing explanations of the past, need to be linked closely to "observable implications" that help a data collector or a participant to know which of the stories they believe or are living through. Although early indicators of future histories are in principle no different from what King, Keohane, and Verba (1994) and others call "observables" in thinking about the past, the scenario process again has a different emphasis. Scenarios rely more on process-tracing of a few stories about the future than on increasing the number of (supposedly) independent observables by increasing the number of cases.[14] Thinking into the future blurs the distinction between these two strategies, which I find a good thing. That is mainly because I find the notion of independent observations in the past much more troubling and problematic than King, Keohane, and Verba seem to.

I also find that thinking about early indicators of alternative futures predisposes toward the development of evocative and powerful images that can pass Daniel Kahneman's "clairvoyance" test, which calls upon experts to advance scenarios that are sufficiently precise that one could turn the scenarios over to a *genuine* clairvoyant who, in turn, could tell one—without equivocation or need for clarification of the original scenario—whether the scenario did indeed come to pass (Tetlock 1992a). The test is a good benchmark for breaking down biases toward an official future (or, for that

---

[14] On this point compare King, Keohane, and Verba (1994) with George (1980) and George and McKeown (1985).

matter, an official past). Scenarios are not about point predictions and there
is no underlying notion that they should be if only that were possible. The
emphasis is on developing a set of expectations along the lines of "these
kinds of things should start to happen more frequently, and these other kinds
of things less frequently." Built into this is a healthy skepticism that emerges
in part from *not* having firm standards of "proof," be they $p < .05$ or whatever else. Because I am generally skeptical of using firm statistical standards
to evaluate results when the raw data itself is so murky, I am more comfortable in discussions that legitimate this kind of existential uncertainty. Keeping that kind of challenge in the forefront of peoples' minds is certainly
possible in formal statistics, but how often does it really happen in discussions about world politics? I would like to see it happen more frequently,
because I think it matters greatly for the ultimate rationale of the discussion—the implications for action.

Implications

Because scenarios are directed explicitly at decision making and action, developing sets of implications that attach to different scenarios is a central
part of the process. The social-psychological value here lies in forcing people who are going to make decisions to ask themselves what life would be
like in more than one future world, and what they would do if they found
themselves in a world different from their official future. They might also
recognize the extent to which their own actions could be an important pivot
or determinant of what kinds of futures were likely to evolve. This is again a
difference of emphasis from more standard retrospective-oriented theory-
testing exercises in world politics. Balance of power theory is a good example of an argument that Waltz, Walt, and others have used effectively in an
action-oriented dialogue, with persuasive results.[15] What scenario thinking
adds is a greater direct emphasis on this kind of discussion, along with a
stress on flexibility and responsiveness to change. It does this by forcing
discussants to consider at once the behavioral implications of more than one
scenario, which helps to clarify the stakes, risks, and uncertainties connected with any single course of action that an individual, a firm, or a state
might choose.

Six Criteria

Tetlock and Belkin's six criteria for judging the plausibility of counterfactuals take on slightly different qualities in the context of thinking about the

[15] See, for example, Walt (1989).

future. I discuss them briefly here to raise further issues about just how different thinking forward and backward in time with counterfactuals is or should be.

Tetlock and Belkin recognize that to generate "clearly specified" antecedents and consequents it is frequently necessary to add compound statements to counterfactuals, as a way of saying something more precise than "all other things being equal." I have already noted the slipperiness of this tactic: "all other things" tend to be limited to the things we are comfortable talking about and are almost certainly not *all* other things. The human mind cannot deal with *all* other things, even if we knew what they were—and we do not. Thinking about the future tends to put (and keep) that limitation in central focus, whereas in thinking about the past we forget it too easily. The narrative logic of scenarios falls somewhere between the stark parsimony of a single variable counterfactual (which Tetlock and Belkin recognize is often a coverup for poorly specified antecedents or consequents) and an "all other things being equal" statement.

Whether it is possible to judge the cotenability of antecedents and connecting principles depends on how much shared faith those who are doing the judging have in the connecting principles. The Fogel-Elster debate illustrates this problem. Does Fogel need to have a theory of innovation that requires the invention of cars fifty years earlier in a world without railroads? When we think about the future, we generally apply softer standards. We might ask instead, from the vantage point of (say) 1950, would nuclear fusion as a source of energy have been developed more quickly if fission reactors failed or if governments had ruled them out as too dangerous? I can certainly tell a story about shifting research priorities that would make that future plausible, despite the fact that the same laws of physics underlie both technological trajectories. On what grounds can we justify asking for more than this when developing counterfactuals about the past?

Judgments about consistency with well-established historical facts depend, as Tetlock and Belkin acknowledge, on what people consider "well established" and "factual" in history. But a counterfactual is precisely about manipulating one or more of these supposedly well established facts in a manner, according to Tetlock and Belkin, that does not require the manipulation of too many others. Why is that necessarily a sign of a "good" counterfactual, when we know from historical observation that truly important ideas can change many things about the way the world works all at once? And can we really be confident about how much manipulation is necessary, possible, or legitimate?

Judgments about consistency with well-established theoretical laws are even more problematic, as Tetlock and Belkin realize, because different schools of thought in world politics have very different notions of what constitutes a theory or a law or what is "well established." Seeing that this principle will not help to establish consensus about counterfactuals, Tetlock and Belkin mostly skip over it and hope that the other five criteria will do the job. That would be manageable if the discussion about consistency with well-established theoretical laws ended by leaving things open and on the table, to be ferreted out by other criteria that people can more easily agree on. But in my experience that is not what generally happens. Instead, we tend to get an active dissensus which pushes arguments *off* the table, perhaps too quickly. The result is a conversation that is overly constrained, precisely the opposite of what Tetlock and Belkin seem to fear.

Consistency with well-established statistical generalizations in world politics almost always depends, at some deeper level, on agreements about general theory and the conceptualization of variables. Arguing out these points in statistics is frequently a proxy for more profound debate and is a favorite tactic for crass political rhetoric. The Geddes (1990) critique of "if no labor repression, then lower growth" shows the importance of forcing the discussion to the deeper issues behind the chosen "variables." The problem here is not with counterfactuals per se; it is a problem of bad thinking and bad reasoning.

The Tetlock and Belkin discussion of projectibility prejudices, in a peculiar way, what we think we know about the past. Dawes's (1993) arguments about search bias are good reminders of how causal complexity in the real world makes projectibility a very tricky problem. My question is this: why, if we "cannot avoid the many-many complexity of possible relationships among antecedents and consequents" when thinking forward into the future, do we put more stock in "our knowledge of past causal relationships" constructed ideally in one-to-one fashion (Chapter 1, Tetlock and Belkin)? If there are complex interactions among causes and potential for randomly distributed small forces to be amplified into large effects in world politics, why would we think that is only true in the future? Surely it was also true in the past, which suggests that projectibility can break down for common as well as low-frequency events.

Finally, the notion of proximity tests (Lewis 1973) or the semantics of possible worlds pulls us back to a discussion about "distance" between actual and possible worlds. But this concept seems no different to me than a probability judgment or confidence estimate. Tetlock and Belkin rightly suggest that we should try to specify conditions for the emergence of a possible world (I would soften this to "tell a story about how it could come to pass"), but in neither case is this the equivalent of a probability estimate or a distance metric. It can't even be thought of as a crude measure unless we know reasonably well the probability of the conditions and the probability that they will interact in the way the story says is plausible. Do we really have on hand an understanding of world politics that would produce these numbers? Scenarios do not include probability estimates precisely for this reason. If people carry around with them versions of an official future, then they probably also have implicit probability estimates about different sorts of events that fall inside, on the margins of, or outside that story. Breaking down those probability estimates is one of the major objectives of scenarios.

Conclusion

Scenarios are counterfactual histories of the future. They focus attention on what is most uncertain and most important, in an effort to force people to look straight on at critical junctures and possible surprises that might change the world they live in. This encourages flexibility and maximum responsiveness to change. It also encourages questioning, after the future becomes the past. What was left out of the scenarios? What important driving forces did we miss, underestimate, overestimate, or misinterpret? Why were we surprised? I have tried in this chapter to pose two challenges to the main thrust of this book: To what extent can counterfactuals be used to liberate scholars from certainty of hindsight and overconfidence about comfortable causal paths? And if counterfactuals can play this role, how can they do so most effectively?

There is an obvious challenge that the rest of the book throws back at me. How do we know if scenarios succeed? My answer is that there is no "test" of what is "right" in this exercise, and a scenario that "predicts" the future may not be any more "right" than one that does not.[16] The standard of success is a practical, social-psychological one. Scenarios are effective if they open people's minds to possibilities that they did not previously consider, so that their level of surprise on encountering the future is reduced. Scenarios are effective, more fundamentally, if they cause changes in perception, and in turn in behavior, that matter to the actors as they move through that future.

The "big-miss" errors that make social scientists feel helpless, and that sometimes underlie massive decision-making errors by governments, firms, and individuals, are usually driven more by misaligned perceptions and obsolete world views than by poor tactics or marginal errors of measurement in variables. To change tactics is relatively easy; to change perceptions is much harder. Counterfactuals used in scenarios can help in that task. By focusing minds on what is possible and on the power of the unexpected idea, technological surprise, or whatever else to wreak creative destruction on an official future, the act of writing counterfactual histories of alternative futures is itself a move toward greater freedom and away from what may very well be self-imposed constraints.

---

[16] As Tetlock (1992a) has said, it is easy to look "right" for the wrong reasons, particularly if you have on hand more than one alternative history.

I have stressed repeatedly this notion of undue or unnecessary constraints because I want to keep raising questions about what I see as underlying biases in this volume. I could make essentially the same points with regard to reasoning about the past, but I have found it easier to do so by using the future as a model. Thinking forward in time seems to demand different methods. Scenario thinking is an interpretive method, and I use that term neither as a polemic nor as a commendation but simply as a description of reality. I believe also that the knowledge conditions of forward thinking do not seem very different from those of thinking into the past. At a minimum, I hope I have shown why they are less different than most people assume. Therefore, projectibility should not only be from past to future but from future to past as well, at least in principle.

A longer, more interesting paper remains to be written about interpretive methods and the status of counterfactual arguments in that philosophical-epistemological world. The debate about counterfactuals could help us to make judgments about whether there really exists an "interpretive method" by which we understand or "grow" consensus around stories—and to what extent that is a function of culture, language, the hardwired structure of the brain, something else that can be defined, or simply context. I am not expert enough in these literatures to write that paper, but I believe such a paper should be written and given serious, equal attention.

Part Six

COMMENTARIES

1

Conceptual Blending and Counterfactual Argument in the Social and Behavioral Sciences

MARK TURNER

A COUNTERFACTUAL ARGUMENT arises by virtue of an essential cognitive mechanism: conceptual blending.[1] Blending has been studied in detail by Fauconnier and Turner (1994; and forthcoming), Turner and Fauconnier (1996), Fauconnier (forthcoming), Turner (1996), Coulson (1995), Mandelblit (1994; 1995), and Oakley (1995).

Consider a prototypical counterfactual claim: *If Churchill, instead of Chamberlain, had been prime minister in 1938, Hitler would have been deposed and World War II averted.* This counterfactual claim asks us to blend conceptual structures from different mental spaces to create a separate, counterfactual mental space. The input spaces include: (1) Churchill in 1938 as outspoken opponent of Germany; and (2) Chamberlain in 1938 as prime minister facing the threat from Germany. To construct the blend, we project parts of each of these spaces to it, and develop emergent structure there.

From the first mental space the blend takes Churchill. From the second mental space the blend takes the role of prime minister. In the blend, Churchill is prime minister by 1938. The blend is contrary to fact with respect to both of its input spaces. The antecedent and the consequent exist in the blend; neither exists in either of the input spaces.

Because the process of blending is largely unconscious it seems easy, but in fact it is complex. Blending has the following characteristic features.

The blend exploits and develops counterpart connections between input spaces. The space with Churchill and the space with Chamberlain share many identity-counterparts: date, England, Germany, Hitler, tension. Churchill and Chamberlain are additionally frame-counterparts: each is an English political figure, holding a certain political office, with views about Germany.

[1] This paper was written while the author was a fellow at the Center for Advanced Study in the Behavioral Sciences in 1994. He is grateful for financial support provided during that time by the Andrew W. Mellon Foundation. He is grateful to David Collier, Bruce Bueno de Mesquita, Phil Tetlock, and Aaron Belkin for comments, and to Gilles Fauconnier for both his original work on counterfactuals and his collaboration in developing the theory of blending on which this commentary is based.

Counterparts may or may not both be brought into the blend, and may or may not be fused in the blend. Many paired counterparts are brought into the blend as fused units: Hitler in the blend is a single fused entity corresponding to Hitler in each of the inputs but not equal to them—the Hitler in the blend has a different life. Churchill is brought into the blend but not fused with his frame-counterpart, Chamberlain. Chamberlain's political office is brought in but not fused with its frame-counterpart.

The projection from the input spaces is selective. The blend takes from the space with Churchill his opposition to Germany but not his political office or his reputation for having poor judgment of the sort that would prevent him from obtaining a position of leadership. The blend takes from the space with Chamberlain the role *prime minister* and the situation faced by the prime minister in 1938, but not Chamberlain himself or the default knowledge attached to *prime minister* that world leaders facing aggression are concerned greatly to avoid unnecessary war. We frame Chamberlain according to this default knowledge but keep it out of the blend, where we need a prime minister who views conflict as inevitable.

Blends recruit a great range of conceptual structure and knowledge without our recognizing it. Very little of the structure needed for the contrary-to-fact blended space is mentioned. The Churchill blend recruits conceptual frames of world leaders, political aggression, and wars. It recruits the relevant history of Germany and England. These recruitments are needed for the reasoning to work properly in the blend. Academic theories may also be recruited to the blend: game-theoretic interaction during political aggression, or deterrence by "power-maximizing" actors. These recruitments may drive the elaboration of the blend in one direction or another.

Blending is a process that can be applied repeatedly, and blends themselves can be inputs to other blends. Someone might respond to the Churchill counterfactual, "That is only because Hitler was irrational: a more rational Hitler would have seen that his strategic chances were still excellent, and would not have backed down." This new counterfactual blend takes part but not all of the original Churchill blend, and additionally takes part but not all of the characteristics of Hitler from spaces that refer to actual situations. In the new counterfactual hyperblend, World War II is not averted.

Blends develop structure not provided by the inputs. Typically, the blend is not a simple cut-and-paste reassembly of elements to be found in the input spaces but instead resembles what Kahneman (1995) calls a "mental simulation." Usually we focus on additional structure that develops only in the blend. For example, in the blend, but not in any of its inputs, Hitler backs down and World War II is averted.

Inferences, arguments, and ideas developed in the blend can have effect in cognition, leading us to modify the initial inputs and to change our view of the corresponding situations. A student of historicist patterns that led to

World War II might know Churchill's personality well but not have brought what she knows to bear on her conception of appeasement in 1938. The Churchill blend might challenge her to reconsider the causal weight of personality.

How does structure develop in the counterfactual blend? How does structure developed in the blend lead us to reconsider input spaces?

Blends develop by three mechanisms: *composition, completion, and elaboration*. We selectively *compose* structure from input spaces into the blend. To do so, we exploit counterpart connections between the input spaces. Partial composition provides a working space for further composition. *Completion* provides additional structure once a few elements have been brought in. A minimal framing of Churchill and Hitler as adversarial heads of state invites us to complete that structure by recruiting any amount of specific or general knowledge we have about personal opposition, international relations, negotiation, and so on. *Elaboration* develops the blend through imaginative mental simulation according to principles and logic in the blend. Some of these principles will have been brought to the blend by completion. Continued dynamic completion can recruit new principles and logic during elaboration. But new principles and logic may also arise through elaboration itself.

Composition and completion often draw together conceptual structures usually kept apart. As a consequence, the blend can reveal latent contradictions and coherences between previously separated elements. It can show us problems and lacunae in what we had previously taken for granted. It can equally show us unrecognized strengths and complementarity. In this way, blends yield insight into the conceptual structures from which they arise.

Composition, completion, and elaboration all recruit selectively from our most favored patterns of knowing and thinking. Consequently, blending is very powerful but also highly subject to bias. It is hard to evaluate bias in blends for two reasons. First, composition, completion, and elaboration operate for the most part automatically and below the horizon of conscious observation. Therefore, we rarely detect consciously the infrastructure in the blend that makes it effective. Second, since the emergent structure in the blend comes from our favored patterns of knowing and thinking, we are likely to regard biased infrastructure in the blend as unobjectionable even if we somehow manage to detect it.

For example, in trying to reason about a blend only on the basis of its proper historical structure, we may unwittingly complete the blend with evidence from a later historical moment. In the Churchill counterfactual, we use what we know of 1938. But once we have Churchill as prime minister in the blend, it is almost impossible to prevent completion from another (covert) input space—Churchill as prime minister later in time. In this way, our ex post knowledge can affect our supposed ex ante reasoning in ways detectable only on analysis. Even the selection of objects of ex ante reasoning can be influenced by ex post knowledge: Had Churchill never been prime minister, it is less likely that we would think of constructing a blend in which he was prime minister in 1938. Ex post input spaces seep into ex ante counterfactual blended spaces, and in fact prompt us covertly to construct them.

The model of conceptual blending, like all scientific models, reveals a set of constraints on the phenomena it describes. It demands mapping between counterparts in inputs, selective projection to the blend, and so on. There are also optimality constraints that pressure blends in one direction or another. The *integration constraint* requires that blends constitute a tightly integrated scene that can be manipulated as a unit. The *web constraint* requires that manipulation of the blend as a unit maintain the web of appropriate connections to the input spaces easily and without additional surveillance. The *unpacking constraint* requires that the blend alone enable the understander to unpack it to reconstruct the inputs and the connections between spaces. The *topology constraint* requires that any element in a blend that has been projected from an input have relations in the blend that match the relations of its corresponding element in the input.

An optimality constraint naturally has more or less power depending on the purpose of the blend. When blending is used to conceive of a new policy, model, or activity (like using the "desktop" interface for operating a computer), the integration constraint may play a dominant role, because the blend is meant to provide the mental basis for extended integrated activity.

But in cases where the blend has been constructed to help solve a puzzle in one of the input spaces, the web and topology constraints may dominate relevant structure, because abandoning certain connections to the input and altering relations between elements may make the blend locally less useful as an instrument for analyzing the input.

Perhaps the principal practical function of counterfactual blends in the social sciences is the spotlight function: to spotlight features of a space we care about, usually an input space. Pascal's counterfactual statement, *If Cleopatra's nose had been an inch longer, Antony might not have been so infatuated and the history of Rome and the West might have been entirely different*, spotlights the potential effect of specific private and personal affairs on large impersonal public political events. Fauconnier's counterfactual statement, *In France, Watergate would not have harmed Nixon*, spotlights differences in cultural attitudes toward actions taken by politicians.

The authors of spotlight counterfactual blends are typically indifferent to the kinds of restrictions that have been proposed for counterfactual arguments in the social sciences. But spotlights have their own restrictions. Because they are constructed to pick out important features—often causal—in an input space, they must contain structure that is easy to see once it is pointed out, and that leads us to recognize the related interesting features in the input. The spotlight must therefore obey the integration constraint over the relevant structure; but it can ignore integration for peripheral or subtle structure in the blend that is inconsequential for its spotlight function. Antecedents, consequents, and connecting principles must be compatible as judged by the logic and structure intended for the blend, but only to the extent that they bear on the spotlight function, and not otherwise. This restricted kind of "cotenability" for spotlight counterfactual blends arises from integration as controlled by the spotlight function. Other optimality constraints show the same governance: a constraint has effect only to the extent needed for accomplishing the spotlight function.

Some spotlight counterfactual blends deviate greatly from actuality, statistical probability, or theoretical possibility. Others deviate very little. For example, *If Napoleon had been Alexander's son, Alexander's empire would not have fragmented so quickly* deviates radically from actuality, from a comfortable level of statistical probability, and from theoretical possibility. We lack methods of measuring this deviation, but we judge it to be enormous. By contrast, *If a butterfly in the Amazon had flapped its wings one more time, we might at this instant have completely different weather on the East Coast* has as its antecedent the smallest imaginable deviation from actuality, from a comfortable level of statistical probability, and from theoretical possibility. This minimal deviation is the central feature of this spotlight, and of its claim that a minute difference in causes can make an enormous difference in effects. This spotlight has been so successful as to become the premier symbol of chaos theory.

2

Psychological Biases in Counterfactual Thought Experiments

JAMES M. OLSON, NEAL J. ROESE, AND RONALD J. DEIBERT

COUNTERFACTUAL THINKING refers to reconstructive thoughts about a past event, in which antecedents to the event are mentally mutated and possible changes to the outcome are contemplated (Kahneman and Miller 1986; Kahneman and Tversky 1982). In world politics, scholars use such thinking to speculate about the causes of historical events. Cognitive and social psychologists are interested in how lay perceivers use counterfactual thinking in everyday life. The goal of these researchers is to understand both when counterfactual thinking normally occurs and which counterfactual reconstructions of reality, from the infinite number of possible ones, are most likely to be generated by the average person.

Psychological research has identified many factors that can bias naturally occurring counterfactual thoughts (for reviews, see Kahneman and Miller 1986; Miller, Turnbull, and McFarland 1990; Roese and Olson 1995a). Counterfactual thinking is guided and constrained by both motivational and cognitive processes. These biasing factors can introduce systematic distortions into counterfactual reconstructions.

The purpose of the present commentary is to consider the implications of this psychological literature for counterfactual thought experiments in world politics. We argue that some of the same factors that bias naturally occurring counterfactual thinking can also affect the counterfactual reconstructions generated by theorists in world politics.

It might seem likely that scholars would be relatively immune to the factors that bias the counterfactual thoughts of everyday perceivers. For example, scholars are trained in scientific methods and are socialized into epistemic communities in which they are held accountable for certain standards of evidence and proof. Thus, they may be aware of potentially biasing factors and work to avoid them in their empirical analyses. Also, psychologists have been primarily interested in spontaneous, unplanned counterfactual thoughts, what Kahneman (1995) calls "automatic" counterfactual thinking. By contrast, scholars in world politics conduct counterfactual thought experiments deliberately and very self-consciously (what Kahneman calls "elaborative" counterfactual thinking). Perhaps different principles guide these two types of counterfactual thinking.

Although scientific training undoubtedly enhances objectivity in scholarly discourse, there is little reason to believe that all biases, some involving unconscious motivations, are eliminated by education. In this commentary, we focus on three sources of bias that can be clearly identified in counterfactual thought experiments. For each factor, we describe an experiment from the psychological literature that documents its biasing impact and then cite an example from world politics that illustrates its operation in this domain of scholarship.

Preferred Theories and Ideologies

Perceivers construct counterfactual thoughts to be consistent with their understanding of and theories about the world. A simple (and perfectly reasonable) example of this tendency is that people rarely violate physical, natural laws in their counterfactual musings (e.g., they are relatively unlikely to think about how their life would have been different if gravity did not exist; see Seelau, Seelau, Wells, and Windschitl 1995). Potentially more problematic is perceivers' tendency to conform in their counterfactual thinking to intuitive beliefs and theories about how antecedents and outcomes are related in the focal domain. That is, preferred theories, political ideologies, and other subjective perspectives bias counterfactual thoughts in a predictable manner. Specifically, intuitive theories lead people to believe that particular antecedents probably caused a given outcome; their counterfactual reconstructions of the event will mutate the antecedents implicated by the theories.

For example, people with high self-esteem (chronically positive appraisals of themselves) believe that, in general, they are responsible for their positive outcomes but are not responsible for their negative outcomes (i.e., that they personally cause successes, whereas failures are caused by factors external to themselves; see Taylor and Brown 1988). In two studies of counterfactual thinking, Roese and Olson (1993) induced high and low self-esteem subjects to imagine themselves in scenarios with another actor that resulted in either success or failure. Subjects were then asked to list any things that, had they been different, could have changed the outcome. When asked how a successful outcome might have been different, high self-esteem subjects were more likely than low self-esteem subjects to focus on their own actions ("If not for me, we would have failed"). By contrast, when asked how a failure might have been different, high self-esteem subjects were more likely than low self-esteem subjects to focus on the other actor's actions ("If not for him, we would have succeeded"). Thus, the counterfactual thoughts of high self-esteem individuals conformed to their intuitive theories about the causes of their own successes and failures.

In counterfactual thought experiments in world politics, scholars also mutate events in ways that are consistent with their relevant intuitive theories, including ideologies, theoretical perspectives, and pet hypotheses. It makes sense for counterfactual analyses to be consistent with widely accepted or highly general theories, but counterfactuals in world politics often emerge from subjective, particularized views for which there is no wide consensus or empirical support. For example, in contrasting interpretations of the end of the Cold War, realists and conservatives have tended to mutate the existence of strong deterrents and an unremitting arms buildup during the Reagan era (e.g., "had the West succumbed to the pacifists, the Cold War would still be ongoing"; see Perle 1992). By contrast, liberals have tended to mutate "learning" and epistemic community interaction within a growing network of informal and formal security regimes (e.g., "it is in spite of the arms buildup that superpower cooperation ensued"; see Adler 1992; Levy 1994). In these cases, differences in counterfactual content reflect the competing underlying presuppositions of each theoretical perspective about the values and interests that motivate states in the international system. These counterfactuals are self-serving in that they imply the existence of evidence and argument that support rather than weaken the foundational positions of the author. Of course, scholars' preferred theories and ideologies can bias not only how they generate counterfactual hypotheticals, but also how they evaluate the thought experiments of others. That is, researchers may apply different standards of proof to counterfactual thought experiments that are consistent versus inconsistent with their ideologies, ascribing greater plausibility to those reconstructions that conform to their preferred theories.

Exceptional or Unusual Antecedents

Perhaps the most widely cited idea in the psychological literature on counterfactual thinking is that perceivers focus on exceptional, unusual, or salient antecedents when constructing counterfactual thoughts. That is, in naturally occurring counterfactual thoughts, perceivers typically mutate exceptional or unexpected antecedents to be more routine or expected (and then contemplate whether the outcome would have been different if things had been more normal). In terms of norm theory (Kahneman and Miller 1986), exceptional or unexpected events are more cognitively "mutable" (i.e., easier to imagine being different).

For example, in an often-replicated scenario study, Kahneman and Tversky (1982) had subjects read about a man who was killed in an automobile accident on the way home from work. Some subjects learned that he left work early but drove home via his usual route. Other subjects learned that he left work at his usual time but took an unusual route home. When asked how the accident could have been avoided, the former subjects mutated the exceptional departure time (he would still be alive if he had left work at his normal time) but not his route, whereas the latter subjects mutated the exceptional route home (he would still be alive if he had taken his normal route) but not his departure time. Of course, either mutation was theoretically possible in either condition; presumably, subjects' attention was drawn to the exceptional, unusual antecedent.

Similarly, in counterfactual thought experiments in world politics, exceptional or unexpected antecedents are likely to be seized upon for mutation toward more routine, normal, or default values. To put it another way, rare or low base-rate events will be replaced with more common or higher base-rate events. Crop failures, market crashes, and sudden technological innovations tend to be mutated in counterfactual thought experiments to reestablish the trajectory of historical trends that were interrupted by the unusual events. Rarely do scholars in world politics speculate about how a routine election would have turned out differently if one of the candidates had been assassinated. On the other hand, when an assassination actually occurs, scholars often wonder about what would have happened if things had proceeded routinely (Chapter 3, Breslauer; Chapter 8, Kiser and Levi). For example, speculation about how the religious affairs of Europe would have been different had Henry of Navarre not been assassinated and the Edict of Nantes not repealed is common among historians of early modern European politics (see Toulmin 1990). This observation reflects the powerful fact that counterfactual thoughts are more compelling when they replace unusual events with normal events.

Negative Outcomes

Certain kinds of events trigger counterfactual thinking. That is, people are more likely to think about "what might have been" after particular kinds of outcomes. Perhaps the primary "engine" for counterfactual thinking is a negative outcome (Roese and Olson 1995a). Indeed, negative outcomes command more intense and effortful attention in a variety of ways than do positive outcomes. The evolutionary significance of this asymmetry is clear: Negative outcomes are acute, signifying a state of affairs that must be addressed immediately. Hence, across many species, internal systems igniting "flight or fight" responses are highly reactive to negative stimuli, producing rapid physiological, cognitive, affective, and behavioral changes (see S. E. Taylor 1991). Increased counterfactual thinking is just one example of such responses.

In recent experiments, Roese and Olson (1995c) gave subjects a description of either a success or a failure in an academic achievement context. A subsequent, open-ended "thought-listing" task revealed a far greater proportion of spontaneously produced counterfactual thoughts in the negative (failure) than positive (success) outcome condition.

Negative events are also more likely to capture the attention of scholars in world politics than positive events. One difficulty in assessing this issue in world politics is the ambiguous valence of many historical events. For example, was the Cuban missile crisis positive (because it was resolved peacefully) or negative (because it pushed the world to the brink of nuclear war)? But despite ambiguity in characterizing some historical events, there does seem to be a strong tendency for theorists in international relations to focus on explaining (counterfactually or otherwise) negative outcomes in general, and war in particular (Gilpin 1981; Waltz 1959). Although the field has broadened its concerns enormously over the last twenty years, its development as a formal discipline evolved out of a desire to understand the recurrence of war (Holsti 1985). Thus, events such as the First World War have traditionally received a far greater proportion of scholarly attention than, say, the undefended border between the United States and Canada (Christensen and Snyder 1990; Sagan 1986).

Why Should Scholars Care about These Biases?

We have argued that scholars in world politics may construct counterfactual thought experiments that are biased by preferred theories, exceptional antecedents, and negative outcomes. Why should scholars care about these biases? On the one hand, analyses might be deliberately tailored to conform to these (and other; see Roese and Olson 1995a) lay constraints; such arguments will seem more plausible and persuasive to other scholars. But more importantly, awareness of these cognitive and motivational constraints may open new ways of examining issues and illuminate previously untested variables that have been foreclosed by unrecognized biases. For example, researchers might give deliberate consideration to alternative realities that would be plausible only with revisions to their preferred theories. Also, thoughts about whether alterations to routine antecedents would have changed an outcome might provide a novel perspective on historical events. Scholars could also give greater attention to positive events in history; how might these events have been changed?

Thus, scholars might profit from an assessment of the extent to which their counterfactual arguments are constrained by the factors we have discussed, inasmuch as such factors maintain and reinforce conceptual parochialism. By deliberately avoiding these constraints, scholars may realize more creative, novel, and insightful analyses. This observation underscores the relevance of psychological approaches to counterfactual thinking for improving the use of counterfactual thought experiments in world politics.

3

Counterfactual Inferences as Instances of Statistical Inferences

ROBYN M. DAWES

FEARON (Chapter 2) asserts that the underlying logic of hypothesis testing and counterfactual inference is the same. In this comment I suggest that he is correct, with the qualification that the underlying logic of hypothesis testing and *good* counterfactual inferences—i.e., those that are productive, reasonable, and helpful—is the same. Fearon, however, goes on to suggest that unlike hypothesis testing and statistical estimation, "evidence always comes from consideration of particular cases, rather than from blunt regularities of association across multiple cases." Here I disagree. In this comment I argue that good counterfactual inferences—again, productive, reasonable, helpful ones—should be point predictions arising from statistical expectations. A corollary of my argument is that good counterfactual inferences must be derivable from, or at least justified by, statistical analyses for which there is some empirical or rational justification.

Here I am in agreement with Kahneman (1995) and Herrmann and Fischerkeller (Chapter 6). Kahneman argues that "if only" is often (usually? always?) a linguistic equivalent of "because." That is, to maintain that "if only X had occurred, Y would have been different" is to assert that the nature of Y is dependent—at least in part—on X. The more extreme statement—"If only Z had not occurred, Y would not have occurred"—is the assertion that Y occurred *because* Z did, i.e., that Z was a necessary condition for Y. (Not-Z implying not-Y is equivalent to Y implying Z; in the earlier assertion, X is a sufficient condition for Y to be different.)

Such statements of necessity or sufficiency can, however, be established only on the basis of general principles. If they are equivalent to "good" counterfactuals, then these "what might have been" assertions must be compatible with assertions about what is, what was, and what will be—as argued by Herrmann and Fischerkeller (Chapter 6). If so, then such statements when they concern people and society must be probabilistic in nature because we do not know enough to make deterministic causal statements (Dawes 1991), and they must be justified nomothetically—even if they appear on the surface to be of a purely idiographic nature.[1] The reason for the latter condition is that statistical generalizations, even when applied to a single instance (e.g., the generalization that in poker one is more likely to be dealt a flush than a straight flush), have at least potential applicability to a class of instances. (More usually, the individual instance is analyzed as the expectation of a class, defined either empirically or in terms of a theoretically constructed sample space.)

Consider, by contrast, a counterfactual inference in the absence of a statistical justification. If p then q; therefore, if not-p then not-q. That is simply the contrapositive form of the mundane fallacy of affirmation of the consequent. As is well established, people do commit the fallacy (see, for example, Wason and Johnson-Laird 1972) *in particular contexts*.

But now consider another counterfactual inference. An actor fails at a task and makes the counterfactual inference that "if only" she had put forth more effort, she would have succeeded. Is such reasoning a simple instance of affirmation of the consequent? If "effort" and "outcome" are considered in isolation of other instances relating effort to outcome, yes. But effort and outcome more reasonably refer to multiple instances in this person's life in which she has put forth varying amounts of effort and experienced varying outcomes. There is undoubtedly a positive correlation between effort and quality of outcome in her experience—not as positive a correlation as would be estimated in retrospect (Dawes 1993), but a positive correlation nevertheless. Thus, it is perfectly reasonable to conclude that higher effort in general yields better outcomes, and hence would have done so in this particular instance. It is only the counterfactual "if only" language—coupled with an apparently deterministic point prediction—that yields the difference between the counterfactual assertion and what is most probably a valid statistical inference about the potentially different outcome.

But why did the counterfactual inference not involve greater ability rather than greater effort? Psychologists present hypotheses involving stability (effort less so than ability), controllability, and "mutability" (Roese and Olson 1995c). These explanations are purely psychological without any reference to normative principles. Here, however, I suggest that there is a perfectly good statistical reason for choice of effort rather than choice of ability. Most individuals have undoubtedly experienced greater variance in the effort they put into a particular task than variance in their ability at the outset, and hence a greater covariance between effort and outcome than between ability and outcome. A major exception would be variance in outcome that results

---

[1] My former colleagues in clinical psychology often claim to make "purely idiographic" analyses of "individuals in their unique entirety" (whom these colleagues, of course, understand in their unique entirety). The problem with this claim, however, is that virtually every descriptor claimed to be true of the individual qua individual (e.g., "passive-aggressive") has meaning only with reference to classes of people who can and who cannot be accurately described by it.

from an ability developed over time. But even ability changes over time are often too gradual to be noticed (e.g., consistent deterioration from age twenty-nine or so, which is extremely gradual, barring disasters such as stroke). "I 'yam what I 'yam," proclaims Popeye, which does not prevent him from experiencing various levels of effort and success (e.g., after ingesting spinach or being deprived of it). However illusory the magnitude of the resulting correlation, the correlation itself is there. Conversely, even though we may speak of being a "better person" than in the past, or "not the man I used to be," the actual experience of having differing aptitude is not as available to a single individual as the experience of putting forth varying amounts of effort on a task.

Now consider the same example of failure after less than optimal effort from the perspective of a professor who is evaluating the outcome. The professor has had indirect contact with changes in effort within people and how they are tied to variability in success. (Note that the professor has not had direct *experience* with students' differential effort, whether on a within- or between-student basis; the variance is an inference.) The easiest variability in effort for the professor to observe is that between students—and the professor may well be willing to make a *valid* (Dawes 1989) inference from between to within. The experience of students differing in aptitude is, however, more direct for the professor. Thus, the professor, noting a positive correlation between aptitude and success,[2] can easily create the counterfactual inference that "if only" this particular (hard-working, enthusiastic, engaged) student were brighter, the student would have succeeded, or at least done better. A professor who has had experience teaching at universities of varying degrees of student selectivity may be even more likely to refer to "if only" aptitude rather than effort, not only because of the greater psychological ease of "doing and undoing," but also because of the actual experience with enhanced variability of aptitude.

Recall that, as Tversky and Kahneman (1974) pointed out in their classic article, heuristics that may lead to grievous errors in some contexts are often generally helpful "rules of thumb." For example, ease of recall and generation is, in fact, correlated with experience in life in general, even though factors other than frequency readily create "availability biases." Here, the degree to which a variable is considered static, controllable, or mutable may well be correlated with the degree to which it has actually varied in a person's experience in general.

Now consider another example, this one Fearon's. "If I had not gotten stuck in a traffic jam, I would have arrived on time." In asking whether it is possible to evaluate the correctness of this counterfactual inference, Fearon

---

[2] Those of us who teach elementary statistics sometimes wonder whether performance in this area reflects anything but aptitude.

writes (Chapter 2): "I do not see any obviously correct answer here." But some others may. Some people will reply sarcastically, "Oh, sure!" When? When the person making the counterfactual assertion is always late anyway. In this case it is possible to conclude that the counterfactual inference is incorrect, or at least that we can form a reasonable (statistical) expectation that it is incorrect. (Of course, this conclusion also requires a side assumption that there are instances in which the person is not caught in a traffic jam; if the probability of a traffic jam equals the probability of being late equals one, we have an instance of "paradoxical implication," which is necessarily "true." In what follows, I will assume that all probabilities are nonzero.)

In fact, the probability of being late *in general* if there is not a traffic jam can be inferred from the probability of being late, the probability of being late if there is a traffic jam (which can be assumed to be close to one), and the base-rate probability of a traffic jam (the probability of no jam being one minus the probability of a jam). If we have knowledge that allows reasonable estimates of these probabilities, we are justified in inferring what the probability is of being late given no jam. If it is close to zero, we are justified in concluding that the counterfactual inference is justified in this instance; if not, not.

My major point is that counterfactual inferences are justified—or deemed incorrect—if and only if they are embedded in a system of statistical contingency for which we have reasonable evidence. Sometimes the evidence can be fairly explicit, sometimes "fuzzy" but nevertheless reasonable, if not established. Here, I agree with Elster (1978) that we must evaluate both "actual possibility" and the potential realizability—but of *both* the counterfactual condition and the possibility of sampling from it, or having sampled from it in the past, even though I also agree with Fearon (Chapter 2) that this requirement creates "substantial difficulties."

Now consider: "If Bobby Kennedy had not been assassinated, our war against Vietnam would have ended sooner." Again, consider not just that statement isolated from other knowledge, but whether there is some statistical justification for it. First, Bobby Kennedy expressed opposition to the war, and although people elected to the presidency do not always follow policies enunciated during campaigns (e.g., Johnson's reasonableness in the 1964 campaign, Reagan's fiscal conservatism in the 1980 campaign), they generally do. Which policies? I admit that my conclusion is based on "fuzzy" intuitive contingency, but a study testing it is at least potentially realizable. Second, Kennedy was popular in the opinion polls, and there is undoubtedly a positive correlation between popularity in opinion polls in June and election in November. (Again, we could test that, in part to determine the reasonableness of the counterfactual inference.) Third, there appears to be some historical contingency between the assassination of liberal political leaders and the ascendancy of conservative to reactionary ones who pursue war. Examples include the 1925 assassination of Ebert in Germany and the string of assassinations of prime ministers in Japan preceding the success of the war party in the late 1930s.

Now it is possible to gather data to support or refute my statistical assertions regarding the Robert Kennedy assassination. My point, however, is that it *is* possible to evaluate it, once it is framed in terms of general statistical contingencies, and only then. Without at least the potential for such support, I see no distinction between the counterfactual assertion "If Robert Kennedy had not been assassinated, the war would have been over sooner" and the statements "Robert Kennedy was assassinated and the war against Vietnam continued" and the (totally vacuous) counterfactual inference "If Robert Kennedy had not been assassinated, subsequent events would have been different."

Thus, for example, if a person switched flights at the last minute and was subsequently killed in an accidental airplane crash, it would not be *normatively* valid, in my view, to conclude that "if only" the person hadn't switched flights, the person would be alive. The reason is that we have no basis for concluding that flights switched to are more likely to crash than flights switched from. Of course, it may be psychologically compelling to argue "if only," or death may appear more "tragic" on a flight switched to than one routinely scheduled several days or weeks in advance,[3] but we know that people experience psychologically compelling conclusions that are not normatively justified. Perhaps someone will someday find some contingency between switching and dying, but I doubt it, given that dying in accidental airplane crashes results from flights' crashing, independent of which passengers happen to be on them.

My position also implies that in addition to the switched flight example, some of the examples in Tetlock and Belkin (Chapter 1) cannot be normatively justified. These authors appear to be in search of "butterfly effects." But as Maruyama (1963) so brilliantly pointed out more than twenty years before "chaos" theory became popular, the essence of a butterfly effect is that it cannot be discovered. (His example of what he termed an "initial kick" was of a beautiful morning on a western U.S. plain that the first white invader took as a sign that he and his family should settle there rather than somewhere else. The "reason" a city ended up being built there rather than somewhere else would be literally "undiscoverable.")

In summary, the expectation of "what would have happened" must be a "reasonable" one based on a supportable statistical argument. Many different types of argument may suffice, for example, arguments based on:

---

[3] The more I think about this example, the less compelling it is. Is it not possible that switching is as inevitable as not switching? There is, after all, the story about fleeing to Sumeria to avoid Death only to meet Death there.

1. Past sampling of specific instances
2. Past sampling of patterns (a particular type of specific instance)
3. Beliefs about "how things are" based on indirect generalizations from the past or principles believed to be established, perhaps "fuzzily," from an analysis of the past, e.g., beliefs about how rational people would behave "off the equilibrium path" in games (see Chapter 9, Bueno de Mesquita; and Chapter 10, Weingast)
4. Simulations or theories with some support (outside the particular "case")
5. Good common sense[4]
6. Other good reasons.

The forgoing brings me to my major example, which follows from the view that counterfactual inferences are normatively justified if and only if they are embedded as instances in generally valid statistical relationships. This example could convince the reader of this view's value or lack thereof.

Suppose that someone is required to wager her entire wealth on a single roll of a pair of fair dice. Her wealth will be doubled if she wins the bet; if she loses, she will be bankrupt. Her choice is to bet either for or against a roll of snake eyes. Being wise, she bets against snake eyes. The dice are rolled and they come up snake eyes. She loses. She is bankrupt.

Is it normatively valid to state that "if only" she had bet on snake eyes she would have won? Well, it is true that she bet against snake eyes and that she lost. But does the "if only" add anything to the analysis? I suggest that the answer is no.

Suppose instead that she had bet *on* snake eyes and had lost. Here, the regretful counterfactual inference that "if only" she had bet against snake eyes she would have won is normatively justified. Why? Because the odds are thirty-five to one against snake eyes, and those odds justify the expectation that she would have won had she bet against snake eyes. It is an expectation; one can insert "probably won" if one wishes. But it is a fairly "tight" expectation, moreover one that is broadly applicable.

Now compare this example to that of switching flights. We might note that for a particular deceased individual, switching flights was unusual behavior that led to death. But this particular form of unusual behavior is not in general tied to life versus death; there is no general contingency between it and death comparable to the contingency between betting against snake eyes and winning. (Once again, however, avoiding unusual behavior may be a reasonable "rule of thumb" in general. New behavior may be risky; hence, like other heuristics that are generally valid but grievously erroneous in particular situations, the heuristic of forming the counterfactual "if not unusual, no disaster" may have some general applicability.)

---

[4] Stern (1993) argues that a major policy goal of psychological and social science should be to "separate common sense from common nonsense and make common sense more common." I agree.

Thus, I suggest that when Fearon and Tetlock and Belkin *contrast* counterfactual inferences with those derived from experiments or observational statistical inference they are incorrect—at least when considering counterfactual inferences that are normatively justifiable. I argue, instead, that counterfactual inferences are normatively justified only when they are embedded in a broader experimental or statistical context and justified in terms of *expectation*, which may be applied to an individual instance.

A challenge to my view comes from the concept of "normativeness" (as distinct from statistical expectation) that has been introduced by Dale Miller and his colleagues (Miller, Turnbull, and McFarland 1990; Miller and Turnbull 1990). Let me share an example of this distinction. You know that a child prefers a chocolate cookie to a plain one, but you believe that the child should have the plain one (so that the child's expected longevity is increased one microsecond at the expense of several seconds of enjoyment). You tell the child to reach into a cookie jar without looking and draw a cookie. The child draws a chocolate cookie. In situation 1, there is a single chocolate cookie and nine plain cookies in the jar. In situation 2, there are ten chocolate cookies and ninety plain ones in the jar. In which situation are you more suspicious that the child has peeked?

Miller and his colleagues suggest that most people are more suspicious in the first situation, and these researchers present other situations in which suspicion is independent of probability, which they believe clearly to be .10 in both cookie jar situations. Their argument is in part an argument *against* considering counterfactual inferences in purely probabilistic terms.

Yes, it is true that people will state that the probability of blindly picking a chocolate cookie is exactly .10 in both situations *if asked*. But there is another way to assess probability belief, by inferring it from choice behavior. Thus, for example, Gold and Hester (1987) find that subjects who explicitly state a belief in independence of successive coin tosses nevertheless act as if they don't believe in independence; specifically, they accept a sure payment X in preference to betting on heads after four heads in a row have been tossed, where X is substantially less than an amount Y that is rejected in preference to betting on tails after four heads. With payoffs for winning the coin toss a constant, the discrepancy between X and Y cannot be explained by a transformation of the payoffs to utilities, but only by a difference in implicit probabilities. An important result of this research is that the effect was as strong for subjects who explicitly stated that successive coin tosses are independent as for those (fortunately a minority) who stated a belief in the gambler's fallacy.[5]

Now consider the following choice. You receive $1,000 for drawing a

---

[5] An actual comment: "I studied probability at Pitt, so I know that when a coin comes up heads it is more likely to come up tails the next time."

white ball three successive times in a row. Urn 1 contains one white and two blue balls, and drawing is done with replacement. Urn 2 contains ten white and twenty blue balls, and drawing is done without replacement. Quick calculation reveals that the probability of winning the \$1,000 is $(1/3)^3 = .0370$ when drawing from Urn 1 and $(10/30) \times (9/29) \times (8/28) = .0295$ when drawing from Urn 2. But bet on drawing the same solitary ball three times in succession?! If our probability judgments are behaviorally revealed by choices carefully constructed to elicit them ("revealed probability"), then we should not be too quick to reject the idea of justifying counterfactual inferences on a statistical basis simply because our implicit judgment does not correspond to one that we would form explicitly after calculation. There may be no need to add an idea of "normativity" to expectation in order to justify and explain counterfactual inference. (And remember, once again, that there may be a confounding between normativeness, broadly conceived, and safety; for evolutionary or functional reasons, belief in behavior as normative, usual, or proper that systematically deviates from behavior that is rewarded on a probabilistic basis will be extinguished; some silly deviations can, of course, be maintained, especially in the absence of feedback, especially if errors do not matter much for our survival. How often has any of us, for example, drawn a ball from an urn?[6])

It is all a matter of statistics.

[6] When writing this section, I became aware of the fact that despite discussing drawing balls from urns *ad nauseam* in my work, I have never actually drawn a ball from an urn!

4

Counterfactuals, Causation, and Complexity

ROBERT JERVIS

> When you pick up one piece of this planet, you find that, one way or
> another, it's attached to everything else—if you jiggle over here, something
> is going to wiggle over there. . . . We need this sense of the continuing
> interconnectedness of the system as part of the common knowledge, so that
> politicians feel it and believe it, as so that voters feel it and believe it, as so
> that kids feel it and believe it, so that they will grow up with an ethic.
> Because what we do—or not do—now will be an inheritance for all
> time. . . .
> 　　[To minimize oil spills] we should . . . mandate double-hulled vessels and
> compartments in tankers.
> 　　(*Sylvia Earle, quoted in White 1989, 56 and 46*)

> Scientific medicine has done little to add years to people who have already
> reached their maturity. In the last 50 years only about four months have been
> added to the expected lifespan of the person who is already 60 years old.
> 　　(*Lewontin 1993, 42–43*)

These two statements make implicit counterfactual claims, one about the
future and the other about the past. Both are undermined by a failure to
appreciate the dynamics of the systems in which the elements are imbedded
and which they constitute. The reader who immediately understands this has
little need to read the rest of this commentary. But my suspicion that the fallacies are not self-evident is bolstered by the fact that Earle and Lewontin are not
only experts in their fields, but distinguished systems theorists as well.

A system exists when elements or units are interconnected so that the
system has emergent properties—i.e., its characteristics and behavior cannot
be inferred from the characteristics and behavior of the units taken individually—and when changes in one unit or the relationship between any two of
them produce ramifying alterations in other units or relationships.[1] The result
often is a high degree of complexity as causation operates in ways that
defeat standard forms of common sense and scientific method. On the one
hand, this means that when we are dealing with a system, counterfactuals
cannot be used in as simple and straightforward a way as our intuition leads

[1] This conception of systems and many of the ideas that inform this commentary are drawn
from Jervis (forthcoming).

us to expect. On the other hand, it means that counterfactual thinking can be extremely useful for thought experiments that assist us in developing our ideas about how elements are connected and how results can arise. Counterfactuals can alert us to the possible operation of dynamics and pathways that we would otherwise be prone to ignore (Chapter 12, Weber). They cannot, of course, offer proof, but they may get us to think more productively.

A great deal of thinking about causation, both in science and in everyday life, is based on comparing two situations that are the same in all ways except one. Any differences in the outcome, whether actual or expected (this method is used for both prediction and postdiction), can be attributed to the difference in the state of the one element. Thus in nonexperimental social science we generally teach our students to select cases that allow them to hold everything constant except the variable on which they are focusing. This can be done either by looking at different cases or at one case in which the variable changes over time. Under many circumstances, this method is powerful and appropriate. But it runs into serious problems when we are dealing with systems because other things simply cannot be held constant: as Garrett Hardin nicely puts it, in a system, "we can never do merely one thing" (Hardin 1963, 80; Chapter 11, Cederman).

Let me explain what I mean by returning to the quotations with which I started this chapter. Earle's reasoning is straightforward and, at first glance, impeccable: when oil tankers go aground, even a fairly small rend in their hauls will cause the cargo to spill. Double hulls would provide a significant measure of protection because only the most severe collisions would produce spills; past pollution would have been reduced if tankers had been equipped with second hulls because many impacts would have penetrated only the outer, but not the inner, skin. Implicitly, Earle is rerunning past cases by using a counterfactual and imagining that the only difference was a single element. But this is unlikely in a system, especially one that includes actors who have knowledge and beliefs about the other elements and the system itself. In a system, one always does more than one thing; worlds in which one element is different will differ in other ways as well. In other words, cotenability problems arise when we think that the rest of the world would stay the same if tankers were outfitted with an outer hull. Although we cannot be sure what would happen, we can make some guesses. The shipping companies, forced to purchase more expensive tankers, might cut expenditures on other safety measures, in part because of the belief that this is justified by the greater protection supplied by the double hulls. The relative cost of alternative means of transporting oil would decrease, perhaps moving spills from the seashore to the areas traversed by new pipelines. But even tanker spills might not decrease. The current trade-off between costs and spills may reflect the preferences of shippers and captains, who might take advantage of the greater safety by going faster and taking more chances than they did when their ships were more vulnerable.[2]

In the case Lewontin presents, the implicit counterfactual is complicated by a form of systemic selection effects: the world that modern medicine has helped to shape is a very different one from that which existed earlier. More specifically, many people who live to age sixty would have died much younger in earlier eras. Lewontin's data refer only to those who live past that age, but if modern health science has saved the lives of people who otherwise would have died young and—what is crucial—if these people are not as strong and healthy as others, then the fact that life expectancy after sixty has grown a bit indicates, not the weakness of modern medicine, but its potency. The comparison to a world without modern medicine implies that we can infer that modern medicine's influence has been negligible from the fact that there has been only a slight change in the life expectancy of the elderly. The problem is that this ignores the fact that the variable Lewontin is trying to understand has strongly affected the characteristics of people over sixty, thereby precluding the use of a counterfactual that rests on the hidden assumption that this crucial factor has remained constant.

Of course modern medicine is also connected with other aspects of industrial and postindustrial society, some of which may undermine people's health. Thus modernity may bring—or be composed of—pollution, stress, and a variety of associated dangers. Indeed, people may even engage in more health-threatening activities because modern medicine has made them less threatening.[3] If these effects are operating, then even in the absence of selection effects of the kind discussed in the previous paragraph, any increase in life expectancy of the elderly would show the power of improvements in health care. But note also that this implicit counterfactual runs afoul of systems thinking because it asks us to imagine a world in which all the effects of modernity are present except for health science, and it is doubtful that such a world could exist: the kinds of medical treatments now available are an inextricable part of our social system.

In everyday thought experiments we ask what would have happened if

---

[2] Many readers may be especially skeptical of the claim that captains would be less careful if they thought their ships were safer, but there is a good deal of evidence that this dynamic has at least partly undermined the effectiveness of safety devices in automobiles (see Peltzman 1975; Perrow 1984, 179–80). The empirical analyses necessary to tease out the influence of regulations from the multiplicity of other factors at work is extremely difficult and therefore all the studies are controversial. A review of the evidence argues that safety regulations in fact have had at least some desired effect (Crandall 1986, 56–84).

[3] When we deal with actors whose behavior is influenced by their expectations of how others will behave, game theory is extremely illuminating. Thus it is not surprising that my analysis reaches conclusions similar to those in two other chapters in this volume (see Chapter 9, Bueno de Mesquita; and Chapter 10, Weingast).

one element in our world had been different. Living in New York, I often hear people speculate that traffic would be unbearable (as opposed to merely terrible) had Robert Moses not built his highways, bridges, and tunnels. But to try to estimate what things would have been like, we cannot merely subtract these structures from today's Manhattan landscape. The traffic patterns, the location of businesses and residences, and the number of private automobiles that are now on the streets are in significant measure the product of Moses's road network. Had it not been built, or had it been built differently, many other things would have been different. Traffic might now be worse, but it is also possible that it would have been better because a more efficient public transportation system would have been developed or because the city would not have grown so large and prosperous without the highways. In any event, the thought experiment cannot be carried out in a simple way.

A similar error (among others) mars the counterfactual that underpins Newt Gingrich's arguments that American society would be more moral, stable, and prosperous were it not for the pernicious values of the 1960s and 1970s, which undermined the ethic of individual responsibility. Even if we grant the claim that the protests of that era led to a loosening of social bonds and a diminished sense of social responsibility, they may also have helped shape other aspects of our current world, ones that Gingrich approves of. Thus it is possible that the norms that led to an increased divorce rate also unleashed creative individualism, which encouraged such innovations as the computer revolution; that the resistance to authority that made society more turbulent also led conservatives to feel empowered to challenge big government; that the increased salience of equality that spawned excessive affirmative action programs also destroyed some of the unfair barriers to equal opportunity. In other words, Gingrich would like us to imagine a world that is like our own only without what he sees as the evil legacy of the 1960s and 1970s. But such a world could not exist: that era had many consequences, including ones that may have made possible the arrangements Gingrich and his colleagues seek.

Simple counterfactuals will also be misleading when the actors in a system are in conflict. Here a change that would advantage one of them if all things remained the same will have quite a different effect as all the actors respond to the new situation. For example, if we were not in a system, then lifting the arms embargo on Bosnia would strengthen that state. But we are in a system, and Serbia and Croatia are likely to react by buying more arms and increasing their aggression. The reaction of third parties may be crucial: if all other things remained equal, a regime plagued by guerrillas could safely employ repression. But this course of action will have multiple consequences, perhaps including alienating previously neutral citizens and so generating greater support for the rebels. In a parallel manner, external intervention in a civil war may not help the side being aided if it also has the effect of mobilizing nationalism on the other side. Here as elsewhere in complex systems the dynamics of the biological world provide instructive parallels. In looking at the evolution of animals in nonsystemic terms, one would think that as a species improves, its members will catch more prey. But this would be to disregard the fact that the prey's defenses are also improving under the pressures of natural selection; predators and prey are engaging in a dynamic arms race.[4]

Counterfactuals When Comparisons Will Not Do

Our standard techniques for testing the validity of propositions assume that factors are independent in a way that is not likely to be true in a system. We cannot readily hold all else constant when the variable on which we are focusing influences the composition of the set of cases we are studying, the processes that occur in those cases, and the policies the actors choose to adopt. Here counterfactuals both show the limits of our standard comparative method and make us look for the hidden connections that tie the system together. For example, one central implication of deterrence theory is that in situations resembling the game of chicken an actor can increase his chance of prevailing by showing the other side that he is committed to standing firm (Schelling 1960). The obvious way to test this proposition is to compare the outcomes of two sets of crises, one in which a defender had committed himself and another in which he had not. But crises that occur when the defender has made a commitment are likely to be different from those that occur in the absence of such pledges; it is extremely difficult to construct comparisons in which all variables save one are either the same or are randomly different because the variables of interest are connected with each other. A challenge will take place in the face of a commitment only when the challenger is either unable to understand the situation or is extremely strongly motivated to prevail. In either case, the challenger will be difficult to dissuade. Commitment thus might decrease the number of challenges that occur, but not increase the defender's chance of prevailing when the challenger does choose to create a crisis.[5] Similarly, to see whether deterrence is easier than compellence, the obvious thing to do is to look at the success rates of these policies (see, for example, Petersen 1986). But if statesmen believe that it is very difficult to get the other side to change its behavior by the use of threats, they will resort to compellence only under unusual cir-

---

[4] For a good discussion see Dawkins and Krebs (1979).

[5] To use Morgan's terms, commitment may then be positively correlated with the success of general deterrence and negatively correlated with the success of immediate deterrence (see Morgan 1977, 25–45).

cumstances, circumstances that will be not unrelated to whether the effort is likely to succeed.

A related problem for testing propositions by the normal use of the comparative method is that different tactics are selected by actors on the basis of their expectations of the results that are likely to be produced. For example, assume that by comparing cases in which a state tried to discourage the adversary from changing the status quo by building up its defenses with cases in which it sought to deter the other by threatening it with punishment, we discover that one method worked in a higher percentage of cases than the other. Such a finding would be interesting, but what could we make of it? Because the state selected its approach by estimating how alternative policies would work in each particular circumstance, we could not infer that the state would have done better if it had used the more successful tactic in the other set of cases. The tactic that failed more often may have been applied in cases that were more difficult or were not suited to the "more successful" approach. Furthermore, thinking about evolutionary processes reminds us that the additional application of the "more successful" tactic might have led to changes in the beliefs, behaviors, and even identities of other actors that could have radically altered the effects of using the tactic. Our methods must take account of the fact that the outcomes are produced by the interaction of actors who are not choosing their behavior at random.

For the same reason, one cannot determine the influence of nuclear weapons by looking for differences in the course of conflicts depending on whether either side had them. One study tries, and concludes that "the possession of nuclear weapons appears to have no deterrent effect in disputes with non-nuclear states. Specifically, nuclear targets are much more likely to de-escalate such conflicts than are non-nuclear targets. . . . In conflicts between nuclear and non-nuclear states, the possession of nuclear weapons has no apparent inhibitory effect on the escalatory behavior of the opponent." But while the data indeed do show that "nuclear disputes are more likely to escalate (short of war) than are non-nuclear disputes," the other conclusions are unwarranted (Geller 1990, 302). A nation without nuclear weapons is likely to enter into a dispute with a nuclear power only if the stakes are very important to it and/or if it believes that there are especially good reasons why it should be able to prevail. The other side of this coin is that the possession of nuclear weapons may enable states to enter into disputes they otherwise would have avoided. The apparent similarity of behavior between nuclear and non-nuclear states during active conflicts may then mask a large role for nuclear weapons in influencing decisions on whether to engage in a confrontation.

In these cases counterfactuals cannot be employed in the simple form of imagining a world different in only one way from the existing one, but they are a very fruitful aid to thinking about systemic connections. Thus if the standard argument about commitment is correct, it follows that in a situation in which the state had actually failed to commit itself, adopting the alternative policy would have made the adversary more likely to see a challenge as very risky. But this is quite different from arguing that we can determine the efficacy of the tactic by comparing the outcomes of challenges to commitments with the results of challenges that were issued when there had been no such signals. We can also see that because states do not undertake commitments randomly, the counterfactual may be difficult: we cannot imagine a world in which the state chose a tactic different from the one it actually did unless we also imagine other changes that provide good reasons for that decision.

Actors and analysts often judge a policy's success by using indicators or yardsticks to compare two cases, or one case over an extended period of time. The implicit counterfactual reference is to a world in which the indicator is different, and the implication is that if it were, the policy would be producing the desired effect. But because the elements in a system are interconnected, the changes that are occurring may alter the meaning of the yardstick, bending it if you will. For example, many colleges use the yield rate as a measure of their quality: if this year 40 percent of the people we accept enroll in our program, we must be doing worse than we were five years ago when 60 percent enrolled. This inference seems especially compelling if competitors' yield rates did not drop. But the data do not rule out an alternative explanation—the program's reputation may have improved, thus attracting better applicants. Because of their quality, the applicants will also gain admittance to other programs, and so the yield may fall. This could be the case even if the total number of applicants did not increase, because weaker ones may no longer be applying. Similarly, interactions would render problematic an attempt to determine which professors are easy and hard graders by looking at the distribution of marks they give: if students know who is lenient and who is tough, then those who are less motivated and able will disproportionately take classes from the former. As a result, there may not be any relationship between a professor's standards and the number of As and Cs she gives. For the same kind of reasons, one cannot judge the competence of a doctor or hospital by the rate at which patients survive. Excellent physicians and facilities will attract (and select) harder cases and sicker people.[6]

Giving an actor incentives to do well according to an indicator that previously measured success can be self-defeating; expressing a counterfactual can change not only the behavior, but what it signifies. If I value the (hypothetical) fact that my daughter keeps her room neat because I think this

[6] As the government tries to rate the providers of medical services it has sought to control for this effect, but there are limits to how well this can be done.

shows admirable values and I tell her how glad I am about it, her future neatness may reflect not these values, but the desire to please me. For strategic reasons as well, many yardsticks will be valid only if those being measured are not aware of them. Thus even if the skill of health care providers was initially reflected in the survival rate of patients, dispensing rewards and punishments on this basis would give the providers incentives to avoid hard cases. This would not only be unfortunate, but would alter the link between the indicator and what it indicates. Charles Goodhart of the Bank of England identified what he calls Goodhart's law which, with the indicated modification, has much validity: "If an economic statistic becomes focus of attention [and if actors have the ability and incentives to affect the statistic, then] that statistic is likely to distort" (Barge 1985, 31).[7] Thus Soviet statements about the importance of nuclear superiority ceased shortly after many American defense analysts argued that they showed that the USSR was aggressive. Perhaps the Soviets changed their views, but they may also have seen that their speeches were having an undesired effect and altered them to try to create a more desired image.[8]

In summary, counterfactuals are both useful and tricky when we deal with a system. They can help us think through the connections we believe to be at work, but cannot be employed to help us imagine a world that is like our own in all ways except for one. A change will inevitably have many effects; often the change itself is only possible if other factors change as well, in which case, the counterfactual will violate the minimal-rewrite rule (Chapter 1, Tetlock and Belkin). When we act, we often intend a direct consequence, as we seek to reduce oil spills by requiring tankers to have double hulls. But in a world of many actors with many goals, deflection is more the rule than the exception. This does not mean that purposeful behavior is impossible: systems are not completely interconnected and there are methods of acting to effect change despite—and sometimes because of—a system's dynamics.[9] The use of counterfactuals to test propositions or guide action can be designed to help us trace consequences, but the complex interconnections involved are likely to make the exercise a difficult one.

[7] For further discussion of this problem see Jervis (1989, chapter 3).

[8] Recently declassified documents do not allow us to choose between these explanations (Korniyenko 1995).

[9] See Jervis (forthcoming, chapter 7) and the discussion of "Leibnizians" and more moderate systems thinkers in Tetlock and Belkin (Chapter 1).

References

Abelson, R. P. 1959. Modes of resolution of belief dilemmas. *Journal of Conflict Resolution* 3: 343–52.

Aberbach, J. D. 1990. *Keeping a watchful eye: The politics of congressional oversight*. Washington: Brookings Institution.

Achen, C. H., and D. Snidal. 1989. Rational deterrence theory and comparative case studies. *World Politics* 41 (2): 143–69.

Adler, E. 1992. The emergence of cooperation: National epistemic communities and the international evolution of the idea of nuclear arms control. *International Organization* 46 (1): 101–45.

Alker, H. R. 1981. From political cybernetics to global modeling. In *From national development to global community*, ed. K. L. Merritt and B. M. Russett, 353–78. London: George, Allen & Unwin.

Allyn, B. J., J. G. Blight, and D. A. Welch. 1992. *Back to the brink: Proceedings of the Moscow Conference on the Cuban Missile Crisis, January 27–28, 1989.* Lanham, Maryland: University Press of America.

Almond, G. A., and S. J. Genco. 1977. Clouds, clocks, and the study of politics. *World Politics* 29 (4): 489–522.

Altfeld, M. F. 1984. The decision to ally: A theory and test. *Western Political Quarterly* 37 (4): 523–44.

Altfeld, M. F., and B. Bueno de Mesquita. 1979. Choosing sides in wars. *International Studies Quarterly* 23 (1): 87–112.

Anderson, R. D., Jr. 1993. *Public politics in an authoritarian state: Making foreign policy during the Brezhnev years*. Ithaca: Cornell University Press.

Arthur, W. B. 1989. Competing technologies, increasing returns, and lock-in by historical events. *The Economic Journal* 99 (394): 116–31.

———. 1990. Positive feedbacks in the economy. *Scientific American* 262 (Feb.): 92–99.

Aster, S. 1989. "Guilty men": The case of Neville Chamberlain. In *Paths to war: New essays on the origins of the Second World War*, ed. R. Boyce and E. M. Robertson, 233–68. New York: St. Martin's Press.

Axelrod, R. 1984. *The evolution of cooperation*. New York: Basic Books.

———. 1987. The evolution of strategies in the iterated prisoner's dilemma. In *Genetic algorithms and simulated annealing*, ed. L. Davis, 32–41. Los Altos, Calif.: Kaufmann.

———. 1995. The convergence and stability of cultures: Local convergence and global polarization. Discussion Paper No. 375, Institute of Public Policy Studies, University of Michigan.

Axelrod, R., and R. O. Keohane. 1985. Achieving cooperation under anarchy: Strategies and institutions. *World Politics* 38 (1): 226–54.

Babst, D. V. 1964. Elective governments: A force for peace. *Wisconsin Sociologist* 3 (1): 9–14.

Bak, P., and K. Chen. 1991. Self-organized criticality. *Scientific American* 264 (Jan.): 46–53.

Baldwin, J. W. 1986. *The government of Philip Augustus: Foundations of French royal power in the Middle Ages*. Berkeley: University of California Press.

Barge, J. 1985. Goodhart's law strikes again. *The Banker* 135 (July): 27–31.

Barry, B. 1980. Superfox. *Political Studies* 28 (1): 136–43.

Beattie, A. 1977. Neville Chamberlain. In *British prime ministers in the twentieth century*, ed. J. Mackintosh, 1:219–71. New York: St. Martin's Press.

Bercovitch, J. 1991. International mediation and dispute settlement: Evaluating the conditions for successful mediation. *Negotiation Journal* 7 (1): 17–30.

Berger, P. L., and T. Luckmann. 1966. *The social construction of reality: A treatise in the sociology of knowledge*. Hammondsworth, Eng.: Penguin Books.

Berk, G. 1990. Constituting corporations and markets: Railroads in gilded age politics. *Studies in American Political Development* 4: 130–68.

———. 1994. Regionalism in economic practice: The Chicago Great Western Railway. In *Alternative tracks: The constitution of American industrial order, 1865–1917*, 116–49. Baltimore: Johns Hopkins University Press.

Berkowitz, B. D. 1983. Realignment in international treaty organizations. *International Studies Quarterly* 27 (2): 77–96.

Bernstein, B. J. 1976. The week we almost went to war. *Bulletin of Atomic Scientists* 32 (3): 13–21.

———. 1980. The Cuban missile crisis: Trading the Jupiters in Turkey? *Political Science Quarterly* 95 (1): 97–125.

Bernstein, M. A. 1994. *Foregone conclusions: Against apocalyptic history*. Berkeley: University of California Press.

Betts, R. 1987. *Nuclear balance and nuclear blackmail*. Washington: Brookings Institution.

Bill, J. A. 1990. The U.S. overture to Iran, 1985–1986: An analysis. In *Neither East nor West: Iran, the Soviet Union, and the United States*, ed. N. R. Keddie and M. J. Gasiorowski, 166–79. New Haven: Yale University Press, 1990.

Billington, J. H. 1966. Six views of the Russian revolution. *World Politics* 18 (3): 452–73.

Binmore, K. 1990. *Essays on the foundations of game theory*. Oxford: Blackwell.

Blake, R. 1993. How Churchill became prime minister. In *Churchill*, ed. R. Blake and W. R. Louis, 257–73. Oxford: Oxford University Press.

Blight, J. G., B. J. Allyn, and D. A. Welch. 1993. *Cuba on the brink: Castro, the missile crisis, and the Soviet collapse*. New York: Pantheon.

Blight, J. G., D. Lewis, and D. A. Welch. 1994. *Cuba between the superpowers: The Antigua Conference on the Cuban Missile Crisis*. Savage, Maryland: Rowman & Littlefield.

Blight, J. G., and D. A. Welch. 1989. *On the brink: Americans and Soviets reexamine the Cuban missile crisis*. New York: Hill & Wang.

Brandes, L. 1994. Public opinion, international security policy, and gender: The United States and Britain since 1945. Ph.D. diss., Yale University.

Brawley, M. R. 1993. *Liberal leadership: Great powers and their challengers in peace and war*. Ithaca: Cornell University Press.

Brecher, M. 1993. *Crises in world politics: Theory and reality*. Oxford: Pergamon.

Bremer, S. A. 1992. Dangerous dyads: Conditions affecting the likelihood of interstate war, 1816–1965. *Journal of Conflict Resolution* 36 (2): 309–41.

———. 1993. Democracy and militarized interstate conflict, 1816–1865. *International Interactions* 18 (3): 231–49.

Breslauer, G. W. 1992. In defense of Sovietology. *Post-Soviet Affairs* 8 (3): 197–238.

Brown, F. 1968. *Chemical warfare: A study in restraints*. Princeton: Princeton University Press.

Brown, L. C. 1984. *International politics and the Middle East: Old rules, dangerous game*. Princeton: Princeton University Press.

Bueno de Mesquita, B. 1981. *The war trap*. New Haven: Yale University Press.

———. 1988. Nuclear peace through selective nuclear proliferation. Manuscript, Hoover Institution, Stanford University.

Bueno de Mesquita, B., and D. Lalman. 1992. *War and reason: Domestic and international imperatives*. New Haven: Yale University Press.

Bueno de Mesquita, B., and R. Siverson. 1995. Nasty or nice? Political systems and the removal of adversaries. Paper presented at the annual meeting of the American Political Science Association, Chicago.

Bundy, M. 1988. *Danger and survival: Choices about the bomb in the first fifty years*. New York: Random House.

Burawoy, M. 1989. Two methods in search of science: Skocpol versus Trotsky. *Theory and Society* 18 (6): 759–805.

Burks, A. W., ed. 1970. *Essays on cellular automata*. Urbana: University of Illinois Press.

Calvin, W. H. 1994. The emergence of intelligence. *Scientific American* 271 (Oct.): 100–7.

Campbell, D. T., and J. C. Stanley. 1966. *Experimental and quasi-experimental designs for research*. Chicago: Rand McNally.

Carr, E. H. 1961. *What is history?*. New York: Knopf.

"Cato." 1940. *Guilty men*. London: Gollancz.

Cederman, L.-E. 1994. Emergent polarity: Analyzing state-formation and power politics. *International Studies Quarterly* 38 (1): 501–33.

———. 1995. Competing identities: An ecological model of nationality-formation. *European Journal of International Relations* 1 (3): 331–65.

———. 1997. *Emergent actors in world politics: How states and nations develop and dissolve*. Princeton: Princeton University Press.

Chan, S. 1993. Democracy and war: Some thoughts on future research agenda. *International Interactions* 18 (3): 205–13.

Chandler, A. D., Jr. 1977. *The visible hand: The managerial revolution in American business*. Cambridge, Mass.: Belknap Press.

Christensen, T. J., and J. Snyder. 1990. Chain gangs and passed bucks: Predicting alliance patterns in multipolarity. *International Organization* 44 (2): 137–68.

Churchill, W. S. 1950. *The grand alliance*. Boston: Houghton Mifflin.

Cohen, J., and I. Stewart. 1994. *The collapse of chaos: Discovering simplicity in a complex world*. New York: Viking.

Cohen, R. 1994. Pacific unions: A reappraisal of the theory that "democracies do not go to war with each other." *Review of International Studies* 20 (3): 207–23.

Cohen, S. F. 1985a. Bolshevism and Stalinism. Chapter 2 in *Rethinking the Soviet experience: Politics and history since 1917*, 38–70. New York: Oxford University Press.

———. 1985b. *Rethinking the Soviet experience: Politics and history since 1917.* New York: Oxford University Press.

Collier, D. 1995. Translating quantitative methods for qualitative researchers: The case of selection bias. *American Political Science Review* 89 (2): 461–66.

Cooper, D. 1953. *Old men forget.* London: Hart-Davis.

Cottam, R. W. 1988. *Iran and the United States: A Cold War case study.* Pittsburgh: University of Pittsburgh Press.

———. 1989. Inside revolutionary Iran. *Middle East Journal* 43 (2): 168–85.

Coulson, S. 1995. Analogic and metaphoric mapping in blended spaces. *Center for Research in Language Newsletter* 9 (1): 2–12.

Crandall, R. W. 1986. *Regulating the automobile.* Washington: Brookings Institution.

Crawford, N. C. 1994. A security regime among democracies: Cooperation among Iriquois nations. *International Organization* 48 (3): 345–85.

Dallin, A. 1992. Causes of the collapse of the USSR. *Post-Soviet Affairs* 8 (4): 279–302.

Davidson, D. 1980. *Essays on actions and events.* Oxford: Clarendon Press.

Dawes, R. M. 1988. *Rational choice in an uncertain world.* San Diego: Harcourt Brace Jovanovich.

———. 1989. The potential non-falsity of the false consensus effect. In *Insights in decision making: A tribute to Hillel J. Einhorn*, ed. R. M. Hogarth, 179–99. Chicago: University of Chicago Press.

———. 1991. Probabilistic versus causal thinking. In *Thinking clearly about psychology: Essays in honor of Paul Everett Meehl*, ed. D. Cicchetti and W. Grove, 235–64. Minneapolis: University of Minnesota Press.

———. 1993. The prediction of the future versus an understanding of the past: A basic asymmetry. *American Journal of Psychology* 106 (1): 1–24.

Dawkins, R., and J. R. Krebs. 1979. Arms races between and within species. *Proceedings of the Royal Society, London* B 205 (Sept.): 489–511.

Deutsch, K. W. 1954. Cracks in the monolith: Possibilities and patterns of disintegration in totalitarian systems. In *Totalitarianism*, ed. C. J. Friedrich, 308–33. Cambridge: Harvard University Press.

Deutsch, K. W., and J. D. Singer. 1964. Multipolar power systems and international stability. *World Politics* 16 (3): 390–406.

Deutscher, I. 1970. *Russia, China, and the West: A contemporary chronicle, 1953–1966*, ed. F. Halliday. New York: Oxford University Press.

Dilks, D. 1987. "We must hope for the best and prepare for the worst": The prime minister, the cabinet and Hitler's Germany, 1937–1939. *Proceedings of the British Academy* 73: 309–52.

Dinerstein, H. S. 1959. *War and the Soviet Union: Nuclear weapons and the revolution in Soviet military and political thinking.* New York: Praeger.

Dion, D. 1995. Evidence and inference in the comparative case study. Mimeograph, University of Michigan.

Dittmer, L. 1992. *Sino-Soviet normalization and its international implications, 1945–1990.* Seattle: University of Washington Press.

Dixon, W. J. 1993. Democracy and the management of international conflict. *Journal of Conflict Resolution* 37 (1): 42–68.

———. 1994. Democracy and the peaceful settlement of international conflict. *American Political Science Review* 88 (1): 14–32.

Durkheim, E. 1938. *The rules of sociological method.* Glencoe, Ill.: Free Press of Glencoe.

———. 1951. *Suicide: A study in sociology.* Glencoe, Ill.: Free Press of Glencoe.

Dutton, D. 1994. Simon and Eden at the Foreign Office, 1931–1935. *Review of International Studies* 20 (1): 35–52.

Eden, A. 1962. *Facing the dictators: The memoirs of Anthony Eden, earl of Avon.* Boston: Houghton Mifflin.

Elster, J. 1978. *Logic and society: Contradictions and possible worlds.* New York: John Wiley.

———. 1983. *Explaining technical change: A case study in the philosophy of science.* New York: Cambridge University Press.

———. 1989. *Nuts and bolts for social scientists.* Cambridge: Cambridge University Press.

———. 1993. *Political psychology.* Cambridge: Cambridge University Press.

Erlich, A. 1960. *The Soviet industrialization debate, 1924–1928.* Cambridge: Harvard University Press.

Evangelista, M. 1982. Stalin's postwar army reappraised. *International Security* 7 (3): 110–39.

Farber, H. S., and J. Gowa. 1995. Politics and peace. *International Security* 20 (2): 123–46.

Fauconnier, G. 1985. *Mental spaces: Aspects of meaning construction in natural language.* Cambridge, Mass.: MIT Press, 1985; reprint, Cambridge, Eng.: Cambridge University Press, 1994. Page references are to the reprint edition.

———. Forthcoming. *Mappings in thought and language.* Cambridge: Cambridge University Press.

Fauconnier, G., and M. Turner. 1994. Conceptual projection and middle spaces. *UCSD Cognitive Science Technical Report 9401*, April. San Diego: University of California.

———. Forthcoming. Blending as a central process of grammar. In *Conceptual structure, discourse, and language*, ed. A. Goldberg. Stanford: Center for the Study of Language and Information, Stanford University.

Fearon, J. D. 1991. Counterfactuals and hypothesis testing in political science. *World Politics* 43 (2): 169–95.

———. 1994a. Domestic political audiences and the escalation of international disputes. *American Political Science Review* 88 (3): 577–92.

———. 1994b. Ethnic war as a commitment problem. Working paper, University of Chicago.

———. 1994c. Signaling versus the balance of power and interests: An empirical test of a crisis bargaining model. *Journal of Conflict Resolution* 38 (2): 236–69.

Ferejohn, J. A., and C. R. Shipan. 1989. Congressional influence on administrative behavior: A case study of telecommunications policy. In *Congress reconsidered*, ed. L. C. Dodd and B. I. Oppenheimer, 4th ed., 393–410. Washington: CQ Press.

Festinger, L. 1957. *A theory of cognitive dissonance.* Stanford: Stanford University Press.

322   REFERENCES

Fiorina, M. P. 1981. Congressional control of the bureaucracy: A mismatch of incentives and capabilities. In *Congress reconsidered*, ed. L. C. Dodd and B. I. Oppenheimer, 2nd ed., 332–48. Washington: CQ Press.

Fischhoff, B. 1975. Hindsight is not equal to foresight: The effect of outcome knowledge on judgment under uncertainty. *Journal of Experimental Psychology: Human Perception and Performance* 1 (3): 288–99.

Fisher, D. H. 1970. *Historians' fallacies: Toward a logic of historical thought.* New York: Harper & Row.

Fiske, S. T., and S. E. Taylor. 1991. *Social cognition.* Reading, Mass.: Addison-Wesley.

Floyd, D. 1963. *Mao against Khrushchev: A short history of the Sino-Soviet conflict.* New York: Praeger.

Fogel, R. 1964. *Railroads and American economic growth: Essays in econometric history.* Baltimore: Johns Hopkins University Press.

Fontana, W., and L. W. Buss. 1994. What would be conserved if "the tape were played twice"? *Proceedings of the National Academy of Sciences of the USA* 91 (2): 757–61.

Foot, M. 1986. *Loyalists and loners.* London: Collins.

Foreign relations of the United States (FRUS). Washington: US Government Printing Office.

Friedman, M. 1953. *Essays in positive economics.* Chicago: University of Chicago Press.

Gaddis, J. L. 1992. International relations theory and the end of the cold war. *International Security* 17 (3): 5–58.

———. 1993. The tragedy of Cold War history. *Diplomatic History* 17 (1): 1–16.

Gardner, M. 1970. Mathematical games: The fantastic combinations of John Conway's new solitaire game "life." *Scientific American* 223 (Oct.): 120–3.

Garfinkel, A. 1981. *Forms of explanation.* New Haven: Yale University Press.

Garfinkel, M. R. 1994. Domestic politics and international conflict. *American Economic Review* 84 (5): 1294–1309.

Garrett, B. 1979. China policy and the strategic triangle. In *Eagle entangled: US foreign policy in a complex world*, ed. K. A. Oye, D. Rothchild, and R. J. Lieber. New York: Longman.

Garthoff, R. L. 1987. *Reflections on the Cuban missile crisis.* Washington: Brookings Institution.

Gasiorowski, M. J. 1991. *U.S. foreign policy and the Shah: Building a client state in Iran.* Ithaca: Cornell University Press.

Geddes, B. 1990. How the cases you choose affect the answers you get: Selection bias in comparative politics. *Political Analysis* 8: 131–50.

———. 1991. Paradigms and sand castles in the comparative politics of developing areas. In *Political science: Looking to the future*, Vol. 2, *Comparative politics, policy, and international relations*, ed. W. Crotty, 45–75. Evanston, Ill: Northwestern University Press.

———. 1994. Big questions, little answers. Paper presented at the annual meeting of the American Political Science Association, New York.

Geller, D. S. 1990. Nuclear weapons, deterrence, and crisis escalation. *Journal of Conflict Resolution* 34 (2): 291–310.

George, A. L. 1979. Case studies and theory development: The method of structured, focused comparison. In *Diplomacy: New approaches in history, theory, and policy*, ed. P. G. Lauren, 43–68. New York: Free Press.

———. 1980. The causal nexus between cognitive beliefs and decision-making behavior: The "operational code" belief system. In *Psychological models in international politics*, ed. L. Falkowski, 95–124. Boulder: Westview.

———. 1993. *Bridging the gap: Theory and practice in foreign policy*. Washington: U.S. Institute of Peace.

George, A. L., and T. J. McKeown. 1985. Case studies and theories of organizational decision making. In *Advances in information processing in organizations*, Vol. 2, *Research on public organizations*, ed. R. Coulam and R. Smith, 21–58. Greenwich, Conn.: JAI Press.

George, A. L., and R. Smoke. 1974. *Deterrence in American foreign policy: Theory and practice*. New York: Columbia University Press.

Gerschenkron, A. 1960. Problems and patterns of Russian economic development. In *The transformation of Russian society*, ed. C. E. Black, 42–72. Cambridge: Harvard University Press.

———. 1966. *Economic backwardness in historical perspective*. Cambridge: Harvard University Press.

Gibbs, N. H. 1976. *Grand strategy*, Vol. 1, *Rearmament policy*. London: HMSO.

Giddens, A. 1984. The constitution of society: Outline of the theory of structuration. Berkeley: University of California Press.

Gilbert, M. 1976. *Winston S. Churchill*, Vol. 5, *1922–39*. London: Heinemann.

Gilpin, R. 1981. *War and change in world politics*. Cambridge: Cambridge University Press.

Glaser, C. L. 1990. *Analyzing strategic nuclear policy*. Princeton: Princeton University Press.

Gleick, J. 1987. *Chaos: Making a new science*. New York: Viking.

Goertz, G., and P. F. Diehl. 1993. Enduring rivalries: Theoretical constructs and empirical patterns. *International Studies Quarterly* 37 (2): 147–71.

Gold, E., and G. Hester. 1987. The gambler's fallacy and the coin's memory. Manuscript, Department of Social and Decision Sciences, Carnegie Mellon University.

Goldgeier, J. M. 1994. *Leadership style and Soviet foreign policy: Stalin, Khrushchev, Brezhnev, and Gorbachev*. Baltimore: Johns Hopkins University Press.

Goldman, M. 1994. *Lost opportunity: Why economic reforms in Russia have not worked*. New York: Norton.

Goldstone, J. A. 1991. *Revolution and rebellion in the early modern world*. Berkeley: University of California Press.

———. 1994. Why we could (and should) have foreseen the revolutions of 1989–91 in the USSR and eastern Europe. In *Debating revolutions*, ed. N. R. Keddie, 39–64. New York: New York University Press.

Goodman, N. 1983. *Fact, fiction, and forecast*. Cambridge: Harvard University Press.

Gould, J. D. 1969. Hypothetical history. *Economic History Review* 22 (2): 195–207.

Gould, S. J. 1981. *The mismeasure of man*. New York: Norton.

Graebner, N. A. 1969. Cold War origins and the continuing debate: A review of recent literature. *Journal of Conflict Resolution* 13 (1): 123–32.

Greif, A., P. Milgrom, and B. R. Weingast. 1994. Coordination, commitment, and enforcement: The case of the merchant guild. *Journal of Political Economy* 102 (4): 745–76.

Griffith, W. E. 1964. *The Sino-Soviet rift*. Cambridge: MIT Press.

Griffiths, F. 1984. The sources of American conduct: Soviet perspectives and their policy implications. *International Security* 9 (2): 3–50.

Grosnell, H. F. 1980. *Truman's crises: A political biography of Harry S. Truman*. Westport, Conn.: Greenwood.

Gruner, W. D. 1980. The British political, social and economic system and the decision for peace and war: Reflections on Anglo-German relations, 1800–1939. *British Journal of International Studies* 6 (3): 189–218.

Hagopian, M. N. 1974. *The phenomenon of revolution*. New York: Dodd, Mead.

Haimson, L. 1964. The problem of social stability in urban Russia, 1905–1917 (Part one). *Slavic Review* 23 (4): 619–42.

———. 1965. The problem of social stability in urban Russia, 1905–1917 (Part two). *Slavic Review* 24 (1): 1–22.

Hannan, M. T., and J. Freeman. 1989. *Organizational ecology*. Cambridge: Harvard University Press.

Hardin, G. 1963. The cybernetics of competition: A biologist's view of society. *Perspectives in Biology and Medicine* 7 (1): 58–84.

Harkness, R., and G. Harkness. 1954. The mysterious doings of the CIA. *Saturday Evening Post*, 6 Nov., 66–68.

Hart, H. L. A. 1961. *The concept of law*. Oxford: Clarendon Press.

Hart, H. L. A., and A. M. Honoré. 1959. *Causation in the law*. Oxford: Oxford University Press.

Hawkins, S. A., and R. Hastie. 1990. Hindsight: Biased judgments of past events after the outcomes are known. *Psychological Bulletin* 107 (3): 311–27.

Hawthorn, G. 1991. *Plausible worlds: Possibility and understanding in history and the social sciences*. New York: Cambridge University Press.

Hayek, F. A. 1967. *Studies in philosophy, politics and economics*. Chicago: University of Chicago Press.

Hempel, C. 1965. *Aspects of scientific explanation, and other essays in the philosophy of science*. New York: Free Press.

Herrmann, R. K. 1985. *Perceptions and behavior in Soviet foreign policy*. Pittsburgh: University of Pittsburgh Press.

Holland, J. H. 1992. Complex adaptive systems. *Daedalus* 121 (1): 17–30.

Holland, J. H., K. J. Holyoak, R. E. Nisbett, and P. R. Thagard. 1986. *Induction: Processes of inference, learning, and discovery*. Cambridge: MIT Press.

Holland, J. H., and J. H. Miller. 1991. Artificial adaptive agents in economic theory. *American Economic Review* 81 (2): 365–70.

Holloway, D. 1994. *Stalin and the bomb: The Soviet Union and atomic energy, 1939–1956*. New Haven: Yale University Press.

Holsti, K. J. 1985. *The dividing discipline: Hegemony and diversity in international theory*. Boston: Allen & Unwin.

Hook, S. 1943. *The hero in history: A study in limitation and possibility*. New York: John Day.

Hudson, G. F., R. Lowenthal, and R. MacFarquhar, eds. 1961. *The Sino-Soviet dispute*. London: China Quarterly.

Humphreys, P. 1989. *The chances of explanation: Causal explanation in the social, medical, and physical sciences*. Princeton: Princeton University Press.

Hunter, H., and J. M. Szyrmer. 1992. *Faulty foundations: Soviet economic policies, 1928–1940*. Princeton: Princeton University Press.

Huth, P. 1988. *Extended deterrence and the prevention of war*. New Haven: Yale University Press.

———. 1990. The extended deterrent value of nuclear weapons. *Journal of Conflict Resolution* 34 (2): 270–90.

Huth, P., and B. Russett. 1984. What makes deterrence work? Cases from 1900 to 1980. *World Politics* 36 (4): 496–526.

———. 1988. Deterrence failure and crisis escalation. *International Studies Quarterly* 32 (1): 29–45.

Isaacson, W. 1992. *Kissinger: A biography*. New York: Simon & Schuster.

Janis, I. L., and L. Mann. 1977. *Decision making: A psychological analysis of conflict, choice and commitment*. New York: Free Press.

Jervis, R. 1976. *Perception and misperception in international politics*. Princeton: Princeton University Press.

———. 1981. Beliefs about Soviet behavior. In *Containment, Soviet behavior, and grand strategy*, ed. R. E. Osgood, 55–59. Berkeley: Institute of International Studies, University of California.

———. 1989. The manipulation of indices. Chapter 3 in *The logic of images in international relations*, 2nd ed., 41–65. New York: Columbia University Press.

———. 1991. The future of world politics: Will it resemble the past? *International Security* 16 (3): 39–73.

———. 1993. Systems and interaction effects. In *Coping with complexity in the international system*, ed. J. Snyder and R. Jervis, 25–46. Boulder: Westview.

———. Forthcoming. *Systems: Dynamics and effects*. Princeton: Princeton University Press.

Jowitt, K. 1971. *Revolutionary breakthroughs and national development: The case of Romania, 1944–1965*. Berkeley: University of California Press.

———. 1978. *The Leninist response to national dependency*. Berkeley: Institute of International Studies, University of California.

———. 1992. *New world disorder: The Leninist extinction*. Berkeley: University of California Press.

Kahneman, D. 1995. Varieties of counterfactual thinking. In *What might have been: The social psychology of counterfactual thinking*, ed. N. J. Roese and J. M. Olson, 375–96. Mahwah, New Jersey: Erlbaum.

Kahneman, D., and D. T. Miller. 1986. Norm theory: Comparing reality to its alternatives. *Psychological Review* 93 (2): 136–53.

Kahneman, D., P. Slovic, and A. Tversky, eds. 1982. *Judgment under uncertainty: Heuristics and biases*. New York: Cambridge University Press.

Kahneman, D., and A. Tversky. 1982. The simulation heuristic. In *Judgment under uncertainty: Heuristics and biases*, ed. D. Kahneman, P. Slovic, and A. Tversky, 201–8. New York: Cambridge University Press.

Kaminski, A. Z. 1992. *An institutional theory of communist regimes: Design, function, and breakdown*. San Francisco: Institute of Contemporary Studies Press.

Kellert, S. H. 1993. *In the wake of chaos: Unpredictable order in dynamical systems*. Chicago: University of Chicago Press.

Kennedy, P. M. 1976. The tradition of appeasement in British foreign policy, 1865–1939. *British Journal of International Studies* 2 (3): 195–215.

———. 1978. "Appeasement" and British defence policy in the inter-war years. *British Journal of International Studies* 4 (2): 161–77.

Keohane, R. O. 1984. *After hegemony: Cooperation and discord in the world political economy*. Princeton: Princeton University Press.

Kerensky, A. 1934. *The crucifixion of liberty*. New York: John Day.

Khong, Y. F. 1992. *Analogies at war: Korea, Munich, Dien Bien Phu, and the Vietnam decisions of 1965*. Princeton: Princeton University Press.

———. 1993. Structural constraints and decision-making: The case of Britain in the 1930s. In *Ideas and ideals: Essays on politics in honor of Stanley Hoffmann*, ed. L. B. Miller and M. J. Smith, 296–312. Boulder: Westview.

Khrushchev, N. 1992. Letter to John F. Kennedy, Oct. 30, 1962. *Problems of Communism* 41 (special issue, Spring): 62–73.

Kiewiet, D. R., and M. D. McCubbins. 1991. *The logic of delegation: Congressional parties and the appropriations process*. Chicago: University Chicago Press.

Kilgour, D. M. 1991. Domestic political structure and war behavior: A game-theoretic approach. *Journal of Conflict Resolution* 35 (2): 266–84.

King, G., R. O. Keohane, and S. Verba. 1994. *Designing social inquiry: Scientific inference in qualitative research*. Princeton: Princeton University Press.

Kiser, E. 1994. Markets and hierarchies in early modern tax systems: A principal-agent analysis. *Politics and Society* 22 (3): 284–315.

———. 1995. What can sociological theories predict: Comments on Collins, Kuran, and Tilly. *American Journal of Sociology* 100 (6): 1611–15.

Kiser, E., and M. Hechter. 1991. The role of general theory in comparative-historical sociology. *American Journal of Sociology* 97 (1): 1–30.

Kissinger, H. 1993. *Diplomacy*. New York: Simon and Schuster.

Kornai, J. 1992. *The socialist system: The political economy of communism*. Princeton: Princeton University Press.

Korniyenko, G. M. 1995. A "missed opportunity": Carter, Brezhnev, SALT II, and the Vance mission to Moscow, November 1976-March 1977. *Cold War International History Project Bulletin* 5 (Spring): 141–43.

Koslowski, R., and F. V. Kratochwil. 1994. Understanding change in international politics: The Soviet empire's demise and the international system. *International Organization* 48 (2): 215–47.

Kotkin, S. 1991. "One hand clapping": Russian workers and 1917. *Labor History* 32 (4): 604–20.

Krasner, S. D. 1988. Sovereignty: An institutional perspective. *Comparative Political Studies* 21 (1): 66–94.

Kreutzer, W. 1986. *System simulation: Programming styles and languages*. Sydney: Addison-Wesley.

Kreps, D. M. 1990. *Game theory and economic modelling*. Oxford: Clarendon Press.

Kuniholm, B. R. 1980. *The origins of the Cold War in the Near East: Great power conflict and diplomacy in Iran, Turkey, and Greece*. Princeton: Princeton University Press.

Kupchan, C. A. 1994. *The vulnerability of empire*. Ithaca: Cornell University Press.

Kuran, T. 1991. Now out of never: The element of surprise in the East European revolution of 1989. *World Politics* 44 (1): 7–48.

———. 1994. Why revolutions are better understood than predicted: The essential role of preference falsification: Comment on Keddie. In *Debating revolutions*, ed. N. R. Keddie, 27–35. New York: New York University Press.

Kvart, I. 1986. *A theory of counterfactuals*. Indianapolis: Hackett Publishing.

Lake, D. A. 1992. Powerful pacifists: Democratic states and war. *American Political Science Review* 86 (1): 24–37.

Lalman, D., and D. Newman. 1991. Alliance formation and national security. *International Interactions* 16 (4): 239–54.

Lane, D. A. 1992. Artificial worlds and economics. Working Paper 92-09-048, Santa Fe Institute.

Laqueur, W. 1994. *The dream that failed: Reflections on the Soviet Union*. New York: Oxford University Press.

Layne, C. 1994. Kant or cant: The myth of the democratic peace. *International Security* 19 (2): 5–49.

———. 1995. On the democratic peace. *International Security* 19 (4): 175–77.

Lebow, R. N. 1984. Windows of opportunity: Do states jump through them? *International Security* 9 (1): 147–86.

———. 1989. Interview with Sergei Khrushchev, Moscow, May 17, 1989.

Lebow, R. N., and J. G. Stein. 1994. *We all lost the Cold War: Can we win the peace?* Princeton: Princeton University Press.

Leites, N. C. 1951. *The operational code of the politburo*. New York: McGraw-Hill.

Leng, R. J. 1993. Reciprocating influence strategies in interstate crisis bargaining. *Journal of Conflict Resolution* 37 (1): 3–41.

Levi, M. 1988. *Of rule and revenue*. Berkeley: University of California Press.

———. 1995. Contingencies of consent. Manuscript, Department of Political Science, University of Washington, Seattle.

Levy, J. S. 1989. The causes of war: A review of theories and evidence. In *Behavior, society, and nuclear war*, ed. P. E. Tetlock, J. L. Husbands, R. Jervis, P. C. Stern, and C. Tilly, 209–333. Oxford: Oxford University Press.

———. 1994. Learning and foreign policy: Sweeping a conceptual minefield. *International Organization* 48 (2): 279–312.

Lewin, M. 1968. *Lenin's last struggle*. New York: Pantheon.

———. 1974. *Political undercurrents in Soviet economic debates: From Bukharin to the modern reformers*. Princeton: Princeton University Press.

Lewis, D. K. 1973. *Counterfactuals*. Cambridge: Harvard University Press.

Lewontin, R. C. 1993. *Biology as ideology*. New York: HarperCollins.

Lieberthal, K. 1978. *Sino-Soviet conflict in the 1970s: Its evolution and implications for the strategic triangle*. Santa Monica: Rand Corporation.

Lindblom, C. E. 1990. *Inquiry and change: The troubled attempt to understand and shape society*. New Haven: Yale University Press.

Malia, M. 1994. *The Soviet tragedy: A history of socialism in Russia, 1917–1991*. New York: Free Press.

Mandelblit, N. 1994. Blending in causative structures. Manuscript.

————. 1995. The theory of blending as part of the general epistemological developments in cognitive science. Manuscript.

Manninen, O. 1983. Operation Barbarossa and the Nordic countries. In *Scandinavia in the Second World War*, ed. H. S. Nissen, 139–81. Minneapolis: University of Minnesota Press.

Maoz, Z. 1996. *Domestic sources of global change*. Ann Arbor: University of Michigan Press.

Maoz, Z., and N. Abdolali. 1989. Regime types and international conflict, 1816–1976. *Journal of Conflict Resolution* 33 (1): 3–35.

Maoz, Z., and B. Russett. 1993. Normative and structural causes of democratic peace, 1946–1986. *American Political Science Review* 87 (3): 624–38.

March, J. G. 1978. Bounded rationality, ambiguity, and the engineering of choice. *Bell Journal of Economics* 9 (2): 587–608.

March, J. G., and J. P. Olsen. 1984. The new institutionalism: Organizational factors in political life. *American Political Science Review* 78 (3): 734–49.

————. 1995. *Democratic governance*. New York: Free Press.

Maruyama, M. 1963. The second cybernetics: Deviation-amplifying mutual causal processes. *American Scientist* 51 (2): 164–79.

McCubbins, M. D., R. G. Noll, and B. R. Weingast. 1989. Structure and process, politics and policy: Administrative arrangements and the political control of agencies. *Virginia Law Review* 75 (2): 431–82.

McCubbins, M. D., and T. Schwartz. 1984. Congressional oversight overlooked: Police patrols versus fire alarms. *American Journal of Political Science* 28 (1): 165–79.

McDaniel, T. 1988. *Autocracy, capitalism and revolution in Russia*. Berkeley: University of California Press.

Mearsheimer, J. J. 1990. Back to the future: Instability in Europe after the Cold War. *International Security* 15 (1): 5–56.

————. 1993. The case for a Ukrainian nuclear deterrent. *Foreign Affairs* 72 (Summer): 50–66.

Mendel, A. P. 1965. Peasant and worker on the eve of the First World War. *Slavic Review* 24 (1): 23–33.

Menon, R. 1994. Post-mortem: The causes and consequences of the Soviet collapse. *Harriman Review* 7 (10–12): 1–10.

Meyer, S. M. 1991. How the threat (and the coup) collapsed: The politicization of the Soviet military. *International Security* 16 (3): 5–38.

Mill, J. S. 1900. *A system of logic*. London: Longmans.

Millar, J. 1976. What's wrong with the "standard story"? *Problems of Communism* 25 (4): 50–55.

Miller, B. 1995. *When opponents cooperate: Great power conflict and collaboration in world politics*. Ann Arbor: University of Michigan Press.

Miller, D. T., and W. Turnbull. 1990. The counterfactual fallacy: Confusing what might have been with what ought to have been. *Social Justice Research* 4 (1): 1–19.

Miller, D. T., W. Turnbull, and C. McFarland. 1990. Counterfactual thinking and social perception: Thinking about what might have been. In *Advances in Experimental Social Psychology*, ed. M. Zanna, 305–31. New York: Academic Press.

Moe, T. M. 1985. Control and feedback in economic regulation: The case of the NLRB. *American Political Science Review* 79 (4): 1094–1116.

———. 1987. An assessment of the positive theory of "congressional dominance." *Legislative Studies Quarterly* 12 (4): 475–520.

Moore, B., Jr. 1966. *Social origins of dictatorship and democracy: Lord and peasant in the making of the modern world*. Boston: Beacon Press.

Morgan, P. M. 1977. *Deterrence: A conceptual analysis*. Beverly Hills: Sage.

Morgenthau, H. J. 1973. *Politics among nations: The struggle for power and peace*, 5th ed. New York: Knopf.

Morrow, J. D. 1991. Alliances and asymmetry: An alternative to the capability aggregation model of alliances. *American Journal of Political Science* 35 (4): 904–33.

———. 1993. Arms versus allies: Trade-offs in the search for security. *International Organization* 47 (2): 207–33.

Morson, G. S. 1994. *Narrative and freedom*. New Haven: Yale University Press.

Mueller, J. 1988. The essential irrelevance of nuclear weapons: Stability in the postwar world. *International Security* 13 (2): 55–79.

———. 1989. *Retreat from doomsday: The obsolescence of major war*. New York: Basic Books.

Nash, P. 1991. The use of counterfactuals in history: A look at the literature. *The SHAFR Newsletter* (March): 2–12.

Nathan, J. A. 1975. The missile crisis: His finest hour now. *World Politics* 27 (2): 256–81,

National Security Archive. 1987. *The chronology: The documented day-by-day account of the secret military assistance to Iran and the Contras*. New York: Warner Books.

Newman, S. 1976. *March 1939: The British guarantee to Poland: A study in the continuity of British foreign policy*. Oxford: Clarendon Press.

Nisbett, R., and L. Ross. 1980. *Human inference: Strategies and shortcomings of social judgment*. Englewood Cliffs, New Jersey: Prentice-Hall.

Noonan, J. T. 1957. *The scholastic analysis of usury*. Cambridge: Harvard University Press.

North, D. C. 1990. *Institutions, institutional change, and economic performance*. New York: Cambridge University Press.

Nove, A. 1964. *Economic rationality and Soviet politics; or, Was Stalin really necessary? Some problems of Soviet political economy*. New York: Praeger.

———. 1976. The logic and cost of collectivization. *Problems of Communism* 25 (4): 55–59.

Nove, A., and J. A. Newth. 1967. *The Soviet Middle East: A communist model for development*. London: Allen & Unwin.

Nozick, R. 1993. *The nature of rationality*. Princeton: Princeton University Press.

Oakley, T. 1995. Presence: The conceptual basis of rhetorical effect. Ph.D. diss., University of Maryland.

O'Neill, B. 1995. Weak models, nil hypotheses and decorative statistics: Is there really no hope? *Journal of Conflict Resolution* 39 (4): 731–48.

Overy, R., and A. Wheatcroft. 1989. *The road to war*. London: Macmillan

Owen, J. 1994. How liberalism produces democratic peace. *International Security* 19 (2): 87–125.

Parker, R. A. C. 1993. *Chamberlain and appeasement: British policy and the coming of the Second World War*. London: MacMillan.

Pattee, H. 1973. *Hierarchy theory*. New York: George Braziller.

Peltzman, S. 1975. The effects of automobile safety regulation. *Journal of Political Economy* 83 (4): 677–725.

Perle, R. 1992. *Hard line*. New York: Random House.

Perrow, C. 1984. *Normal accidents: Living with high-risk technologies*. New York: Basic Books.

Petersen, W. J. 1986. Deterrence and compellence: A critical assessment of conventional wisdom. *International Studies Quarterly* 30 (3): 269–94.

Pipes, R. 1993. *Russia under the Bolshevik regime*. New York: Knopf.

———. 1994. Did the Russian Revolution have to happen? *The American Scholar* 63 (Spring): 215–38.

Post, G., Jr. 1993. *Dilemmas of appeasement: British deterrence and defense, 1934–1937*. Ithaca: Cornell University Press.

Powell, R. 1990. *Nuclear deterrence theory: The search for credibility*. Cambridge: Cambridge University Press.

———. 1995. Remarks at the Conference on Counterfactual Thought Experiments in World Politics, Berkeley.

Proceedings of the Cambridge Conference on the Cuban Missile Crisis, 11–12 October 1987. 1988. Mimeograph, Center for Science and International Affairs, Harvard University.

Przeworski, A., and F. Limongi. 1993. Political regimes and economic growth. *Journal of Economic Perspectives* 7 (3): 51–69.

Ragin, C. C. 1987. *The comparative method: Moving beyond qualitative and quantitative strategies*. Berkeley: University of California Press.

Ramazani, R. K. 1989. Iran's foreign policy: Contending orientations. *Middle East Journal* 43 (2): 202–17.

Ray, J. L. 1990. Friends as foes: International conflict and wars between formal allies. In *Prisoners of war? Nation-states in the modern era*, ed. C. S. Gochman and A. N. Sabrosky, 73–91. Lexington, Mass.: Lexington Books.

———. 1993. Wars between democracies: Rare or nonexistent? *International Interactions* 18 (3): 251–76.

———. 1995. *Democracy and international conflict: An evaluation of the democratic peace proposition*. Columbia: University of South Carolina Press.

Raymond, G. A. 1994. Democracies, disputes, and third-party intermediaries. *Journal of Conflict Resolution* 38 (1): 24–42.

Reisch, G. A. 1991. Chaos, history, and narrative. *History and Theory* 30 (1): 1–20.

Richards, D. 1990. Is strategic decision making chaotic? *Behavioral Science* 35 (3): 219–32.

Richardson, J. L. 1988. New perspectives on appeasement: Some implications for international relations. *World Politics* 40 (3): 289–316.

Richter, J. G. 1994. *Khrushchev's double bind: International pressures and domestic coalition politics*. Baltimore: Johns Hopkins University Press.

Risse-Kappen, T. 1995. *Cooperation among democracies: The European influence on U.S. foreign policy*. Princeton: Princeton University Press.

Rodgers, R., and O. Hammerstein II. 1951. *The king and I*. New York: Random House.

Roese, N. J. 1995. Determinants of counterfactual thinking. Manuscript.

Roese, N. J., and J. M. Olson. 1993. Self-esteem and counterfactual thinking. *Journal of Personality and Social Psychology* 65 (1): 199–206.

———. 1995a. Counterfactual thinking: A critical overview. In *What might have been: The social psychology of counterfactual thinking*, ed. N. J. Roese and J. M. Olson, 1–59. Mahwah, New Jersey: Erlbaum.

———. 1995b. Functions of counterfactual thinking. In *What might have been: The social psychology of counterfactual thinking*, ed. N. J. Roese and J. M. Olson, 169–197. Mahwah, New Jersey: Erlbaum.

———, eds. 1995c. *What might have been: The social psychology of counterfactual thinking*. Mahwah, New Jersey: Erlbaum.

Roosevelt, K. 1979. *Countercoup: The struggle for the control of Iran*. New York: McGraw-Hill.

Rosecrance, R. 1986. *The rise of the trading state: Commerce and conquest in the modern world*. New York: Basic Books.

Rousseau, D., C. Gelpi, D. Reiter, and P. Huth. 1996. Assessing the nature of the democratic peace, 1918–1988. *American Political Science Review* 90.

Rummel, R. J. 1975–81. *Understanding conflict and war*, 5 vols. Beverly Hills: Sage.

Russett, B. M. 1993. *Grasping the democratic peace: Principles for a post–Cold War world*. Princeton: Princeton University Press.

———. 1995. The democratic peace: "And yet it moves." *International Security* 19 (4): 164–75.

Russett, B., and J. L. Ray. 1995. Why the democratic peace proposition lives. *Review of International Studies* 21 (3): 319–23.

Sabrosky, A. 1980. Interstate alliances: Their reliability and the expansion of war. In *The correlates of war: II. Testing some realpolitik models*, ed. J. D. Singer, 161–98. New York: Free Press.

Sagan, S. D. 1986. 1914 revisited: Allies, offense, and instability. *International Security* 11 (2): 151–75.

Saunders, E. M., Jr. 1993. Stock prices and Wall Street weather. *American Economic Review* 83 (5): 1337–45.

Schelling, T. C. 1960. *The strategy of conflict*. Cambridge: Harvard University Press.

———. 1966. *Arms and influence*. New Haven: Yale University Press.

———. 1978. *Micromotives and macrobehavior*. New York: Norton.

Schlesinger, A. M., Jr. 1965. *A thousand days: John F. Kennedy in the White House*. Boston: Houghton, Mifflin.

———. 1992. Four days with Fidel: A Havana diary. *New York Review of Books*, 26 March, 22–29.

Schoemaker, P. J. H. 1991. When and how to use scenario planning: A heuristic approach with illustration. *Journal of Forecasting* 10 (6): 549–64.

Schroeder, P. 1976. Munich and the British tradition. *The Historical Journal* 19 (1): 223–43.

Schultz, K., and B. Weingast. 1994. The democratic advantage: The institutional sources of state powers in international competition. Paper presented at the annual meeting of the American Political Science Association, New York.

Schurmann, H. F. 1974. *The logic of world power: An inquiry into the origins, currents, and contradictions of world politics*. New York: Pantheon Books.

Schwartz, P. 1991. *The art of the long view*. New York: Doubleday/Currency.

Schweller, R. L. 1992. Domestic structure and preventive war: Are democracies more pacific? *World Politics* 44 (2): 235–69.

Scott, J. C. 1985. *Weapons of the weak: Everyday forms of peasant resistance*. New Haven: Yale University Press.

Seelau, E. P., S. M. Seelau, G. L. Wells, and P. D. Windschitl. 1995. Counterfactual constraints. In *What might have been: The social psychology of counterfactual thinking*, ed. N. J. Roese and J. M. Olson, 57–79. Mahwah, New Jersey: Erlbaum.

Selten, R. 1975. Reexamination of the perfectness concept for equilibrium points in extensive games. *International Journal of Game Theory* 4 (1): 25–55.

Sewell, W. H., Jr. 1985. Ideologies and social revolutions: Reflections on the French case. *Journal of Modern History* 57 (1): 57–85.

Shultz, G. P. 1993. *Turmoil and triumph: My years as secretary of state*. New York: Scribner's.

Sigmund, K. 1993. *Games of life: Explorations in ecology, evolution, and behaviour*. Oxford: Oxford University Press.

Simon, H. A. 1957. *Models of man*. New York: Wiley.

———. 1985. Human nature in politics: The dialogue of psychology with political science. *American Political Science Review* 79 (2): 293–304.

Siverson, R. M., and J. Emmons. 1991. Birds of a feather: Democratic political systems and alliance choices in the twentieth century. *Journal of Conflict Resolution* 35 (2): 285–306.

Skocpol, T. 1979. *States and social revolutions: A comparative analysis of France, Russia, and China*. New York: Cambridge University Press.

———. 1982. Rentier state and Shiá Islam in the Iranian revolution. *Theory and Society* 11 (3): 265–83.

Skyrms, B. 1980. *Causal necessity*. New Haven: Yale University Press.

———. 1988. Probability and causation. *Journal of Econometrics* 39 (1–2): 53–68.

Sloman, A. 1978. *The computer revolution in philosophy: Philosophy, science, and models of mind*. Hassocks, Eng.: Harvester Press.

Small, M., and J. D. Singer. 1982. *Resort to arms: International and civil wars, 1816–1980*. Beverly Hills: Sage.

Smith, A. 1995. A theory of alliances. Ph.D. diss., University of Rochester.

Sniderman, P. M., R. A. Brody, and P. E. Tetlock. 1991. *Reasoning and choice: Explorations in political psychology*. Cambridge: Cambridge University Press.

Snyder, S., and B. R. Weingast. 1994. The American system of shared powers: Congress, the president, and the NLRB. Working paper, Hoover Institution, Stanford University.

Speer, A. 1970. *Inside the third reich: Memoirs*. New York: Macmillan.

Spiro, D. E. 1994. The insignificance of the liberal peace. *International Security* 19 (2): 50–86.

———. 1995. The liberal peace: "And yet it squirms." *International Security* 19 (4): 177–80.

Stalnaker, R. C. 1968. A theory of conditionals. In *Studies in logical theory: Essays*, ed. N. Rescher, 98–112. Oxford: Blackwell.

————. 1984. *Inquiry*. Cambridge: MIT Press.

Steel, R. 1969. End game. *New York Review of Books*, 13 March, 5–22.

Stern, P. C. 1993. A second environmental science: Human-environment interactions. *Science* 260 (June 25): 1897–99.

Strassfeld, R. N. 1992. If . . . : Counterfactuals in the law. *George Washington Law Review* 60 (2): 339–416.

Streit, C. K. 1940. *Union now: A proposal for an Atlantic federal union of the free.* New York: Harper.

Stone, I. F. 1966. The brink. *New York Review of Books*, 14 April, 12–16.

Taylor, A. J. P. 1954. *The struggle for mastery in Europe, 1848–1918*. Oxford: Clarendon.

————. 1961. *The origins of the Second World War*. London: Hamilton.

Taylor, M. 1976. *Anarchy and cooperation*. London: Wiley.

————. 1988. Rationality and revolutionary collective action. In *Rationality and revolution*, ed. M. Taylor, 63–97. Cambridge: Cambridge University Press.

Taylor, S. E. 1991. Asymmetrical effects of positive and negative events: The mobilization-minimization hypothesis. *Psychological Bulletin* 110 (1): 67–85.

Taylor, S. E., and J. D. Brown. 1988. Illusion and well-being: A social psychological perspective on mental health. *Psychological Bulletin* 103 (2): 193–210.

Taylor, T. 1979. *Munich: The price of peace*. New York: Vintage Press.

Tetlock, P. E. 1991. Learning in U.S. and Soviet foreign policy: In search of an elusive concept. In *Learning in U.S. and Soviet foreign policy*, ed. G. W. Breslauer and P. E. Tetlock, 20–61. Boulder: Westview.

————. 1992a. Good judgment in international politics: Three psychological perspectives. *Political Psychology* 13 (3): 517–39.

————. 1992b. The impact of accountability on judgment and choice: Toward a social contingency model. *Advances in Experimental Social Psychology* 25: 331–76.

————. 1994. Good judgment in world politics: Who gets what right, when and why? Paper presented at the annual meeting of the American Psychological Society, Washington, DC.

Tetlock, P. E., and A. Levi. 1982. Attribution bias: On the inconclusiveness of the cognition-motivation debate. *Journal of Experimental Psychology* 18: 68–88.

Tetlock, P. E., and A. S. R. Manstead. 1985. Impression management versus intrapsychic explanations in social psychology: A useful dichotomy? *Psychological Review* 92 (1): 59–77.

Thompson, N. 1971. *The anti-appeasers: Conservative opposition to appeasement in the 30s*. Oxford: Clarendon Press.

Thorne, C. 1967. *The approach of war, 1938–1939*. London: Macmillan.

Thucydides. 1959. *History of the Peloponnesian War*, tr. T. Hobbes. Ann Arbor: University of Michigan Press.

Tilly, C. 1984. *Big structures, large processes, huge comparisons*. New York: Russell Sage.

Toulmin, S. 1990. *Cosmopolis: The hidden agenda of modernity*. New York: Free Press.

Tower, J., E. Muskie, and B. Scowcroft. 1987. *The Tower Commission report: The full text of the president's Special Review Board*. New York: Bantam Books/Times Books.

Tucker, R. C. 1977a. Stalinism as revolution from above. In *Stalinism: Essays in historical interpretation*, ed. R. C. Tucker, 77–108. New York: Norton.

Tucker, R. C., ed. 1977b. *Stalinism: Essays in historical interpretation*. New York: Norton.

Turner, M. 1996. *The literary mind*. New York: Oxford University Press.

Turner, M., and G. Fauconnier. 1996. Conceptual integration and formal expression. *Metaphor and Symbolic Activity* 10 (3): 183–203.

Tversky, A., and D. Kahneman. 1974. Judgment under uncertainty: Heuristics and biases. *Science* 185 (Sept. 27): 1124–31.

U.S. Department of State. 1964. *Bulletin* 50 (Mar. 23).

———. *Foreign relations of the United States* (FRUS). Washington: U.S. Government Printing Office.

Von Laue, T. H. 1971. *Why Lenin? Why Stalin? A reappraisal of the Russian Revolution, 1900–1930*, 2nd ed. Philadelphia: Lippincott.

———. 1981. Stalin among the moral and political imperatives, or How to judge Stalin? *Soviet Union/Union Sovietique* 8 (1): 1–17.

Von Neumann, J. 1966. *Theory of self-reproducing automata*, ed. A. W. Burks. Urbana: University of Illinois Press.

Waldrop, M. M. 1992. *Complexity: The emerging science at the edge of order and chaos*. New York: Simon & Schuster.

Walt, S. M. 1987. *The origins of alliances*. Ithaca: Cornell University Press.

———. 1989. The case for finite containment: Analyzing US grand strategy. *International Security* 14 (1): 5–49.

Waltz, K. N. 1959. *Man, the state, and war: A theoretical analysis*. New York: Columbia University Press.

———. 1979. *Theory of international politics*. Reading, Mass.: Addison-Wesley.

Wandycz, P. S. 1986. Poland between East and West. In *The origins of the Second World War reconsidered: The A. J. P. Taylor debate after twenty-five years*, ed. G. Martel, 187–209. Boston: Allen & Unwin.

Wason, P. C., and P. N. Johnson-Laird. 1972. *Psychology of reasoning: Structure and content*. Cambridge: Harvard University Press.

Watt, D. C. 1989. *How war came: The immediate origins of the Second World War, 1938–1939*. New York: Pantheon.

———. 1993. Churchill and appeasement. In *Churchill*, ed. R. Blake and W. R. Louis, 199–214. Oxford: Oxford University Press.

Weart, S. R. 1994. Peace among democratic and oligarchic republics. *Journal of Peace Research* 31 (3): 299–316.

———. 1995. Never at war: Why democracies will not fight one another. Manuscript.

Weber, M. [1905] 1949. Objective possibility and adequate causation in historical explanation. In *The methodology of the social sciences*, 164–88. Glencoe, Ill.: Free Press of Glencoe.

Weede, E. 1992. Some simple calculations on democracy and war involvement. *Journal of Peace Research* 29 (4): 377–83.

Weinberg, G. L. 1988. Munich after 50 years. *Foreign Affairs* 67 (1): 165–78.

Weingast, B. R. 1984. The congressional-bureaucratic system: A principal-agent perspective (with applications to the SEC). *Public Choice* 44 (1): 147–91.

————. 1995a. Institutions and political commitment: A new political economy of the American Civil War era. Manuscript, Hoover Institution, Stanford University.

————. 1995b. Constructing trust: The political and economic roots of ethnic and regional conflict. Manuscript, Hoover Institution, Stanford University.

Weingast, B. R., and M. J. Moran. 1983. Bureaucratic discretion or congressional control? Regulatory policymaking by the Federal Trade Commission. *Journal of Political Economy* 91 (5): 765–800.

Wendt, A. E. 1987. The agent-structure problem in international relations theory. *International Organization* 41 (3): 335–70.

————. 1992. Anarchy is what states make of it: The social construction of power politics. *International Organization* 46 (2): 391–425.

White, W. 1989. Profiles (Sylvia Earle). *New Yorker* 65 (20).

Wilber, C. K. 1969. *The Soviet model and underdeveloped countries.* Chapel Hill: University of North Carolina Press.

Wills, G. 1982. *The Kennedy imprisonment: A meditation on power.* Boston: Little Brown.

Wilson, J. Q., ed. 1980. *The politics of regulation.* New York: Basic Books.

With the historical truth and morale of Baraguá. 1990. *Granma,* 2 Dec., 2.

Wolfram, S. 1983. Statistical mechanics of cellular automata. *Review of Modern Physics* 55 (3): 601–44.

————. 1984. Universality and complexity in cellular automata. In *Cellular automata: Proceedings of an interdisciplinary workshop,* ed. D. Farmer, T. Toffoli, and S. Wolfram, 1–35. Amsterdam: North-Holland Physics Publishing.

————, ed. 1986. *Theory and applications of cellular automata: Including selected papers, 1983–1986.* Singapore: World Scientific.

Wright, G. H. von. 1971. *Explanation and understanding.* Ithaca: Cornell University Press.

Zagoria, D. 1962. *The Sino-Soviet conflict, 1956–1961.* Princeton: Princeton University Press.

Index